Crime in the Art and Antiquities World

Stefano Manacorda · Duncan Chappell
Editors

Crime in the Art and Antiquities World

Illegal Trafficking in Cultural Property

Springer

Editors
Stefano Manacorda
Centro Nazionale di Prevenzione
e Difesa Sociale Piazza Castello 3
20121, Milano, Italy
and
Université Paris 1 Panthéon Sorbonne
Paris, France
stefano.manacorda@unina2.it

Duncan Chappell
Faculty of Law
University of Sydney
NSW 2006, Australia
chappell@bigpond.net.au

ISBN 978-1-4419-7945-2 e-ISBN 978-1-4419-7946-9
DOI 10.1007/978-1-4419-7946-9
Springer New York Dordrecht Heidelberg London

Library of Congress Control Number: 2011922987

Printed on acid-free paper

Springer is part of Springer Science+Business Media (www.springer.com)

Preface

The genesis of this book can be traced directly to the activities of the International Scientific and Professional Advisory Council (ISPAC) of the United Nations Crime Prevention and Criminal Justice Program. Established in 1991, ISPAC's secretariat is located in Milan, Italy, at the Centre Nationale di Prevenzione e Difesa Sociale (CNPDS).

ISPAC's tasks have been defined as

> channelling to the United Nations professional and scientific input and creating a capacity for the transfer of knowledge and exchange of information in crime prevention and criminal justice drawing on the contributions of non-governmental organisations (NGO's), academic institutions and other relevant entities, so as to assist the United Nations in program formulation and implementation in this field.

In December 2008 ISPAC, together with the Courmayeur Foundation and the United Nations Office on Drugs and Crime (UNODC), sponsored an international conference on "Organised Crime in Art and Antiquities". It should be noted that this was not the first occasion on which ISPAC had been involved in such a gathering. In June 1992 ISPAC, in collaboration with the Division of Cultural Patrimony of the United Nations Educational Scientific and Cultural Organisation (UNESCO), held an international workshop on the "Protection of Artistic and Cultural Property" in Courmayeur, Mont Blanc in Italy. This workshop resulted in the formulation of the so called Charter of Courmayeur, urging national and international action against the illicit trade with objects belonging to the cultural patrimony of nations (see Annex #24??).

The 2008 conference also took place in Courmayeur and was attended by 145 experts from 27 different countries including, among others, representatives of national governments and international organisations, NGOs, academia and the private sector. Selected papers from the conference were subsequently published as an edited collection by ISPAC/CNPDS (Manacorda 2009). Following this publication, which had only limited circulation, it was decided by ISPAC that a broader audience needed to be reached and subsequently an agreement was entered into with Springer, an international publisher based in New York in the USA, to produce the current book. This agreement provided for the joint editorship of Stefano Manacorda, who had coordinated the 2008 conference and edited its proceedings, and Duncan Chappell who had participated as an expert at the conference, and is a member of the Board of Management of ISPAC.

As is seen from the list of contents of this book a number of the chapters, revised and updated, have been drawn from the papers presented at Courmayeur in 2008 while others are newly commissioned works. In addition, as an Annex, a collection of the major international instruments and related documents concerned with the protection of art and antiquities of cultural significance has been reproduced. As anyone involved in this area of academic and scientific endeavour quickly discovers many of these documents are by themselves very difficult to locate – a problem which, it is hoped, is overcome through the provision of the material contained in the Annex.

As editors, we wish to express our warm gratitude to ISPAC for permitting us to participate in the production of this book, and for supporting us in so many ways throughout a quite lengthy gestation period. During this period, we have also engaged with ISPAC in the organisation of an ancillary meeting, titled "Protecting Cultural Property: The State of the Art", held at the Twelfth United Nations Congress on Crime Prevention and Criminal Justice in Salvador, Brazil in April 2010, and a subsequent workshop on this topic conducted in May 2010 at the Vienna meeting of the United Nations Commission on Crime Prevention and Criminal Justice.

This book could not have been produced without the encouragement and assistance of Eleni Papageorgiou and Camilla Beria di Argentine at ISPAC. We owe a special debt of gratitude to Eleni who did so much to smooth the frustrations and logistics involved in working with editors, authors and a publisher scattered across the globe. We also wish to convey our thanks to each of the contributors to this book who have given so freely of their time and expertise. Last, but not least, we express our appreciation to our publisher, Springer, and in particular to Welmoed Spahr and Katherine Chabalko, for their patience and understanding over the number of months it has taken to bring this venture to a successful conclusion.

Naples, Italy — Stefano Manacorda
Sydney, Australia — Duncan Chappell
August 2010

Reference

Manacorda, S. (Ed.) (2009) Organised crime in art and antiquities. Milano, Italy: ISPAC.

Contents

Contributors

Mathew Bogdanos
Colonel, US Marine Corps, New York, NY, USA
mbogdanos@aol.com

Blythe Bowman Proulx
Wilder School of Government and Public Affairs,
Virginia Commonwealth University, Richmond VA, USA
bbproulx@vcu.edu

Neil Brodie
Archaeology Center, Stanford University,
94305 Stanford, CA, USA
njb1012@gmail.com

Duncan Chappell
Faculty of Law, University of Sydney,
NSW 2006, Australia
chappell@bigpond.net.au

Karl-Heinz Kind
INTERPOL General Secretariat, Lyons, France
kh.kind@interpol.int

Simon Mackenzie
Scottish Centre for Crime and Justice Research, University of Glasgow,
Glasgow, UK
simon.Mackenzie@glasgow.ac.uk

Stefano Manacorda
Centro Nazionale di Prevenzione e Difesa Sociale Piazza Castello 3,
20121, Milano, Italy;
Université Paris 1 Panthéon Sorbonne, Paris, France
stefano.manacorda@unina2.it

Giovanni Nistri
Heritage Protection Unit, Carabinieri Corps, Rome, Italy
giovanni.nistri@carabinieri.it

Nikos Passas
College of Criminal Justice, Northeastern University, Boston, MA, USA
n.passas@neu.edu

Kenneth Polk
University of Melbourne, Parkville VIC, Australia
kpolk@unimelb.edu.au

Folarin Shyllon
Olabisi Onabanjo University, Ago-Iwoye, Ogun State, Nigeria
fshyllon@yahoo.co.uk

Edgar A.J.G. Tijhuis
Netherlands Institute for the Study of Crime and Law Enforcement, Amsterdam, The Netherlands;
VU University, Amsterdam, The Netherlands
tijhuis@nscr.nl

Chapter 1
Introduction

From Cairo to Vienna and Beyond: Contemporary Perspectives on the Dialogue About Protecting Cultural Artefacts from Plunder

Stefano Manacorda and Duncan Chappell

Context

Cultural heritage officials from 20 nations gathered earlier this year in Cairo, Egypt, to discuss how to recover ancient treasures which had been stolen in the past and placed on display in foreign museums and galleries (BBC 2010a). The meeting, convened by Egypt's Supreme Council of Antiquities (SAC) and chaired by its head, Zahi Hawass, included representatives from Greece, Italy, China and Peru – all countries which over centuries have lost countless antiquities to plunderers. Hawass urged delegates from all countries to work together to recover their lost treasures. "Every country is fighting alone, every country suffered alone, especially Egypt" he said. "We will battle together" (BBC 2010b).

This Cairo meeting, and especially its leadership by the SAC and Zahi Hawass, represents the face of a new and assertive international movement to redress historic wrongs among nations that have been in the past, and in most cases continue today to be the principal suppliers of the illicit market in art and antiquities. In the countries that fall on the demand side of this market, primarily those of the rich and developed world, this movement has already begun to have an impact. Hawass, for example, has claimed to have secured the return by a number of countries of more than 6,000 objects held in their museums and galleries (De Roquefeuil 2010). His much publicised activities include the 2009 breaking of archaeological ties with the Louvre Museum in Paris until France returned to Egypt fragments chipped from a wall in an ancient tomb (BBC 2010a). He also continues to pursue the recovery of a number of other treasures, including the Rosetta Stone kept in the British Museum, and the statue of Queen Nefertiti on display in the Neues Museum in Berlin (Tierney 2009).

S. Manacorda (✉)
Centro Nazionale di Prevenzione e Difesa Sociale Piazza Castello 3, 20121, Milano, Italy
and
Université Paris 1 Panthéon Sorbonne, Paris, France
e-mail: stefano.manacorda@unina2.it

S. Manacorda and D. Chappell (eds.), *Crime in the Art and Antiquities World: Illegal Trafficking in Cultural Property*, DOI 10.1007/978-1-4419-7946-9_1,

A related international development that has occurred, largely in tandem with that just described, has been a surge of interest in the United Nation's Commission on Crime Prevention and Criminal Justice (UNCCP) in combatting the illicit trade in art and antiquities (Economic and Social Council 2010). The UNCCP, comprising 40 elected nations from among the members of the UN, oversights the programme and activities of the Vienna-based UN Office on Drugs and Crime (UNODC). The latter body has now recognised that the actions of illicit traffickers in art and antiquities have many similarities to those engaged in other organised transnational criminal activities, including drugs and arms trafficking. As such, they are also the activities which might be better targeted by collaborative law enforcement efforts utilising the powers already given by an international instrument like the UN Convention against Transnational Organised Crime, agreed in 2000 in Palermo, Italy. The UNCCP has also given fresh consideration to the acceptance of a model treaty for the prevention of crimes that infringe on the cultural heritage of peoples in the form of movable property – a model treaty whose terms were first proposed nearly two decades ago at the 1990 Eighth UN Congress on the prevention of crime and the treatment of offenders held in Havana, Cuba (see Annex # 4).

It is within this general contemporary and international context that this book is set. The book is concerned with the illegal trafficking in art and antiquities linked to the cultural heritage of the nations of the world – a highly lucrative and global trade whose true dimension and scope is only slowly becoming realised by many in the international community. For those source countries whose rich cultural heritage has been subjected to systematic plunder, often over many generations, an awareness of the losses involved and a desire to achieve the restitution of looted items has already tended to become deeply embedded in their respective national psyches. Now, there would seem to be a new and broader appreciation in the demand countries, which provide the principal and largely unfettered markets for this international trade in art and antiquities that this situation can no longer be allowed to continue.

Evidence to support these statements is found in the chapters which follow. They are the chapters which have been contributed by a range of invited scholars and practitioners. The scholars come from a mix of disciplines, including law, criminology, anthropology, and archaeology while the practitioners represent both national and international law enforcement bodies involved in the investigation of this area of crime. Many of the contributors participated originally in an international conference on the topic of "Organised crime in art and antiquities" held in Courmayeur, Italy, in December 2008, under the auspices of the International Scientific and Professional Advisory Council of the United Nation's Crime Prevention and Criminal Justice Program (ISPAC), the Centro Nazionale di Prevenzione e Difesa Sociale (CNPDS), the Courmayeur Foundation in cooperation with UNODC (Manacorda 2009).

The book is in three parts – first, a survey across a number of disciplines of some of the principal issues and perspectives surrounding this topic; second, a series of case studies which provide a graphic illustration of the nature and gravity of this illicit trade; and third, a consideration of the role law enforcement can and does play in combatting this aspect of criminal activity. In addition, in an annex, a comprehensive range of international treaties, conventions, and allied documents, concerned with the protection of cultural heritage items and their restitution, is reproduced. This annex is intended to provide a ready and immediate access to documents which are often difficult to obtain and locate through regular sources.

Brief attention is now turned to a number of significant themes and issues which emerge from these various authors and the associated international illicit trade in art and antiquities that is subject to analysis.

Dimension and Scope of the Illicit Trade

There would now seem to be quite widespread consensus, as evidenced by the authors in this book that the illicit trade in art and antiquities is both profitable and extensive crossing international boundaries and presenting a challenge to law and policy makers in all regions of the world. As noted earlier, the North South divide among the rich and poorer nations of the world is reflected here as well with source countries for the art and antiquities in high demand being concentrated largely in the South, and demand countries in the North. There is not, however, agreement regarding the magnitude of the illicit trade, nor its true value in a monetary sense. Elsewhere, Charney has asserted that the illegal profits of art crime in general amount to an "astounding $6 billion per annum by conservative estimates". He goes on to add that art crime is the

> third highest-grossing annual criminal trade worldwide, run primarily by organised crime syndicates and therefore funding their other enterprises, from the drug and arms trades to terrorism (Charney 2009, p. xvii)

In their chapter, Passas and Bowman subject estimates like these to critical scrutiny, concluding that this particular figure and comparison with the profitability of drug and arms trafficking is not based on fact but gets recycled nonetheless simply because it is sensational. They point to the diverse and multiple dilemmas that confront anyone seeking to provide a more reliable estimate of the illicit trade in art and antiquities, including the fact that Interpol, the international police agency, has stated that less than half of all its member countries provide it with annual art crime information. Another barrier to accurate estimation of the extent of this illicit trade is the fact that most looting of cultural objects, and the subsequent laundering of the proceeds of their sale and distribution, takes place under the radar screens of law enforcement agencies across the globe. Few of these incidents result in any official reports, and they remain part of the "dark figure" of this particular aspect of crime.

Despite these data gathering and interpretation problems, the three case studies provided in the book – two relating to Iraq and the third to the African continent – do allow some appreciation of the dimension and scale of the problems presented by the destruction of cultural heritage sites and the plunder of objects from them. In his chapter, Bogdanos gives a graphic account of his investigation into "one of the greatest art crimes in recent memory" – the looting of the Iraq National Museum in Baghdad in 2003 during the US led invasion to topple the regime of Saddam Hussein. Bogdanos' account includes a penetrating analysis of the law of armed conflict and the obligations upon warring parties to protect cultural property against any act of hostility. These obligations were clearly haphazardly observed at best by the US and its allies during and after the invasion. But no one seems to have planned for or suspected the scale of plunder that occurred at the National Museum.

Thousands of objects were stolen from the National Museum and even today only a fraction has been recovered. Among the investigative team led by Bogdanos three approaches were adopted depending on the level of sophistication shown in selecting and removing looted items. Professional thieves were believed to have taken 40 of the museum's most treasured objects, 16 of which have since been recovered from within Iraq as well as from a range of foreign countries, including the USA. One object, for example, was seized by the US customs in 2006 having moved through Damascus to Beirut to Geneva and then New York. Other objects were believed to have been taken primarily by looters off the street, or insiders within the museum. A large number of these objects have since been found on international markets, including E Bay as Brodie makes clear in his chapter. Some have been recovered, in part because of an amnesty programme offered by Iraqi authorities.

Brodie's chapter contains a detailed analysis of the market in Iraqi antiquities between 1980 and 2009. He too shows how a significant number of the objects stolen from the National Museum, and elsewhere from looted sites across the country, found their way to auction houses in places like London and New York. He also identifies the nature of the continuing and thriving market for unprovenanced Iraqi artefacts on the Internet, and elsewhere, and seeks to place valuations on the types of objects being offered for sale. He indicates that it would seem possible to sell illegally obtained and exported Iraqi material with relative impunity. The auction houses, however, now seem less willing to run the risk of damage to their reputations from such sales although their motivations may also have been influenced by a slump in the value of these items over recent years.

In the third case study, Shyllon focuses attention on the losses of cultural heritage suffered through the illegal excavation of archaeological sites and the trade in stolen antiquities across the African continent. Shyllon claims that this trade has assumed massive proportions over recent decades from countries like Egypt, Mali, and Nigeria. He notes, for example, the comment of the Nigerian Minister of Culture in 1996 who said that the country was losing its cultural heritage at such a rate "that unless the trend is arrested soon we may have no cultural artefacts to bequeath to our progeny". Shyllon also observes that the looting of objects from Nigeria has occurred for well over a century following the infamous invasion of Benin in 1897 by the British and the subsequent plunder and exportation of thousands of works of art from that city.

The Organisation of the Market

As already noted, Charney has suggested that the art crime market is dominated by organised crime syndicates whose illicit activities are multivarious and intertwined with the trafficking of arms and drugs. This view of the market is, of course, not limited to the illicit trade in art and antiquities linked to the cultural heritage of the world's nations but incorporates as well, as Passas and Bowman indicate, the theft of contemporary art objects and the fraudulent reproduction of both ancient and modern art works. This book is not concerned with these aspects of the art market. Even so, some attention needs to be given to this view expressed by Charney and others since if it is accurate it suggests that the approach taken to the repression of other areas of organised criminal activity, both nationally and internationally, may be applied without question to the illicit market in art and antiquities.

A number of the book's authors offer insights into the way in which the illicit market in art and antiquities is organised which differ from that offered by Charney. Significantly, Nistri, who is the commander of the elite Italian law enforcement body devoted to the protection of that nation's cultural heritage, observes that his investigators have found no evidence at the judicial level of an involvement of "mafia type organisations in the direct and continuing organisation of the activities related to the traffic of cultural artefacts", although some affiliations had been found at the local level between criminals looting artefacts and mafia type clans. Nistri's investigators have, on the other hand, found overwhelming evidence of the highly sophisticated and internationally connected "cordata" or chain through which illegally excavated and exported cultural objects find their way onto the legal market for art and antiquities in Europe and North America. No single case illustrates the nature and power of this "cordata" more than that of the so-called "Medici Conspiracy", mentioned in Chappell and Polk's chapter but described in an entertaining and comprehensive way in a book by investigative journalist Peter Watson and a colleague (Watson and Todeschini 2006).

The "cordata" unveiled in the Medici case led from the tomb robbers who initially dug up antiquities through to various local dealers who then supplied Giacomo Medici, a prominent Italian dealer with offices in various places, including Rome and Geneva. From Medici the "cordata" went on to involve a series of well-known individual dealers, auction houses, collectors and museum officials in Europe, North America and elsewhere, all of whom were allegedly handling artefacts whose original plundered provenance had been laundered in various ways since the objects were illegally excavated and exported from their Italian sources.

When the Italian authorities eventually unravelled the "cordata", they were able to prosecute and convict Medici on a number of charges relating to the receipt of stolen antiquities although Medici's case remains subject to appeal in the Italian courts. Medici has not as yet served any of the prison sentence of 10 years he received upon his conviction, reduced to 8 years on appeal. Nor have others charged with him, including the former antiquities curator of the Getty Museum in California, Marilyn True, and the prominent American antiquities dealer Robert Hecht, been convicted in trials in Italy which have dragged on for a number of years (Scherer 2009; Povoledo 2010).

More is said later in this introduction about the impact these trials in the Medici conspiracy have had upon the illicit international market in art and antiquities. But first mention must be made of the views expressed about the nature of this market in the chapters by Mackenzie, Chappell and Polk, and Tijhuis. Each of these authors writes from primarily a criminological perspective, and each emphasises the importance of understanding how the market operates in considerable detail before offering suggestions about how best to restrict its operations and growth.

Mackenzie considers the dual questions of whether the illegal market in art and antiquities is an example of organised crime simply because of its organised market nature and the fact that many of its transactions are illegal, or whether various types of more conventionally conceived organised criminals operate within the market, and if so where and how. His analysis suggests that there are elements of both the market as criminal and criminals in the market – a finding with implications for the application of any prevention strategies as is discussed in greater detail below. In relation to the "market as criminal" Mackenzie, Chappell and Polk, and Tijhuis each indicate how the illicit market for art and antiquities runs in tandem in most cases with a perfectly licit market–illicit activities are concealed and embedded within the framework of quite lawful auction, gallery, and allied sales of artefacts which is in marked contrast to the illicit trade in drugs, where the product for sale is tainted with illegality no matter how it is marketed. The same is not necessarily true for the illicit traffic in arms, where lawful transactions may be used to clothe illegal dealings in much the same way as is the case with art and antiquities. Tijhuis describes how within this framework certain notorious jurisdictions facilitate this laundering process and allow looted or illegally exported artefacts to be provided with a false provenance and placed on the legal market. His own research on this issue concentrated on the Netherlands and Belgium which for years have been used as the laundering grounds for stolen French art and artefacts, and for plundered antiquities from other countries.

Evidence of criminals in the market is mentioned by Bogdanos in his chapter where he recounts the discovery of looted antiquities among weapon seizures made from violent groups involved in the Iraq insurgency. He concludes that like the insurgents in Afghanistan who learned to finance their activities through opium, insurgents in Iraq have discovered a new source of funding in Iraq's cash crop of artefacts. Bogdanos says that hard evidence is lacking regarding the scope and dimensions of the art for weapons trade, and much of the information on this topic is classified because of its association with terrorism. It is, nonetheless, a worrying trend which can only fuel the looting of the thousands of poorly guarded archaeological sites scattered around Iraq.

Responses: Law Enforcement and the Criminal Law

In July 2010, the Carabinieri del Reparto Operativo Tutela Patrimonio Culturale, Italy's elite police cultural heritage protection unit, held a press conference in Rome's Colosseum to display more than 300 looted archaeological objects discovered in a warehouse in Geneva, Switzerland following an extensive investigation, code named Andromeda, led by the Carabinieri and Swiss authorities (Davis 2010; Heritage Thieves 2010). The investigation, which mirrored many of the facets of the Medici case mentioned earlier, was said to have involved the tracing of a series of illicit trafficking activities associated with a prominent British art dealer, Robin Symes, and an unidentified Japanese art dealer, which eventually led to the warehouse in

Geneva's Freeport used as a clearing centre for this unlawful business. Twenty thousand artefacts were in fact stored at this and other facilities, many of them believed to have been taken from illicitly excavated sites in Italy. The repatriated objects on display were said to be valued at more than EUR 15 million.

The Andromeda investigation is but one of a series of well publicised and successful law enforcement operations conducted against the illicit trade in looted art and antiquities by the Carabinieri's cultural heritage protection unit over the past decade or so, as is made clear in the chapter in this book by the current commander of the unit, Giovanni Nistri. The unit is unique in many respects, including its formation as a national squad in 1969 prior to the passage in 1970 of the UNESCO Convention on the means of prohibiting and preventing the illicit import, export, and transfer of ownership of cultural property (UNESCO Convention 1970; see Annex # 10). Nation states subscribing to this Convention are now encouraged to establish specific agencies and measures designed to protect their cultural heritage but none have done so, to date, in a way which matches Italy's commitment to a well-resourced and expert law enforcement unit like that set up by the Carabinieri.

In his chapter, Bogdanos is scathing in voicing his criticisms of the failure of countries like the USA and Britain to devote adequate investigative resources to combatting the illicit trafficking of art and antiquities. He also notes that the world policing body, Interpol, has been able to assign only two part time officers to tracking down objects looted from Iraq. His criticisms can probably be extended to most if not all countries which subscribe to the UNESCO Convention 1970 with, of course, the notable exception of Italy.

There seems little doubt that Italy's response in using the tools of law enforcement and the criminal law as primary weapons in the protection of the nation's cultural heritage has had an impact on the market for stolen antiquities, both locally and abroad. The Carabinieri reported that nationally in 2009 cultural heritage thefts declined by almost 15% compared with the previous year, and more than 60,000 looted artefacts worth almost an estimated USD 240 million were recovered during the year (Harris 2010). Nistri, in his chapter, also notes that the number of clandestine excavations discovered has dwindled from a peak of more than 1,000 per year to 103 in 2008.

Internationally, Italy's assertive actions to repatriate looted objects which have found their way into some of the world's most prestigious museums and galleries have produced major dividends. In the wake of the Medici case in particular, where a virtual library of documents and photographs of illicitly excavated and trafficked artefacts was seized from Medici and his co-conspirators which enabled them to be traced to their ultimate destinations, dozens of treasured objects have been returned to Italy by institutions like the Metropolitan Museum of Art in New York , the J. Paul Getty Museum in Los Angeles, the Museum of Fine Arts in Boston, and the Cleveland Museum of Art in Ohio (Povoledo 2010). The past failure of such institutions to undertake due diligence inquiries into the provenance of these repatriated objects should now be less likely to be repeated in the future as both museums and collectors alike realise their purchasing conduct will be subjected to much closer scrutiny, and possibly lead to criminal proceedings being brought against them.

In particular, artefacts of questionable provenance appearing on the open market since 1970, the benchmark year for the introduction of the protections offered by the UNESCO Convention, are now far less attractive objects of desire at public auctions and sales. As observed at the outset of this introduction, there is also now a surge of interest and activity among numbers of countries on the supply side of the stolen artefact market in pursuing the recovery of looted objects, even if they have been in the hands of institutions for substantial periods of time.

Despite these positive developments, the majority of the authors in this book acknowledge, directly or indirectly, that the role to be played by law enforcement and the criminal law in responding to the illicit trafficking of art and antiquities must at best be seen as a palliative for a problem whose scope and dimensions is such as to require other remedies as well. Thus Manacorda, in a far reaching survey of trends at the international level towards a strengthening of criminal sanctions for illicit activities in cultural property, issues a cautionary warning about such actions. He suggests, for example, that proposals for the extension of international instruments like the UN Convention against Transnational Organised Crime to this area of crime are based on shaky evidence about the involvement of major organised cartels in the illicit art and antiquities trade. Laws of this type can be unduly repressive in their reach and impact, affecting the civil liberties of citizens without being proven to improve protections over the cultural heritage of nation states.

Mackenzie also questions the effectiveness of using the criminal law, as was attempted quite recently in the United Kingdom with the introduction of legislation intended to ban dealing in illicit antiquities within its jurisdiction. Research conducted by Mackenzie and a colleague regarding the implementation of this new law found it had a negligible impact on such dealing, most of those involved in the trade believing quite correctly that the risks of detection were minimal and the possibility of being prosecuted successfully even slimmer because of flaws in the definition of offences, and the associated evidence required to establish guilt.

Responses: Market Regulation and Reduction

If law enforcement and the criminal law do not possess the exclusive power or the ability to deal comprehensively with the trade in looted artefacts, what other remedies are there that might be effective? Two possible approaches, which offer promise and are referred to by several authors in the book, relate to market regulation and reduction.

An extensive literature exists in regard to the regulation of many different types of market, including those tainted by criminal activities like those described in this book. Braithwaite (1993, 2002), for one, has proposed what he terms a regulatory pyramid, whereby various forms of soft persuasion at the base of the pyramid are used to try and gain compliance with acceptable rules of behaviour in a market like that in art and antiquities. Such persuasion may be couched in the guise of codes of ethical conduct set by those involved in the market which, if breached, may lead to censure by colleagues. Ultimately, however, if compliance is not gained by persuasion harsher and stepped up measures towards the peak of the pyramid may be required, such as a loss of licence to do business. The step of last resort may be the use of a criminal sanction.

Codes of ethics do exist (see Annex #'s 19–21) although their levels of acceptance and compliance among the groups involved – primarily museum directors and art and antiquities dealers – remains uncertain. One of the weaknesses of such professional codes is that they apply in practice only to members of the groups who formulate them. Frequently, questionable practices occur among outsiders who have no formal ties to these groups and who can still operate their businesses with impunity because typically no official regulatory system is in place to licence their dealings in art and antiquities. It would seem that most dealers, whether or not members of their professional bodies, are opposed to the imposition of any new government regulation upon their activities.

Mackenzie, after considering the forces that drive the demand for looted artefacts, advances some persuasive arguments for the adoption of a number of market reduction measures in this field. Drawing upon the general criminological literature concerned with organised crime and its involvement in markets, he suggests a combination of three associated types of crime prevention response – first, reducing the demand for illegal product and services; second, increasing the awareness of abuse by facilitators (often lawyers and accountants) and making it more difficult for them to operate illicitly; and third, diminishing the tools in the licit environment which can be used by organised criminals through measures like stronger anti-money laundering provisions. Each of these measures, labelled the Market Reduction Approach (MRA), when applied to the broader market in stolen goods was believed to instil an appreciation among thieves that the transportation, storing and selling of stolen goods was at least as risky as it was to steal goods, and that active trading in such goods was appreciably more risky for all involved. The same effect might apply, according to Mackenzie, to the related marketing of stolen antiquities.

Chappell and Polk also offer proposals for a market reduction approach which relate to but are also different from those advanced by Mackenzie. Their emphasis is directed more towards public awareness and education programmes within demand environments for stolen artefacts. These programmes, like the successful campaigns against smoking, drink-driving, wearing of seat belts or preventing the spread of AIDS, are designed to alter community attitudes and behaviour in a particular area without primary resort to criminal laws and sanctions. Such laws and sanctions, if used at all, are seen as being a tool of last resort. In the context of stolen artefacts, the message to be conveyed is that their acquisition is wrongful, and that the purchase of any such object should only proceed, where lawful provenance can be established. Turning a blind eye to questions about the legitimacy of the source of an object of art or antiquity, as has tended to be the practice in the past, should be viewed as totally unacceptable behaviour.

It is suggested that there are some signs that this form of a market reduction approach is already having some effect at the level of institutional directors, boards of trustees and other high-level actors within the art and antiquities world following the well-publicised prosecutions flowing from the Medici case. None of these actors can be keen to be portrayed in the media as the purveyors or beneficiaries of stolen artefacts. Equally the wealthy patrons, upon whom so many of the world's museums rely for the donation of art and antiquity treasures, are unlikely to wish to have their gifts labelled as being from dubious sources, or rejected outright because they are believed to be stolen.

Significantly, in 2008 the Association of Art Museum Directors (AAMD) adopted a new policy on the acquisition of archaeological materials and ancient art which reflects a more principled view on this topic. It was agreed by the AAMD that its members "should not acquire a work unless research substantiates that the work was outside its country of probable modern discovery before 1970 or was legally exported from its probable country of modern discovery after 1970" (AAMD 2008, p. 5). As commentators have noted the choice of 1970 is significant because it coincides with the UNESCO Convention of that year (Gill 2008).

It remains to be seen whether this more principled behaviour by the AAMD is now displayed among the broader collecting public who may be less moved by altruistic considerations, or the potential shame and opprobrium associated with the handling of stolen goods. The AAMD has also strengthened its stand by establishing an "Object Registry" which places in the public domain all relevant information about any newly acquired artefacts that had no recorded collecting histories prior to 1970. Already it would seem certain private collectors in the US have expressed concern that archaeological items they at present own will no longer be welcomed as gifts, purchases or bequests (Gill 2008).

Future Directions

From Cairo to Vienna and beyond, as this brief introduction to this book has sought to demonstrate, there is now an energetic, at times controversial but generally civilised dialogue at many levels about how best to address the long standing and seemingly intractable problems associated with the illicit trafficking of cultural artefacts. The dialogue is no longer limited to exchanges between nation states within forums like the United Nations, nor to countries whose cultural heritage has been subjected to past plunder. Across the globe no one involved in any aspect of the acquisition, sale, restoration or display of cultural artefacts can really remain aloof from questions about the provenance of such artefacts and their possible links, contemporary or ancient, with the illicit market we have described.

If we are on the cusp of a more principled and comprehensive approach towards the protection of cultural artefacts from plunders, as has been suggested above, what are some of the broad brushed and future directions that this movement might take? At the international level, there is the increasing prospect that countries like those represented at the Cairo gathering in 2010 achieve the repatriation of some of the high profile looted items they have identified as theirs, and which currently are on display in foreign museums. This is not the place to enter the debate, stimulated by people like James Cuno (2008), about who should own antiquity and where it is best kept and displayed. Regardless of this debate, the return of stolen artefacts by national authorities, museums, and galleries across several continents is a real and growing phenomenon.

A recent example of this can be found in the repatriation in 2010 by the US authorities of an Egyptian sarcophagus, seized in 2008 by vigilant customs officials at Miami International Airport in Florida (Gill 2010). Investigations revealed that the coffin, exported from a Spanish gallery in Barcelona, was being imported by a US citizen who was neither an art dealer nor broker but who claimed to have already sold it to a Canadian. Neither the exporter nor importer could demonstrate that the sarcophagus had been lawfully removed from Egypt. Lacking a genuine provenance the object was deemed to be owned by Egypt, through its cultural patrimony laws, and the coffin was seized as an item of imported stolen property.

The stolen sarcophagus story has a happy ending due largely to the professional capabilities of the US border officials who queried and then investigated the circumstances surrounding this particular object. Unfortunately, such capabilities are still rare in many parts of the world, as are the resources to inspect in any detail the vast numbers of trafficked objects that are moved on a regular basis across international borders. Often such movements are facilitated by corrupt officials along the supply chain. This leads to a further future direction that the dialogue on this topic may take us, namely, towards capacity building at various levels of law enforcement in the measures that might be taken to identify, investigate, and prosecute those involved in the illicit trafficking of cultural artefacts. Bogdanos suggests that such actions should extend to the establishment of a coordinated international law enforcement response to tackle the looted antiquities market, including a much more assertive role being played by Interpol and greater cooperation between law enforcement agencies and the cultural heritage community. These proposals have substantial merit but implementing them requires leadership and commitment at many levels of government across the globe.

Another future direction, and one which we believe to be essential, must be the continuation and extension of the public awareness campaigns about the evils of the trade in stolen antiquities to a much broader audience than the elites who currently set acquisition and related policies in the museums and galleries of the rich countries of the world, and the high profile dealers and collectors who fuel this illicit market. Already certain members of these groups have displayed a lack of sympathy with the recent bout of repatriations of objects to Italy and elsewhere by various museums and galleries. In the US, for instance, it was reported in June 2010 that a prominent curator at the Princeton University Art Museum, J. Michael Padgett, along with a Princeton alumnus, were being investigated by Italian authorities regarding their alleged involvement in acquiring looted artefacts (Barksdale Maynard 2010a; Eakin 2010). The alumnus named in the case was a former New York antiquities dealer, Eduardo Almagia, who it was claimed had from the mid 1990s to the early 2000s, through Padgett, sold, donated or lent a number of artefacts to the Princeton museum which were believed to have been looted from Italian sites. Almagia was also alleged to have been involved in the sale of other looted objects to a range of prominent US museums during the 1980s (Eakin 2010).

The Princeton Alumni Weekly (PAW) magazine conducted an interesting interview with Almagia, who now lives in Italy, about his reaction to the various allegations made against him (Barksdale Maynard 2010b). Almagia claimed that the investigation was meant to punish him for his political activism in campaigning against a long standing Italian law, first passed during Mussolini's time in office in 1939, by which the Italian government claimed ownership of all antique objects in the country, including those in private homes. He went on to say:

> You are immediately equated with a criminal nowadays by being a collector...... Its like prohibition in the United States – there's a criminal underworld. Italian law leads to crime. By legalising the market in antiquities you destroy the black market and eliminate the incentive to forgeries (Barksdale Maynard 2010b).

Almagia was also asked about his views on an agreement reached between the Princeton museum and Italian authorities in 2007 to return certain objects to Italy. He said that the agreement was ridiculous and that the Italians "had set up an operation to scour every American dealer and museum coast to coast" for looted artefacts. "It's a publicity stunt" he said. "Every American museum should fight for its right to acquire objects in the market. The museum has a right to collect; the dealers have right to deal" (Barksdale Maynard 2010b).

The expression of such obdurate opinions illustrates how the apparent lack of any current rigorous ethical codes among antiquities dealers still allows the market to trade in unprovenanced objects looted from multivarious sites. The opinions also seem somewhat at odds with the views noted earlier of the AAMD about the importance of principled collecting. It appears further at odds with the recent trend among numbers of the US museums, including Princeton, to resolve antiquities disputes through a series of bilateral agreements with the Italian government (Eakin 2010). Associated with these restitution agreements have been arrangements which permit museums to have long-term loans of various objects previously viewed as having a disputed provenance – a beneficial outcome for all concerned.

The Princeton investigation is also interesting from the perspective of the involvement of academia in the illicit market in antiquities. Brodie, in his chapter, draws attention to this issue, and to the facilitating role played by academic experts in archaeology who are able to provide an attribution of authenticity and authorship to objects of dubious provenance, increasing their value and smoothing their passage through the marketplace. In the Princeton investigation, this facilitating role was alleged to have been undertaken by curator J. Michael Padgett. As Brodie indicates, the academic community needs to consider carefully what are the legitimate boundaries of expert archaeological involvement in providing authentication and allied services of this type. From an ethical perspective alone it would seem hard to justify continuing advice being provided about the authentication of any object believed to have been unlawfully obtained. There might also be a duty to report any suspicions about an unlawful provenance to the appropriate authorities.

If in the future efforts to reduce the demand for illicitly obtained cultural objects are successful, they may well have some side effects which need to be recognised and dealt with. One of these side effects is the potential for the demand to be taken up by the creation of fake objects – a practice which is already evident in some art and antiquities markets (Polk and Chappell 2009; Spencer 2004). It is not within the framework of this book to consider fake objects, but it is a hazard present in the marketplace and one which offers lucrative rewards for certain skilled criminals.

Another potential side effect of successful demand reduction is likely to be the price inflation for objects which are known to have a lawful provenance. Volatility is already part of the art and antiquities market so price inflation may simply be absorbed, along with the other economic factors that drive the market at any given time (Thompson 2008). A further factor which may drive up prices is the changing influence and impact of the market in Chinese cultural objects. In the past, China has been viewed as principally a supplier of art and antiquities, many of them obtained from illicit excavations and exported illegally to external markets through ports like Hong Kong and Bangkok (Alder et al. 2009). More recently, however, with growing prosperity and economic power, the Chinese have begun to develop their own internal market for antiquities, and have also sought to secure treasured objects taken from the country by past occupying powers like Britain and France (Levin 2010; McDonald 2009).

With price inflation, and what would seem eventually to be an inevitable diminution in the supply of new cultural objects available from licit or illicit excavations across the globe as fresh sites for exploitation become rarer and the old ones are exhausted, concern about looting may shift to concern about theft of treasured objects from their places of display in public and private collections. This trend may not occur immediately but there do seem some signs that well-organised criminals are now turning their attention to the theft of high value art and antiquities (Carvajal 2010). This is a trend which requires monitoring.

It is hoped that this book stimulates not only better monitoring of issues like this, but also informs the contemporary dialogue about the best ways in which to protect cultural artefacts from plunder in the future. Making progress in curbing looting may at times appear a forlorn and distant goal, but there is now at least a growing cohort of concerned and involved nations prepared to move onwards from Cairo to Vienna and beyond.

References

Alder, C., Chappell, D. and Polk, K. (2009). Perspectives on the organisation and control of the illicit traffic in antiquities in South East Asia. In Manacorda, S. (Ed.) Organised Crime in Art and Antiquities. Milano, Italy: ISPAC.

Association of Art Museum Directors (AAMD) (2008). Report of the AAMD Task Force on the Acquisition of Archaeological Materials and Ancient Art (Revised 2008). New York: AAMD.

Barksdale Maynard, W. (2010a). Art museum curator targeted by Italian prosecutors. Alumnus also reportedly named in probe of looted works of ancient art. Princeton Alumni Weekly. July 7, 2010. Vol. 110(16). http://paw.princeton.edu/issues/2010/07/07/pages/8023/index.xml. Accessed August 4, 2010.

Barksdale Maynard, W. (2010b). Italy's antiquities and US museums: A Q&A with Edoardo Almagia '73. Princeton Alumni Weekly. July 7, 2010. Vol. 110(16). http://paw.princeton.edu/issues/2010/07/07/pages/8254/index.xml. Accessed August 4, 2010.

BBC News (2010a). Egypt hosts antiquities meeting on recovery of 'stolen treasures'. BBC News. http://news.bbc.co.uk/2/hi/middle_east/8606458.stm. Accessed August 2, 2010.

BBC News (2010b). Egypt calls for antiquities unity. BBC News. http://news.bbc.co.uk/2/hi/middle_east/8608513.stm. Accessed August 2, 2010.

Braithwaite, J. (1993). Business Regulation and Australia's Future. Canberra: Australian Institute of Criminology.

Braithwaite, J. (2002). Restorative Justice and Responsive Regulation. New York: Oxford University Press.

Carvajal, D. (2010). Seeking clues, Paris examines security after art theft. New York Times. June 2, 2010. http://www.nytimes.com/2010/05/22/world/europe/22iht-paris.html. Accessed May 21, 2010.

Charney, N. (2009). Introduction. In Charney, N. (Ed.). Art and Crime. Exploring the Dark Side of the Art World (p. xvii). Santa Barbara, CA: Praeger.

Cuno, J. (2008). Who Owns Antiquity. Museums and the Battle over Our Ancient Heritage. Princeton: Princeton University Press.

Davis, A. (2010). Italy repatriates EU15 million of antiquities from Switzerland. Bloomberg. July 16, 2010. http://www.bloomberg.com/news/2010-07-16/italy-repatriates-eu15-million-of-looted-antiquities-found-in-switzerland.html. Accessed August 4, 2010.

De Roquefeuil, C. (2010). Zahi Hawass, media savvy guardian of Egypt's past. Agence France Presse. February 14, 2010. http://www.google.com/hostednews/afp/article/ALeqM5g8YEXuhBvWwwzpjIAw9NwaKCGmHA. Accessed August 2, 2010.

Eakin, H. (2010). Italy focuses on a Princeton curator in an antiquities investigation. New York Times. June 2, 2010. http://www.nytimes.com/2010/06/03/arts/design/03curator.html?pagewanted=1. Accessed August 2, 2010.

Gill, D. (2008). AAMD and antiquities: A revised position. Looting Matters. June 5, 2008. http://lootingmatters.blogspot.com/2008/06/aamd-and-antiquities-revised-position.html. Accessed August 4, 2010.

Gill, D. (2010). Egyptian sarcophagus returned. Looting Matters. March 13, 2010. http://looting-matters.blogspot.com/2010_03_01_archive.html. Accessed August 4, 2010.

Harris, J. (2010). Crackdown on culture crime: Italy's proud Carabinieri art squad. Association for Research into Crimes against Art. January 19, 2010. http://art-crime.blogspot.com/2010/01/crackdown-on-culture-crime-italys-proud.html. Accessed August 4, 2010.

Heritage Thieves (2010). 300 looted antiquities displayed in the Colosseum. July 17, 2010. http://heritagethieves.blogspot.com/2010/07/300-looted-antiquities-displayed-in.html. Accessed August 2, 2010.

Levin, D. (2010). Reactionaries? Make that 'collectors'. New York Times. February 3, 2010. http://www.nytimes.com/2010/02/04/garden/04chinese.html. Accessed August 2, 2010.

Manacorda, S. (Ed.) (2009). Organised crime in art and antiquities. Milano, Italy: ISPAC.

McDonald, M. (2009). Chinese bidder says he will not pay for looted bronzes. New York Times. March 2, 2009. http://www.nytimes.com/2009/03/02/arts/02iht-03auction.20522775.html. Accessed August 4, 2010.

Polk, K. and Chappell, D. (2009). Fakes and deception: Examining fraud in the art market. In Charney, N. (Ed.). Art and Crime. Exploring the Dark Side of the Art World (p. xvii). Santa Barbara, CA: Praeger.

Povoledo, E. (2010). Rome trial of ex- Getty curator ends. New York Times. October 13, 2010. http://www.nytimes.com/2010/10/14/arts/design/14true.html?_r=1&scp=11&sq=povoledo+2008&st=nyt. Accessed October 14, 2010.

Scherer, S. (2009). Rome court upholds conviction of antiquities smuggler Medici. Bloomberg News. July 15, 2009. http://www.bloomberg.com/apps/news?pid=newsarchive&sid=a4JP7NRy5BFM. Accessed August 2, 2010.

Spencer, R. (Ed.) (2004). The Expert Versus the Object. Judging Fakes and False Attributions in the Visual Arts. Oxford: Oxford University Press.

Thompson, D. (2008). The $12 Million Stuffed Shark. The Curious Economics of Contemporary Art. London: Palgrave Macmillan.

Tierney, J. (2009). A case in antiquities for 'finders keepers'. New York Times. November 17, 2009. http://www.nytimes.com/2009/11/17/science/17tier.html?_r=1&ref=john_tierney. Accessed August 2, 2010.

United Nations Economic and Social Council (ECOSOC) (2010). Protection against trafficking in cultural property. Report of the Secretary General. ECOSOC February 23, 2010. E/CN.15/2010/4.

Watson, P and Todeschini, C. (2006). The Medici conspiracy. Prahran, Victoria: Hardie Grant Books.

Chapter 2
Criminal Law Protection of Cultural Heritage: An International Perspective

Stefano Manacorda

Introduction: The Criminal Law Dimension in the Protection of Cultural Goods

For more than 50 years – and a good deal longer in certain areas – the international community has exerted considerable efforts to protect the world's cultural heritage in its various facets. These efforts, whether to protect movable or immovable assets, reflects their importance which far transcends their mere economic value, since they represent a significant expression of the history and traditions of nations, reflected in the concrete choices that the law is required to address. Further strong calls for juridical protection have also arisen since the end of the colonial era with the growing demands of States that were victims of despoliation in earlier centuries, demanding restitution of their assets and works of global importance that had been appropriated, often in highly questionable ways.[1]

However, there is a growing recognition among observers that the past development of international instruments regarding the protection of cultural heritage has pursued a protective aim, giving only a primarily marginal, disorganized and fragmentary role to their punitive element. Indeed, in some areas, international law has widely favoured recourse to extra-penal instruments, commercial or civil law in nature (with special emphasis, as is well known, to the remedy of return and restitution). In other areas, while compelling States to impose penal sanctions, the juridical framework outlined by international instruments has often been muddled, convoluted and incomplete. From this starting-point, the aim of this paper is to *analyse critically the criminal law dimension emerging at the international level in the field of safeguarding cultural assets* and to examine the prospects for possible reforms. By way of introduction, however, there is a need to look at the extent of the theme from a

[1]On *cultural internationalism* as compared to *cultural nationalism*, see Merryman (1985, 1986).

S. Manacorda (✉)
Centro Nazionale di Prevenzione e Difesa Sociale Piazza Castello 3, 20121, Milano, Italy
and
Université Paris 1 Panthéon Sorbonne, Paris, France
e-mail: stefano.manacorda@unina2.it

S. Manacorda and D. Chappell (eds.), *Crime in the Art and Antiquities World: Illegal Trafficking in Cultural Property*, DOI 10.1007/978-1-4419-7946-9_2,

methodological point of view as well as its inherent content. *In methodological terms*, one has to ask whether we should focus so strongly today on the punitive dimension in the protection of cultural assets. As is well known, criminal law scholars in recent decades have tended to concentrate primarily on restricting the punitive response to comply with the fundamental principles of *extrema ratio* and proportionality, pursuing instead conceptual schemes moving progressively from reduced to minimalist sanctions and ultimately to abolish them altogether. In this scenario, international law has tended to act in a contrary direction, pressing criminal law legislators towards the definition and adoption of further and ever broader criminal offences and operating as one of the most influential factors pushing towards the expansion of domestic legislation. It is precisely this one-way direction (real or supposed) of international norms, accompanied moreover by a general inadequacy of institutional procedures with regard to the traditional canons of legality, which has given rise to extremely severe criticisms in a large area of penal science relative to this "criminalisation engine". International law, in its various articulations, has thus come to represent the main object of critical analysis from the "classical" quarter of penology, which moreover is currently reviving – not without some controversy – concerning the strong trends inspired by social defence and the concept of dangerousness. We must then wonder whether we should subscribe in theoretical terms to a standpoint in favour of recourse (or greater recourse) to the punitive instrument even in an apparently marginal area like the protection of artistic, archaeological and cultural assets.

Such a fundamental interrogation cannot be wholly discarded with an assumption that it is essential to proceed in this direction (in other words that there exists an "ontological necessity" connected to the abstract importance of the interests concerned) or by merely asserting that a trend towards criminalization is spreading among international organizations (so as to reveal, in other words, an "institutional necessity"), while contrarily demanding a close scrutiny of possible reasons militating for an intensification of political–criminal instruments. This paper, therefore, must *first of all address the supposed need for a justification* (which must be demonstrated) for a greater move towards criminalisation in *cultural heritage* protection, by examining the empirical and value-based arguments underlying this choice. Yet, it must not be forgotten that favouring a greater use of international instruments in the punitive field does not exempt one from verifying the extent to which such an approach should be adopted.

Practical considerations also necessitate *limiting the aims*, in order to comply with the permitted length of this contribution. The cultural heritage theme in fact embraces a wide range of issues that are difficult to unify, and involves an extremely difficult definition, given the absolute relativity of the concept of art and culture.[2]

[2]Lalive (2009a), page 4: "a movable object may only be characterized as "artistic" or "cultural" as a result of a value judgment, i.e. of a personal and subjective opinion. Contrary to ordinary movables or chattels, it can hardly be described with precision by its weight or measure – and its value does not depend on physical characteristics but rather on aesthetic or historic factors. Hence, the difficulty of regulating sales of works of art and, for instance, the responsibility of the seller and the relevance of an expertise. So the definition of cultural property is clearly an obstacle, first to legislation (national and "international") on the subject, and then to its implementation".

At this point it is opportune to introduce a *summa divisio* which, however approximately, allows the exclusion of a good proportion of objects from the scope of the study and thereby facts which (potentially) may come within the scope of criminal law. Thus, no analysis is made in the present study of the heritage of immovable property – unless purely incidentally – although it is important and is dealt within specific provisions in the international field (especially in humanitarian international law and international criminal law). Immoveable property includes historical and religious buildings, whole urban centres, monuments erected as part of mankind's heritage. More widely, we also exclude natural resources from the scope of this study which could otherwise be covered in a broad definition of cultural heritage, even though these certainly deserve to be protected under criminal law for the high value they embody within their social environment, being both unique and irreplaceable.

International law today appears to focus on the *strengthening of protection for movable assets, notably including artistic and archaeological assets*, which might be packaged within the overall definition of *cultural property*. Furthermore, while the protection of immovable property is now included in the international normative framework, at least with reference to extremely serious phenomena (war crimes and other violent acts arising during armed conflict), the movable property sector – as we see – appears, by comparison, defenceless in terms of criminal law protection. Having thus defined our area of study, further precision still is called for, since the diversity of objects endowed with cultural importance has already led to a diversity of choices in the international instruments devoted to this subject.

With the scope of our examination thus set out, we can proceed to the main issues requiring analysis. Initially, we have to ask what basic contemporary factors have led to a potential extension of the international criminal law sector to cultural heritage protection? Two different issues then require consideration: first an identification of the empirical–criminological components of criminal activity in the artistic and cultural field, and second the identification of the objects to be protected and thereby the importance that the cultural and common heritage of mankind is destined to assume in the face of harmful or dangerous assaults.

Secondly, we proceed to a review of the punitive components of the conventional regulation of artistic and cultural assets. In looking forward to the basic elements expected to emerge from this analysis, which occupies a major part of our study, we emphasize both the heterogeneity and a certain "criminal minimalism" in the international juridical scene.

The aspect to be examined immediately after setting out the areas for the application of important internationally sourced norms concerns an evaluative component of great substance, capable of providing a number of critical leads on the concrete choice for criminalisation crystallized in the texts contained in international pacts but remitted for their practical application to national legislatures.

Finally, we reflect on some issues arising in the debate in order to reform the present legal framework.

The Punitive Option for the Protection of Movable Cultural Assets: Its Fundamentals and Limits in the Light of a Criminological Evaluation

Crimes variously related to artistic, cultural and archaeological assets present a very diffuse phenomenon, nationally as well as internationally and little is known about their nature and extent.[3] Today, we still do not have a systematic approach to the gathering of criminal statistics which would permit an accurate analysis of such crimes, most of which are likely to be unreported or "hidden statistics" (*chiffre noir*).[4]

Some information may be gleaned from the limited official data provided by national authorities, but although these are certainly useful to a degree, they offer only an extremely restricted tranche of criminal typologies and trends.

In Italy, for example, in view of the richness of the national heritage, useful elements appear in the 2009 report of the Comando tutela Patrimonio Culturale (Heritage Protection Command) of the Carabinieri,[5] which highlights, relative to the previous year: a significant diminution of *thefts* in general (95 cases, a reduction of c. 14.5%); a continuing persistence of the phenomenon of *falsification*, as seen in the high number of people pursued before the Judicial Authority (299 cases, an increase of 424%); a major reduction in *illicit excavations* (161 cases, −76%); a slight but significant increase of counter activity in terms of both persons pursued before the Judicial Authority (+2%) and of the variety of typology of the offences prosecuted.

There are a good number of official data banks, from which it is possible to deduce, albeit in extremely summary form, the totality of crime in the field of art and antiquities. For example, the French authority appointed to take charge in this sector (*Central office for combating trafficking in cultural assets*) has a specific data-bank, the *Thesaurus of electronic and image research in artistic matters* ("TRIMA"), which since 1985 has assembled data on stolen objects (names of the victims, details of thefts, photographs), including up to now some 20,000 items. In recent years, however, there has been a decrease: the count of cases handled by the police authorities has moved from some 8,000 cases recorded annually to 2,023 in 2008.[6]

Recently, the inadequate and fragmentary nature of available data on the extent of crime in this area has been underlined in the work of the UN *Commission on Crime Prevention and Criminal Justice*: "Analysis of data over time for the States reporting a continuous time series for police-recorded offences involving theft of cultural property for the period 2003–2008 (10 States) suggests a consistent decreasing trend". Caution must be exercised in such analysis, however, due to the small number of States for which data are available and to differences in the definition of theft of cultural property.[7]

---

[3] Polk (1999).

[4] Brodie et al. (2000). See also Calvani (2009).

[5] Comando Tutela patrimonio Culturale dei Carabinieri. *Relazione per l'anno 2009* (December, 2009).

[6] Gauffeny (2009).

[7] Commission on Crime Prevention and Criminal Justice (2010).

Apart from the quantitative data, thus summarized, studies in this field lead one to underline certain prevalent characteristics in this area of crime, which may be summarized as set out below.

(a) A *paradigm of transnational crime*. Unlawful activities in the field of art and antiquities often involve the use of highly specialized techniques and skills, which operate across frontiers so that the structural elements of the crime are rarely confined to the territory of a single country. In view of the exponential increase in the circulation (including unlawful trafficking) of individual cultural objects, the transnational nature of the crimes shows a continuous growth, and this results in a corresponding attention to trafficking phenomena (in drugs, arms and human beings), all of them highly profitable, which can easily extend into the field of cultural assets.[8] A number of factors explain this trend. First, the international traffic, including legitimate trade, is stimulated by the presence of States particularly rich in terms of their artistic and archaeological heritage, that are traditionally victims of looting, and of States which, for basically economic reasons, act as importers of such assets. The transnational dimension of the crime, moreover, is supported by the diversity of juridical frameworks (both in the field of private as well as criminal law) which prevail in different national systems and by the presence of national legislations favouring the import of cultural assets.[9] Further, the development of *e-commerce* currently represents a valid mechanism for putting assets of dubious provenance on the international market. This development can be seen in the case study elsewhere in this book (Brodie) concerning looting from Iraq which highlights the commercialization, through the internet, of numerous finds of questionable provenance.[10] This combination of factors fully justifies the attention that we are now paying to set out the punitive responses offered from international sources, in a perspective of closer cooperation between state authorities and, marginally, of a growing measure of closer harmonization in domestic penal legislation.
(b) A second characteristic of undoubted interest is the *porosity between the legal and the illegal market* in antiquities.[11] Licit and illicit trade in *objets d'art* and in antiques passes through the same channels. This is particularly true for the intermediaries: auction houses, antiques dealers and galleries can find themselves, often unknowingly, handling illegally sourced goods, as a series of instances coming to light in recent years have amply demonstrated. Moreover, this applies also to the final consignees (museums, private collections) who – in the majority of cases through sheer negligence – may come to acquire cultural assets which have been stolen or illegally exported.

[8]Tijhuis (2009).

[9]Lalive (2009b), page 9: "theft or cultural property nearly always involves the crossing of a frontier. Why? Not only (in fact) because the thieves (often organised but also individuals) hope to better escape the police! but also in order to benefit from the diversity of national laws regulating the acquisition by the so-called 'purchaser in good faith' ".

[10]Brodie (2009).

[11]Massy (2008).

(c) Finally, we must mention the correlation of crime in the artistic and archaeological sector with these *unlawful phenomena on a broader scale*, such as receiving of stolen goods, money-laundering and financial and tax offences, that are systematically highlighted by the police authorities and are relevant also in our present study. As the United Nations has emphasized, this associated area is especially problematic at the present time as it concerns the role played by *organized crime* in this field, Thus *Resolution 2004/34 of 21 July 2004, Protection Against Trafficking in Cultural Property*,[12] of the Economic and Social Council notes that "organized criminal groups are involved in trafficking in stolen cultural property and that the international trade in looted, stolen or smuggled cultural property is estimated at several billion United States dollars per year". As we see later, various political–diplomatic initiatives have been undertaken on the basis of such a (problematic) premise.

Undoubtedly, there are criminal activities which, in the great majority of cases, have organized and many-faceted forms: international trafficking in works of art is rarely the work of a single individual. Nor are we to ignore the fact that notorious organized crime groups, such as the Mafia, are giving close attention to the art and antiquities market for a number of reasons that have recently come to light: the undoubted huge profit margins available; probably also for the high symbolic value of works of art in terms of personal status; finally, for their importance as a common heritage, whose removal and destruction may be perceived as a *vulnus* to the whole national community and an element of the might of the criminal organization. Having said this, it is doubtful if one should go further and maintain that this represents a "typical" activity of the major criminal organizations in the way in which drug trafficking, extortion, or certain forms of forgery are.[13]

In terms of punitive responses, on the basis of the characteristics just examined, a very important contest is emerging in the protection of antiquities. Not infrequently recourse is had in the systems where they are established to crimes of criminal association or conspiracy, provided that the offences against antiquities meet the level of gravity required by the relevant legislative provisions. Influenced by some States particularly active in taking a punitive approach to the protection of cultural heritage items, the international community is now endeavouring to include illicit actions involving such items within the all-embracing category of organized crime. The outcome of such endeavours (or perhaps the main objective) is to then apply the range of especially effective penal instruments and procedures developed over recent years (like "invasive"

[12]ECOSOC (2004).

[13]In the Report of the General Secretary, entitled *Protection against trafficking in cultural property*, presented to the Commission on Crime Prevention and Criminal Justice 15th Session held in Vienna from 24 to 28 April 2006, Italy declared that: "As far as the involvement of organized crime in trafficking in cultural property was concerned, reference was made to the analysis of results of investigations carried out in the country showing that only in a few limited circumstances were Mafia-type organizations involved in that specific field. *Such trafficking was more often organized by individuals or criminal groups that utilized international contacts* consolidated over the years and managed to set up illicit markets abroad" (emphasis added).

investigative techniques, under-cover operations, evidential assistance such as the reversal of the burden of proof, mechanisms for seizure and confiscation, inclusion of offences among those on which money-laundering is based, etc.) to the field of cultural property. However, caution needs to be exercised when broadening the concept of organized crime in this way since it is a nebulous concept at the best of times and often involves the application of quite draconian measures affecting individual liberties.

(d) Finally, it must be stated that an important element in the expansion of crime is this sector derives from the contrast between its economic scope, with the vast profits produced, and the *relatively modest penalties* which can be imposed. This element, moreover, is accentuated by the diversity of penalties applied between jurisdictions which can lead to "forum shopping" among the most cunning criminals, who adopt strategies to avoid prosecution in those jurisdictions known for the severity of their penal responses.

The Cultural Heritage as the Property of Mankind

Identification of the juridical assets to be protected, as an essential basis for the punitive response, presents a series of difficulties, beginning with the extreme variability of the definition of *cultural heritage*.[14] Here, we confine ourselves to underline how, even on an international plane, there is growing awareness of the enormous range of artistic and archaeological assets that need to be protected. This knowledge has been evidenced by the way in which a number of Penal Codes have now added cultural property offences to their contents.[15]

Cultural assets are then considered in legal doctrine as part of mankind's rights, both in their individual dimension, relative to the law applying to each cultural object and to the rights of peoples' historical and cultural identity.[16] They receive the public attention appropriate to their universality. A special importance is attributed to religious objects, a symbol of the collective identity. Recent conflicts have strongly evidenced the importance of such items, which have been subjected to wide and indiscriminate assaults, sometimes tending even to destroy the identity of a people. Examples can be found in the forms of ethnic cleansing perpetrated in the former Yugoslavia, including the burning of the Sarajevo library and the attack on the ancient historical centre of Dubrovnik; in the destruction of the statue of the Bayman Buddha in Afghanistan; and in the looting of the Baghdad museum during the occupation of Iraq.[17]

Various international texts recognize the crucial importance of cultural assets: the norms to protect property and basic freedoms contained in the Universal Declaration of Human Rights and in the International Convention on Economic and Social Rights

---

[14] Merryman (1990); Blake (2000a).

[15] Merryman (1990); Blake (2000a).

[16] Blake (2000b); Francioni (2004).

[17] Phuong (2004).

indirectly support this recognition. At a generic level, the protection of "*the common heritage of mankind*" represented by assets such as books, monuments, works of art or science, lies within the province of UNESCO (Article 1 of the Statute).[18] This corresponds to the progressive growth of knowledge in the international community, especially in the wake of two World Wars, that the damaging, looting and destruction of cultural assets represents a threat to the whole of mankind. So *human common heritage* must be understood as that whole entity of assets of "outstanding universal value", which, in the territory of some States and subject to their sovereignty, become by their intrinsic value important to the whole international community. Since these are assets subject to the sovereignty of individual States, the application of the protective regime laid down by UNESCO – and in particular the 1970 Convention[19] – needs the request of the proprietary State, accepting thereby a self-limitation of national sovereignty over the assets in recognition of their common value for all of mankind.

Gradually, all the instruments adopted in this sector emphasize the correlation between *cultural property* and national identity, including the latest document being developed within the United Nations, namely, that of the Commission for the Prevention of Crime and Criminal Justice. The Commission referred in Vienna in 2010 to "the significance of cultural property as part of the common heritage of humankind and as unique and important testimony of the culture and identity of peoples and the necessity of protecting it".[20] Of great importance is the declaration on the international destruction of the cultural heritage adopted by the General Conference of UNESCO in 2003, with some punitive dimensions, where it is asked that: "States should take all appropriate measures, in accordance with international law, to establish jurisdiction over, and provide effective criminal sanctions against, those persons who commit or order to be committed, acts of international destruction of cultural heritage of great importance for humanity, whether or not it is inscribed on a list maintained by UNESCO or another international organization" (Art VII – *Individual criminal responsibility*).[21]

Review of the Punitive Components of the Conventional Rules for the Protection of Artistic and Cultural Assets: Identification of the Principal Juridical Frameworks

The juridical framework hitherto available shows a marked *heterogeneity* with a plurality of texts (essentially arising from international pacts) and formulations adopted in different eras and meeting the concerns that have arisen in the international community at various historical moments. Among this mass of different

[18] Canino (1997).

[19] O'Keefe (2004).

[20] *Draft Resolution 2010. "Protection against trafficking in cultural property".*

[21] UNESCO *Declaration concerning the Intentional Destruction of Cultural Heritage*, 17 October 2003.

texts, albeit to a variable degree according to the different sectors involved, there is a certain "reluctance" to identify the precise obligations incumbent upon Party States, which sometimes results in a sort of "*penal minimalism*". Brevity and simplicity of exposition compel us to concentrate on two main juridical areas within the international area:

- First, the regime for the protection of the artistic and cultural heritage in conditions of armed conflict (*the juridical framework of exception*), which essentially is contained in the texts of international humanitarian law and international criminal law
- Second, rules governing the circulation of cultural assets in export, import or transfer of them in the broadest sense (*the juridical framework of circulation*) to which the UNESCO and UNIDROIT Conventions, adopted respectively in 1970 and 1995, are dedicated

We will not be looking at *other specific and intermediate juridical regimes*, standing between the paradigms of the exception linked to armed conflict and the everyday circulation of assets, like the regime concerning archaeological assets, which are specifically protected by UNESCO (the UNESCO 2001 Convention on the protection of the submarine cultural heritage)[22] and the Council of Europe.[23]

The "Juridical Framework of Exception": Protection of the Cultural Heritage in Conditions of Armed Conflict. The 1954 Hague Convention in a Penal Perspective

In the first of the normative assets upon which we concentrate lie all those provisions dealing with the protection of the cultural heritage of mankind in case of armed conflict.

In the modern era, the starting point is represented by the *Convention for the protection of cultural property in the case of armed conflict*, signed at The Hague on 14 May 1954, which came into force on 7 August 1956, as a reaction to the acts of barbarism committed during World War II, and which apply when war is declared or international or non-international armed conflict occurs, or a foreign territory is invaded.

The historical antecedents of this discipline lie back in history: first, as the object of a purely *indirect* protection as a result of the propagation of rules for humanizing conflicts, and subsequently, with the bursting on to the scene of military techniques endowed with a massive destructive capability, with the creation of instruments

[22] UNESCO *Declaration concerning the Intentional Destruction of Cultural Heritage*, 17 October 2003.

[23] European Convention on The Protection of The Archaeological Heritage, London, 6 May 1969 and European Convention on The Protection of The Archaeological Heritage (Revised), Valletta, 16 January 1992.

aimed *directly* at protecting cultural assets. Article 35 of the US *Lieber Code* of 1863, which is considered to be the first legislative provision in this field, provides that: "Classical works of art, libraries, scientific collections, or precision instruments, such as astronomical telescopes, as well as hospitals, must be secured against all avoidable injury, even when they are contained in fortified places whilst besieged or bombarded".[24] Later, we have the *Regulations concerning the Laws and Customs of War on Land* linked with the Second Hague Convention of 1907 to intervene in the argument[25]: they lay down the duty of all States to protect immovable assets,[26] while the protection of movable assets was provided, albeit indirectly, through the prohibition of confiscation and injury, with intensified provisions applying in relation to occupied territories.[27]

Nevertheless, we must focus on the 1954 Hague Convention because this was inspired by the experiences of the Military Tribunal of Nuremburg, which signals a fundamental transformation of the juridical framework, resorting to individual liability for offences against the cultural heritage. With regard to the entirety of the cultural heritage, broadly defined by Article 1 of the 1954 Convention as the "movable or immovable property of *great importance*" – and this specification is obviously important because it confines the protection to works of major value – of the cultural heritage of each people, it includes monuments, archaeological sites, works of art and so on, as well as the buildings and historical centres containing them. This is a highly innovative definition, founded on the two criteria of importance to the cultural heritage of any people and the artistic, historical and archaeological interest involved, although this has been criticized in legal doctrine for its vagueness.[28]

[24] General Orders No. 100: *The Lieber Code (Instructions for the Government of Armies of the United States in the Field Prepared by Francis Lieber, promulgated as General Orders No. 100 by President Lincoln, 24 April 1863).*

[25] *Convention (II) with Respect to the Laws and Customs of War on Land and its annex: Regulations concerning the Laws and Customs of War on Land*, The Hague, 29 July 1899. Article 27: "In sieges and bombardments all necessary steps should be taken to spare as far as possible edifices devoted to religion, art, science, and charity, hospitals, and places where the sick and wounded are collected, provided they are not used at the same time for military purposes. The besieged should indicate these buildings or places by some particular and visible signs, which should previously be notified to the assailants".

[26] *Convention (IV) with Respect to the Laws and Customs of War on Land and its annex: Regulations concerning the Laws and Customs of War on Land*, The Hague, 18 October 1907. Article 27: "In sieges and bombardments all necessary steps must be taken to spare, as far as possible, buildings dedicated to religion, art, science, or charitable purposes, historic monuments, hospitals, and places where the sick and wounded are collected, provided they are not being used at the time for military purposes. It is the duty of the besieged to indicate the presence of such buildings or places by distinctive and visible signs, which shall be notified to the enemy beforehand".

[27] Article 56: "The property of municipalities, that of institutions dedicated to religion, charity and education, the arts and sciences, even when State property, shall be treated as private property. All seizure of, destruction or wilful damage done to institutions of this character, historic monuments, works of art and science, is forbidden, and should be made the subject of legal proceedings". See Maugeri (2008a).

[28] Maugeri (2008b).

These are added to the general protection laid down in Articles 2 et seq. the special protection of Articles 8 et seq., based on the mechanism of inscription, under the aegis of the Director General of UNESCO, in an international register of cultural assets covered by special protection, although this does not relate to movable goods except insofar as they are located in the relevant protected sites.

With regard to such assets, the States parties to the 1954 Convention engage themselves to ensure their protection, and prohibits their use for purposes that might expose them to danger in the course of armed conflict (e.g. use of a monument as cover for military action) or involves directly hostile acts (e.g. the bombardment of museums). Additionally, there are express prohibitions of thefts, damaging or improper acquisition, while reprisals – considered legitimate under certain conditions of humanitarian international law – are not permitted against such specifically protected assets.

Further, in the sense of Article 28 of this Convention, "The High Contracting Parties undertake to take, within the framework of their ordinary criminal jurisdiction, all necessary steps to prosecute and impose penal or disciplinary sanctions upon those persons, of whatever nationality, who commit or order to be committed a breach of the present Convention". While this norm comes within the punitive province, it does not seem very demanding, on the one hand because of its extreme generality linked with the imprecise definition of prohibited acts, and on the other by the admissibility of alternative protective instruments by the typical disciplinary sanctions of military law. Nor, despite what was envisaged in the preparatory work, it was stated that only wilful actions were to be the subject of sanctions.[29]

This initial basic text has led to further instruments generated by the international community for the protection of the cultural heritage in conditions of armed conflict. It is significant, in evaluating such an evolution, that the 1954 Convention has had an unsatisfactory reception on the international plane: it was not until 25 September 2008 that the American Senate agreed to its ratification – some 50 years after its signature – and this came into effect on 13 March 2009, bringing the number of adherent States up to 123.

Subsequent Developments: Protocols Additional to the Geneva and Hague Conventions and International Criminal Courts

This subsequent process of evolution has led to the adoption of numerous instruments, among which particular mention – in a much later period – must be made of the Protocols additional to the Geneva Convention and the Hague Convention.

(a) In the first group of texts (*Geneva law*), of particular interest is the *Protocol I of 1977*, which introduces the prohibition of "indiscriminate attacks" and of attacks and reprisals against the civil population,[30] while specific protection is accorded

[29] O'Keefe (2006a).

[30] *Protocol Additional to the Geneva Conventions of 12 August 1949, and relating to the Protection of Victims of International Armed Conflicts (Protocol I)*, 8 June 1977, Articles 51(4) e 52(1).

to cultural assets, even if purely in a subsidiary capacity to the 1954 Convention. Particular interdicts are: (a) to commit any acts of hostility directed against historical monuments, works of art or places of worship which constitute the cultural or spiritual heritage of peoples; (b) to use such objects in support of the military effort and (c) to make such objects the object of reprisals (Art 53. Protection of cultural objects and of places of worship). Further, in the sense of Article 85, are addressed "grave breaches of this Protocol, when committed wilfully and in violation of the Conventions or the Protocol: [...] making the clearly-recognised historic monuments, works of art or places of worship which constitute the cultural or spiritual heritage of peoples and to which special protection has been given by special arrangement, for example, within the framework of a competent international organization, the object of attack, causing as a result extensive destruction thereof, where there is no evidence of the violation by the adverse Party of Article 53, subparagraph (b) and when such historic monuments, works of art and places of worship are not located in the immediate proximity of military objectives" [Article 85(4)(d)]. For such serious violations, deemed to be war crimes [Article 81(5)], domestic law is required to impose sanctions and States are obliged to apply the principle of universal jurisdiction. Individual liability is extended, with an innovative norm destined to lead to important developments in international criminal law and to the so-called *command responsibility*. It has been rightly observed that the norm, in requiring conduct "causing as a result extensive destruction" introduces an instance of damage, although this is superseded by Protocol II of the 1990 Hague Convention, which instead speaks of protecting from the risk of damage.[31] The Second Protocol to the Geneva Convention equally gives protection to cultural property in the course of armed conflicts which are not international in nature (Article 16).[32]

(b) In the second normative area (*The Hague law*) is contained the *First additional Protocol to the 1954 Hague Convention*, adopted at the same date that the main Convention (which requires adherent States to prevent exportation of protected assets from occupied territories) and the *Second Protocol*, adopted on 26 March 1999, which came into force on 9 March 2004 and has currently been ratified by 56 States of whom the latest is Germany (25 November 1999); this extends the Conventional protection to conditions of conflict within States. As has been underlined, the major contribution of these texts lies in a more efficient regulation of individual criminal liability for violations committed intentionally or in excess of military necessity.[33]

In the sense of Article 15 of II Protocol ("Serious violations of this Protocol"), five different instances are set out: "(a) making cultural property under enhanced protection (and thus only in this specific case) the object of attack; (b) using cultural property under enhanced protection or its immediate surroundings in support of military

[31] Maugeri (2008c).

[32] *Protocol Additional to the Geneva Conventions of 12 August 1949, and relating to the Protection of Victims of International Armed Conflicts (Protocol II)*, 8 June 1977.

[33] Maugeri (2008d).

action; (c) extensive destruction or appropriation of cultural property protected under the Convention and this Protocol; (d) making cultural property protected under the Convention and this Protocol the object of attack; e. theft, pillage or misappropriation of, or acts of vandalism directed against cultural property protected under the Convention". As already indicated, each of these instances significantly looks to the threshold of penal protection without requiring, unlike Protocol 1 of the Geneva Convention, the infliction of actual damage.[34] The actions which they describe embrace the extremes of the abstract concept of damage: the legislator presumes, in the particular cases mentioned in letters a, b and d (attack and abuse of property subject to *enhanced protection* or attacks on property protected by the Convention) that such acts expose the protected property to danger, thereby meriting an appropriate punitive response on the part of the States.

In relation to such acts, and differently from the "1954 Convention, there is imposed on each State an obligation to prescribe *criminal offences* under its domestic law [...] and to make such offences punishable by appropriate penalties. When doing so, Parties shall comply with general principles of law and international law, including the rules extending individual criminal responsibility to persons other than those who directly commit the act", with the further obligation, for each of the detailed acts to introduce a universal penal jurisdiction,[35] to introduce provisions for extradition,[36] to recognize the principle *aut dedere aut iudicare* in the case, where there is no current scope for extradition, and to encourage judicial cooperation.

For provisions different from those contemplated by Article 15 the State obligations are much less demanding. One reads, for instance, in Article 21 ("Measures regarding other violations") that: "Without prejudice to Article 28 of the Convention, each Party shall adopt such legislative, *administrative or disciplinary measures* as may be necessary to suppress the following acts when committed intentionally: (a) any use of cultural property in violation of the Convention or this Protocol – as well as, a significant aspect for our present purpose – (b) any illicit export, other removal or transfer of ownership of cultural property from occupied territory in violation of the Convention or this Protocol".

In this context, only deliberate crimes are punishable and a residual role is always given to military necessity.[37] Legal theory debates whether the responsibility extends to every form of participation, e.g. the so-called *command responsibility*: Article 15(2) provides in this regard that: "With respect to the exercise of jurisdiction

[34] O'Keefe (2006b).

[35] Article 16 Jurisdiction: "1. Without prejudice to paragraph 2, each Party shall take the necessary legislative measures to establish its jurisdiction over offences set forth in Article 15 in the following cases: a. when such an offence is committed in the territory of that State; b. when the alleged offender is a national of that State; c. in the case of offences set forth in Article 15 sub-paragraphs (a) to (c), when the alleged offender is present in its territory"; O'Keefe (2006c).

[36] Article 18 Extradition: "1. The offences set forth in Article 15 sub-paragraphs 1 (a) to (c) shall be deemed to be included as extraditable offences in any extradition treaty existing between any of the Parties before the entry into force of this Protocol. Parties undertake to include such offences in every extradition treaty to be subsequently concluded between them". See also Article 20 – *Grounds for refusal.*

[37] Maugeri (2008e).

and without prejudice to Article 28 of the Convention: (a) this Protocol does not preclude the incurring of individual criminal responsibility or the exercise of jurisdiction under national and international law that may be applicable, or affect the exercise of jurisdiction under customary international law", which would lead us to conclude that they embrace the provisions of Article 86(1) of the First Protocol to the Geneva Conventions as well as those of the Statute of the International Criminal Court (Articles 25 and 28), which we now consider briefly.

As a token in this juridical framework, the same international penal jurisdictions, starting with Nuremburg and going on to the ad hoc tribunals of the 1990s and finally the International Criminal Court, have recognized their competence to impose penal sanctions for those acts serious enough to constitute international crimes. There is a very useful examination on this point in cases decided before the *International Criminal Tribunal of the former Yugoslavia (ICTY)*.[38] These deal with "Violations of the laws or customs of war" in the sense of Article 3 *ICTY* Statute (the seizure of, destruction or wilful damage done to institutions dedicated to religion, charity and education, the arts and sciences, historic monuments and works of art and science [Article 3(d)]), but a wider indirect protection is to be found in the other instances contemplated by the same Article 3 and in the succeeding Articles 4 and 5, relating respectively to the crime of genocide and to crimes against humanity.[39]

Finally, it has to be mentioned that the protection afforded by the Rome Statute enables punishment for "Intentionally directing attacks against buildings dedicated to religion, education, art, science or charitable purposes, historic monuments, hospitals and places where the sick and wounded are collected, provided they are not military objectives" [Article 8(2)(b) IX and 2(e)(iv) – ICC Statute].

The "Juridical Framework of Circulation" and the 1970 UNESCO Convention in a Penal Perspective

The second ground for intervention by the international community on illicit imports, exports and transfers of ownership of cultural property was realized – some 40 years ago – in the *UNESCO Convention on the Means of Prohibiting and Preventing the Illicit Import, Export and Transfer of Ownership of Cultural Property*, signed in Paris on 14 November 1970, which came into force on 24 April 1972. At the present time, this is the principal international instrument setting out minimum rules for legislative provisions which the Party States are required to adopt to repress the illegal circulation of cultural property.

The UNESCO Convention is structured in accordance with a double order of considerations. On the one hand, it relies, like other instruments of the Organization, on emphasizing the importance to be accorded to cultural property, as "the basic elements

[38] Abtahi (2001).

[39] Maugeri (2008f).

of civilization and national culture". On the other hand, by focusing strongly on the dangers resulting from illicit acts directed at cultural property, the Preamble underlines how "illicit import, export and transfer of ownership of cultural property is an obstacle to that understanding between nations which it is part of UNESCO's mission to promote". This last element represents the main *raison d'être* of the instrument, recalling the provisions of Article 2, paragraph 1 of which more specifically underlines how "the illicit import, export and transfer of ownership of cultural property is one of the main causes of the impoverishment of the cultural heritage of the countries of origin of such property". Thus, the specific aim of the Convention is defined as "enhancing the international cooperation for protecting each country's cultural property against all the danger resulting from", in particular "by removing their causes, putting a stop to current practices, and by helping to make the necessary reparations" (paragraph 2).

As regards the field of application, we now witness an instrument which has a very broad spectrum of cultural property: this covers items which the State, for religious or secular reasons, has declared to have great importance on the archaeological, pre-historic, historical, literary, artistic or scientific levels and which belong to specified normative categories (Article 1). Article 4 then sets out the criteria by which individual cultural assets can be declared to form part of the cultural heritage of an individual State.

With regard to this broad extent of cultural property, the Convention identifies a framework of regulations for States to observe with regard to the import, export or transfer of ownership of property. The first group is generic in nature and concerns the creation of "one or more national services" charged with formulating norms in this field, drawing up and updating of lists of objects to be protected and establishing rules meeting the "*ethical principles*" established by the Convention. This last provision, contained in Article 5(c), indirectly recalls the existence of rules of conduct, not covered by sanctions, which result from the text of the Convention, as well as being particularly rich in other instruments of *soft law* adopted in this field.

The core of the Convention, however, in which the more demanding obligations are articulated, concerns the export and import of assets, which – by virtue of a marked divergence between exporting and importing countries coming to light during the preparatory works – are the subject of significantly varying treatment.[40]

The most stringent regulations regard *export* activities. For these, provision is made for the issue of a certificate by the national authorities, permitting transfer abroad of the item. In particular – and this is a significant element in the perspective of criminal law – the Party State is given the obligation to "prohibit the exportation of cultural property from their territory unless accompanied by the above-mentioned certificate" [Article 6(b)].

Less exacting are the provisions concerning the *import* of cultural assets, which are formulated at two levels, according to whether they are dealing with items illegally exported or to items stolen abroad. In the first case, national legislations must introduce

[40]Frigo (2001a).

norms suitable "to prevent museums and similar institutions from their territories from acquiring cultural property originating in other Party States which have been illegally exported". In the second case, they must place a ban on the "import of the cultural property stolen", but only when it comes "from a museum or a religious or secular monument or similar institution in another Party State", provided of course that the property is of major value. In this case, provision is made for the duty to "recover and return" the property, provided that "just compensation" is paid to the "purchaser or to a person who has valid title to the property". This supersedes the obligation, envisaged in the original draft, to introduce penal sanctions against officials of public or private institutions who acquire cultural property without having ascertained their provenance; likewise, it was decided not to make the certificate a control instrument to cover also importation because of the excessive complexity of such a mechanism.

As is well known, this last mechanism analysed, contemplated by Article 7, represents the essential nucleus of the whole import of the Convention. In fact, it determines the obligation, which previously was extremely rare and difficult to implement, to create a mechanism to restore illegal acquired property to the victim State. It is important to underline for our purposes that this is an option which does not involve the penal system. The fulcrum of the system controlling the illicit circulation of cultural assets lies, instead, in instruments of an administrative or private law nature which require a certificate accompanying the assets (Article 6) and in their restitution where they have been illegally transferred [Article 7(b)(ii) and Article 13], even when the transfer itself involved acts of penal significance, such as theft. Nevertheless, there are practical difficulties in the mechanism of restitution, whether in relation to those countries that are not party to the Convention or to those Party States when the possessor can claim a proprietary title validly created in good faith in the consignee State, or, a fortiori, when the declaration of ownership is supported by a legislative provision in that State.[41]

Passing more specifically to prohibitions, in terms of entire generality, Article 3 provides that "The import, export or transfer of ownership of cultural property effected contrary to the provisions adopted under this Convention by the States Party thereto, shall be illicit". However, that has not translated into a renewed obligation of States to impose penal sanctions against such conduct. There seem to be two reasons for this: evidential difficulties and the lack of an international willingness to move against crimes committed against the cultural heritage of a foreign country.[42]

The few exiguous obligations of criminal law intervention, which, in the broader ambit of the 1970 Convention, bear upon States, are represented by the succeeding Articles 8, 10 and 13. The first of these provides that Party States "impose penalties or administrative sanctions" for the acts identified in Articles 6(b) and 7(b). The route of penalization is thus pursued in terms that are purely possible, in the sense that States are able to favour alternative purely administrative and thus highly generalized sanctions in view of the vagueness of the Conventional provisions. As we have already observed, Article 6(b) covers the case of "exportation of cultural property"

[41] Frigo (2001b).

[42] O'Keefe (1992).

that is not accompanied by the relevant certificate; however, both Article 7(b) and Article 8 call for it without exception, the scope of the obligation to impose penalties is limited interpretively to the first paragraph concerning the importation of stolen property, and cannot be extended to acts attributable to States in the same way as those dealing with recovery and restitution.

The other provision of interest in the perspective of sanctions is contained in Article 10(a), under which every Party State must "oblige antique dealers, subject to penal or administrative sanctions, to maintain a register recording the origin of each item sold and to inform the purchaser of the cultural property of the export prohibition to which such property may be subject". Even in this case, the criminal law route is only one of the possible alternatives for States, who alternatively may choose administrative sanctions, and for acts that are not described with sufficient precision and details under the terms of the Convention, with regard to which the systems of the Party States enjoy ample space for manoeuvre in the description of punishable acts.

Vaguer still are the obligations that spring from Article 13 of the Convention which – at the conclusion of the system – endeavours to establish that Party States, in a way compatible with their domestic law, avoid the transfer of title to cultural property susceptible to promoting illegal export or import and establish a swift procedure for restitution to the true owner, as well as the exercise of judicial proceedings to protect individual juridical positions for the recovery of the property in question.

So in a very initial evaluation of the Convention, we see how, in widening the object of protection, the punitive scope of the instrument is weakened: in explicit terms, the actions for which the adoption of penal sanctions is required are few and extremely generalized and also have the express provision of an alternative recourse to administrative sanctions.

Thus, in the face of such bland obligations, it is interesting to see that some States especially active in the acquisition of cultural assets (like Australia and the USA) have put interpretative reservations on the norms in question, in order to exclude the need to provide new specific legislation in this area. So the first of these States, has placed an express restriction on Article 10, declaring that "Australia is not at present in a position to oblige antique dealers, subject to penal or administrative sanctions, to maintain a register recording the origin of each item of cultural property, names and addresses of the supplier, description and price of each item sold [...]", thus imposing a very significant redimensioning of the field of application of domestic legislation containing penal sanctions. The reservations of the USA have gone much further, showing the clearest intention to exempt themselves from the most penetrating of the Conventional obligations,[43] to such a point that Mexico has considered "that these comments and reservations are not compatible with the purpose and aims of the Convention". Primarily, on the American side, it has been asserted that the provisions in question are not "neither self-executing nor retroactive". With regard to the important provision, already frequently mentioned, of Article 7(a) relating to the acquisition by museums of illegally exported items, it is stated that it is "not (to) require the enactment of new legislation". With regard to Article 7(b), moreover, is

[43]Herscher (1985).

intended that it should not exclude instruments for the recovery of stolen items with the payment of some compensation. Finally, the requirement contained in Article 10, that the obligation imposed on antique dealers is introduced "as appropriate for each country" must be deemed to be wholly remitted to State and municipal authorities, whom the adoption of the relevant legislation would affect.

Finally, legal doctrine has highlighted that the provisions of the UNESCO Convention will come up against significant limits in the absence of a general acceptance on the international plane: for example, Switzerland ratified the Convention only in 2003[44] and Great Britain, which traditionally has a flourishing art market, joined it in 2002; moreover, there are very few signatory States that have enacted the requisite legislation under the Convention.[45]

The 1995 Unidroit Convention and Rejection of the Penal Route

Motivated by the difficulties that have marked the UNESCO Convention, when in the stage of negotiation, on the issue of adjusting national domestic legislations, and later at the point of concrete application of its provisions in the courts, the decision was made to entrust to Unidroit, with its specific competence in dealing with the unification of private law, the task of formulating an instrument that more effectively enables illegally exported or stolen items to be returned to their original owners. The outcome of this initiative is to be found in the *UNIDROIT Convention on Stolen or Illegally Exported Cultural Objects*, adopted in Rome on 24 June 1995. This sets out precise rules of private international law for the recovery and restitution of the items in question, with derogatories relative to the principles commonly applied in private law on account of the importance attached to them, while at the same time instituting a fair and reasonable measure of compensation for the people who have been holding them in good faith and have made the necessary preliminary enquiries with regard to them.[46]

In the Preamble to the text, there is an examination, carried out with thoroughness and recognition of the limits of the instrument, of the two essential themes that inspire it. In the first case, it reaffirms as usual "the fundamental importance of the protection of cultural heritage and of cultural exchanges for promoting understanding between peoples and the dissemination of culture for the well-being of humanity and the progress of civilisation". There is, however, further development of the themes leading to the introduction of a mechanism aimed at combating the illicit traffic: on the one hand, it underlines that need to proceed to the "important step of

---

[44] Widmer (2009).

[45] Frigo (2001c).

[46] See Prott (1997, 2009); Carducci (1997); Lalive (1999); On the preparatory works see Schneider (1992). On the *bona fide* concept see Prott (1992).

establishing common minimal legal rules for the restitution and return"; on the other hand, however, it does not hide the fact that "this Convention will not by itself provide a solution to the problems raised by illicit trade, but that it initiates a process that will enhance international cultural co-operation". In short, the private law route is significantly strengthened, even though it cannot be entirely relied upon – in the words of the draftsmen – to provide a complete solution to the complex problems inherent in illicit activities to the detriment of the cultural heritage.

Precisely because of the extra-penal nature of the solutions adopted in Rome, it is not our present remit to examine the detailed and complex mechanism of this Convention; let us, however, simply glance at the overall scheme, if only to bring to light the insufficiency of the instruments adopted.

Since the field of application of the Convention is extremely wide (Article 1) and not founded on any particular merit, value or importance of the cultural property, in order to enhance its deterrent effect, it should be observed that two discrete juridical regimes are put forward, according to whether the items in question have been stolen or illegally exported: in the latter case, they are the subject of "return", while in the former case they are subjected to a broader mechanism of "restitution" regardless of whether it comes from a Party State (Article 1). Both of these are measures that are not unknown to private international law but here are the subject of a different and more restrictive definition.[47]

The duty of restitution and its relative procedures, laid down in Articles 3 and 4, require the possessor to restore the stolen property even if he has acquired it in good faith. This is a particularly innovative provision, introducing a derogation to general rules applying in many of the States party to the Convention,[48] even if some problematic aspects remain in matters of limitation periods.[49]

More controversial is Chapter II of the Convention dealing with the "return" mechanism for illegally exported assets which permits importance to be accorded to provisions of public law which a State may have adopted in protection of its own cultural heritage. Here too, there is recognition of the right of the possessor of the property to receive fair compensation.

In short, the assessment contained above is confirmed: the whole Unidroit Convention, in line with the premise inspiring it and within the range of the institution which drew it up, concentrates entirely on ameliorating the instruments in the field of private law, without giving the least attention to the criminal or, more broadly, punitive element. This fact does not prevent Party States from adopting them, as is indirectly confirmed by which: "does not in any way legitimize any illegal transaction of whatever has taken place before the entry into force of this Convention or which is excluded under paragraphs (1) or (2) of this Article, nor limit any right of a State or other person to make a claim under remedies available outside the

---

[47] For an overall picture, see Prott (1997, 2009); Carducci (1997); Lalive (1999); On the travaux préparatoires see Schneider (1992); On the *bona fide* concept see Prott (1992).

[48] Frigo (2001d).

[49] O'Keefe (2006d).

framework of this Convention for the restitution of return of an cultural, object stolen or illegally exported before the entry into force of this convention" (Article 10, paragraph 3). The compass of this obligation is embodied in the right to "fair and reasonable compensation" for the holder in good faith, which represents a balanced compromise as between importing and exporting States.

The Model Treaty of the United Nations: An Interesting Tool with No Binding Force

One of the instruments of interest in a criminal law context is the *Model treaty for the prevention of crimes that impinge on the cultural heritage of peoples in the form of movable property*, adopted in the course of the United Nations 8th Congress on crime and criminal justice in 1990.[50] It must be said, however, that this instrument, unlike other *model treaties* adopted at Havana, has not been accepted by any Resolution of the General Assembly, so that, in its capacity purely as a model-treaty, it has no binding juridical value, and simply represents a schema which could be helpful in relations between States who wish to cooperate in combating crime in the sector of movable cultural property. In the Preamble, States who wish to introduce "measures for impeding illicit transnational trafficking in movable cultural property whether or not it has been stolen", agree to have recourse to the "imposition of appropriate and effective administrative and penal sanctions and the provision of a means of restitution". Although the restitution is common – as has been seen – to the main existing Conventions (UNESCO Convention and the UNIDROIT Convention), we see the idea of sanctions for illicit importation and exportation as the real innovation here. In this respect, States would undertake three different obligations.

First of all, in generic terms, they would undertake "To take the necessary measures to prohibit the import and export of movable cultural property (1) which has been stolen or (2) which has been illegally exported from the other State Party [Article 2(a)]. The provision is accompanied by the requirement to adopt sanctions, including possible minimal penal sanctions to given offences of illicit exportation and – what is more innovative – illicit importation of movable cultural property.

Secondly, after having accepted the duty to "take the necessary measures to prohibit the acquisition of, and dealing within its territory with, movable cultural property which has been imported, Article 3 extends the provision of penal sanctions to acts perpetrated in breach of such norm. Here, the *Model Treaty* requires as a condition for the imposition of penal sanctions that the acts have been perpetrated by "Persons or institutions that knowingly acquire or deal in stolen or illicitly imported movable property". The scope for its application seems to be confined by the requirement that the acquiring person be aware of the illicit provenance of the property; even

[50] Eighth United Nations Congress on the Prevention of Crime and the Treatment of Offenders, Havana, 27 August–7 September 1990: report prepared by the Secretariat (United Nations publication, Sales No. E.91.IV.2), chapter I, section B.1, annex.

if that would cause evidential problems, one must still approve such a normative choice, which is in line with general principles in terms of subjective responsibility, while rejecting forms of presumption of guilt of a serious offence or the acceptance of negligent offences, as indeed some legal theory would advocate.[51]

Extremely vague, and connected to the prospect of the growing incursion of organized crime into this sector, is the final paragraph of Article 3, which requires the adoption of penal sanctions also for "Persons or institutions that enter into international conspiracies to obtain, export or import movable cultural property by illicit means". This provision would seem to refer to the possibility of applying sanctions to both physical and juridical persons.

Some of the provisions in this Model-treaty might provide a point of departure for the introduction of new international instruments to fight the illicit trafficking. As proof of the interest of the instrument, it should be said that the Economic and Social Council in the *United Nations Resolution 2003/29 on the Prevention of crimes that infringe on the cultural heritage of peoples in the form of movable property*, "Encourages Member States to consider, where appropriate and in accordance with national law, when concluding relevant agreements with other States, the Model Treaty".[52]

A Look at the European Instruments: Convention of the Council of Europe and Legal Texts Adopted by the European Union

Only limited attention can be given here to the European juridical context – a true laboratory for the regionalization of criminal law – which has progressively developed in many varying forms, namely, to the two institutions that are important from a juridical point of view: the Council of Europe, currently comprising 47 countries, has for some time followed the route of Conventions, within which some attention has been given to the penalistic dimension; the European Union, which for its part has 27 Members, all of whom are also in the Council of Europe, has expended its efforts solely in the private law and commercial law fields.

The Council of Europe has generated the June 1985 *European Convention on Offences relating to Cultural Property*, signed at Delphi on 23 June 1985, although this has remained a dead letter since it was signed only by six States, none of which went on to ratify it.[53] From the point of view of criminal law, this has to be considered as a "lost opportunity": the Conventional provision in fact gives particular

[51]Mackenzie, S. *The Model treaty for the prevention of crimes that infringe on the cultural heritage of peoples in the form of movable property*: "these only work if the legal context is one where wilful blindness constitutes knowledge (i.e. where a dealer 'ought to have known')".

[52]E/2003/INF/2/Add.4, 22 July 2003.

[53]Cunha (1992); Möhrenschlager (1992).

attention to this dimension, focusing on three distinct assets. These are: direct protection of the assets, their restitution and the repression of crime in this sector. It is very significant that the chapter on restitution includes a series of measures regarding judicial cooperation (Article 8): the execution of Letters Rogatory "for the purpose of procuring evidence or transmitting articles to be produced in evidence, records or documents", "for the purpose of seizure and restitution of cultural property which has been removed to the territory of the requested Party subsequent to an offence relating to cultural property" or simply "relating to the enforcement of judgments delivered by the competent authorities of the requesting Party in respect of an offence relating to cultural property for the purpose of seizure and restitution of cultural property". Similarly, provision is made for restitution in the case of extradition, provided that this has been agreed but cannot be executed "owing to the death or escape of the person claimed or to other reasons of fact". Finally, "The requested Party may not refuse to return the cultural property on the grounds that it has seized, confiscated or otherwise acquired rights to the property in question as the result of a fiscal or customs offence committed in respect of that property".

It is very important that an effort has been made towards harmonizing some rules of criminal law, the third intervention aim under the Delphi Convention. In the terms of Article 12 (*Sanctioning*): "The Parties acknowledge the gravity of any act or omission that affects cultural property; they shall accordingly take the necessary measures for adequate sanctioning", which moves in the direction of an effective system of protection, even if not expressly correlated to the punitive dimension. For our purpose, also important are the succeeding provisions aimed at extending the scope of criteria for the application of criminal law, within the appropriate balance whereby the rights of the accused are safeguarded.

As regards the other regional normative area, the European Union, it must be said at the outset that the principle of free circulation of goods, one of the four fundamental freedoms of an economic nature recognized by the Treaties, permits the introduction of prohibitions or restrictions on imports, exports or goods in transit justified on grounds of […] the protection of national treasures possessing artistic, historic or archaeological value (now Article 36, Treaty on the Functioning of the European Union). Nevertheless, recognizing that "such prohibitions or restrictions shall not, however, constitute a means of arbitrary discrimination or a disguised restriction on trade between Member States", the Court of Justice of the European Union has allowed an extremely restrictive interpretation of the scope for derogation.[54]

The "conservation and safeguarding of cultural heritage of European significance" recognized by the treaties (now Article 167, Treaty on the Functioning of the European Union) has led in the past to the adoption of two important instruments: Regulation No. 3911/92 of 9 December 1992 on the export of cultural property outside the European space and Directive 93/7/EEC of the Council of 15 March 1993 on the restitution of cultural property that has illicitly left the territory of a Member State; both of these have had subsequent amendments.

[54]Manacorda (2010).

The Regulation had been amended on a number of occasions and is now codified in the *Council Regulation (EC) No. 116/2009 of 18 December 2008 on the export of cultural goods*[55]: it is founded on the mechanism of export authorization for allowing the transfer of goods out of the EU area (the so-called export licence), leaving one Member State, which is valid in all the other States for transfer to a non-EU country. Although the Regulation is an instrument endowed in general with direct application, some of its provisions necessitate legislative acceptance by the national authorities. This is the case – which is important for our purposes – of Article 9 on *Penalties*, under which "The Member States shall lay down the rules on penalties applicable to infringements of the provisions of this Regulation and shall take all measures necessary to ensure that they are implemented". In utilizing a formula which is very common within the EU, it requires that these penalties shall be "effective, proportionate and dissuasive", although this does not preclude recourse to penal sanctions when such criteria have been deemed to have been satisfied exclusively by such typology of instrument.

The Directive,[56] modified in 1997[57] and in 2001,[58] is less important for our purposes. It proposes to complete the mechanism of restitution provided by the Unidroit Convention in the cases of goods that have been illicitly exported from one or more Member States. Under Article 15, there is an express reservation for the use of sanctions including penal ones, by Member States: "This Directive shall be without prejudice to any civil or criminal proceedings that may be brought under the national laws of the Member States, by the requesting Member State and/or the owner of a cultural object that has been stolen".

An Overall Assessment of Criminal Law Components in International Texts to Be Adopted within National Legislations

Taking together the quantity of detailed normative elements, upon which we have focused in this analysis, we are able to draw up a comprehensive balance-sheet of the lines adopted on the international plane in the political–criminal field. It is possible to look into the choices of criminalization both at the macro-system level (in order to assess the underlying political–criminal options regarding recourse to

[55]Council Regulation (EC) No. 116/2009 of 18 December 2008 on the export of cultural goods (Codified version), in OJEU, L39/1, 10.02.2009.

[56]Council Directive 93/7/EEC of 15 March 1993 on the return of cultural objects unlawfully removed from the territory of a Member States, in OJEC, L74/74, 27.03.1993; See Frigo (1992).

[57]Directive 96/100/EC of the European Parliament and of the Council of 17 February 1997 amending the Annex to Directive 93/7/EEC on the return of cultural objects unlawfully removed from the territory of a Member State, in OJEU, L60/59, 1.3.1997.

[58]Directive 2001/38/EC of the European Parliament and of the Council of 5 June 2001 amending Council Directive 93/7/EEC on the return of cultural objects unlawfully removed from the territory of a Member State, in OJEU L187/43, 10.07.2001.

penal sanctions (*when should one punish?*) and on the micro-system level, with the aim of identifying the mechanisms for protection, the levels of penalty or the geographical range for applying the criminal laws: choices which are rarely pursued in international texts although more frequently requested by the domestic legislator (*how is one to punish?*).

In the macro-systematic perspective, the choices made in the two sectors on intervention that have been analysed, correspond to very different philosophies between them concerning the use of the penal instrument. In the first area of intervention, humanitarian criminal law and international criminal law both refer to extreme situations of armed conflict and focus on the most important cultural assets forming part of a nation's heritage. In line with this premise, they opt *notably in favour of the punitive instrument*, laying down *a level – albeit minimal – of harmonization*, whose concrete implementation, however, is actually required from States.

As may easily be seen, the other areas of intervention of international law in the protection of cultural property – if we ignore the extreme circumstances of armed conflict and look at a broader spectrum of assets, and not only those of the highest cultural and historical eminence – display a greater caution in mobilizing the punitive weapon in this field. So in the second aspect of intervention dealing with the circulation of cultural property, international law, although on the one hand it embraces a great swathe of protection for cultural property; on the other hand, it relegates *criminal law to a purely residual role*, relying essentially on the private law instruments of return, restitution and compensation, although it refrains from focusing on the promotion of harmonization among the domestic legal systems. Paradigmatically, as we have perceived, penal sanctioning in the UNESCO Convention remains only one of the possible routes that Party State legislators have open to them, as opposed to embracing the administrative route.

Altogether, these basic political–criminal options – thus briefly summarized – should be considered to be justified, insofar as they represent an adequate adaptation of the plurality of interests in play, even if, to the criminal lawyer, they reveal a number of problematical facets.

For situations of armed conflict, providing these affect property of the highest and most exceptional importance to mankind at large, Party States are required to impose penal sanctions, especially for those actions so serious as to amount to war crimes. To launch an attack against a cultural site or a historical monument, so as to assault the identity of a people, as so often has occurred in recent conflicts, is conduct which, without question, deserves the most severe responses from the system. Here, the balance between interests has to lie between the legitimate conduct of hostilities on the one hand and the *fil rouge* of the whole of international law for armed conflicts on the other, which is that of progressive humanization of warfare: apart from the cases covered by the vast and still controversial concept of military necessity, whether one of typicality or as grounds for justification, the formulation of an individual criminal liability fits the context of *cultural heritage*. Yet, we may observe critically that in the texts under observation there appears no precise choice as to the essential elements of the offence: *theft* or *pillage* are mere labels for which there is not even a tentative minimum definition.

For the case of illegal circulation of goods, however, the juridical framework is essentially dominated by elements of an administrative law flavour (cataloguing of assets and system of certification) or of private law (restitution and compensation for the *bona fide* holder). By contrast, the criminal law is allocated a subsidiary and accessory, a fragmentary and residual, function. Here, the punitive choice is more tentative and is not unanimously applied by the international texts, having to give due regard to the existence of opposing interests needing to be protected, especially the principle of free circulation of the artistic and cultural property which represent a physiological dimension – insofar as it is strictly regulated – of the property in question and the rights of the *bona fide* possessor. This is a situation which, alongside the premises, leads to a limited recourse to penal sanctions (the penal minimalism mentioned above), in a perspective which seems understandable from a pragmatic point of view, especially in view of the difficulties in reconciling in the course of negotiations the positions of exporting and importing countries, but which nonetheless holds a crucial importance.

To renounce out of hand the national embodiment of the *ius punendi* is a policy not without inconsistencies and not without a price. With regard to the first proposition, it is notable that States, whether in the UNESCO Convention or the Unidroit Convention, concentrate their attention on property acquired by theft – which is unanimously and globally punished at law – while refraining, however, from any sort of coordination of the provisions protecting the property in question. It is as if the legislator, paradoxically, has recognized the existence of unquestionably criminal acts in national law but "forgotten" to draw from them the necessary consequences. Considerable attention could well be given here to consider whether models–offences should be put forward so as to induce domestic systems to view criminal conducts in a homogenous way, even if only with regard to *standard* minimum punishments and recovery procedures of an entirely penal nature such as attachment and confiscation.

On the other hand, the substantial failure by the Conventions to penalize, incurs a price in terms of the capacity to fight the object phenomenon, since the disparity, which is sometimes very great, between the choice of measures available to control illegal conduct adopted by national systems, a direct consequence of the great gaps in international law, ends by encouraging those illicit phenomena which the same Conventions with their bias towards civil law treatment endeavour to combat. We have occasion, in the last part of this paper, to judge developments that might prove possible in the area of Conventions with regard to illegal circulation to endow themselves finally with a well-considered and balanced response in punitive terms.

It is much harder to evaluate the penal juridical scene in micro-systematic terms (*how to punish?*) especially as these figure minimally in international texts. Strictly speaking, only a comparative study, which would consider those legislatures that have pursued the criminal path, could determine whether, and in what terms, this failing exists, but this is an objective that lies outside the scope of our present study. Let us simply take a brief look of the principle choices adopted in Conventions on this theme.

For war crimes, we have already seen – compliant with the classical structure of the criminally punished prohibition – how examination of the damage caused predominates.

In the most recent texts, however, we can see the use of instances of danger, which would seem to find adequate justification relative to the collective dimension of the juridical asset protected, to the serial or systematic nature of the criminal conduct in this area, and to the appropriateness of safeguarding the *cultural heritage* of this before it is irreversibly destroyed or dispersed.

From the point of view of subjective criteria for responsibility, the prohibited acts have a fundamentally willing nature: for instance, a deliberate attack on a cultural site when the so-called military necessity justification does not exist, but certainly deserves to be severely punished. However, the exceptional importance of the protected property raises the question of whether the ability of punishment should also extend to cases characterized by a lesser degree of deliberateness. Should utilizing an archaeological site of exceptional interest for concealing arms, while impervious to the risk that it may be destroyed, incur criminal sanctions? The problem of opening the door to *dolus eventualis* is, on the other hand, practically posed in relation to Article 30 of the Rome Statute: if opinions in criminal science diverge on this point, the first decided cases before the ICC – albeit in an entirely different situation – incline towards its acceptance. On the other hand, the role of criminal intent seems minimal in this area: even if the conventions lay down the precautionary measures to be followed in the case of an attack or in the concrete outbreak of hostilities, there does not follow the obligation to punish an involuntary infringement. Indeed, it should not be underestimated that a good part of offences occurring during hostilities result from negligence, inexperience or rashness of soldiers in the field, as may be seen recently in connection with *peacekeeping* operations, leading one to reflect on the possible criminalization of such conduct even if only culpable in such ways.

In the second aspect of intervention, in relation to the illicit circulation of property, the response in the form of penal sanctions is moving at the level of minor criminal offences or administrative ones: this is not only the consequence of a trend towards "moderation" in resorting to the penal instrument, but results from favouring a model of penalization organized in an accessory form, through recourse to the declared schema for the protection of the cultural heritage. Consequently, on the structural plane, normative intervention of a criminal sort hinges on a system for the protection of functions, which could militate towards a broad recourse in domestic law to the issue of risk of damage.[59]

Proposals for Reform in the International Penal Context: Towards a New Offence of "Trafficking in Works of Art"

In the international panorama, there has recently been a move in favour of strengthening the range of penal instruments, although this has not yet translated into the adoption of a new Convention text; nevertheless a number of standpoints have been established at the scientific as well as the political–diplomatic level.

[59]De Muro (2002); Manna (2005).

(a) To take a first trend, the protection of the cultural heritage could make use of international-type norms – both existing and possible future ones – to fight organized crime. In this direction, strong support has been expressed for applying the *United Nations Convention against Transnational Organized Crime*, adopted by the General Assembly in *Resolution 55/25* of 15 November 2000 (UNTOC). The real nub of this Convention lies famously in requiring the introduction of criminal offences connected with organized criminal acts having an international dimension (from participation in a criminal association to money laundering) as well as the creation of stronger instruments for an international cooperation.

In this direction, there has been talk of introducing a new Protocol in addition to the three existing ones,[60] which would focus solely on the phenomenon of traffic in artistic and archaeological assets. This route seems to have reached a dead end in negotiating forums, partly due to the difficulty in mobilizing the entire international community into action to achieve intensified penal responses for an issue which only concerns in practice a limited number of States – as victims of the phenomenon.

As an alternative, the idea has been put forward to permit – interpretatively and legislatively – an application of the same UNTOC in such a way as to embrace the phenomena which now concern us. Specifically, Party States would be induced to impose the highest levels of penalty (a minimum of 4 years imprisonment) for illegal acts in the field of cultural property, so as to qualify in the "Serious Crimes" category in Article 2 of the Convention. The immediate consequence would be – *inter alia* – the extension of acts participating in organized crime (*Criminalization of participation in an organized criminal group*) relative to trafficking in works of art and archaeological artefacts. The inclusion of the *cultural heritage* in UNTOC's field of application has been advocated on various occasions in recent years. A first major step in this direction may be seen in *Resolution ECOSC 2004/34 of 21 July 2004*, "*Protection against trafficking in cultural property*", in which it is stressed that "the entry into force of the United Nations Convention against Transnational Organized Crime is expected to create a new impetus in international cooperation to counter and curb *transnational organized crime*, which will in turn lead to innovative and broader approaches to dealing with the various manifestations of such crime, including trafficking in movable cultural property". In the same way, the *11th United Nations Congress on Crime Prevention and Criminal Justice*, held in Bangkok 18–25 April 2005, "took note of the increased involvement of *organized criminal groups* in the theft of and trafficking in cultural property and reaffirmed the fundamental importance

[60] Protocol to Prevent, Suppress and Punish Trafficking in Persons, especially Women and Children, adopted by General Assembly resolution 55/25; Protocol against the Smuggling of Migrants by Land, Sea and Air, adopted by General Assembly resolution 55/25; Protocol against the Illicit Manufacturing and Trafficking in Firearms, Their Parts and Components and Ammunition, supplementing the United Nations Convention against Transnational Organized Crime, adopted by General Assembly resolution 55/255 of 31 May 2001.

of implementation of existing instruments and the further development of national measures and international cooperation in criminal matters, calling upon Member States to take effective action to that effect". Likewise, in ECOSOC Resolution No. 2008/23, the Council said it was "*Alarmed* at the growing involvement of organized criminal groups in all aspects of trafficking in cultural property", once more strongly? supporting recourse to UNTOC. Further discussion of the question took place at the United Nations Congress on Crime at Salvador de Bahia in March 2010, with the agreement to "invite the Commission on Crime Prevention and Criminal Justice for an appropriate follow-up including, *inter alia*, exploring *the need for guidelines for crime prevention with respect to trafficking cultural property*, (…) *bearing in mind the existing relevant international instruments, including the United Nations Convention against Transnational Organized Crime* where appropriate".

(b) A second route in the relative development of punitive tools has been put forward recently in the work of the United Nations, and in particular two objectives: the creation of a model–offence of trafficking, and also one of confiscation. The fuller development of this strategy (even if ambiguously characterized by a certain superimposition upon the prospect of a similar utilization of the provisions of UNTOC) is to be found in the work of the group of experts convened at the end of 2009 at the *United Nations Office on Drugs and Crime*, whose proposals were embodied in the Report presented by the Secretary General to the *19th Session Commission on Crime Prevention and Criminal Justice*, Vienna 17–21 May 2010.

First of all the Party States were asked to make "legislation that is appropriate for *criminalizing trafficking in cultural property* and that takes into account the specificities of such property". More specifically: "States should criminalize *activities related to trafficking* in cultural property *by using a wide definition* that can be applied to stolen and illicitly exported cultural property. They *should also criminalize the import, export or transfer of cultural property* in accordance with Article 3 of the 1970 Convention. States should also consider making trafficking in cultural property (including stealing and looting at archaeological sites) a serious crime in accordance with their national legislation and Article 2 of the Organized Crime Convention, especially when organized criminal groups are involved".

Moreover, the group of experts asked for confiscation – already mentioned in the *ECOSOC Resolution 2008/23*: "If consistent with their legal systems, including the fundamental principles of their legal systems, States are invited to consider: (a) Allowing cultural property to be seized when those in possession of the property cannot prove the licit provenance of the objects or that they have a reasonable belief in the licit provenance of the objects". In this regard, "the Organized Crime Convention may constitute a useful basis".

In conclusion, international law is currently moving towards a substantial strengthening of penal instruments that could in future lead to a notable intensification of criminal sanctions for illicit activities in the field of cultural property. However, reservations immediately come to mind over such a broad and nebulous prospect, characterized by a general compression of individual civil liberties. In particular, the incisive legislation against organized crime, inspired by a widening of the control, would forthwith be extended to a sector upon which empirical evidence at least throws some doubt regarding the involvement of the major criminal cartels. Allowing that trafficking in works of art and antiquities may become the object of such an international instrument, it could open the door, as to a "Trojan horse", to ever new emergencies destined to appear on the international plane, with mechanisms creating perplexity both in constructive deliberation and democratic representation: tomorrow, trafficking in animals and the day after, dangerous waste and so on.

That does not mean that all prospects for reform should be rejected. As we have already seen, there are many inconsistencies in the existing system and an impetus towards the introduction of well-considered reforms, particularly in three directions.

First – as we have often seen – progress must be made towards a *growing harmonization of the definition of crimes*, through a precise identification of the objects to be protected and the constituent elements of the offences. Probably, there should be a convergence of views on the insertion in international texts of a model–offence of trafficking in works of art and archaeological artefacts, to resolve the dichotomy between import and export and to outline carefully the elements of the case and other minimum requirements from the point of view of imposing penal sanctions.

There is, further, to be seen a more general consensus for strengthening the instruments of *seizure and confiscation*. This would call for a consensus to overcome the mere recourse to private law mechanisms for restitution and return, although careful thought needs to be given to protect *bona fide* third parties and their property rights. In very brief terms, it should be pursued only if it is accompanied by an adequate level of safeguards, both from the substantive point of view (one thinks of the recent issue of corollaries of non-retroactivity and retroactivity *in bonam partem* in this sector in many European systems) and procedurally (with the provision of guarantees of fair process). However, one would not favour, as mooted in the work of the United Nations, a reversal in this field of the burden of proof.

Finally, a last probable prospect could see the extension of *criminal responsibility* from physical persons to *juridical persons*; the pressure in this direction results from a number of criminological features in this sector (strong group pressures on individual participants, porosity between licit and illicit markets), as well as some normative peculiarities (a high presence in the sector of deontological codes, supported by a possible attribution of liability to juridical persons).

We are looking here at reform hypotheses that could only perhaps be confirmed by future developments in the international normative framework: juridical science needs to concentrate continuously on normative processes, in order that criminal law finds its proper place in that prospect of a careful balance of relevant interests and moderation of punitive interventions, subject to the guiding principles of *ultima ratio* and proportionality which have inspired this study.

References

Abtahi, H. (2001). The Protection of Cultural Property in Times of Armed Conflict: The Practice of the International Criminal Tribunal for the Former Yugoslavia. *Harvard Human Rights Journal*, vol. 14, 1 et seq.

Blake, J. (2000a). On Defining the Cultural Heritage. *The International and Comparative Law Quarterly*, vol. 49, No. 1 (January), 61–85.

Blake, J. (2000b). On Defining the Cultural Heritage. *The International and Comparative Law Quarterly*, vol. 49, No. 1 (January), 77, 84.

Brodie, N. (2009). The market in Iraqi antiquities 1980–2008. In *Organised Crime in Art and Antiquities* (63 et seq.). Milano: ISPAC.

Brodie, N., Doole, J., Watson, P. (2000). *Stealing History: The Illicit Trade in Cultural Objects*. Cambridge, UK: Mc Donald Institute for Archeological Research.

Calvani, S. (2009). Frequency and figures of organized crime in Art and Antiquities. In Manacorda, S. (ed.). *Organised Crime in Art and Antiquities. (Selected papers and contributions from the International Conference on "Organised crime in art and antiquities", Courmayeur Mont Blanc, Italy, 12–14 December 2008)* (29 et seq.). Milano: ISPAC.

Canino, G. (1997). Il ruolo svolto dall'UNESCO nella tutela del patrimonio culturale e mondiale. In Ciciriello, M. G. (ed.), *La protezione del patrimonio mondiale culturale e naturale a venticinque anni dalla convenzione dell'UNESCO* (44 et seq.). Napoli: Editoriale Scientifica.

Carducci, G. (1997). *La restitution internationale des biens culturels et des objets d'art volés ou illicitement exportés*. Paris: L.G.D.J., 486.

Commission on Crime Prevention and Criminal Justice, 19th Session, Vienna, 17–21 May 2010. Thematic discussion on Protection Against Illicit Trafficking in Cultural Property. World crime trends and emerging issues and responses in the field of crime prevention and criminal justice.

Cunha, C. (1992). Le système européen: le rôle du Conseil de l'Europe. In *La tutela penale delle opere d'arte/The penal protection of works of art*. Atti del Convegno, Siracusa 22–26 March 1992, 29 et seq.

De Muro, G. P. (2002). *Beni culturali e tecniche di tutela penale*. Milano: Giuffrè, 235 et seq.

ECOSOC, *Resolution 2004/34 of 21 July 2004 "Protection against trafficking in cultural property"*, 47th plenary meeting, 21 July 2004.

Francioni, F. (2004). Beyond State Sovereignty: The Protection of Cultural Heritage as a Shared Interest of Humanity. *Michigan Journal of International Law*, vol. 25, 1212.

Frigo, M. (1992). La proposta di Direttiva del Consiglio CEE relativa alla restituzione dei beni culturali esportati illecitamente. In *La tutela penale delle opere d'arte/The penal protection of works of art*. Atti del Convegno, Siracusa, 22–26 March 1992, 49 et seq.

Frigo, M. (2001a). *La circolazione internazionale dei beni culturali. Diritto internazionale, diritto comunitario e diritto interno*. Milano: Giuffrè, 7–8.

Frigo, M. (2001b). *La circolazione internazionale dei beni culturali. Diritto internazionale, diritto comunitario e diritto interno*. Milano: Giuffrè, 10–12.

Frigo, M. (2001c). *La circolazione internazionale dei beni culturali. Diritto internazionale, diritto comunitario e diritto interno*. Milano: Giuffrè, 14–15.

Frigo, M. (2001d). *La circolazione internazionale dei beni culturali. Diritto internazionale, diritto comunitario e diritto interno*. Milano: Giuffrè, 25.

Gauffeny, S. (2009). *La lutte contre le trafic illicite des biens culturels en Europe*. Proceedings of the Conference "La lutte contre le trafic illicite des biens culturels en Europe". Paris: Institut National du Patrimoine. Available at http://inp.fr/index.php/fr/mediatheque_numerique/les_retransmissions_audio/colloques/la_lutte_contre_le_trafic_illicite_des_biens_culturels_en_europe/intervention_de_stephane_gauffeny. Accessed at December 3, 2009.

Herscher, E. (1985). The Antiquities Market. *Journal of Field Archaeology*, vol. 12, No. 4, 469–481.

Lalive, P. (1999). A Disturbing International Convention: UNIDROIT. In *Art Antiquity and Law*. London: Kluwer London, vol. 4, Issue 3 (September).

Lalive, P. (2009a). *The UNIDROIT Convention on Stolen or Illegally Exported Cultural Objects (Rome, June 24, 1995)*. Proceedings of the Conference "Governance of Cultural Property: Preservation and Recovery", Basel, Switzerland, 29 September 2009.

Lalive, P. (2009b). *The UNIDROIT Convention on Stolen or Illegally Exported Cultural Objects (Rome, June 24, 1995)*. Proceedings of the Conference "Governance of Cultural Property: Preservation and Recovery", Basel, Switzerland, 29 September 2009.

Manacorda, S. (2010). Public Policy and the Court of Justice: The "Combinatorial Logic" in the Framework of Criminal Law. *New Journal of European Criminal Law*, 59–843.

Manna, A. (2005). *Il codice dei beni culturali e del paesaggio. Gli illeciti penali*. Milano: Giuffrè.

Massy, L. (2008). The Antiquity Art Market: Between Legality and Illegality. *International Journal of Social Economy*, vol. 35, No. 10, 729 et seq.

Maugeri, A. M. (2008a). *La tutela dei beni culturali nel diritto internazionale penale. Crimini di guerra e crimini contro l'umanità*. Milano: Giuffrè, 11 et seq.

Maugeri, A. M. (2008b). *La tutela dei beni culturali nel diritto internazionale penale. Crimini di guerra e crimini contro l'umanità*. Milano: Giuffrè, 29–30.

Maugeri, A. M. (2008c). *La tutela dei beni culturali nel diritto internazionale penale. Crimini di guerra e crimini contro l'umanità*. Milano: Giuffrè, 53–54.

Maugeri, A. M. (2008d). *La tutela dei beni culturali nel diritto internazionale penale. Crimini di guerra e crimini contro l'umanità*. Milano: Giuffrè, 61.

Maugeri, A. M. (2008e). *La tutela dei beni culturali nel diritto internazionale penale. Crimini di guerra e crimini contro l'umanità*. Milano: Giuffrè, 70 et seq.

Maugeri, A. M. (2008f). *La tutela dei beni culturali nel diritto internazionale penale. Crimini di guerra e crimini contro l'umanità*. Milano: Giuffrè, 102 et seq.

Merryman, J. H. (1985). Thinking about the Elgin Marbles. *Michigan Law Review*, vol. 83, No. 8 (August), 1880–1923.

Merryman, J. H. (1986). Two Ways of Thinking About Cultural Property. *The American Journal of International Law*, vol. 80, No. 4 (October), 831–853.

Merryman, J. H. (1990). "Protection" of the Cultural "Heritage". *The American Journal of Comparative Law*, vol. 38, 513–522.

Möhrenschlager, M. (1992). The applicability of European conventios on prosecution and punishment of illegal exports of cultural goods. In *La tutela penale delle opere d'arte/The penal protection of works of art*. Atti del Convegno Siracusa 22–26 March 1992, 33 et seq.

O'Keefe, P. (1992). Penal protection of cultural property. The role of UNESCO. In *La tutela penale delle opere d'arte/The penal protection of works of art*, Atti del Convegno, Siracusa, 22–26 March 1992, 10.

O'Keefe, R. (2004). World Cultural Heritage: Obligations to the International Community as a Whole? *The International and Comparative Law Quarterly*, vol. 53, No. 1 (January), 189–209.

O'Keefe, R. (2006a). *The Protection of Cultural Property in Armed Conflict*. Cambridge, New York: Cambridge University Press, 188.

O'Keefe, R. (2006b). *The Protection of Cultural Property in Armed Conflict*. Cambridge, New York: Cambridge University Press, 278.

O'Keefe, R. (2006c). *The Protection of Cultural Property in Armed Conflict*. Cambridge, New York: Cambridge University Press, 274.

O'Keefe, P. (2006d). Cultural Heritage: Dispute Resolution and Avoidance: Article: Using UNIDROIT to Avoid Cultural Heritage Disputes: Limitation Periods. *The Willamette Journal of International Law and Dispute Resolution*, vol. 14, No. 2 (Winter), 227.

Phuong, C. (2004). The Protection of Iraqi Cultural Property. *The International and Comparative Law Quarterly*, vol. 53, No. 4 (October), 985–998.

Polk, K. (1999). *Illegal Property Markets*. Paper given at the 3rd National Outlook Symposium on Crime, sponsored by the Australian Institute of Criminology, Canberra, 23 March 1999.

Prott, L. V. (1992). Standards of good faith for the acquisition of cultural objects. In *La tutela penale delle opere d'arte/The penal protection of works of art*. Atti del Convegno, Siracusa 22–26 March 1992, 103 et seq.

Prott, L. V. (1997). *Commentary on the UNIDROIT Convention*. London: Institute of Art and Law. Editions UNESCO (2000).

Prott, L. V. (2009). The UNIDROIT Convention – Ten Years On. *The Uniform Law Review*, vol. 14, 215–237.

Schneider, M. (1992). L'acquérer de bonne foi: dimensions internationale et européenne. In *La tutela penale delle opere d'arte/The penal protection of works of art*. Atti del Convegno, Siracusa, 22–26 March 1992, 91 et seq.

Tijhuis, A. J. G. (2009). The trafficking problem: a criminological perspective. In *Organised Crime in Art and Antiquities* (75 et seq.). Milano: ISPAC.

Widmer, Ra B. (2009). *The Cultural Property Transfer Act in Switzerland and its impact*. Proceedings of the Conference "Governance of Cultural Property: Preservation and Recovery", Basel, 29 September 2009.

Part I
Illicit Trafficking in Cultural Heritage: The Criminological Perspective

Chapter 3
Overview of Crimes and Antiquities

Nikos Passas and Blythe Bowman Proulx

Preface

In 1987, grave robbers in Peru stole the largest gold object ever found from an ancient royal tomb in the archeological site of Sipàn (Atwood 2004). Weighing in at just under 3 pounds, the piece was a backflap, ripped off the skeletal remains from the tomb of an important warrior–priest. Ten years later, the backflap was recovered in the parking lot of a hotel in Philadelphia as part of sting operation conducted on the part of the Federal Bureau of Investigation (FBI) (FBI 2009). The undercover agents had offered $1.6 million for it (Brodie et al. 2000: 15). In 1998, the backflap was finally returned to Peru and is now on display in the Museo de la Nación in Lima (Rose 1998).

In a world beset by political unrest, corruption, poverty, crime, violence, threats to international security, environmental crimes, discrimination, and social injustice, why would anyone, much less the FBI, care about what happened to that Peruvian backflap? Why should anyone, for that matter, care about the cultural heritage of distant times and far off places?

Introduction: The Changing Scope of Transnational Crime

The complex web of sociocultural, economic, political, and technological changes characterizing the twenty-first century has yielded disparate effects on countries around the world (Woods 2000; Williamson 1996), and shifts in the patterns of transnational crime are but one result of the ever-increasing interconnectedness and global character of life. Despite scholarly discord regarding the extent to which globalization has in fact accentuated transnational organized criminal activity, one fact upon which there is substantial agreement is that transnational crime today is

---

N. Passas (✉)
College of Criminal Justice, Northeastern University, Boston, MA, USA
e-mail: n.passas@neu.edu

S. Manacorda and D. Chappell (eds.), *Crime in the Art and Antiquities World: Illegal Trafficking in Cultural Property*, DOI 10.1007/978-1-4419-7946-9_3,

not what it was even a few years ago (Bowman 2008). Crime now traverses both time and space at such an alarming pace that, while transnational crime itself may be nothing new, there is still something unprecedented and particularly ominous about the contemporary threat of transnational crime (Berdal and Serrano 2002).

While transnational crime itself is old news, the contemporary threat of transnational crime differs in two important respects. First, processes of globalization and changes in international political relations have meant a marked increase in integrated markets and the transnational movement of people, capital, goods, and services. Like legitimate businesses, criminal enterprises have had to adjust to the complexities of this nascent globalized economy, and as such have expanded their geographic sphere of influence beyond national borders (Naylor 2002; Passas 2002; Joyce 1999). In many respects, then, physical distance has become a nonissue for crime problems (Robinson 2000), and the menace of transnational crime – crime that affects more than one country either directly or indirectly – has wormed its way into each and every corner of the globe. Crime is, in other words, less constrained by national boundaries than ever. Transnational crime is a moving target – where it is today is not where it may be tomorrow.

Second, in addition to exerting a broader geographic influence, the scope of transnational criminal activities has also steadily diversified (Robinson 2000). Intensified international enforcement efforts mean that new forms of transnational criminal activity are springing up on a regular basis (Passas 1998). While traditional transnational criminal activities remain the same (i.e., drug and human trafficking, corruption, money laundering, extortion, etc.), criminals have learned to increase their profits exponentially by broadening their spheres of illicit activity to include cybercrime, trade in human body parts, trafficking in flora and fauna, and theft of art and antiquities, just to name a few (Mueller 2001; Williams 1999). Diversified activities, coupled with broader geographic capabilities have further turned the black and white line between the licit *upperworld* and illicit *underworld* (van Duyne et al. 2002) a decidedly murky shade of gray (Ruggiero 1998, 2000).

In this paper, we explore but one dynamic of contemporary transnational crime: crimes involving art and antiquities. We begin with a discussion of the significance of cultural heritage, followed by an overview of art and antiquities crimes. After an exploration of criminogenic asymmetries and the role they play in producing transnational criminal activity, we conclude with a discussion of policy implications of the legal–illegal interface in terms of crimes involving art and antiquities.

Why Crimes Against Cultural Heritage Matter

Art crime, which can be defined as *criminally punishable acts that involve works of art*, generally entails damage, theft, deceit, or a combination of these (Conklin 1994: 2). Subsumed under the rubric of *art crime* are such activities as diverse as art thefts and confiscations, vandalism, faked and forged art, illicit excavation and export of antiquities and other archeological materials. While the men involved in the Peruvian backflap were eventually convicted of smuggling, conspiracy, and interstate transportation of stolen property (FBI 2009), it is essential to note that crimes involving culturally relevant material are crimes that embody a unique spectrum of harm beyond what can be legally construed as simple tangible loss. Since art, antiquities, and other culturally significant resources represent the physical vestiges of cultural heritage and the human experience, crimes against art and antiquities instead result in two types of broader, interrelated consequences: the material and the intellectual (Gill and Chippindale 1993). Antiquities and archeological resources, for example, are finite and irreplaceable; once they are gone, they are gone forever. Gone too is valuable information about the human past: objects ripped from archeological sites to be traded as commercial commodities cannot contribute much to existing knowledge about human adaptation and the development of human civilization. We are left with random objects that might be valuable or esthetically pleasing, but tell us nothing about the people or culture that produced them (Atwood 2004).

In addition to their importance as sources of cultural information, the tangible remains of human cultural heritage are also a critical component of national identity. For the Greeks, for example, the Acropolis at Athens represents central themes in modern Greek national identity: democracy, exemplary classical art, philosophy, humanism, architectural purity, the ancient *polis* at its height, and refinement of the dramatic arts (Athanassopoulos 2002). It is a cultural treasure upon which much of the modern Greek sense of national identity and cultural heritage is based. For Americans, something similar is captured in the symbolism of the Statue of Liberty, and what that represents for American cultural heritage. If the Statue of Liberty were carted off to grace some wealthy art collector's backyard, it would likely strike a chord deep in the hearts of most American citizens.

Art, antiquities, and cultural heritage thus play an integral role in the formation and perpetuation of national identity and self-image, and the destruction of such resources inevitably contributes to the destruction of a people's identity. In 2001, for example, the Taliban ordered the destruction of the Buddhas of Bamiyan in Afghanistan. These monumental sculptures, carved into sandstone cliffs during the third through fifth centuries AD, were among the most significant treasures in Afghan cultural heritage (Francioni and Lenzerini 2003). Despite public outcry over the cultural and historical value of the sculptures, the Taliban deemed them insulting to Islam. In an act that some have labeled *cultural terrorism*, the statues were blown up following the orders of the Taliban's supreme leader (Francioni and Lenzerini 2006: 31). Subsequent to the destruction of the Buddhas, Afghanistan's ruling Taliban sacrificed dozens of cows as an act of atonement for not acting sooner in destroying these statues and others (Salahuddin 2001), and Buddhist art and antiquities from Afghanistan began appearing on the international market in vast quantities (Bohlen 1996).

The loss of historical memory is not a modern problem,[1] but the recent processes of globalization, colonization, exploration, and advances in technology have meant

[1]With the advent of farming, for example, empires and cities largely replaced hunter–gatherer, pastoral, and nomadic ways of life (Stille 2002: xiv).

that Western culture and its acquisitive nature have descended on every corner of the globe in an unprecedented manner. We are now faced with a troubling paradox: these modern technologies and global processes are as central in the destruction of global cultural heritage as they are in its preservation (Stille 2002). Ultimately, archeological resources, as part of universal cultural heritage, play a critical role in collective cultural identity and a sense of human history.[2] Clearly, then, there is much more at stake than the welfare of art, antiquities, and other culturally relevant resources.

Overview of Crimes Involving Art and Antiquities

As noted above, art crime can be construed to refer to thefts, fakes and forgeries, confiscations, vandalism, illicit excavation and export of antiquities, and other archeological resources. Many such art crimes avoid criminal punishment, however. Like other types of crime, art crime is not always reported to police, offenders are not always apprehended, and frequently cases are instead handled as civil actions (Conklin 1994). The following provides a brief overview of various criminally punishable acts involving art and antiquities, as well as some examples.

Art Theft

Of all crimes involving art and antiquities, art theft is perhaps most well-known. Dozens of articles have been published, for example, that chronicle the high-profile 1990 theft of a number of paintings from the Isabella Stewart Gardner Museum in Boston. Having entered the museum dressed as police officers, the thieves removed 13 artworks valued at over $300 million (FBI 2009).[3] While there has been much speculation on the whereabouts of the artworks,[4] they have yet to resurface.

Many other high-profile art thefts have achieved similar legendary status. In 1969, for example, Caravaggio's *Nativity with Saints Lorenzo and Francesco*, reportedly worth over $20 million, was stolen off the wall of a Sicilian church (FBI 2009). Its theft is rumored to have been part of a Mafia vendetta (Conklin 1994). Indeed, the fate of the painting is subject to speculation that has taken on the air of urban legend. In addition to stories of its outright destruction, it is also rumored to

[2]Moreover, the tangible remains of the past as they relate to collective cultural heritage are also essential elements in the perpetuation of a thriving tourist economy. Greece, for example, is a relatively poor country that relies heavily on tourism as a source of national income.

[3]http://www.fbi.gov/hq/cid/arttheft/northamerica/us/isabella/isabella.htm.

[4]At one point, for example, there was speculation that the heist had been perpetrated by individuals with ties to local organized crime groups and even the Irish Republican Army (Boston Globe 2004). See the full article online at http://www.boston.com/news/local/articles/2004/03/11/ new_theory_airs_on_gardner_museum_theft/.

have been given as an Italian Mafioso wedding gift and even buried in a Sicilian treasure chest (Clarke 2005). Despite numerous appeals by local Palermo residents for its return, the painting has yet to resurface, and to this day the painting is reported to remain in Mafia hands (McMahon 2005; Isman 2001). It is high-profile cases such as these that have captured scholarly attention, the public's imagination, and carved out a unique niche within the entertainment industry. Based on cases such as these, there is no shortage of popular film and fiction devoted to the portrayal of sophisticated art heists and the debonair, sexy, *Thomas Crown* sorts who mastermind them.

It is clear that when art theft makes news, the focus is on high-value thefts from museums or private collections. As entertaining and sensational as these multimillion dollar art crimes may be, however, most art thefts do not take place in museums, and many objects are in fact stolen alongside other objects in run-of-the-mill burglaries (Tijhuis 2006). Other common loci of art theft include places of worship, galleries, castles, and art dealers' collections, auction houses, and libraries.[5]

Art Vandalism

Art vandalism refers to the intentional damage or destruction of an artwork (Conklin 1994).[6] In its most conventional, deliberate sense, art vandalism can best be seen as an "intermediate form between an attack on a thing and an attack on a person in so far as it entails an attack on a particular image… or on an idea or concept depicted by an image" (Cordess and Turcan 1993: 95). Many motivations for art vandalism are often construed manifestations of mental illness. No crime was charged, for example, when in 1972 Hungarian-born geologist Laszlo Toth attacked Michelangelo's Vatican *Pietà* with a hammer shouting, "I am Jesus Christ risen from the dead;" he was instead committed to a psychiatric hospital for 2 years (Cowell 1991). Other typical motivations for vandalism include: attention-seeking; self-expression; social or political protest; an expression of personal morality or standards of taste; religious motives; or purely for entertainment purposes (Conklin 1994).

In other cases, art vandalism tends toward the pragmatic; that is, damage to artwork is done for a practical purpose. In moving antiquities transnationally, for example, smugglers are clever. In Peru, ancient pottery was regularly doctored to look like modern ceramics so that they could be legally exported. The ancient pots

[5]Many libraries have fallen vict im to theft of rare books and manuscripts. See, for example. Sandra Laville's recent article in The Guardian on William Jacques, a thief who stole £1 million worth of rare and ancient texts from the British Library. (See at http://www.guardian.co.uk/uk/2009/feb/02/antiquarian-book-theft-library-crime.)

[6]A more expansive definition of art vandalism could also include unintentional damage caused by thieves in the course of a theft; damage to an artwork caused by a neglectful caretaker; restorative efforts that instead mutilate an artwork; and damage to artworks caused during war or civil unrest (Conklin 1994: 227–228).

were given false bottoms made of mud and latex and stamped with *Hecho en Bolivia* (Atwood 2004: 83). Once the Peruvian antiquities had been shipped to Bolivia, where customs procedures were less stringent, objects were shipped by plane to the USA by way of Canada (ibidem).

Hamblin (1970) recounts a similar method of destructive transnational transport: "Pots, statues, and vases are much more difficult to conceal, and yet they are smuggled out regularly in false-bottomed car trunks or suitcases, in packing crates, and in small boats. In Basel, Switzerland, art lovers with good connections may be shown Etruscan vases that have been cut into two or three pieces to make them fit more easily into suitcases. A whole generation of Italian experts now makes a tidy living in Switzerland putting these pieces back together again, on order..." (ivi: 108).

In addition to facilitating their transnational movement, the damage to art and antiquities is pragmatic in that it may also help thieves and smugglers minimize the chance that they will be arrested and punished. Whether the damage is intentional or occurs through ignorance or neglect, vandalism of art, antiquities, and other cultural objects represents a substantial loss of cultural heritage (Conklin 1994).

Art Confiscation

Art confiscation generally refers to the plunder and widespread confiscation of art across Europe that was conducted under the auspices of the Nazi Party during the reign of the Third Reich (Nicholas 1995). Beginning even before World War II, the Nazis systematically looted thousands of cultural objects across Western Europe and elsewhere, gathering the most prominent public and private art collections and keeping some works for the *super museum* that Hitler intended to build in Austria and reselling others through the international art market (Gerstenblith 2004). The Nazis' goal, in other words, was to "preserve art objects either for their value abroad or for the enrichment of the Nazi leadership" (Gerstenblith 2004: 480). Thousands of items of cultural significance were stolen from Holocaust victims, including but not limited to paintings, religious treasures, books, silver, crystal, sculpture, jewelry, china, and ceramics (Nicholas 1995). While many objects were returned to their owners by the Western Allies subsequent to the war, restitution is far from complete. Countless works both sold abroad and retained by the Nazis remain unaccounted for, heirs of the original owners remain difficult to locate, survivors and their heirs are not always able to identify missing works accurately, and countries in which looted works appeared have not always been cooperative in restitution efforts (Gerstenblith 2004). Moreover, the restitution of confiscated art presents a number of complex legal issues, and many artworks looted during the Nazi regime are currently the subject of intense legal battles.[7] In the meantime,

[7]For example, a lawsuit involving the seizure of Egon Schiele's Portrait of Wally, was initially commenced by the U.S. Government in 1999, claiming that the current holding institution knew that the painting had been stolen in 1938 from a Jewish owner's private collection (Hoffman 2006). To this day, the painting is still tied up in litigation (Artinfo 2008).

claims continue to be brought seeking restitution, and it is unknown how many cultural treasures looted during wartime have yet to resurface. As Gerstenblith (2004) notes, "conflicts in the former Yugoslavia, Afghanistan, and Iraq serve as continuing reminders that war often brings destruction to cultural objects and monuments" (ivi: 470).

Art Fraud[8]

The sale of counterfeit art is a globally pervasive problem with annual profits estimated in the millions (Conklin 1994). The difference between faked and forged art is that the former is an object made to resemble the style of an original artwork, while the latter is an exact copy of an original artwork which is sold as the original.[9] While the faking or forgery of an artwork is not a criminal act per se, the attempt to disguise a work of art as someone else's certainly constitutes forgery, which is without doubt a type of fraud (Conklin 1994).

Faked and forged art, antiquities, and other objects of cultural significance are an unfortunate but well-known element of the international art market. Forgeries are, as Radnoti (1999) notes, the *steady companion of art* (ivi: 6) which inevitably find their way into collections because art collecting increases demand for that art, and such demand fosters more forgery (ibidem). As Tijhuis observes, faked or forged art has a transnational dynamic in two respects: first, that faked artworks and forged antiquities are moved internationally in order to be sold; second, that forged antiquities that are illegally exported may initially be considered looted or smuggled, but upon discovery that they are in fact fake, it may be determined that no crime in fact was committed (2006).

It is unknown just how many fraudulent pieces are on the market or in any established collection (Conklin 1994). Regardless of its esthetic value, the commercial value of an artwork is lost when it has been shown to be counterfeit. In spite of such issues, some experts have suggested that the parallel trade in faked and forged art, antiquities, and cultural objects may in fact be a blessing of sorts in that the prevalence of fakes throughout the international art market can make theft and illicit export of original pieces less profitable (Tijhuis 2006). Charles Stanish, an archeologist who has been tracking the sale of antiquities on eBay, suggests that many

---

[8]While the art fraud discussed here is, for the sake of space, limited to a cursory discussion of fakes and forgeries, a broader examination of art fraud should include fraudulent activities committed on the part of dealers, collectors, auction houses, and museums. Such examples of art fraud include but are not limited to: insurance fraud, tax fraud, and investment fraud committed on the part of collectors; fraud committed on the part of dealers against artists, other dealers, collectors, auctions houses, museums; fraud committed on the part of auction houses (e.g., insider trading, the sale of stolen or counterfeit art); fraud committed on the part of museums (e.g., purchasing stolen or looted art for a collection; customs violations). For an excellent, in-depth discussion of such fraudulent activities, we refer the reader to John Conklin's Art Crime (Praeger Press 1994).

[9]http://www.spurlock.uiuc.edu/explorations/research/collecting.pdf.

original *producers* of antiquities have shifted from looting sites for the purpose of locating saleable items to faking antiquities: "People who used to make a few dollars selling a looted artifact to a middleman in their village can now produce their own *almost-as-good-as-old* objects and go directly to a person in a nearby town who has an eBay vendor account. They will receive the same amount or even more than they could have received for actual antiquities. I have visited a number of these workshops in Peru and Bolivia. Using local materials and drawing on their cultural knowledge, small manufacturers can produce pieces that are, in some cases, remarkably accurate reproductions of actual artifacts. The really smart ones do not reproduce pieces at all but create an ever-so-slightly modified version of real artifacts that have the look and feel of an authentic ancient object…" (Stanish 2006: paragraph 5).

Archeological Site Looting and Export of Antiquities

Inevitably, archeological site looting and subsequent trafficking in antiquities and other archeological materials involve irreversible destruction of cultural resources. As Papa Sokal (2006) notes, for every marketable object that a tomb-raider unearths, many more objects and sites have been despoiled in the process (ivi: 4). In recounting the story of the looted Peruvian backflap, Atwood (2004) confirms this: "[The looters] destroyed hundreds, perhaps thousands, of copper and ceramic objects that they thought they couldn't sell… Like grave robbers everywhere, they went straight for the best merchandise and trashed everything else along the way" (ivi: 77). In his study of Classical ceramics from southern Italy, Elia (2001) reached a similar conclusion: "It is clear that several thousands, even tens of thousands, of ancient tombs have been plundered to obtain the more than 13,6000 Apulian red-figure vases that exist throughout the world and were recovered in a nonarcheological manner" (ivi: 151).

The illicit antiquities trade is a transnational *gray* market in that it is a market with both licit and illicit elements. While the means by which antiquities are obtained may be illegal (e.g., fed by looting at archeological sites), it should be noted that on the demand end of the market, trading in antiquities is perfectly legal (Alder and Polk 2002). Owning an antiquity thus becomes illegal only when it has been stolen, smuggled, or illicitly exported (Tijhuis 2006). Therefore, in order to be profitable, the illicit means by which antiquities are obtained must be disguised in order to be profitable. This is often done by faked or forged provenance[10] documents or the

[10]Provenance refers to the previous ownership history of an object. The term is most frequently used in the art community to refer, in other words, to what has happened to an antiquity since it came out of the ground.

exploitation of differences in the international legal landscape, such as differing statutes of limitation, legal conceptions of *ownership*, and allocation of the burden of proof.[11] The result is that licit and illicit antiquities become hopelessly mixed on the international art market, and because illegal excavations yield never-before-seen undocumented antiquities, they cannot easily be identified and therefore legally construed as stolen or illicitly exported (Brodie 2006).

The trade in illicitly obtained antiquities involves local, small-scale thieves, larger groups of looters, and international connections with auction houses, galleries, museums, dealers, and collectors. With the help of middlemen, antiquities looted from archeological sites are generally smuggled transnationally, laundered, and end up in the open, legal antiquities market. While many efforts have been undertaken to curb the looting problem[12] and thus eliminate supply to satisfy international demand, the global situation does not appear to be improving (Bowman 2008). Improvements in the means, ease, and speed of travel and communications, for example, have opened up regions of the world that used to be unreachable (Brodie 2002). Advancements in technology have increased the destructiveness of illegal digging, and archeological sites are scavenged at an increasingly accelerated pace (Bowman 2008). Indeed, the existence of a *gray* antiquities market facilitated by legal loopholes and fed by theft from archeological sites has led a number of scholars to conclude that the looting situation has reached epidemic proportions, and that the world's archeological resources are vanishing at an alarming rate (Hoffman 2006; McCalister 2005; Brodie 2002; Brodie et al. 2000; O'Keefe 1997).

---

[11] Since property varies from one legal framework to the next, so too do legal conceptualizations of ownership. Following the Anglo–American nemo dat rule, for example, a thief can neither convey good title nor can someone claim good title through a thief even if the property is transferred to a good faith purchaser (Gerstenblith 2004). Unlike common law countries such as the USA, however, good title to a stolen object can be conveyed in the bulk of European continental civil law countries if the object was purchased in good faith. This means that even if an antiquity was looted and illegally exported from its country of origin, if it was subsequently purchased in good faith in a civil country, then the good faith purchase is favored and the object is no longer legally construed as stolen (Brodie 2002). Civil countries, then – most famously, Switzerland – become transit ports in which antiquities change hands and title is obtained. With a good title secured, an antiquity can now obtain legal export documentation, be legally imported elsewhere, and thus begin to circulate freely and legally on the antiquities market (Alder and Polk 2002, 2005).

[12] Legislative attempts to curb antiquities trafficking have in general identified the issue as one of theft or illicit export; that is, the enactment of national laws that vest ownership over antiquities to the State, in which case the removal of such objects constitutes theft; or, laws that attempt to prohibit exportation of such objects from national borders (Alder and Polk 2002). The salient difference between these two legislative efforts concerns its enforceability – market nations who top the list of antiquities importers have been reluctant to enforce other nations' export laws, and source nations are more successful in pursuing legal recourse when such items are legally construed as stolen (ibidem).

Estimating the Extent of Crime Involving Art and Antiquities

As Mackenzie keenly observes, "Before we can talk of how best to regulate the market, we must be sure of the existence and form of the looting problem we wish to address" (2005: 1). Accurate estimations of the global extent of crime involving cultural heritage are problematic. For one thing, estimates of economic losses and commercial gains due to transnational criminal activity in general vary wildly. This is not all that surprising given that no one really knows exactly how much illicit money is actually earned, saved, moved, and laundered around the world precisely because it is earned, saved, moved, and laundered illicitly (Naylor 2002). For another, what official statistics exist is often misleading. INTERPOL, for example, collects annual estimates of cultural property thefts from museums, places of worship, castles, archeological sites, art galleries, antique dealers, and private property. But these numbers are limited in that the majority of art crimes remain undetected and unreported to authorities; second, national statistics are recorder according to the circumstances of theft (i.e., breaking and entering; armed robbery) and not by the type of object stolen; lastly, less than half of all member countries reply annually with art crime information (INTERPOL 2009).

A second reason why it is difficult to estimate the financial extent of the losses caused by art crime is that the monetary value of art and antiquities is never fixed. In December 2007, for example, Sotheby's auction house set a new world record for the highest price for any antiquity with the sale of the Guennol Lioness, which sold for upwards of $57.1 million25, more than tripling its high presale estimate of $18 million (Artdaily 2007; New York AFP 2007).

Despite such reservations, the FBI estimates annual losses due to art crimes as high as $6 billion (FBI 2009).[13] Art crime does not appear to discriminate; that is, trade in stolen and illicitly exported cultural heritage is globally pervasive. In 2002, for example, Italy reported to INTERPOL the theft of 18,715 art objects; Russia claimed the loss of 4,563 objects; Turkey reported 725 objects stolen (INTERPOL 2005).

Attempts to estimate the extent of archeological site looting and its contribution to the illicit antiquities trade are even more problematic. Firstly, looting is necessarily a clandestine activity, making it difficult to document the scope of looting activity. Secondly, looting involves two types of sites: sites that are known to archeologists and sites that have not yet been discovered (Conklin 1994). In combination with the sheer number of archeological sites (Italy, for example, like many countries with a long history, is teeming with a rich archeological heritage the whole of the

[13] Another figure often attributed to INTERPOL by scholars and journalists alike is that art crime is the third highest-grossing criminal industry, just behind drugs and arms. INTERPOL, on the other hand, has carefully and explicitly stated for years on its Web site that "We do not possess any figures which would enable us to claim that trafficking in cultural property is the third or fourth most common form of trafficking, although this is frequently mentioned at international conferences and in the media" (INTERPOL 2009). We suspect that this figure gets recycled over and over simply because it is sensational, not because it is necessarily based in fact.

country is littered with archeologically significant structures both known and as of yet undiscovered), it is difficult to assess the extent of damage to cultural heritage.

Despite these difficulties, there is a substantial body of research that paints a dismal picture of the scale of on-the-ground damage around the world through archeological field surveys and photographic testimony. In Beijing between 1989 and 1990, for example, Chinese officials estimated that nearly 40,000 tombs had been stripped of their antiquities (Anderson 2002; Murphy 1995; Platthy 1993), and in 2003 it was reported that an additional 220,000 tombs had been pillaged in the preceding 5 years (Beech 2003). In Peru, where there are an estimated 200,000 archeological sites and monuments, "[a]ll of them… including the furthest or most overgrown, have been partially affected by looting" (Alva 2001: 91).

That the damage to archeological resources is as devastating as it is pervasive is recently reiterated in a recent study by Bowman (2008). In her survey of over 2,350 archeologists working throughout the world, she found that 98% of the study participants reported that looting was happening in some capacity in the area where they conducted archeological research. The majority (68%) of respondents also reported having personally encountered evidence of looting activity on site (holes, pits, stolen excavation equipment, stashes of artifacts hidden elsewhere for later removal), and 24% reported having encountered looting in progress (Bowman 2008). When asked to estimate whether they perceived looting to be getting worse, better, or remaining constant where they work, the majority (34%) of respondents felt that it was fluctuating; that is, some years were worse than others. Only 7% of responding archeologists felt that the site looting where they work was decreasing. Indeed, if archeologists' assessments of the presence and magnitude of looting is any indication of the true scope of the problem, then the damage is as pervasive as it is devastating. The scope of the looting problem is a reflection of the size of demand for antiquities, and it is likely that, as Bator (1982) remarks, "so long as there is a world market for beautiful objects, a substantial amount of looting will persist no matter what regulatory system is installed" (ivi: 49).

Theoretical Framework: Global Anomie, Criminogenic Asymmetries, and Trafficking in Art and Antiquities

The theoretical framework we propose as appropriate for the study of markets and networks involved in the illicit trade art and antiquities is that of "global anomie theory" (Passas 2000, 2005) and criminogenic asymmetries (Passas 1999). In a nutshell, the premises of this framework are as follows.

People act most frequently purposefully and seek to attain their goals. Some of these goals are basic – such as food, health, education, security. Other goals can be loftier, such as economic success, job promotion, etc. When these goals are blocked and people in a given society or region are unable to reach them through legitimate avenues, this causes stress. In this context, people may consider also deviant options. Many people remain law-abiding, but some actually turn to deviance in pursuit of their goals: they may take risks, migrate illegally, turn to crime, join a gang or other criminal group, turn a blind eye and seek rents or bribes, etc.

Some social systems are unable to meet these basic needs and thus this sort of crime and deviance are expected to be high. Other societies that are wealthy confront very (analytically) similar problems because they raise expectations and promote ever higher goals for the population at large without providing at the same time legal opportunities for everyone to accomplish these higher goals. The USA, Europe, and other countries fall into this category.

The inability to meet legitimate goals (more money, better clothes, fancy cars, higher profits, etc.) through legal means causes the same sort of stress because the point of comparison (reference groups) is different for each class, stratum, or peer group – everyone compares themselves with their peers, so the rich are not immune to such pressures. But the more a social system promotes goals that unrealistic for most of the population and the more it systematically frustrates members of society, the stronger the strain, the higher the likelihood to produce deviance. Antiquity rich countries also have people who turn to crime, corruption and illegal exploitation or violence for such reasons. Similar motives underlie white-collar professionals who may allow and facilitate art destruction or smuggling, engage in purchases they know or suspect to be illegal and participate in "art laundering" to hide the true origin and circumstances through which an artifact is produced or discovered. In short, this analytical framework lends itself for the study of all nodes and contributors to illicit art networks and markets.

This process is reinforced by the globalization process and forces. Just as the American Dream keeps producing successful people as well as high levels of stress and thus deviance too in the USA, so does globalization encourage people to want and "need" things they cannot achieve or get. All this increases the likelihood that a minority of people turn to crime. If these deviant acts end up solving the problem at hand (the source of the stress or suffering), this becomes a model/example for yet others to follow, and the deviance spreads. The more it spreads, the less people feel committed to the particular rules that are so often broken and unenforced, the more people imitate it or follow peers. The extreme (which occurs extremely rarely) is anomie, where a significant normative breakdown occurs and everything goes. All this accelerates and continues, unless policies and measures intervene to stop and reverse the process.

So the essence of global anomie theory is that the rates of deviance and crime rise when societal conditions and processes undermine the guiding power of norms, when legitimacy suffers. This can happen not only when socially induced expectations are systematically frustrated, but also as a result of ill-conceived or misapplied control measures. In this sense, global anomie theory does not take effective social control for granted but treats it as potentially problematic, too.

An important set of crime-producing conditions is what has been termed *criminogenic asymmetries*. These are structural discrepancies and inequalities in economy, law, politics, technology, and culture, which emerge when unequal actors or systems with dissimilar features interact. The criminogenic potential grows when the asymmetries fuel the demand for illegal goods and services, increase motives to participate and weaken controls. This is conducive to corruption and illegal markets, opportunities for illicit profit, reduced transparency, impunity, and lack of accountability. For example, one country has strict tax laws while another has no taxation system: this means no international cooperation is offered by the latter in fiscal matters, so controls are weak. A substance is classified as toxic in one country but not in another, thus generating a market for toxic waste. Different prioritization and handling of art theft, theft of cultural property, corruption, smuggling, and other related crimes as serious problems in some countries constitute control weaknesses. Economic asymmetries provide motives for people to turn to crime or vulnerabilities for people to take the ite for better employment elsewhere and then get exploited as victims of trafficking.

Globalization renders cultural asymmetries criminogenic and brings about another sort of more questionable and criminal type of disembeddedness. The increased contact between countries with art-rich past and countries with art-collecting present results to illicit transfers of national treasures from their original sites to artificial contexts. There is a huge global market of art items which are removed or stolen from primarily economically underdeveloped countries and channeled to Western private collections, museums, or galleries. In the process of rooting paintings or frescoes out of their original context, many pieces of art are destroyed or damaged (Margules 1992).

Economic problems in some developing and art-rich countries motivate counterfeiters to sell fake art to rich foreigners, as noted above. As Brooke has remarked, this "activity is looked on favorably as a source of income that can improve the standard of living in the villages where the counterfeiters work" (1988).

Legal and cultural asymmetries allow the cleansing of stolen art through jurisdictions, where laws conveniently legitimate the ultimate possessors. Just as crime proceeds and dirty money are laundered, stolen art is purified, so we could speak of "art laundering," as briefly mentioned earlier. In addition, there is a market for counterfeit art, given that supply is insufficient to satisfy the thirst of art collectors around the world (primarily in developed countries).

The profits in these markets are substantial while the risks of detection and sanction rather low. Asymmetric law enforcement and capacity to control are clearly taken advantage of. For example, we pointed out earlier how Peruvian antiquities get shipped to Bolivia, where customs controls are weaker, and then sent to Canada with final destination the USA. We also pointed out that the illegal origin of antiquities is disguised through fake or forged provenance documents. Moreover, we noted how legal asymmetries are indeed exploited by art traffickers: differences in statutes of limitation, legal conceptions of *ownership* and burden of proof.

As the planet is increasingly interconnected and asymmetries are multiplied, illegal markets can be expected to grow unless effective control systems are put in place. However, controls get weakened by processes conducive to *dysnomie*. Passas has described this concept as follows: "Dysnomie literally means *difficulty to govern* and obtains when the following three conditions are present: a lack of a global norm-making mechanism, inconsistent enforcement of existing international rules, and the existence of a regulatory patchwork of diverse and conflicting legal traditions and practices" (Passas 2000: 37).

Indeed, the illicit market in art and antiquities comes close to a dysnomic context, where we do have an absence of a universally accepted normative framework to regulate cross-border art-related activities and we have at the same time diverse, inconsistent and conflicting legal frameworks. So the illicit art market operates in the midst of an ineffective regulatory patchwork and fragmented controls, which make possible the commission of serious offences without breaking the laws of particular countries where some of the transactions and activities occur. Illicit art marketers, in other words often commit *crimes without lawbreaking* (Passas 1999).

Conclusion

A comprehensive examination of all the national, international, and domestic responses to art and antiquities crime is beyond the scope of our paper. What can be said with certainty, however, is that art and antiquities crime represents a complex transnational market fuelled and facilitated by several types of criminogenic asymmetries, and that the spectrum of solutions is similarly complex. Globalization presents as many opportunities for crime control policy as it does for transnational crime, and there is an urgent need for more systematic research that elicits a clearer picture of the licit–illicit interfacing in the international market of art and antiquities. In the meantime, the world's cultural heritage continues to disappear at an alarming rate unless action is taken.

In broad terms, we need to work towards a reduction of legal asymmetries through harmonization of substantive provisions, procedures, and sanctions. Fewer regulatory asymmetries lower both criminogenesis and compliance costs to the private sector and legitimate concerns.

Nation states may complain about gradually ceding independence and power to act and shape their environment, but it is largely the exercise of their power that generates global crime opportunities for illicit markets and crime facilitation. It is national policies and measures, the use of asymmetric state powers, overemphasis of sovereignty issues, and nationalist resistances against international regulation that breed criminogenic asymmetries.

The kinds of asymmetries that contribute to illicit art markets are to a large extent the making of governments. For instance, their economic policies produce relative or objective deprivation, their subsidization of domestic industries undercuts efforts of less developed countries to narrow the gaps, their initiatives undermine efforts to prevent theft of natural and cultural property from other countries, their inability or unwillingness to reduce the demand for stolen art perpetuates these illegal markets.

In other words, the optimistic message that emerges from this analysis is that, if there is political will to combat the international crime of cultural theft and destruction, it is within the control and power of national authorities to make a significant and positive impact.

References

Alder, C., Polk, K. (2002). Stopping this awful business: the illicit traffic in antiquities examined as a criminal market. *Art, Antiquity, & Law*, 7(1), 35–53.

Alder, C., Polk, K. (2005). The illicit traffic in plundered antiquities. In Reichel, P. (ed.), *Handbook of Transnational Crime and Justice*. Thousand Oaks: Sage.

Alva, W. (2001). Destruction of the archaeological heritage of Peru. In Brodie, N., Doole, J., Renfrew, C. (eds.), *Trade in Illicit Antiquities: The Destruction of the World's Archaeological Heritage* (89–96). Cambridge: McDonald Institute for Archaeological Research.

Anderson, K. (2002). The international theft and illicit export of cultural property. *New England Journal of International & Comparative Law*, 8(2), 1–26. http://www.nesl.edu/intljournal/vol8/anderson_v8n2.pdf. Retrieved 20 December 2007.

Artdaily (2007). Guennol lioness sells for $57.2 million. *Artnews*, December 6. http://www.artdaily.com/indexv5.asp?int_sec=11&int_new=22531. Retrieved 23 January 2008.

Athanassopoulos, E. (2002). An "ancient" landscape: European ideals, archaeology, and nation building in early modern Greece. *Journal of Modern Greek Studies*, 20(2), 273–305.

Atwood, R. (2004). *Stealing History: Tomb Raiders, Smugglers, and the Looting of the Ancient World*. New York: St Martin's Press.

Bator, P. (1982). An essay on the international trade in art. *Stanford Law Review*, 34(2), 275–384.

Beech, H. (2003). Asia's looted treasures spirited away. *Time Asia*, October 13. http://www.time.com/time/asia/covers/501031020/story.html. Retrieved 20 December 2007.

Berdal, M., Serrano, M. (2002). Introduction. In Berdal, M., Serrano, M. (eds.), *Transnational Organized Crime and International Security: Business as Usual?* Boulder, CO: Lynne Rienner Publishers, Inc.

Bohlen, C. (1996). Mafia and a lost Caravaggio stun Andreotti trial. *New York Times*, November 8. http://query.nytimes.com/gst/fullpage.html?res=9507E0DA163BF93BA35752C1A960958260. Retrieved 29 January.

Bowman, B. A. (2008). Transnational crimes against culture: looting at archaeological sites and the gray market in antiquities. *Dissertation Abstracts International*, 69(11A), 4517.

Brodie, N. (2002). Introduction. In Brodie, N., Tubb, K. (eds.), *Illicit Antiquities: The Theft of Culture and the Extinction of Archaeology*. London: Routledge.

Brodie, N. (2006). An archaeologist's view of the trade in unprovenanced antiquities. In Hoffman, B. (ed.), *Art & Cultural Heritage: Law, Policy, & Practice*. Cambridge: Cambridge University Press.

Brodie, N., Doole, J., Watson, P. (2000). *Stealing History: The Illicit Trade in Cultural Material*. Cambridge: The McDonald Institute for Archaeological Research.

Brooke, J. (1988). Faced with a shrinking supply of authentic art, African dealers peddle the illusion. *New York Times*, April 17, H51.

Clarke, H. (2005). Message to the mafia: city wants its stolen Caravaggio returned. *Telegraph*, November 26. http://www.telegraph.co.uk/news/main.jhtml?xml=/news/2005/11/27/wmafia27.xml. Retrieved 29 January 2008.

Conklin, J. (1994). *Art Crime*. Westport, CT: Praeger.

Cordess, C., Turcan, M. (1993). Art vandalism. *British Journal of Criminology*, 33, 95–102.

Cowell, A. (1991). Michelangelo's David is damaged. *New York Times*, 15 September 1991, 3.

Elia, R. (2001). Analysis of the looting, selling, and collecting of Apulian red-figure vases: a quantitative approach. In Brodie, N. et al. (eds.), *Trade in Illicit Antiquities: The Destruction of the World's Archaeological Heritage*. Cambridge: McDonald Institute for Archaeological Research.

Federal Bureau of Investigation (2009). Art theft program. http://www.fbi.gov/hq/cid/arttheft/arttheft.htm. Retrieved 13 November 2009.

Francioni, F., Lenzerini, F. (2003). The destruction of the Buddhas of Bamiyan and international law. *European Journal of International Law*, 14(4), 619–651.

Francioni, F., Lenzerini, F. (2006). The obligation to prevent and avoid destruction of cultural heritage: from Bamiyan to Iraq. In Hoffman, B. (ed.), *Art & Cultural Heritage: Law, Policy & Practice*. Cambridge: Cambridge University Press.

Gerstenblith, P. (2004). *Art, Cultural Heritage, and the Law: Cases & Materials*. Durham, NC: Carolina Academic Press.

Gill, D., Chippindale, C. (1993). Material and intellectual consequences of esteem for Cycladic figures. *American Journal of Archaeology*, 97(3), 602–673.

Hamblin, D. (1970). *Pots and Robbers*. New York: Simon & Schuster.

Hoffman, B. (2006). Introduction to parts II and III: cultural rights, cultural property, and international trade. In Hoffman, B. (ed.), *Art & Cultural Heritage: Law, Policy & Practice*. Cambridge: Cambridge University Press.

INTERPOL (2005). 2003 statistics on stolen works of art by place of theft. http://www.interpol.int/Public/WorkOfArt/woafaq.asp. Retrieved 13 December 2005.

INTERPOL (2009). Stolen works of art: frequently asked questions. http://www.interpol.int/Public/WorkOfArt/woafaq.asp. Retrieved 20 December 2007.

Isman, F. (2001). For that stolen Vermeer, follow the art squad. *UNESCO Courier*. http://www.unesco.org/courier/2001_04/uk/doss24.htm. Retrieved 29 January 2008.

Joyce, E. (1999). Transnational criminal enterprise: the European perspective. In Farer, T. (ed.), *Transnational Crime in the Americas*. New York: Routledge.

Mackenzie, S. R. M. (2005). *Going, Going, Gone: Regulating the Market in Illicit Antiquities*. Leicester: Institute of Art and Law.

Margules, P. L. (1992). International art theft and the illegal import and export of cultural property: a study of relevant values, legislation, and solutions. *Suffolk Transnational Law Journal*, 15, 609–647.

McCalister, A. (2005). Organized crime and the theft of Iraqi antiquities. *Trends in Organized Crime*, 9(1), 24–37.

McMahon, B. (2005). Mafia informer asked to solve mystery of stolen Caravaggio. *The Guardian*, November 28. http://www.guardian.co.uk/italy/story/0,12576,1652146,00.html. Retrieved 29 January 2008.

Mueller, G. (2001). Transnational crime: definitions and concepts. *Transnational Organized Crime*, 4, 13–21.

Murphy, J. (1995). Stealing China's past. The People's Republic reports a hemorrhage of artefacts. *Archaeology*, 48(6), 71–77.

Naylor, R. (2002). *Wages of Crime: Black Markets, Illegal Finance, and the Underworld Economy*. Ithaca, NY: Cornell University Press.

New York AFP (2007). Mesopotamian sculpture sells for record 57 million dollars. *The Carved Guennol Lioness*, December 5. http://www.freerepublic.com/focus/f-news/1935404/posts. Retrieved 15 November 2009.

Nicholas, L. (1995). *The Rape of Europa: The Fate of Europe's Treasures in the Third Reich and the Second World War*. New York: Vintage Books.

O'Keefe, P. (1997). *Trade in Antiquities: Reducing Destruction and Theft*. London: Archetype Publications.

Papa Sokal, M. (2006). *Antiquities Collecting and the Looting of Archaeological Sites*. Proceedings of the 2nd Annual Ename International Colloquium, "Who Owns the Past? Heritage Rights and Responsibilities in a Multicultural World", held at Ghent, Belgium, 22–25 March 2006. http://www.savingantiquities.org/pdf/PapaSokal_Antiquities.pdf. Retrieved 13 March 2008.

Passas, N. (1998). Globalization and transnational organized crime: the effects of criminogenic asymmetries. *Transnational Organized Crime*, 4(3, 4), 22–56.

Passas, N. (1999). Globalization, criminogenic asymmetries and economic crime. *European Journal of Law Reform*, 1(4), 399–423.

Passas, N. (2000). Global anomie, dysnomie, and economic crime: hidden consequences of globalization and neo-liberalism in Russia and around the world. *Social Justice*, 27(2), 16–44.

Passas, N. (2002). Cross-border crime and the interface between legal and illegal actors. In van Duyne, P. C. et al. (eds.), *Upperworld and Underworld in Cross-Border Crime*. Nijmegen, The Netherlands: Wolf Legal Publishers.

Passas, N. (2005). Global anomie theory and crime. In Henry, S., Lanier, M. (eds.), *The Essential Criminology Reader* (174–182). Boulder, CO: Westview Press.

Platthy, J. (1993). UNESCO and trafficking in illicit treasures. *Journal of Prehistoric Religion*, 7, 42–48.

Radnoti, S. (1999). *The Fake: Forgery and Its Place in Art*. Lanham, MD: Rowman & Littlefield Publishers, Inc.

Robinson, J. (2000). *The Merger: The Conglomeration of International Organized Crime*. Woodstock, NY: Overlook Press.

Rose, M. (1998). Backflap sting. *Archaeology*, 51(5). http://www.archaeology.org/9809/newsbriefs/backflap.html. Retrieved 13 November 2009.

Ruggiero, V. (1998). Transnational criminal activities: the provision of services in the dirty economies. *International Journal of Risk, Security, and Crime Prevention*, 3(2), 121–129.

Ruggiero, V. (2000). *Crime and Markets: Essays in Anti-criminology*. New York: Oxford University Press.

Salahuddin, S. (2001). Taliban atone for delay in destroying statues. *Reuters*, March 19. http://hss.fullerton.edu/comparative/b%C3%A2mi%C3%A2n_buddhas_exart.htm. Retrieved 13 March 2008.

Stanish, C. (2006). Forging ahead. *Archaeology*, 62(3). http://www.archaeology.org/0905/etc/insider.html. Retrieved 15 November 2009.

Stille, A. (2002). *The Future of the Past*. New York: Picador.

Tijhuis, E. (2006). *Transnational Crime and the Interface Between Legal and Illegal Factors: The Case of the Illicit Art and Antiquities Trade*. Nijmegen: Wolf Legal Publishers.

van Duyne, P. C. et al. (2002) (eds.), *Upperworld and Underworld in Cross-Border Crime*. Nijmegen, The Netherlands: Wolf Legal Publishers.

Williams, P. (1999). Emerging issues: transnational crime and control. In Newman, G. (ed.), *Global Report on Crime and Justice*. New York: Oxford University Press.

Williamson, J. (1996). Globalization, convergence, and history. *Journal of Economic History*, 56(2), 103–132.

Woods, N. (2000). The political economy of globalization. In Woods, N. (ed.), *The Political Economy of Globalization*. Basingstoke: Macmillan.

Chapter 4
The Market as Criminal and Criminals in the Market: Reducing Opportunities for Organised Crime in the International Antiquities Market

Simon Mackenzie

Introduction: The Market as Criminal and Criminals in the Market

What is the relationship between organised crime and the antiquities market? There are two senses in which we can use the term "organised crime" here. In the first sense, we can see the international market in illicit antiquities as a criminal market (Polk 2000), organised into a structure of relations between thieves, smugglers, facilitators, sellers, and buyers of illicit commodities. We might therefore suggest that this illicit part of the trade is an example of "organised" crime. That argument could proceed without reference to the presence of conventionally stereotyped organised criminals in the market, in the sense of groups or networks of professional criminals who use violence and corruption in the pursuit of illegal financial gain. This view of the antiquities market proceeds with reference to the "spectrum of enterprise" approach to defining organised crime that sees global trade as always more or less legitimate or illegitimate, moral or immoral (Smith Jr. 1980; Edwards and Gill 2002, 2003). However, there are also of course many reports of antiquities being used as laundering mechanisms for drug money, as being linked to other international illicit markets, and as being colonised at the source end of the chain of supply and in transit to some extent by local political and bureaucratic corruption, the state military, other militias in conflict states, and organised crime groups, such as mafia-type organisations in Russia, Italy, and China. So we have, on the one hand, the argument that the international illicit market in antiquities is, even without reference to this type of organised criminality, an example of organised crime simply by dint of its organised market nature and the fact that many of its transactions are illegal according to the criminal laws of the jurisdictions where they take place. But we also have, on the other hand, the question whether various types of more conventionally conceived "organised criminals" are operating within the market, and if so at which points and in what form.

S. Mackenzie (✉)
Scottish Centre for Crime and Justice Research, University of Glasgow, Glasgow, UK
e-mail: Simon.Mackenzie@glasgow.ac.uk

S. Manacorda and D. Chappell (eds.), *Crime in the Art and Antiquities World: Illegal Trafficking in Cultural Property*, DOI 10.1007/978-1-4419-7946-9_4,

I will attempt to address both of these questions here – of the "market as criminal", and of "criminals in the market" – while pressing the argument that one of the key points of crime reductive intervention "market" (i.e., buyer) countries such as the UK have is through controlling demand for illicit antiquities within our jurisdiction. The major problem in the UK, as with other market countries such as the USA, remains that illicit trading in antiquities subsists in the global and local trade relations which are part of the most basic architecture of formal and informal markets that continue to function in relatively plain view, and therefore have become normalised to the point that their organised ties to underlying wrongdoing or immorality have become effectively invisible.

In this chapter, I therefore want to address the problem of the presence of looted antiquities in the market as well as consider the question of opportunities for the entry of organised crime groups or networks into the market chain of supply. Rather than undertaking a review of all international criminal policy responses, I want to focus on one particular policy response – market-end criminalisation – outline its problems as it has been recently manifested in the UK, and work towards a framework that sees such criminalisation as one tool in a suite of market reduction measures which can usefully engage with the problematic culture and activities of the antiquities market. The outline for what is to follow is therefore:

1. To briefly review the UK's recent introduction of criminal legislation which purports to ban dealing in illicit antiquities within its jurisdiction.
2. To introduce the idea of sector vulnerability studies in relation to organised crime, and to apply this method as a framework for analysing the international market in antiquities.
3. To consider the market-oriented crime prevention issues raised by the sector vulnerability approach.
4. To note that the sort of criminal policy responses to which such a sector vulnerability analysis gives recommendation in relation to reducing opportunities for organised crime in the market, are broadly the same as the responses thought to be needed to sanitise the market of looted antiquities more generally.

Criminalising the Market in Looted Antiquities in the UK

In interviews with dealers around the world, I found them to be using various among the classic criminological techniques of neutralisation (Sykes and Matza 1957) to justify and excuse their participation in a market in which they knew illicit objects circulated (Mackenzie 2005b). I refer to this work in this chapter as "the 2005 study". Towards the end of that project, in December 2003, the UK passed into law the *Dealing in Cultural Objects (Offences) Act 2003*, a piece of legislation with one main operative provision, creating a new criminal offence in the UK. The Act in Section 1 provides for a sentence on conviction on indictment of up to 7 years imprisonment and/or a fine, where a person:

> dishonestly deals in a cultural object that is tainted, knowing or believing that the object is tainted.

Under Section 2 of the Act, a cultural object is "tainted" if it is excavated, or removed from a monument or other building or structure of historical, architectural, or archaeological interest, and such excavation or removal constitutes an offence. It is stated to be immaterial whether the excavation or removal took place in the UK or elsewhere. The intended effect of this legislation is therefore to criminalise (and by implication deter) the knowing possession or trade in the UK of antiquities looted either there or abroad.

With colleagues, I was funded by the UK's Economic and Social Research Council to conduct a qualitative investigation of the London market's reaction to the introduction of this legislation, focussing again on interviews with significant dealers and other buyers such as museums ("the 2007 study"). Throughout these studies the methodological approach I have taken has been to try to bring a social scientific interpretivism to the study of the trade in illicit antiquities, with a focus on documenting the business processes and worldviews of dealers and collectors in market countries, who provide the demand for the objects the looters are stealing.

There is a range of data which is available from these projects, and I only summarise some of the more interesting findings here. More full expositions of the whole dataset of interviews can be found in the books which have resulted from the set of interviews in the 2005 study (Mackenzie 2005b) and the socio-legal evaluation in the 2007 study (Mackenzie and Green 2009), and further analysis is available in a number of papers (Mackenzie 2002a, b, 2005a, 2006, 2007; Mackenzie and Green 2008).

In the 2007 study, we conducted a survey and a number of in-depth interviews with respondents in and around the London antiquities market to determine the market's reaction to the introduction of the 2003 Act, and our findings can be broadly summarised as follows:

- Despite most respondents being aware of the 2003 Act, only a very small number of the trade respondents thought that they had noticed any change in trade routines which could be seen as a productive response to the Act.
- Likewise, only a very small proportion of trade respondents said that the Act would result in them changing *their own* business routines, and in many of these cases, the change planned was only formal rather than substantive.
- It was acknowledged that where changes to business routines did ensue, they were likely to be purely cosmetic.
- There was a general feeling that the antiquities market was "under fire" from regulators, journalists, and public opinion.
- Dealers, (some) museums, collectors, and officials, such as the UK's Department for Culture, Media and Sport, all tend to work on the assumption that the market is composed of "legitimate" and "illegitimate" dealers and that therefore if the "bad apples" can be excised the "legitimate" market can function without hindrance and will not be in danger of contravening any national criminal laws. This is wrong.

The reason the ideology of the legitimate market is wrong is that the antiquities market is best seen as a grey market (Polk 2000; Bowman 2008). Illegitimate objects pass through the "legitimate" trade and therefore any regulatory attention paid to such objects will directly affect the business of the trade generally, rather than support "legitimate" dealers by eliminating their "illegitimate" peers.[1]

The issue of formal (rather than substantive) responses to formal regulatory requirements is a problem that has been observed by Max Weber, and has persisted as an issue in criminology, finding its most recent place in Doreen McBarnet's observations on "active reception" and "creative compliance" in corporate and white-collar responses to regulation (McBarnet 2003, 2006). Where business ethics do not involve a strong connection with the spirit of the law, formal responses are likely to ensue which simply use documentation and other routine activities to obscure rather than eliminate wrongdoing. This is evident in the antiquities market:

> I'm in the trade, I've seen how things have changed. Even when I'm dealing with friends of mine, I'll say to them 'that's nice', you know, 'how about provenance?' Everybody says that now. 'Got your provenance?' Because if it has a demonstrable good provenance, that helps. It helps with the selling of it. And very often they'll say to me, 'well, not really', you know, 'I bought it from a dealer' and that to me is okay. Because I trust them to buy in the way that I buy. And I'll say the same thing to them (London Dealer 2005 study).

Dealers are apparently out of touch with the reality of the problem of illicit antiquities. As has been argued elsewhere (Mackenzie 2005b), while cases of high-level smuggling are given high profile in the media and therefore provide the most readily-available graphic case-studies of the illicit transit of looted antiquities, these cases must be seen in the context of a market which operates in a routine manner to circulate illicit antiquities in much less remarkable ways. As well as being averse to accepting offers of goods which are clearly illicit, the 2003 Act to be successful in sanitising the market must require of dealers that they take serious steps to investigate the provenance of the objects they routinely purchase from sources they might historically have assumed to be "trustworthy". I will mention at more length in due course the Market Reduction Approach (MRA) to unwinding markets in stolen goods (Sutton 1998; Sutton, Schneider and Hetherington 2001), but here it is worth noting that it predicts that it is the disruption of this routine lack of reflexivity in seeing oneself *qua* buyer as a generative part of the chain of supply of illicit commodities that can have a significant effect on the supply chain, and we might add that in the antiquities market this routine lack of reflexivity manifests itself as an assumption that open market dealing equates to lawful dealing in objects which are not tainted. In light of the evidence we have from sellers on the open market as to the depth of their investigation (or general lack thereof) into object provenance, this faith in the open market appears to be misplaced.

The model of the antiquities market as a grey market captures the reality that flows of licit and illicit objects are intermixed and therefore that rather than being a market characterised by a "clean" public trade and a "dirty" private or "underground" trade, the supposedly clean public trade in antiquities is tainted "grey" by the circulation therein of illicit antiquities. Characteristic of a grey market, dealers

[1]There are of course some dealers who are more pure in their legitimate intent than others, but our interviews found that even these apparently well-intentioned dealers could not always be sure they were not dealing in some looted objects.

who would describe themselves as "legitimate", while at times expressing concern about looted artefacts in the market, are at other more private moments surprisingly complacent about the issue of dealing in stolen goods. In a market which functions without the serious transmission of provenance, such dealing is seen as a standard risk, and remains so in the UK despite the creation of the offence in the 2003 Act:

> So, stolen goods, yes, they must be here. Possibly over the course of time 10% of my stock has probably been stolen at one time or another... I don't know, but it would not surprise me if it was that high... either stolen in China, or wherever, you just don't know (London Dealer 2007 study).

We have documented various problems with the design and implementation of the 2003 Act. Many of these relate to perhaps the most well-known problem in the international regulation of the trade in illicit antiquities; that of proving the origin and transit history of a clandestinely excavated and probably illegally exported artefact. Despite these issues of proof being routine stumbling-blocks to legal action, known to all commentators on the market (e.g., Palmer 1994; Kaye and Main 1995; O'Keefe 1997; Gerstenblith 2007: 179–180), they remain as problems built into the 2003 Act through provisions such as its non-retroactivity, which demands that UK prosecutors have proof of the date an object was "stolen" (i.e., in many cases, illegally excavated or removed from its place as an integral part of a monument or other protected structure). The Act also does not include illegally exported objects within its definition of "tainted". This is problematic since stolen objects are also often illegally exported, and it tends to be easier to prove their illegal export than it does the original theft – or at least a court would be more likely to find fault in a buyer if "taint" were to include unlawful export, the source country had a prohibition on unlicenced export of that type of artefact, and the object had no export documentation. Increased attention to illegal export would therefore be a mechanism for catching some looted objects which might otherwise be evidentially out of reach for a UK court.

The main problem with the 2003 Act, however, is in the requirement for *knowledge of or belief in* the tainted status of the object in question. This wording serves to undermine the basic message that unites all critics of the market: that effective due diligence in relation to object provenance needs to become an essential component of any purchase of antiquities. As the DCMS guidelines state:

> The burden of proving knowledge or belief that an object is tainted rests with the prosecution and such proof must be beyond all reasonable doubt. *This means that a failure by the accused to carry out adequate checks on the provenance of an object will not constitute knowledge or belief* (Department for Culture Media and Sport 2004: 8, my italics).

This major failing of the 2003 Act is well-known to market participants. The problem of proof even acts as a kind of 'pre-emptive' neutralisation of the MRA approach of the 2003 Act, in that 'capable guardians' (Cohen and Felson 1979; Felson 1994) in the chain of supply remain unlikely to report suspicious behaviour. Our research has found the most common reaction of conscientious trade figures to offers suspected of being illicit to be simply to decline to purchase the object rather than report suspicions to the police. Even among the most conscientious dealers, then, there is a culture of self-protection rather than a sense that they might individually contribute to cleaning up the market more generally.

We have accumulated considerable evidence of the "don't ask, don't tell" culture in relation to provenance in the antiquities market. This culture of ignorance in relation to the origin of objects is no longer a fresh revelation, having been raised in almost all of the literature on the illicit market. Not asking provenance-related questions is now enshrined by the 2003 Act and the associated DCMS guidelines as a rational strategy for a dealer who wants to buy antiquities but does not want to risk being prosecuted for the criminal offence of dealing in tainted cultural objects. What is relatively under-researched, and pertinent to the present volume, however, is the further suggestion that the presence of organised crime in the market is itself something that dealers do not want to probe to uncover, for reasons of fear. Whether these stories of organised crime are true or not, they still add to the problem of reluctance among dealers to ask the important, and culturally gauche, questions about provenance. Consider this, from a prominent London Dealer:

> The people in Hong Kong don't tell you [about provenance] because the people who smuggle the goods out of China are not the sort of people you want to talk about. When I've asked about odd pieces, you know, 'Are there any excavation notes? Can you find where something like this came from? It would be fascinating to know.' They just say, 'You don't ask those questions; you don't want to get a reputation for asking questions.' It wasn't me saying that; that's what they say. That's the way presumably, if you're a Hong Kong dealer, to end up in the harbour (London Dealer 2007 study).

The Antiquities Market, Sector Vulnerability, and Organised Crime

In my empirical studies of the antiquities market I have come across only tangential and limited evidence of the presence of organised crime in the market. This may well be an artefact of the particular research methods I have used, and the constituency I have used them on: dealers at the market end of the chain of supply are perhaps the least likely participants in the market to know anything about organised crime if it is present at more distant points further up the chain, and if they do have such knowledge it is likely to be unpalatable and therefore precisely the sort of "fact" that they would tend to ignore or neutralise given their general desire to think of the market as a legitimate trading forum.

In the absence of much first-hand evidence about the participation of organised crime groups or networks in the market, a useful approach to take to the question of the relationship between organised crime groups and antiquities is to try to integrate the "sector vulnerability" approach with a market-oriented crime prevention approach, to provide an outline of a model that can tell us:

(a) Whether the antiquities market is particularly vulnerable to organised crime compared to other commodity markets
(b) What steps can be taken to reduce the attractiveness of the market to organised crime

In terms of sector vulnerability approaches to organised crime, I have found two approaches to be especially helpful: those of Tom Vander Beken in Belgium and Jay Albanese in the USA (Vander Beken and Defruytier 2004; Vander Beken 2004, 2005, 2007a, b; Vander Beken and Van Daele 2008; Albanese 1987, 1995, 2008). Vander Beken's model contains considerably more factors, which makes it an impressively comprehensive tool for considering sector vulnerability. However, its breadth also makes it labour-intensive as a vehicle for regular use by police analysts, and it is rather too extensive for the purposes of a brief review of the vulnerability of the antiquities sector in the space we have here – so I will apply the Albanese model. In terms of preventive approaches to organised crime, I have turned to work by Henk van de Bunt and Cathelijne van der Schoot (van de Bunt and van der Schoot 2003) and considered it alongside the MRA of Mike Sutton and colleagues (Sutton 1998; Sutton et al. 2001).

The risk assessment approach offered by proponents like Vander Beken and Albanese declines to take current knowledge about organised criminals as its focus. Rather than being nominal or group focussed, these authors encourage us to focus on the identification of high-risk products and markets. As Albanese says; "put another way, if you correctly identify the high-risk products and markets, you will know where to look for the offenders" (Albanese 2008: 269). This raises the question whether the antiquities sector can be seen as a high-risk market, or as dealing in high-risk products. A deep knowledge of the opportunity structures of that market allows us to identify the points in the chain of transaction where we should "look for the offenders" and implement measures for the protection of the market against organised crime.

In Albanese's model, four variables contain the essence of prediction of markets which are attractive to organised crime: supply, demand, regulators and competition. Supply factors concern product availability and ease of movement; demand factors include the level of demand and whether it is elastic or inelastic; competition factors include levels of profitability, which are constrained by open competition; and regulation factors include the ease of entry into the market, any special skills needed, law enforcement capacity and levels of corruption among public officials.

Here is the final 10-factor model that Albanese arrives at:

Supply Indicators

1. Objective availability of product or service
2. Ease of movement/sale

Regulation Indicators

3. Ease of entry into market by its regulation and the skills needed
4. Law enforcement capability and competence
5. Level of local government corruption

Competition Indicators

6. History of organised crime in the market
7. Profitability
8. Harm

Demand Indicators

9. Current customer demand for product
10. Nature of the demand – whether elastic or inelastic

I apply this multi-factor approach to the antiquities market here, in order to demonstrate that it is a high–risk market in terms of opportunities presented to organised criminals. It is worth noting that although this analysis takes the form here of a review of the main weaknesses of the market viewed as something of an historical construct, as with any risk analysis the value of the tool increases if it is not seen as a static assessment of organised crime vulnerability, but rather analysis is performed regularly and the level of risk can therefore be subjected to a time series style of analysis. In this way, we can achieve a measure of the effect of the introduction of new initiatives and legislation not in terms of a traditional social scientific outcome evaluation but in terms of effect on market structures and characteristics, and the predicted effects of these changes on opportunities for organised crime.

Supply Indicators

1. *Objective availability of product or service.* Antiquities are a relatively scarce commodity, certainly at the high end, and this contributes to the high prices they can command. Despite this scarcity, they are relatively freely available to anyone interested in looking for them, and low or non-existent levels of security at local sites of archaeological interest mean that very often the only restraint on those who wish to take antiquities is their own conscience or their reluctance to break the law. Demonstrably, these internal psychological controls have not been adequate.
2. *Ease of movement/sale.* Antiquities are sometimes small, and therefore relatively portable. This makes them an attractive commodity in terms of the risk of theft since they embody very high financial values per kilo of weight compared to other commodities. There are of course antiquities which are very large in size, and therefore not especially portable. These can be dismantled, however, to render relatively portable parts which are still independently of very high value, such as where heads are broken from statues or figures, or designs are chiselled from temple walls. In cases where it is desirable to risk moving very large artefacts, contemporary shipping mechanisms combined with corruption among local or regional officials can sometimes accommodate this. Many other factors contribute to the ease of movement and sale of antiquities, including inadequate linking of export controls in source countries with import controls in market countries, and the infamous market culture of not insisting on detailed, explicit and reliable provenance information when purchasing an artefact. Unlike other illicit commodities such as drugs, traffickers in antiquities find an established open and legal structure in market countries for selling these goods, which through chains of dealers and auction houses operates very effectively to maximise the price which can be obtained for art and antiquities.

Regulation Indicators

3. *Ease of entry into market by its regulation and the skills needed.* There are no requirements to obtain an antiquities dealing licence in most countries. The closest most countries get to that is to require application for a generic second-hand dealers' licence, which does not have especially exclusive entry requirements. The private nature of many transactions means that even requirements to hold this kind of licence can be easily evaded, and the high value/low volume of the objects combined with the fact that they do not need any particularly special storage conditions means that people can set themselves up as dealers from home. The overheads are therefore low, contributing to a low barrier to entry into the market. The one most pertinent skill that is needed to function profitably in the antiquities market is to know enough about the objects in question to be able to detect fakes, and to pass objects into the market without raising suspicions (i.e., looking too much like a criminal). While there are therefore some obstacles to be negotiated by way of entry into the market, none of these is burdensome.
4. *Law enforcement capability and competence.* Law enforcement capability is generally low in both source and market countries, where policing and other resources are stretched and antiquities theft and trafficking is likely to be overshadowed by other criminal threats which are perceived to be graver. Law enforcement competence varies from country to country: at best countries have a national art and antiquities enforcement unit, and dedicated specialists within borders agencies. Even where this is the case, issues of competence tend to be overshadowed by issues of capacity, and the culture of secrecy in the trade combined with the relatively high status of dealers, plus the small percentage of shipments which can actually physically be checked by customs, combine to mean that most antiquities in transit and in the market are not subject to extensive law enforcement scrutiny.
5. *Level of local government corruption.* The international market in antiquities tends to operate by taking objects from poor countries and delivering them to rich countries. Problems of corruption can be present at all levels, but are observed to be more widespread in poor countries where economic factors support cultures of bribery which may have become relatively ingrained.

Competition Indicators

6. *History of organised crime in the market.* Recent concern has been expressed at the international level about organised crime in the antiquities market, although it seems to be the case – as is not unusual – that more research is needed to accurately identify the extent to which organised crime operates in the market.
7. *Profitability.* As mentioned above under "portability", antiquities can be a highly profitable commodity, particularly where they can be acquired at source for low or no cost. By way of example as to the high prices provenanced antiquities can command on the open market, in 2007 Sotheby's sold the Guennol

Lioness for US$ 57.2 million – the highest price ever recorded for a sculpture, and especially interesting for criminologists as the statue is a mere 3¼ in. in height, and therefore a very good example of a highly valuable and highly portable commodity.

8. *Harm.* It is clear from the archaeological discourse on looting that these activities cause substantial harm to sites, to objects, and to our historical knowledge base (Brodie et al. 2000, 2001).

Demand Indicators

9. *Current customer demand for product.* In my interviews with antiquities dealers, they have suggested several things about customer demand. They have suggested that the market is not as big or as active as it once was, although this seems to have been an attempt to deflect attention from their activities as I found it to be contradicted by official trade figures (Mackenzie 2005b). As well as arguing that the market is shrinking, they have suggested that the nature of consumer demand is changing. Dealers report that connoisseur collectors, interested in art history and in learning about the objects they buy, are being increasingly replaced by wealthy types who buy objects for speculative investment purposes, or as cultural signifiers (in the sense of mantelpiece status symbols) or both. These buyers, it is said, do not care so much about the history of the object or its place in the overall history of art. Rather than dealers educating their clients over time and cultivating a thirst for knowledge as well as for acquisitions, here as elsewhere the dealing role has become more functionally consumer-oriented, simply delivering attractive objects to rich but underinformed purchasers. So demand remains healthy, albeit changing in demographic in line with the changing times (and we shall consider the implications of this for regulation below).
10. *Nature of the demand – whether elastic or inelastic.* High elasticity signifies a market where when the price of the commodity goes up, demand drops off disproportionately. Low elasticity would be present if price rises did not suppress levels of demand. Demand is inelastic if despite price rises, demand remains the same. A market is taken to be more vulnerable, or attractive to organised crime, if its elasticity is low. We can see that this is most likely to be the case in markets characterised by addiction, where consumers are not in a good position to make rational decisions to suppress their demand. It is also likely to be a feature of markets where there is high finance at the demand end: in drug markets, price rises might be associated with increases in thefts by users to finance the uplift, but in markets with clients who have more money at their disposal, they may simply be prepared to pay more. One would have to conduct an economic analysis of the history of the evolution in prices in the antiquities market in order to determine the level of elasticity in demand. But even without doing so, we can observe that the collection of antiquities is

> performed by affluent individuals, and that it involves a certain kind of object fascination or fetish which can approach addiction. It is in fact a generally accurate diagnosis of the current state of the antiquities market to say that it has been, and still is, driven by buyers who want its objects no matter what, and who therefore find themselves turning a blind eye to suspicions of looting which if investigated with any real energy would probably reveal illegality in a planned purchase. It is, in other words, a market characterised by a knowing reluctance to know, or in a word which accurately captures that state of affairs, denial (Cohen 2001; Mackenzie 2007).

On every measure of a sector vulnerability scale, the antiquities market therefore emerges as presenting opportunities for profit-making through crime. What can we do to reduce some of these opportunities? Where criminal markets involve an interface between legitimate and illegitimate, as is the case in the antiquities market, it is often thought to be productive to focus on that interface, as a means of activating legitimate actors towards taking measures to insulate the market and reducing opportunities for organised crime.

Van de Bunt and van der Schoot identify three categories of "interfaces" between OCGs and the legitimate environment:

1. The demand from the licit environment for illegal products and services
2. The abuse of facilitators in the licit environment
3. The availability of "tools" in the licit environment (van de Bunt and van der Schoot 2003: 9)

These three categories of what van de Bunt and van der Schoot call "red flags" therefore give rise to three associated types of crime prevention response:

1. Reducing the demand for illegal products and services: for example, through social and economic measures.
2. An increase in awareness of abuse of facilitators and measures to increase their defensibility: for example, codes of conduct, screening of personnel and licence requirements that exclude criminals from certain trades or from tendering for public contracts.
3. Diminish the availability of tools in the licit environment which can be used by organised criminals: for example, by strong money laundering regulations combined with the regulation of alternative money transfer mechanisms which might otherwise be used to circumvent regulations.

A study of the antiquities market reveals the interface between illegitimate and legitimate as paramount in allowing crime to profit in the market. The grey market nature of the antiquities trade, where illicitly obtained objects become effectively laundered by insertion into legitimate streams of supply, allows them then to be sold at the high prices they would not command were it indisputable they were illicit. The obfuscation of provenance in the chains of supply of antiquities is relevant to all three of the "red flag" categories: it allows demand for illicit objects to persist even among those who do not know, or do not want to know, that objects are looted. It involves a range of facilitators and complicit actors, including dealers themselves

(Kersel 2006). In studies of other organised criminal activities, professionals who act as facilitators have routinely been found: often lawyers and accountants who can set up front companies or assist in money laundering. The facilitators in the antiquities trade are a range of actors who offer various services, such as customs officials, appraisers, dealers and museums, and even academics (Brodie 2009) who in extreme cases may be bribed but many of whom routinely facilitate the illicit market simply by being reluctant to exercise what power they have to stop it. And the process is constituted by various "tools" of legitimation available to criminals, including fake documents (cf. the Sevso treasure litigation and the Schultz case), auction mechanisms (Watson 1997), movement through numerous jurisdictions (Polk 2000), and so on.

The Market Reduction Approach to Tackling Theft

The three types of crime reductive and preventive measures proposed by van de Bunt and van der Schoot are a useful way to think about approaches to preventing organised crime in the antiquities market. In this market, each of these crime reduction measures requires that purchasers of antiquities be made to care about the origin of their purchases, and not only to reject looted antiquities, but also to report suspicions to the police when they have them. There is some way to go in changing attitudes and routines in this market.

In this regard, the observations made by the dealers on the new class of buyer mentioned above – the art-for-status rather than the art-for-collection purchaser – could be read in an optimistic as well as a pessimistic light. It might be thought that the new brand of purchasers, being apparently little concerned with issues such as object history, prove difficult subjects in whom to inculcate the importance of provenance. In truth though, the sorts of erstwhile art-historian style collectors that dealers say they regret losing did not present great evidence of reluctance to acquire looted pieces (Renfrew 1993; Elia 1994). There may in fact be an opportunity to engage with the modern face of the antiquities trade through public education campaigns geared towards the uncommitted buyer, who might easily be persuaded to turn his or her attentions to other less problematic luxury goods as the antiquities market becomes increasingly tarred with the looting brush, as is now certainly the trend.

In our recent exposition of the 2003 Act in the UK, Penny Green and I have argued that a productive way for criminology to engage with the antiquities market is through the conceptual framework of the MRA (Mackenzie and Green 2009). This is a framework that has proved useful in the practical business of tackling other stolen goods markets. The MRA recommends both general initiatives to reduce demand combined with practical advice for law enforcement measures aimed at key points in the chain of supply, to maximise their potential. We also point out that the MRA contains a philosophy of harm reduction as well as its better-known penal intervention measures. Jacqueline Schneider, an early proponent of the MRA, has recently highlighted the potential of the MRA to apply to commodity markets that are more exotic than domestic stolen goods markets, focussing on the international market in illicit wildlife. She notes that she has previously suggested at the UN Crime Congress 2003 that the MRA might be useful in tackling the property markets which are the concern of the UN Convention on Transnational and Organized Crime, including (as well as wildlife) weapons and ammunition, humans and body parts, and cultural heritage (Schneider 2008).

The MRA is a "strategic, systematic and routine problem solving framework for action against the roots of theft" that provides guidance for "interagency partnerships wishing to tackle stolen goods markets" (Sutton et al. 2001: iii). The general theory of the MRA is that demand affects supply, in other words that "reducing dealing in stolen goods will reduce motivation to steal". The way the MRA attempts to reduce dealing is to:

- instil an appreciation among thieves that transporting, storing, and selling stolen goods has become at least as risky as it is to steal goods in the first place
- make buying, dealing and consuming stolen goods appreciably more risky for all those involved (Sutton et al. 2001: vii)

This approach, which the MRA calls "risk projection", seems to encapsulate quite well many commentators' hopes for the effect of the 2003 Act in the UK, although as we have found, in practice it did not live up to these hopes. The MRA approach of raising the risks faced by those in the chain of supply is particularly apposite to our present discussion because it expressly seeks to engage with "crime facilitators such as business people who buy stolen goods" (Sutton et al. 2001: vii). Among the ways it recommends addressing facilitators is to "seek to implement local legislation requiring traders to require proof of identity, and to keep records of the name and address, of anyone who sells them second-hand goods; to use test-selling to see if businesses are complying with new codes of practice; and to utilise interagency support to crack down on any irregularities committed by businesses known to deal in stolen goods" as well as the use of media campaigns to aid clear delineation between what is and is not acceptable trading, arresting fences and raising awareness of the consequences of being caught dealing in stolen goods, and telephone hotlines for people to report illicit dealing (Sutton et al. 2001: vii).

One of the key findings of the studies that underpinned the development of the MRA was that thieves and fences had very little fear of being caught when selling stolen goods, since their (generally quite accurate) perception was that nobody in the chain of supply was likely to inform on them, even strangers to whom they made offers. They also did not know many people who had been arrested for selling stolen goods, which supported their feelings of safety. There are close parallels here to the antiquities market, and there appear transferable benefits to the MRA model of periodic law enforcement crackdowns followed by periods of consolidation, where progress is reviewed and alternative educative and other market reduction strategies are employed.

These other market reduction strategies relate to the harm–reduction component of the MRA, which tries to create a context in which the deterrent effects of the crackdown phases can bed in. This context involves supporting legitimate markets and encouraging consumers and facilitators to operate in those, removing the base of consumers and dealers who are willing to take up illicit offers by enhancing for them the attractiveness of legitimate offers. In translating this to the antiquities market, we would need to focus on ways to support the legitimate market in recirculating (as opposed to looted) goods, to make dealing in these objects more attractive. Currently, it is the fresh find which thrills the market, with recirculating objects being portrayed by the dealers in my research samples as something of a dull, second-rate choice. This is a deeply ingrained market attitude, but we might consider ways to attempt to engage with dealer attitudes similar to the ways we might engage with public attitudes. Serious sanctions attached to dealing in looted objects would provide some reinforcement here, but as well as fear of arrest there needs to be a commitment from dealers to attempt to eradicate looted antiquities from the market, and currently that commitment is not present. Most of the dealers in the 2005 study (Mackenzie 2005b) said that they disapproved of looting in the abstract (some did not disapprove), but they remained willing to buy the objects since they attributed them with various possible but unproven histories such as being accidental finds or objects that, were it not for the market, would otherwise have been destroyed. It is these sorts of stories that we need to engage with if we want to really begin changing market attitudes, and this kind of discourse and culture based approach can support MRA-style deterrence in addressing the problem of "facilitation" which currently characterises the market.

Cleaning Up the Antiquities Trade and Preventing Opportunities for Organised Crime: Towards Productive Policy Responses

Our research into the 2003 Act found that in the view of some of the most prominent and successful traders in the market, trafficking in looted artefacts is central to its activity (Mackenzie and Green 2009). These market actors equate the cleaning up of the market's activities with its inevitable demise. Dealers and museum respondents reported to us that in relation to dealing in antiquities "it is now almost impossible to do it legitimately if you start asking all of the questions I think" and that restricting oneself only to dealing in recirculating objects as opposed to new looted objects was "professional suicide".

The antiquities market is therefore caught in a serious bind. In its more reflexive moments it accepts that it is, to a not inconsiderable extent, reliant on looting to feed it, yet while it tends to try to construct a picture of that looting as benign acts of "chance finding" by local farmers, and saving artefacts from being destroyed by infrastructure projects like road-building in source countries, it also subsists with some level of knowledge, or at least rumour-based fear, of the notion that the purchase of antiquities in the market is fuelling organised crime activity.

Somewhat ironically, it may be that this relatively new focus on the activities of organised crime groups in the antiquities market provides the catalyst for encouraging national governments in market countries, such as the UK, to take the issue of looted antiquities more seriously. In that regard, it seems that the sorts of measures that have been identified by the cumulative work of a number of commentators as requiring to be put in place if the antiquities market is to be able to seriously argue that it is not complicit in the looting problem, are also the sorts of measures that are likely to lend themselves to achieving a general crime reductive effect, including on organised crime in this market (see for example Bator 1983; Murphy 1995; Renfrew 1999; Brodie et al. 2001; Polk 2002; Gerstenblith 2007). Protecting antiquities at source has always been a difficult proposition, in any country but especially in those with serious resource issues in relation to policing provision, and the problems associated with the policing of rural sites are compounded when the spectre is raised of organised crime gangs doing the looting. Even countries where politics are heavily crime-focussed and where a comparatively large amount of resource is allocated to policing and security, such as the UK, still suffer reports of violent organised gangs looting archaeological sites and intimidating locals (Stead 1998). It is important, of course, to make efforts to apprehend these criminals, but in the long run the antiquities trade is inherently problematic as it currently exists, and the arrest of the key nominals in an organised criminal group will not resolve the tensions in the market which make it vulnerable.

Any measures which actually manage to achieve a reduction in the uptake of purchase opportunities in the market where there is a suspicion of looting involved would decrease the financial incentive for looting and smuggling, and therefore diminish the attractions of the market to organised crime. It is unlikely that this complementarity in approach works the other way round, however – it is by no means clear that measures targeted against organised criminals in the market would substantially impact the key mechanisms and drivers of the market. While there may be organised crime groups operating in the antiquities market, they are not a necessary component of that market, and even if they were removed we would still see the looting of objects and their transit to the market. It therefore appears reasonable to argue that in this case, as in many other cases of systems of enterprise which attract organised crime groups and networks due to their inherent profitability and the ease with which their regulations are circumvented, the central focus in approach should be on addressing those market forces and mechanisms which create and sustain the possibility of a global trade in illicit antiquities. In other words, to return to where this chapter began, it seems productive to see the global trade in illicit antiquities as in key respects an organised criminal enterprise involving transnational traffic flows which require regulation and control, rather than looking first to the presence of serious, violent, organised criminals who may form part of this profitable chain but who do not define the essence of the system.

References

Albanese, J. S. (1987). Predicting the Incidence of Organized Crime: A Preliminary Model. In Bynum, T. (ed.), *Organized Crime in America: Concepts and Controversies*. New York: Criminal Justice Press.

Albanese, J. S. (1995). Where Organized and White-Collar Crime Meet: Predicting the Infiltration of Legitimate Business. In Albanese, J. S. (ed.), *Contemporary Issues in Organized Crime*. New York: Criminal Justice Press.

Albanese, J. S. (2008). Risk Assessment in Organized Crime: Developing a Market and Product-Based Model to Determine Threat Levels. *Journal of Contemporary Criminal Justice*, 24(3), 263–273.

Bator, P. M. (1983). *The International Trade in Art*. Chicago: University of Chicago Press.

Bowman, B. A. (2008). Transnational Crimes Against Culture: Looting at Archaeological Sites and the "Grey" Market in Antiquities. *Journal of Contemporary Criminal Justice*, 24(3), 225–242.

Brodie, N. (2009). Consensual Relations? Academic Involvement in the Illegal Trade in Ancient Manuscripts. In Mackenzie, S., Green, P. (eds.), *Criminology and Archaeology: Studies in Looted Antiquities*. Oxford: Hart.

Brodie, N., Doole, J., Watson, P. (2000). *Stealing History: The Illicit Trade in Cultural Material*. Cambridge: The McDonald Institute for Archaeological Research.

Brodie, N., Doole, J., Renfrew, C. (eds.) (2001). *Trade in Illicit Antiquities: The Destruction of the World's Archaeological Heritage*. Cambridge: McDonald Institute for Archaeological Research.

Cohen, S. (2001). *States of Denial: Knowing About Atrocities and Suffering*. Cambridge: Polity.

Cohen, L. E., Felson, M. (1979). Social Change and Crime Rate Trends: A Routine Activity Approach. *American Sociological Review*, 44, 588–608.

Department for Culture Media and Sport (2004). *Dealing in Tainted Cultural Objects: Guidance on the Dealing in Cultural Objects (Offences) Act 2003* (DCMS Cultural Property Unit Publication PP639). London: DCMS.

Edwards, A., Gill, P. (2002). Crime as Enterprise? The Case of Transnational Organised Crime. *Crime, Law and Social Change*, 37(3), 203–223.

Edwards, A., Gill, P. (2003). Introduction. In Edwards, A., Gill, P. (eds.), *Transnational Organised Crime: Perspectives on Global Security*. London: Routledge.

Elia, R. J. (1994). The World Cannot Afford Many More Collectors with a Passion for Antiquities. *The Art Newspaper*, 41(October), 19.

Felson, M. (1994). *Crime and Everyday Life*. Thousand Oaks, CA: Pine Forge Press.

Gerstenblith, P. (2007). Controlling the International Market in Antiquities: Reducing the Harm, Preserving the Past. *Chicago Journal of International Law*, 8(1), 167–195.

Kaye, L. M., Main, C. T. (1995). The Saga of the Lydian Hoard: From Ushak to New York and Back Again. In Tubb, K. W. (ed.), *Antiquities Trade or Betrayed: Legal, Ethical and Conservation Issues* (150–161). London: Archetype.

Kersel, M. M. (2006). From the Ground to the Buyer: A Market Analysis of the Trade in Illegal Antiquities. In Brodie, N., Kersel, M. M., Luke, C., Walker Tubb, K. (eds.), *Archaeology, Cultural Heritage and the Antiquities Trade* (188–205). Gainesville, FL: University Press of Florida.

Mackenzie, S. (2002a). Illicit Antiquities, Criminological Theory and the Deterrent Power of Criminal Sanctions for Targeted Populations. *Art Antiquity and Law*, 7(2), 125–162.

Mackenzie, S. (2002b). *Regulating the Market in Illicit Antiquities* (Trends & Issues in Crime and Criminal Justice No. 239). Canberra: Australian Institute of Criminology.

Mackenzie, S. (2005a). Dig a Bit Deeper: Law, Regulation and the Illicit Antiquities Market. *British Journal of Criminology*, 45, 249–268.

Mackenzie, S. (2005b). *Going, Going, Gone: Regulating the Market in Illicit Antiquities*. Leicester: Institute of Art and Law.

Mackenzie, S. (2006). Psychosocial Balance Sheets: Illicit Purchase Decisions in the Antiquities Market. *Current Issues in Criminal Justice*, 18(2), 221–240.
Mackenzie, S. (2007). Transnational Crime, Local Denial. *Social Justice*, 34(2), 111–124.
Mackenzie, S., Green, P. (2008). Performative Regulation: A Case Study in How Powerful People Avoid Criminal Labels. *British Journal of Criminology*, 48(2), 138–153.
Mackenzie, S., Green, P. (2009). Criminalising the Market in Illicit Antiquities: An Evaluation of the Dealing in Cultural Objects (Offences) Act 2003 in England and Wales. In Mackenzie, S., Green, P. (eds.), *Criminology and Archaeology: Studies in Looted Antiquities*. Oxford: Hart.
McBarnet, D. (2003). When Compliance is Not the Solution but the Problem: From Changes in Law to Changes in Attitude. In Braithwaite, V. (ed.), *Taxing Democracy: Understanding Tax Avoidance and Evasion*. Aldershot: Ashgate.
McBarnet, D. (2006). After Enron will "Whiter than White Collar Crime" Still Wash? *British Journal of Criminology*, 46(6), 1091–1109.
Murphy, J. D. (1995). *Plunder and Preservation: Cultural Property Law and Practice in the People's Republic of China*. Hong Kong: Oxford University Press.
O'Keefe, P. J. (1997). *Trade in Antiquities: Reducing Destruction and Theft*. London: Archetype.
Palmer, N. (1994). Recovering Stolen Art. *Current Legal Problems*, 47, 215–254.
Polk, K. (2000). The Antiquities Trade Viewed as a Criminal Market. *Hong Kong Lawyer*, September, 82.
Polk, K. (2002). *Controlling the Traffic in Illicit Antiquities: Are Criminal Sanctions Appropriate?* Paper presented at the Implementation of the UNESCO 1970 Convention conference. London: Department for Culture Media and Sport.
Renfrew, C. (1993). Collectors Are the Real Looters. *Archaeology*, 46(3), 16–17.
Renfrew, C. (1999). *Loot, Legitimacy and Ownership: The Ethical Crisis in Archaeology*. Amsterdam: Joh. Enschede.
Schneider, J. L. (2008). Reducing the Illicit Trade in Endangered Wildlife: The Market Reduction Approach. *Journal of Contemporary Criminal Justice*, 24(3), 274–295.
Smith Jr., D. C. (1980). Paragons, Pariahs and Pirates: A Spectrum-Based Theory of Enterprise. *Crime and Delinquency*, 26(3), 358–386.
Stead, I. M. (1998). *The Salisbury Hoard*. Gloucestershire: Tempus.
Sutton, M. (1998). *Handling Stolen Goods & Theft: A Market Reduction Approach* (Home Office Research Study 178). London: Home Office.
Sutton, M., Schneider, J., Hetherington, S. (2001). *Tackling Theft with the Market Reduction Approach* (Crime Reduction Research Series Paper 8). London: Home Office.
Sykes, G. M., Matza, D. (1957). Techniques of Neutralisation: A Theory of Delinquency. *American Sociological Review*, 22, 664–670.
van de Bunt, H. G., van der Schoot, C. R. A. (2003). *Prevention of Organised Crime: A Situational Approach*. Den Haag: WODC.
Vander Beken, T. (2004). Risky Business: A Risk-Based Methodology to Measure Organized Crime. *Crime, Law and Social Change*, 41, 471–516.
Vander Beken, T. (ed.) (2005). *Organised Crime and Vulnerability of Economic Sectors: The European Transport and Music Sector*. Antwerp: Maklu.
Vander Beken, T. (ed.) (2007a). *The European Pharmaceutical Sector and Crime Vulnerabilities*. Antwerp: Maklu.
Vander Beken, T. (ed.) (2007b). *The European Waste Industry and Crime Vulnerabilities*. Antwerp: Maklu.
Vander Beken, T., Defruytier, M. (2004). Methodological Tools for Assessing the Risk of Organised Crime. In van Duyne, P. C., Jager, M., von Lampe, K., Newell, J. T. (eds.), *Threats and Phantoms of Organised Crime, Corruption and Terrorism: Rhetoric and Critical Perspectives*. Nijmegen: Wolf Legal.
Vander Beken, T., Van Daele, S. (2008). Legitimate Businesses and Crime Vulnerabilities. *International Journal of Social Economics*, 35(10), 739–750.
Watson, P. (1997). *Sotheby's: The Inside Story*. London: Bloomsbury.

Chapter 5
The Trafficking Problem: A Criminological Perspective

A.J.G. Tijhuis

Introduction

Crime with art and antiquities often involves cross-border crime (de Roux and Paringaux 1999; Tijhuis 2009a). Both stolen art and illegally excavated antiquities are often, and in the case of antiquities usually, taken abroad to be sold there (Brodie et al. 2001; Middlemas 1975). In this chapter, crime with art and antiquities are limited to situations of cross-border crime. The analysis here is based primarily on a PhD study that focused on the interfaces between legal and illegal actors around transnational crime, and in particular the illicit art and antiquities trade (Tijhuis 2006). The study made use of both official data gathered in the Netherlands, France, and Italy, as well as interviews with experts and open sources like academic literature and (specialized) media reports.

This chapter consists of four parts. First of all, several other types of cross-border or the so-called transnational crime are discussed. By comparing these types of crime, several crucial characteristics of these crimes can be clarified. Secondly, an analytical model that was developed to understand the process of laundering that often takes places with transnational crimes is discussed, and in particular the illicit art and antiquities trade. Thirdly, the model is illustrated by several case studies. Finally, based on the mentioned model, potential preventive strategies against the illicit art and antiquities trade are pointed at. To be sure, outlining these strategies was not the primary aim of the PhD study, but nevertheless appeared as interesting side conclusions.

A.J.G. Tijhuis (✉)
Netherlands Institute for the Study of Crime and Law Enforcement, Amsterdam, The Netherlands
and
VU University, Amsterdam, The Netherlands
e-mail: tijhuis@nser.rl

S. Manacorda and D. Chappell (eds.), *Crime in the Art and Antiquities World: Illegal Trafficking in Cultural Property*, DOI 10.1007/978-1-4419-7946-9_5,

Comparison of the Illegal Art and Antiquities Trade with Other Types of Transnational Crime

The transnational illicit trade in art and antiquities is one of many types of transnational crime. Well-known types are the transnational trade in illegal drugs, as well as the smuggling of human beings and human trafficking. Many criminological studies have looked at these types of crime and their causes, organization and other characteristics (see, e.g., Friman and Reich 2007; Soudijn 2006; Zaitch 2001). Far less attention is given to a range of other transnational crimes, like for example the illegal arms trade, cigarette smuggling, financial crimes, and the illegal trade in ivory, diamonds, toxic waste, and art and antiquities.

Although each crime has its own characteristics, some general observations can be made. First of all, the well-known types of transnational crime and the other types are different in at least one crucial aspect. Drug trafficking, human smuggling, and human trafficking are illegal irrespective of the place where the perpetrators are. For example, when cocaine is smuggled from Colombia to the USA, the trade is illegal in both places and anywhere in between. However, most other types of transnational crime are not by definition illegal everywhere. For example, cigarette smuggling often involves major crimes in some countries and small crimes or no crime at all in others (Auchlin and Gaberly 1990). For different reasons, these types of transnational crimes may be "laundered" into legitimate activities or the other way around. In case of cigarettes or arms, legitimate goods from legitimate producers are destined to either outlawed end users (in case of arms) of the black market (in case of cigarettes).[1] In case of art and antiquities, the opposite trajectory can be seen. Stolen or illegally excavated objects are funneled into the legitimate market (see, e.g., Watson and Todeschini 2006; Atwood 2004). The same goes for the so-called blood diamonds that are destined to legitimate markets abroad.

The two-sided nature of many types of transnational crime can be partly understood because of the fact that these crimes are in fact the illegal variation of legitimate trades.[2] Furthermore, as was said before, a laundering process is crucial here. For the study of the illicit trade in art and antiquities, it is necessary to understand that this type of crime belongs to the category of crimes that are functioning besides, or embedded in, a legitimate market. Whether one can understand this trade as something besides the legitimate market or really as a part of the legitimate market depends very much on the sort of art and antiquities that one looks at, as well as the way one interprets seemingly clear-cut concepts of "legitimate" and "illicit."

---

[1] According to economist T. Naylor, in the year 2000, for example, over a trillion cigarettes were exported around the world. However, only 650 million cigarettes were actually imported. Thus, "about one cigarette in every three of those that entered world trade circuits went up in smoke" (Naylor 2004: 407).

[2] As far as the illegal trade is organized by legitimate companies or states, one could also consider these activities as corporate or state-crime. However, in the analysis here, they are treated as examples of transnational crime, focusing primarily on the activities instead of the actors involved.

The last major difference between the two broad categories of transnational crime is the different way of organization of these crimes. Or, to be more specific, the more varied way of organization. With these transnational crimes, several very distinct ways of organizing can be found. On the one hand, one can find the expected "organized crime" variations like huge criminal organizations or flexible criminal networks. On the other hand, however, one finds very small-scale operations, sometimes by single persons, which seemingly have little in common with traditional "organized crime". In all cases, the role of legal actors is much greater than otherwise the case (Naylor 2001; Passas 1999).

The Lock Model

As was mentioned before, a laundering process is crucial for many types of transnational crime that also have legitimate counterparts, or are part of legitimate markets. Everybody nowadays knows about the laundering of money, but the same laundering takes place with cigarettes, arms, and works of art and antiquities. This latter process, however, is often neglected in studies of these crimes. Usually, the rather questionable assumption of separated markets underlies these studies. That is, that black markets and legitimate markets in certain goods are largely separated worlds. However, looking at these markets, it is obvious that at least some degree of integration between the legitimate and illicit part exists. The arms that end up with boycotted regimes usually come from legitimate producers, often in countries that officially support these boycotts (Farah and Braun 2008; Naylor 2001). And the cigarettes that are sold on the black market are usually coming from the large cigarette producers operating in the legal market place (Beare 2002).

In the PhD study, an analytical model was developed to understand this process of laundering. This model shows how certain transnational crimes are in fact laundered to legitimate activities. Furthermore, the opposite process is also described. While lacking a proper term, this process is called "blackening." The existence of all kind of laundering processes is extremely relevant. Only because of the possibility of laundering art, money, diamonds or other objects, a lively market in tainted objects can continue.

The model uses the mechanism of a lock (or sluice) in shipping to describe the whole process. A lock bridges the gap between two levels, and it is used here as a metaphor for the gap between the legitimate and illicit market. These two markets do not collide but smoothly connect through the lock. And the lock itself cannot be pinpointed to belong to either the legal or illegal domain. The latter characteristic is the main explanation for the reason why transnational crimes can transform into legitimate activities. This transformation is either facilitated by certain unique individuals, legitimate organizations, or jurisdictions. In many cases these three are combined to bridge the gap between illicit and legitimate.

Individuals can have this lock function because of particular qualities. One of these is a base of operation in several countries, with expert knowledge and use of the legal and financial system of these countries. Whereas, ordinary (organized) criminals often have to rely on the knowledge of others to use the opportunities of foreign registered companies, tax havens, and bank secrecy jurisdictions, the persons discussed here were to some extent experts on these matter themselves. Furthermore, the individuals involved often also possess foreign passports. And to be sure, not false or otherwise low-grade passports, like many organized criminal possess. In this case, for example, official diplomatic passports of states other than their home country. Furthermore, a network of (corrupt) contacts with, for example, politicians, customs officials, and other civil servants, helps these individuals to connect the illicit with the legitimate domain. In addition, it makes them partly immune to law enforcement activities against them.

The involved individuals can function as lock in two ways. First of all, they can act as (transnational) brokers between actors in different countries that cannot, or do not want to, deal with each other directly. The broker is arranging a deal in which legal goods or services are delivered to outlawed customers, or illegal goods or services are delivered to legitimate customers. Many arms deals or deals to dispose of toxic waste abroad can be understood in this way. Besides these transnational brokers, the so-called transnational dealers buy from actors in country X to sell to actors in country Y. They thus function as a lock between a source and market country of, for example, blood diamonds.

Legitimate organizations can have the lock function because of their ability to bridge the gap between illicit and legitimate at least for a part by passing goods through their organization. Two different models can be distinguished here. First of all, the so-called coffee shop model. Within this model the legitimate organization can be seen as an extension of a criminal organization or a network of organizations or individuals. The funding of terrorism by certain charities can be seen as an example here. The supporters of this charity legally donate funds to a legitimate organization. Part of these funds is subsequently funneled to terrorist organizations. The opposite trajectory is seen in the Dutch coffee shop. This shop legally sells so called soft-drugs in small quantities to customers. However, the act of supplying the coffee shop itself with large quantities of these drugs is illegal and heavily punished.[3] The second variation involves an organization that is fully independent but has multiple links with both legal and illegal actors. It is called Ambrosiano model, after the case of the Italian Ambrosiano bank.[4] Some banks can be used as examples here. They can either launder proceeds of crimes into legitimate funds or investments or funnel legitimate funds to tax havens or bank secrecy jurisdictions, against the fiscal laws of the country where the funds are leaving (Paoli 1995; Block and Weaver 2004).

[3]To be sure, the punishment if relatively harsh within the Dutch context. Compared to the US, for example, sentences are quite modest.

[4]Banco Ambrosiano was an Italian bank owned by a Luxemburg registered holding company. It was involved in a complex scheme of capital flight, a network of offshore subsidiaries and funding of political parties and several foreign governments. The bank collapsed in 1982, causing a huge scandal. One of the shareholders of the bank was the Vatican Bank (Raw 1992; Trepp 1996).

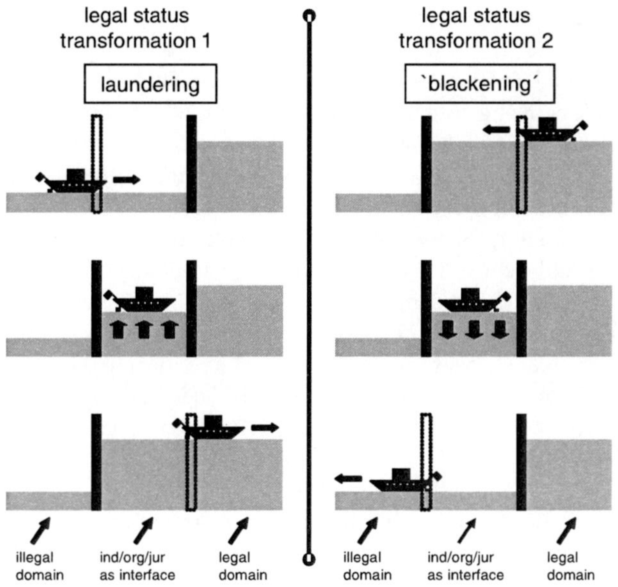

Fig. 5.1 The lock model

The last variation of the lock model involves jurisdictions. Jurisdictions can function as lock in case they lack legislation in branches, where most other jurisdictions have enacted legislation that outlaws certain cross-border activities. Instead of lacking legislation in particular areas, more general provisions in the legal system may also facilitate crimes, like for example short statutes of legislation, protection of good faith purchasers, etc. Ideally, the jurisdiction without legislation does not cooperate with other jurisdictions seeking the perpetrators or persons acting against the specific laws. In that case, transnational flows of goods or money are directed through these jurisdictions. Examples of this interface are, for example, tax havens, bank secrecy jurisdictions, and offshore financial centers (Tijhuis 2007a, b).

In Fig. 5.1, the basics of the lock model are illustrated. On the left, the laundering mechanism is shown and on the right the opposite mechanism is portrayed.

The Lock Model and the Illicit Art and Antiquities

The lock model can be used to understand the process of laundering of stolen art and looted antiquities. The process of laundering is primarily facilitated by jurisdictions without regulation of this market, or failure to enforce the existing regulatory framework. Furthermore, it is facilitated by the favorable general characteristics of the legal system, like short statutes of limitation and protection of good faith purchasers. As a result, looted or at least illegally exported antiquities and stolen art can often be provided with a false provenance and brought into the legal market.

Such notorious jurisdictions were not primarily found in exotic places, but included places like the Netherlands or Belgium (before 2008), that usually are known for an abundant framework of rules and laws. Furthermore, jurisdictions like Switzerland, Hong Kong, and Thailand share the most important characteristics of such jurisdictions as laundering structure. The role of jurisdictions as laundering structure is completed by the corruption of government officials (for example, to grant export licenses in source countries).

As part of the study of the illicit art and antiquities trade, official files from Dutch customs and the Ministry of Culture were studied. A number of cases were found here in which the laundering process was clear. Antiquities from (for example) Cambodia, China, Ghana, Afghanistan and Congo were laundered through the Netherlands. In many cases, it sufficed to simply bring the antiquities to the Netherlands. The reason for this was the lack of adequate legislation and effective law enforcement, except for the mandatory European rules and Holland's own export restrictions.[5]

In other cases, where theft might be proven, it often sufficed to make sure the antiquities were sold through a legitimate dealer. After that, the civil code in most cases ensures that the antiquities involved cannot be claimed back. Short statutes of limitation and the protection of the good faith purchaser are crucial here. In still other cases, the production of some paperwork may be enough to create a false provenance.

To a lesser extent, works of art were also found to be laundered. Especially, from France and also from Russia and other countries. In France, works of art have been stolen and taken to the Netherlands for decades. Although theft and the sale of stolen goods are illegal in the Netherlands, like everywhere, in practice this does not make much of a difference. As there is no art police to check the market, and no laws to go after owners of stolen art after they have changed hands in good faith, there is no way of fighting the trade in stolen objects.

Case Studies

The process of laundering can be illustrated by several case studies. In this section, three cases are discussed from France, Russia and an example of the trade in stolen objects from France is the case of Cornelius M., the Belgian-based Dutch dealer who directed the so-called castle-gang in France. The Cornelius M. case was analyzed at the French police (OCBC) who conducted an extensive investigation of this case. More than 15 persons were involved in dozens of robberies of large French estates,

[5]Within the European Union, the EU Council Regulation 3911/92 regulates the export of cultural goods from member states. Furthermore, EU Council Directive 93/7 provides a set of rules for the return to the (EU) country of origin of cultural objects that were unlawfully removed from the territory of a member state. Finally, EU Council Regulation 1210/2003 provides specific restrictions on the import of cultural goods (and other objects) from Iraq.

capturing precious antiquities, paintings, timepieces, tapestries, and furniture. Many of the estates were only occupied part of the year and the burglaries usually took place when nobody was present. This partly explains why the thieves were never caught red-handed. Sometimes, they burglarized estates that were occupied, but at the same time were so large that the inhabitants did not notice it.

The robberies took place from 1998 to 2000. The thieves were local gypsies and were not involved in the transport or sale of the items. For transport Cornelius M. had hired chauffeurs, including a man named Cipoletti, an Italian driver, who took the items to the Netherlands. When Cipoletti was arrested he admitted to have driven at least 40 loads of antiquities to the Netherlands, and the whole scheme fell apart. In the Netherlands, Cornelius M. sold the items to a number of complicit antiquities dealers who sold the items to international customers. Center of the trade were local markets in the border region of Belgium and the Netherlands, in the South of Limburg, a Dutch province.

Through these markets these objects were "laundered" and funneled into the legitimate market. Factors that enable this laundering process are the lax or non-existent Dutch law enforcement against this trade, the lack of cooperation between the involved states, the lack of a European register of stolen objects, the short statutes of limitation, protection of good faith purchasers, the open borders between EU member states and the absence of specific legislation, except for the EU rules that effectively apply to only a part of the market. Due to these factors, works of art that have made it across the border to Belgium and the Netherlands and have been sold there are practically laundered. This can explain why the Netherlands, as well as Belgium, have acted as an outlet for stolen art and antiquities from France for decades. In a French study on art crimes, this topic was summarized with the well-chosen title *Le Grand bal des receleurs* which can be translated as "The great ball of receivers" (de Roux and Paringaux 1999). To be sure, this book was written before the Cornelius M. case came to light. Two crucial elements have been the basis under this ball for decades. One is the favorable civil code in the Netherlands and Belgium, and the other is the fact that France has innumerable private and state collections of art and antiquities which provide a constant opportunity for art thefts.[6] The result is a persistent system in which art is stolen in France and subsequently sold to dealers in Belgium and the Netherlands. On the one hand, these dealers have established shops and can use this to pass good title on objects to their customers. On the other hand, they are in practice professional receivers at the same time. Most dealers are located in remote areas, in the border region of Belgium and the Dutch province Limburg in the South of the country.

Cornelius M. had a history of involvement in the illicit trade. In 1994 and 1996, he was arrested for theft of and receiving stolen antiquities, and was given a prison

[6]In theory, the EU Directive for the Restitution of illegally exported cultural goods, should erase part of this problem. In practice, this does not change the situation very much. First of all, the directive is very hard to use effectively, and secondly it will by definition be without much effect if local authorities in Belgium or the Netherlands do not actively enforce the national and EU laws.

sentence. The moment he was released coincided with the first robberies of the gang in France. He now serves a 14-year prison sentence in France. His 15 accomplices were given prison sentences from 1 to 6 years.[7]

The Cornelius M. case is just one of many. According to the specialized French art squad, more than 200 cases like this (though differing in scale) are known since 1975. Since the arrest of Cornelius M. several new cases already appeared, even with a more well-known dealer, though on a smaller scale.

Another case that can illustrate the lock model is the case of the Russian dealer Sergej W.[8] His activities in the art trade came to an end in 1998. In that year, he was caught at Schiphol airport in the Netherlands. He had come from St. Petersburg in Russia with a suitcase full of precious objects. When customs opened his suitcase they found, among other items, two volumes of a unique atlas dated 1710. Furthermore, they discovered 185 engravings, almost the whole graphic oeuvre of Jacques Calot, a famous seventeenth century French artist (Leerintveld 2000; Ministry of Finance 2000).

It soon turned out that a number of objects were stolen. Instead of an innocent collector, Sergej W. had been a dealer for a long period of time. He was stopped at customs in Amsterdam four times before during the 1990s, always with precious art and antiquities. He usually stayed in Holland for extended periods. A major part of his business was probably done in Holland due to these and other circumstances. Large cash deposits were found in a number of bank faults at several locations in Amsterdam. In his belongings, a large number of business cards were found which formed an interesting sample from the art trade. As far as could be established, Sergej W. conducted business with at least a number of (legal) art dealers and an auction house in the Netherlands. At the same time, he was supplied with merchandise in Russia. Although this might have been partly legal merchandise, it was not allowed to leave Russia without permits. Furthermore, his involvement in the trade in stolen art in Russia was also proven when the police searched one of his apartments in Russia. They found 300 stolen icons stashed away. As far as could be established, Sergej W. was given a prison sentence of 9 years for this in Russia.

This art dealer partly functioned as a lock. He combined his opportunities as individual with that of the different jurisdictions. As an individual he smuggled the objects from Russia to the Netherlands and was able to funnel the illicit art into the legitimate market through his wide range of productive contacts in the art trade. The differences between the Netherlands and Russia further enabled the successful traffic: the absence of specific legislation in the Netherlands, as well as the lack of effective international registries of stolen and smuggled art, combined with the lack of efficiency in communications between law enforcement agencies across international borders.

---

[7] Judgment of the Montbrison Court, File No. 02/01050, March 6, 2003.

[8] The name of the person meant here is altered.

The last case study involved a shipment of rare items from Ghana, intercepted in Rotterdam harbor in 1996. The owner of the goods was a dealer who had established firm business relations with this African country. According to the Embassy of Ghana, he had been involved in smuggling items at least two times before, in 1992 and 1994 (Van Beurden 2001). In connection with this particular shipment, questions were asked by a Member of Parliament to the Secretary of Justice.[9] In her answer to these questions the Minister stated that the cultural historical value of the goods was substantial, and that Ghana had not given export permits for their transport to the Netherlands. Nevertheless, in the end the owner could not be forced to cede the items.

More or less the same happened in 1992. A large shipment of items was intercepted by Dutch customs in the Rotterdam harbor. Part of the shipment was 92 historic stone sculptures from the Koma region in Northern Ghana. Only after the Embassy of Ghana threatened with summary proceedings, the owner was prepared to surrender the items to Ghana. However, due to the lack of legislation in the Netherlands, he could keep the rest of the smuggled items after he paid the tax based on its real value (Van Beurden 2001). Although the dealer did not want to respond to this particular shipment, he was willing to give his ideas about the trade in Ghana. Every now and then one would engage traders who were selling items from little villages in the bush. They were selling authentic items, as opposed to most dealers in regular shops. This seems to confirm the pattern seen more often in Africa. A network of thieves, smugglers, and middlemen connects the authentic items from illicit excavations, churches, or museums, with the dealers in market countries. It is through a well-connected foreign dealer who ships the items abroad and sells them that they are laundered and placed in the legal market, for example, Belgium, Switzerland, or the Netherlands (Gado 2001; Schmidt and McIntosh 1996).

In this case, the laundering could take place due to the fact that the lack of legislation in the Netherlands created a situation in which smuggled and under circumstances stolen and looted items could be legally sold without any problems.[10] This is especially so in case of antiquities that cannot be traced back to individual owners and therefore not confiscated on the basis of the crime of theft or receiving. This means that the Netherlands as jurisdiction acts as a lock between illicit and licit trade. Through this lock, smuggled objects are turned into legitimate merchandise. The fact that the dealer was obviously very well connected in the source country and organized the transport of the items from source to destination country, helped to reach this result but did not explain it in this case.

---

[9] The written questions in Parliament were raised by MP J. M. Verspaget (Labor Party) on July 11, 1995. The Minister of Justice at the time, W. Sorgdrager, replied on August 26, 1996. See: "Aanhangsel Handelingen", No. 1627, vergaderjaar 1995–96.

[10] All remarks about the Netherlands here should be read within the context of the situation prior to 2008 when the UNESCO Convention was implemented.

Conclusions

Based on the study of the illicit arms and antiquities trade several general conclusions can be drawn. Two conclusions are briefly mentioned here and specifically aim at ways in which the illicit art and antiquities trade can be countered.

First of all, the fact that traditional law enforcement methods have serious limitation in this field of crime and partly necessarily so. First of all, the preventive effect of successful law enforcement is smaller than in other fields. One of the reasons for this is the fact that most successes are connected with large thefts, exactly the type of crime that is often committed by criminals that only incidentally try this type of crime (Tijhuis 2009b). Secondly, most cases of theft are never solved but cost a lot while trying. And thirdly, security of both art and antiquities is generally poor and this will not change dramatically in the future. For a part, it is even impossible to provide more than a very basic level of protection, in particular with unearthed antiquities.

The second main conclusion is partly based on the first conclusion about traditional law enforcement and deals with preventive strategies. These strategies should ideally focus primarily on the legitimate market. The still existing possibility to funnel stolen and looted objects into this market, although this has clearly become more difficult in the last decade, keeps the illicit trade interesting for thieves, fences, dealers, and others. Furthermore, the costs of strategies aimed at the legitimate market will be smaller while the effect will be larger. Examples are the databases that are used by both government agencies (like the Italian Carabinieri) and private actors (like the Art Loss Register) and at least made the trade in stolen art a lot more difficult. Finally, the police can have a consulting role here for museums, dealers, collectors, and other elements of the art world.

References

Atwood, R. (2004). *Stealing History: Tomb Raiders, Smugglers, and the Looting of the Ancient World*. New York: St. Martin's Press.

Auchlin, P., Gaberly, F. (1990). *Das Umfeld eines Skandals: Ein Report über das organisierte Verbrechen und die Rolle der Schweizer Behörden*. Zürich: Werd Verlag.

Beare, M. (2002). Organized Corporate Criminality: Tobacco Smuggling Between Canada and the US. *Crime, Law & Social Change*, 37(3), 225–243.

Beurden, J. van (2001). *Goden, graven en grenzen: Over kunstroof uit Afrika, Azië en Latijns-Amerika*. Amsterdam: KIT Publishers.

Block, A. A., Weaver, C. A. (2004). *All Is Clouded by Desire: Global Banking, Money Laundering and International Organized Crime*. Westport, CT: Praeger.

Brodie, N., Doole, J., Renfrew, C. (2001). *Trade in Illicit Antiquities: The Destruction of the World's Cultural Heritage*. Oxford: Oxbow Books.

Farah, D., Braun, S. (2008). *Merchant of Death: Money, Guns, Planes, and the Man Who Makes War Possible*. New Jersey: Wiley.

Friman, H. R., Reich, S. (2007). *Human Trafficking, Human Security, and the Balkans*. Pittsburgh: University of Pittsburgh Press.

Gado, B. (2001). The Republic of Niger. In Brodie, N., Doole, J., Renfrew, C. (eds.). *Trade in Illicit Antiquities: The Destruction of the World's Cultural Heritage* (57–72). Oxford: Oxbow Books.

Middlemas, K. (1975). *The Double Market: Art Theft and Art Thieves*. Westmead: Saxon House.

Naylor, R. T. (2001). *Economic Warfare: Sanctions, Embargo Busting and Their Human Cost*. Boston: Northeastern University Press.

Naylor, R. T. (2004). *Hot Money and the Politics of Debt*. Montreal: McGill Queen's University Press.

Paoli, L. (1995). The Banco Ambrosiano Case: An Investigation into the Underestimation of the Relations Between Organized and Economic Crime. *Crime, Law & Social Change*, 23, 345–365.

Passas, N. (1999). Globalization, Criminogenic Asymmetries and Economic Crime. *European Journal of Law Reform*, 1(4), 16–44.

Raw, C. (1992). *The Money Changers: How the Vatican Bank Enabled Roberto Calvi to Steal $250 Million for the Heads of the P2 Masonic Lodge*. London: Vintage.

de Roux, E., Paringaux, R. P. (1999). *Razzia sur l'art: Vols, pillages, recels à travers le monde*. Paris: Fayard.

Schmidt, P. R., McIntosh, R. J. (1996). *Plundering Africa's Past*. Bloomington: Indiana University Press.

Soudijn, M. (2006). *Chinese Human Smuggling in Transit*. The Hague: Boom Legal Publishers.

Tijhuis, A. J. G. (2006). *Transnational Crime and the Interface Between Legal and Illegal Actors: The Case of the Illicit Art and Antiquities Trade*. Nijmegen: Wolf Legal Publishers.

Tijhuis, A. J. G. (2007a). Offshore Financial Services: Bank Secrecy Jurisdictions and Offshore Banking. In Shanty, F. G. (ed.), *Organised Crime: From Trafficking to Terrorism* (249–251). Santa Barbara: ABC CLIO.

Tijhuis, A. J. G. (2007b). Money Laundering and the Global Financial System. In Shanty, F. G. (ed.), *From Trafficking to Terrorism* (246–248). Santa Barbara: ABC CLIO.

Tijhuis, A. J. G. (2009a). Trafficking in Cultural Artifacts. In Tonry, M. (ed.), *The Oxford Handbook of Crime and Public Policy* (455–474). Oxford: Oxford University Press.

Tijhuis, A. J. G. (2009b). Who Are Stealing All Those Paintings. In Charney, N. (ed.), *Art and Crime: Exploring the Dark Side of the Art World*. Santa Barbara: ABC CLIO.

Trepp, G. (1996). *Swiss Connection*. Zurich: Unionsverlag.

Watson, P., Todeschini, C. (2006). *The Medici Conspiracy. The Illicit Journey of Looted Antiquities. From Italy's Tomb Raiders to the World's Greatest Museums*. New York: Public Affairs.

Zaitch, D. (2001). *Traquetos: Colombians Involved in the Cocaine Business in the Netherlands*. Dordrecht: Springer.

Chapter 6
Unraveling the "Cordata": Just How Organized Is the International Traffic in Cultural Objects?*

Duncan Chappell and Kenneth Polk

Introduction

In a recent assessment of the nature and gravity of what it loosely termed "art theft," a Zurich-based think tank has asserted that such crime "represents the third most profitable criminal enterprise in the world behind drugs and arms trafficking" (Russell 2009). The assessment goes on to refer to the Association for Research into Crimes Against Art (ARCA 2009) claim that:

> [Most] art crime since the 1960's is perpetrated either by, or on behalf of international organised crime syndicates. They either use stolen art for resale, or to barter on a closed black market for an equivalent value of goods and services (Russell 2009).

There are no doubt many, including the present authors, who would query the accuracy of such claims which seem to attribute a far greater interest in art and cultural objects among well-known traditional mobsters like the mafia and triads than the evidence would support. Thus, neither the latest European Union Organized Crime Threat Assessment (Europol 2008) nor the UK's Threat Assessment of Serious Organized Crime (Serious Organized Crime Agency 2009) makes any mention of either art theft in general or antiquities trafficking in particular, among its list of worrisome offenses engaged in currently by local-, regional-, or transnational-based criminal groups. Similarly, the Italian Carabinieri, almost certainly the world's most experienced police body in dealing with mafia activities, has recently asserted that:

*Revised paper originally presented at Basel Institute on Governance, International Conference: "Governance of Cultural Property: Preservation and Recovery," 29–30 September 2009, Basel, Switzerland.

D. Chappell (✉)
Faculty of Law, University of Sydney, NSW 2006, Australia
e-mail: chappell@bigpond.net.au

S. Manacorda and D. Chappell (eds.), *Crime in the Art and Antiquities World: Illegal Trafficking in Cultural Property*, DOI 10.1007/978-1-4419-7946-9_6,

> [A]t least as regards our own experience... no proof has ever been found of an involvement of mafia-type organizations in the direct and continuing organization of the activities related to the traffic of cultural artifacts, despite the fact that investigations have often demonstrated a link between mafia organizations and the specific criminal sector regarding both the monitoring of the territory and the selection of objectives (Nistri 2009: 98).

In this paper, we are less concerned with the magnitude of the problem of art theft, and just where it stands in the ranking of the profitability of criminal enterprises, than we are with the question of the extent to which the illicit traffic in antiquities, which represents but one facet of the broader term "art theft," can be considered properly as a form of organized crime. To be sure, any complex illegal activity such as that involved in the antiquities trade is at some level "organized." But the term "organized crime," for all of its well-documented ambiguities and imperfections, tends to imply a core of activities such as that it involves behavior which is illicit, complicated, organized around market dynamics, international in character, and likely to produce widespread corruption. Many of these factors would appear to describe, and describe well, the trade in cultural heritage material. However close this correspondence might seem, our argument is that there are key elements of this particular illicit trade that make it different from the more standard forms of organized crime, and further, these differences, it will be argued, are critical when it comes to the question of how this pattern of illicit activity might be brought under some control. We commence with a review of three cases, where it seems considerable organizational capacity and ingenuity was displayed by those involved in the illicit trade in antiquities traffic.

Traffic in Antiquities and the Question of Organization

Case Study 1: The Italian "Cordata"

On September 13, 1995, acting on a tip off, Italian and Swiss law enforcement officials conducted a raid on a warehouse in Geneva Freeport – an area of this Swiss city where goods could be stored without officially entering Switzerland, thus avoiding payment of any tax. Inside the warehouse, the raiders discovered a veritable treasure trove of antiquities, many still with dirt attached suggesting they had only recently been dug from the ground. Also discovered were thousands of photographs of antiquities as well as shipment invoices and other documents relating to business conducted with art dealers and museums in Europe and North America (Watson and Todeschini 2006: 20–22).

Further investigations were to reveal that the owner of the warehouse, an Italian art dealer named Giacomo Medici, had for many years been involved in an elaborate, highly lucrative and clandestine international trade in illicitly obtained antiquities, mostly acquired from the robbery of tombs and other archeological sites in Italy. In a further striking find, investigators also located a handwritten note and diagram listing by name the persons involved in this trade leading from the tombaroli (tomb robbers) to the middle men and art dealers like Medici, and ultimately to museums and collectors in the USA and Europe (Watson and Todeschini 2006: 16–18). This so-called organigram or chart revealed the entire organizational chain or "Cordata" of those involved, and what their links were to some of the most prominent international dealers, auction houses, museums, and collectors in the world.

These unique and damning finds led to the prosecution of Medici by Italian authorities on smuggling and allied charges. Medici was convicted and sentenced in 2004 to 10 years in prison and a fine of ten million Euro. However, he appealed this verdict to a higher court which in July 2009 partly upheld the original decision but reduced the sentence to 8 years imprisonment. Medici has appealed against this latest court decision to Italy's highest court (see in general Scherer 2009).

In addition to the charges laid against Medici the Italian authorities also prosecuted two of those allegedly involved with him in his illicit activities – Robert Hecht, a wealthy and influential US art dealer, and Marion True who until recently was the California-based Getty Museum's antiquities curator.

The entire "Medici Conspiracy," as it has been labeled, is perhaps the most compelling evidence to surface to date of the manner in which looted antiquities are routed through labyrinthine channels and across international borders to the high demand markets centered in places like London, Paris, and New York. The market, with an insatiable appetite for antiquities which is seemingly oblivious to the questionable origins of the artifacts on display, at present represents a highly organized but largely unregulated multibillion dollar transnational industry.

Case Study 2: The Salisbury Hoard

A second case where the evidence of complex organization can be demonstrated concerns the story of the Salisbury Hoard (Stead 1998). These events came to light initially when a well-connected member of the Conservative Party, also a peer of the realm, sold some 22 bronze miniature shields from the British Bronze Age to the British Museum for 55,000 GBP. The sale set in motion a series of investigatory steps which ultimately found that these shields were part of a much larger deposit of some 500 objects, some dating as far back as 2400 BC. The hoard was uncovered as part of an illicit dig by metal detectorists, and the illegal character of that dig was followed by a complex set of steps that involved over a dozen antiquities dealers (some, such as Robin Symes, being quite prominent in the antiquities trade), and Sotheby's and Christie's auction houses. The distribution of material from the hoard involved a pattern of trade that spread the goods widely throughout not only the UK, but as far afield as France, Germany, Japan, and the USA, and ultimately involved the Norwich Castle Museum, Devizes Museum and the British Museum. Stead (1998: 74) prepared a chart illustrating the distribution routes of the artifacts which duplicates some of the central organization themes found in other case studies, including:

1. There was a complex flow of material from source (in this case, the initial theft by the metal detectorists) to multiple and transnational destinations
2. The nature of the dig meant that the market had to respond to the illicit character of the goods
3. Involved, especially with respect to destinations, were persons and/or places of high status and standing

Case Study 3: Khmer Material from Cambodia

In June 2010, in a ceremony associated with much pomp and political significance, the Thai Prime Minister Abhisit Vejjajiva handed over to Cambodian officials in Phnom Penh a number of Khmer treasures seized by Thai authorities from smugglers in 1999. The treasures included six massive stone heads of the Hindu God Shiva dating from the twelfth century Angkorian era (Associated Press 2009). The ceremony came at time of heightened tension between the two countries over the sovereignty of land surrounding the world heritage listed Preah Vihear temple which was judged in 1962 to be in Cambodia.

At the time of the ceremony, the Cambodian Government indicated that the two sides had agreed to cooperate in stamping out smuggling of national antiquities which had already resulted in recent decades in widespread looting of Cambodia's ancient temples and archeological sites with many items, like those just returned, being taken across the border to Thailand for sale on the international market or to private collectors. Nothing was said, however, about just how such large and heavy objects had been cut from their original sites and transported many hundreds of kilometers to places like Bangkok, a well-recognized portal for the sale of illicit antiquities within the South East Asian region. Such objects could only have been removed and smuggled across international borders utilizing significant logistical planning and resources, and probably only with the assistance of corrupt officials prepared to turn a blind eye to items whose export was clearly illegal according to Cambodian law.

This case of smuggled Khmer treasures, happily returned in this instance to their owners, together with our own recent work in parts of Asia, including Cambodia and Thailand (see Alder et al. 2009), provides a third general example of the organized character of the traffic in cultural heritage material, although as yet no source exists to provide the clarity of the market such as that found in the Cordata or organigram in the Medici Conspiracy, or in the chart illustrating the distribution routes of the Salisbury Hoard. The major traffic in Khmer material from Cambodia is certainly transnational, with the initial supply routes from the Angkor sites, for example, flowing onward through Thailand and from there to diverse venues throughout the developed nations. The combination of volume and size has required considerable division of labor for the material to be shipped by truck, and then sometimes by ship, from source to destination.

The original extraction of much of the material undoubtedly requires manpower and expertise at removal (especially in terms of large stone objects like those just mentioned). Payment has to be arranged for the extraction by agents who then must work through the transit problems. The objects have to be lifted and carried from site of origin to some transit point (for example, being lifted by a crane so that they can be carried by truck to a point where they are placed in a container for shipment by sea). Documents also have to be arranged which permit some form of access to both export and import procedures. Dealers who are complicitous in this process must then be found so that the items can be placed on wholesale and ultimately retail markets in destination countries. In turn, buyers must be found who are willing to purchase cultural heritage material without asking questions about provenance.

Both the theft of the material, and its transport (especially across borders), dictate that there are "authorities" involved, and in the course of our research we have obtained many accounts of participation in the traffic of corrupt military and police figures throughout the region. Our observations in numerous destinations in the demand economies demonstrate that these goods can be exceptionally expensive for the ultimate consumers who often represent elite individuals and institutions.

Examining "Organized Crime": Where that Term Fits

While these case examples provide presumptive evidence that the traffic in illicit cultural heritage material is organized, it is not quite so clear that this implies that this makes it part of organized crime. Those close to the study of organized crime, it must be pointed out, are not necessarily comfortable with that term, as for example Tilley and Hopkins (2008: 444) who observe that at best conceptions of organized crime are "loose and ambiguous." There is little doubt that the antiquities traffic does in many cases match the elements of the definition provided by the UN Convention against Transnational Organized Crime (UNODC 2004; see also Bowman 2008), namely that organized crime consists of:

> …a structured group of three or more persons, existing for a period of time and acting in concert with the aim of committing one or more serious crimes or offences established in accordance with this Convention, in order to obtain, directly or indirectly, a financial or other material benefit (Article 2).

A somewhat more complex definition (as discussed by Levi 1998: 335; see also Levi 2007) has been developed by the German Federal Police:

> Organized crime is the planned violation of the law for profit or to acquire power, which offences are each, or together, of a major significance, and are carried out by more than two participants who co-operate within a division of labour for a long or undetermined time span using
>
> a. commercial or commercial like structures, or
> b. violence or other means of intimidation, or
> c. influence on politics, media, public administration, justice and the legitimate economy.

A similar conception is found in the work of Felsen and Kalaitzidis (2005: 6) who emphasize that:

> Many see organized crime as having features such as hierarchical structure, division of labor, organizational codes or taboos, continuity in operations, the practice of corruption, and a capability to inflict violence.

These same authors go on to point out, however, that many others have found that

> ...criminal activities are not at all organized but instead are quite disorganized.

The three case studies we have presented suggest considerable organizational skills and business acumen on the part of those involved. This issue apart, as soon as the focus turns to an examination of the actual trade activity, there is considerable agreement that whatever else it implies, organized crime involves transnational or "cross border" (a term suggested in the work of Levi 1998: 340) activities, although this, as Levi warns does not always imply a high level of sophistication in the nature of that organization (see Edwards and Levi 2008: 365).

Some Distinctive Features of the Traffic in Antiquities

While there are many features that the illicit traffic in antiquities seems to share with other forms of organized crime, there are a number of features that immediately stamp this traffic is different. One of the most important of these, and one which shapes much of our understanding of how this traffic works, is that the sale of antiquities, however illegal their origins, tends to be open and licit in the major commercial centers that provide the demand which drives this market. In any of the major commercial centers, and we have concentrated much of our work in London and New York, one can find a number of elegant venues where high grade antiquities from around the globe are being sold. Emphatically, this is not a market like the illicit drug market, where consumers must contend with the possibility of arrest as they seek out their supply. At the same time, a slight caveat has to be entered here, since as Fred Schultz found in New York (for a review of this case, see Gerstenblith 2002), there is a possibility that thefts which take place in other countries (including thefts of cultural heritage), if their circumstances can be demonstrated beyond reasonable doubt, might be prosecuted. Furthermore, because of various international treaties and conventions, there is also the possibility that an object which has been illegally excavated might be seized by government agents in the destination countries and returned to its country of origin (see the case described by Barnes 2000). These possibilities aside, in general most consumers can openly walk into the shop of an antiquities dealer in places like London or New York (or numerous other cities) and purchase antiquities without fear of police arrest or prosecution.

While the antiquities trade in the demand environments tends to be open and legal, the illicit origins of the material does present a problem because those engaged in the traffic must somehow provide a mechanism whereby what is to be sold becomes transformed into licit goods. The key to this transformation process is played in the transit portals which tend to be the various "duty free" locations which historically have been located in such places as Switzerland or Hong Kong. Once in these locales, various mechanisms are employed so that the material can then be shipped onward with both legal export documents and, in some circumstances, a "provenance" that can be used for purposes of sale to consumers. Thus, the well-known example is provided by objects from the classical world which might appear on the London or New York market with what appear to be perfectly legal export papers from Switzerland with the additional information that they come from the "private collection of a Swiss gentleman." In an interesting recent twist that we encountered in our work in Hong Kong, we were told that an object which had its origins in China was being sold by the shop on "behalf of a collector in Belgium." This need for a process of the transforming of the goods is not found in traditional arenas of organized crime precisely because the sale of such goods as illicit drugs is illegal in destination as in supply environments so there is no need to "clean" the material.

Further, while the traffic involves international movement of objects, this is not always a large-scale or complicated matter. Some dealers, such as those involved in small jade objects from China, do not need large volumes of material. Even venues selling such material as ceramic pots may find that the volumes are small. Combined with the fact that the material has been transformed into legal goods for shipment purposes, transportation routes can be employed that are inconceivable to more traditional forms of organized crime. Thus, it is said that much of the transportation of "clean" objects, replete with a sanitized set of papers regarding their origins, are regularly shipped around the world from supply portals like Hong Kong and Bangkok using regular air freight companies. Upon arrival at their destination, most customs officials are unlikely to question or dispute the legitimacy of the importation, partly because of a lack of awareness of the true value and nature of plundered cultural objects, and partly because of the huge volume of air freight requiring inspection and assessment at most importation sites.

A second feature which provides important contours to this trade is that the high cost of some of the objects assures that wealthy, and thereby socially and politically elite, consumers are involved. To be sure, there is a full range of material available, and many persons who become involved in the purchase of cultural heritage material are far from wealthy. Nonetheless, there is a long tradition of participation of social elites in the purchase, and appreciation, of antiquities. Indeed, English gentlemen in the course of their involvement in a Grand Tour in earlier centuries often returned with works of art acquired along the way.

A third feature of this trade is that it rarely attracts the attention of law enforcement agents, especially in the demand settings. For example, as we noted earlier, the pursuit of art theft and the traffickers of antiquities does not seem to feature among the priorities given to law enforcement officials involved in the investigation and prosecution of serious organized crime in a country like the UK. It is widely acknowledged that London is one of the principal centers in the world for the marketing of art and antiquities through major auction houses like Sotheby's and Christies, and numerous art dealers and galleries. It is also less widely acknowledged that it was through this market that much of the activity of those involved in the Medici Conspiracy was conducted, although this only became fully apparent as a result of the sustained investigative efforts of Italian law enforcement officials.

Italy has had a long tradition of involvement of its national police agency, the Carabinieri, in the protection of its rich cultural heritage (Nistri 2009). The Cultural Heritage Protection Unit of the Carabinieri, staffed by several hundred officers, is currently celebrating its 40th year of existence. During this time, it has established an unrivaled international expertise in the area of art crime investigation and prosecution – an expertise which has been prepared to share with many countries which, like Italy, are on the supply side of the illicit trade in antiquities.

It should also be noted that since 2004 the Federal Bureau of Investigation (FBI) in the USA has taken a more prominent role in tackling art crime and the trafficking of antiquities through the establishment of a specialized Art Crime Team (Wittman 2009). This unit, composed of 12 special agents, has nationwide responsibilities.

A further and fourth feature which distinguishes the illicit antiquities trade from other forms of organized crime relates to the use of violence in achieving certain objectives. As observed in the account given above of the varying definitions and descriptions of the workings of more traditional forms of organized crime, violence is an important component. In the case of the antiquities traffic, this matter is rather more complicated. Certainly, there are numerous accounts of violence in the supply environments (e.g., Watson 1999). Nonetheless, in the demand environments, violence is a rare phenomenon. One does not expect, nor is one likely to find, violence in the refined atmosphere of the elegant antiquities shops of London, New York, or Paris.

The Issue of Public Policy

Effective public policy responses to control organized crime have proven elusive, and this is no less true when we consider the issue of the illicit traffic in cultural heritage material. Throughout the decades, a major thrust of policy has been the attempt to impose heavy sanctions in the hope that potential criminals might be deterred. Particularly, when aimed at the supply end of a market chain, which is where deterrence has played a role in the attempt to restrict the antiquities traffic, the record is sobering. As in the case of drug trafficking, when demand remains high in wealthy nations for costly heritage objects, any attempt to restrict supply in mostly poor nations through deterrence has huge obstacles to overcome to have any positive impact (and the costs in terms of corruption can be more than counterproductive).

Our emphasis here on a market analysis which lays the responsibility for the problem of the illicit traffic squarely upon the demand exerted from wealthy nations results in the direct conclusion that at some point priority needs to be given to policy initiatives that emphasize demand reduction, rather than supply restriction. In his important contribution to this discussion, Mackenzie (2009: 55–58 especially; see also Mackenzie 2005), reviews the history of "market reduction approaches" as applied to the control of organized crime, and analyzes the potential implications of such ideas to the problem of the illicit traffic in cultural heritage material. As he points out, a major thrust of such approaches is the emphasis on the notion that demand affects supply, and that therefore if the dealing in illicit goods is restricted at the market end, the motivation to provide supply will be reduced.

Mackenzie goes on to discuss the many twists and turns that might be taken in applying such approaches, and opens up a path for our discussion of some of the distinctive issues that arise in the consideration of the illicit traffic in antiquities. For our purposes, a major factor that has to be addressed flows out of the observation made above that the antiquities market, unlike most other illicit markets, is legal in most contexts in the demand environments, and can involve persons of exceptional social status, both as dealers and consumers.

Demand reduction in such circumstances cannot rest simply upon the heavy hand of deterrence. As Murphy observed many years ago, those in the art world know full well that the existing attempts to use criminal laws to prohibit the movement of antiquities "...only assures that the traffic goes underground" (Murphy 1995: 155).

Another possibility, of course, is that the various parties, including the governmental authorities, simply ignore the attempt to impose sanctions. For an illustration, we need to look no further than to what has happened recently in our region of the world. Since 2001, there has been a concerted attempt by UNESCO, through the passage of an international convention, to assert that there is no traffic in underwater cultural heritage material. Closing off the market ideally should produce the result of no further plunder, except that is far from the result. In a recent case (Wroe 2009), a German team found the shipwreck of an English vessel off the coast of the Indonesian island of Sumatra. Rather than prohibiting exploration of the site, the Indonesian authorities have worked out an agreement whereby the estimated seven million Euro hoard of objects are sold at auction, with the government receiving half of the proceeds. When so much is at stake, even governments with a stake in preservation of cultural heritage can be tempted to participate in the wealth that results from plunder.

For those like us who approach the problem of demand reduction from the viewpoint of criminology, we are forced to move beyond traditional theoretical discussions which concern various forms of criminal justice sanctions. One possible way of extending such discussions, as we have suggested elsewhere (Alder and Polk 2005), might be to expand upon the approach to restorative justice suggested by Braithwaite (1989, 1993, 2002). In his early work, Braithwaite proposed for such areas of white collar crime as mine safety or occupational health and safety a regulatory approach which called for a "pyramid" of enforcement strategies, with most efforts of regulatory agencies concerned (at the base of the pyramid) with persuasion, negotiation and training, and only a small amount of work aimed at punishment of the most significant and outstanding cases of regulatory or criminal violation.

While this pyramid of enforcement in general is designed for situations where there is a clearly defined statutory body that has a mandate to regulate and control a particular realm of corporate behavior, and thus has a much narrower reach than our concern with the international traffic in antiquities, we think this discussion is relevant because of its emphasis on the techniques of persuasion and negotiation that appear to us to be so central to any process of reduction in the demand for cultural heritage material. The core ideas suggested by Braithwaite call our attention to the need to have a mix of strategies which combine mostly persuasion aimed at demand reduction (through education, training, negotiation, arbitration, and similar processes) with some attention given to major sanctions for the more outstanding criminal ventures.

To be sure, in various forms there are already in existence a number of examples of this emphasis applied with the goal of reducing the market in illicit antiquities. For example, the International Council of Museums (ICOM) has devised an ethical code that stipulates that member museums do not obtain (by purchase or gift) material that has been illegally looted from cultural heritage sites. One aspect of the work of ICOM was to publish a book *Looting in Angkor* (ICOM 1997) which lists "100 stolen objects" taken from Cambodia. Such a book serves both a preventative/control function (identifying works that have been stolen and therefore should not be purchased) and a restorative function (the return of the stolen goods to the source country).

Our own field work has found examples of the importance of such efforts. Thus, in our interviews with one museum curator it was revealed that the museum had items in its collections that were listed among the stolen objects, and these objects were subsequently returned to Cambodia. In Braithwaite's terms, this resulted in a public "shaming" of the institution involved, but then a "restorative" process whereby the material was repatriated to its source nation. Bearing in mind that historically the public museums have consistently been identified as major players in the illicit traffic in antiquities, steps such as this which discourage purchasing on the part of museums are clearly a step in the right direction. In 2001, the Association of Art Museum Directors (AAMD) included within their code of ethics the following provision:

> A museum director should not knowingly acquire or allow to be recommended for acquisition any object that has been stolen, removed in contravention of treaties or international conventions to which the United States is a signatory, or illegally imported in the United States (AAMD 2001).

More recently, the AAMD has added a further caveat to this acquisition policy, indicating that members (of whom there are almost 200 spread across the USA):

> [S]hould not acquire a work unless research substantiates that the work was outside its country of probable modern discovery after 1970, or was legally exported from its probable country of modern discovery after 1970 (AAMD 2008).

The selection of 1970 is significant since it represents the year in which the UNESCO Convention on the means of prohibiting and preventing the illicit import, export and transfer of ownership of cultural property came into effect. It would seem that this position taken by the AAMD was prompted in part by the recent return to Italy by a number of leading US museums of more than 100 cultural objects, including the much vaunted and very valuable Euphonios Krater, purchased originally by New York's Metropolitan Museum from those involved in the Medici Conspiracy (Gill 2009).

These steps are illustrative of how national and international organizations might coordinate efforts to achieve a "market reduction" effect, whereby the demand component in the market of illicit antiquities is reduced. It presumes that there is some level of "organization" that is consistent with both a market analysis of the problem, and our own field work into the various international linkages that make up the "organizational" aspect of this particular form of crime. Such steps are premised in the notion that what is needed are procedures of persuasion and negotiation that presume the presence of a legal and vigorous market in antiquities.

While a virtue of these measures is that they operate in the lower regions of any regulatory pyramid and assume involvement of a licit market of dealers and purchasers, despite the overwhelming legality of that antiquities market there is an important role to be played by deterrence resulting from legal sanctions at the top of the pyramid. Given that the most of the traffic in the demand environments tends to have at least the appearance of being licit, at first any role of "punishment" may seem implausible. There are, however, at least two avenues such steps can take (and have taken). First, countries such as the USA and the UK may try and convict persons of theft (in those countries) when a charge can be laid that a theft has occurred in another country. The Schultz case was tried in New York, for example, on the basis of charges that thefts of cultural heritage material had taken place in Egypt, and Schultz was not only convicted, he was sentenced to 33 months in prison. Although the matter could not proceed, somewhat similar dynamics were involved in the case of an American citizen (resident of Thailand) who was arrested in 2008 in Seattle on comparable charges. The suspect subsequently died in custody during the initial investigation of that case (Wyatt 2008; Felch 2009).

A second important avenue of "punishment" consists of seizing the material, generally by customs officials, which has occurred in a number of cases, where the objects in question have been exceptionally costly (for example, see Barnes 2000). While quite a different process, this step, if it wipes off an investment of hundreds of thousands of dollars, is likely to catch the attention of potential customers.

A third and related avenue of punishment relates to the potential for much greater use of anti-money laundering (AML) and proceeds of crime forfeiture legislation in targeting those involved in the trafficking and purchase of plundered cultural objects (see in general Broome 2005; Millington 2007). While on initial inspection legislation of this type may not seem relevant to the circumstances of those purchasing such objects in demand settings because of the apparent licit nature of the trade through dealers, auction houses and similar outlets, a more detailed analysis suggests that there is still scope for utilizing what have now become well established and effective laws allowing in general the proceeds of crime to be traced and seized from those engaged in a chain of illicit activities.[1] For example, although nations are usually unwilling to enforce within their own jurisdiction the laws of another, including a prohibition on the removal and export of cultural objects without authorization, most nations whether in supply or demand settings now have similar domestic legislation of this type. This means that there is a similar offense in both sets of domestic law. Further, because the original removal of the object and the sale of the illegally removed cultural object are "predicate offenses" under most national AML and forfeiture legislation, any proceeds of the sale are proceeds of crime and recoverable as such.

Depending on the specifics of a nation's AML law, the movement of funds associated with transactions involving cultural object trafficking may also amount to money laundering. Thus, in some countries, any transfer of proceeds may amount to money laundering because the offense involves any transaction involving the proceeds of crime. In other countries, the act may need to involve an intention to hide the source of the funds.

In most situations involving dealings in trafficked cultural objects, it would seem likely that the sale proceeds are paid quite openly by the purchaser to, and be received by an art dealer, gallery, or auction house, depending on the circumstances, for ultimate transmission to the "real seller." In many cases, it is also likely that the "real seller's" identity is not revealed because to do so might disclose that the object was obtained illegally. As such this type of behavior involving the deliberate or reckless hiding of the identity of the true owner of an object, or obfuscating that identity through euphemisms of the type outlined earlier about the object being sold "on behalf of a Belgium collector," all go to strengthen the contention that this movement of the funds amounts to money laundering and a criminal offense by all of those involved, with the presumed exception of a genuine and unwitting ultimate purchaser. Even further strength could be given to this argument if the object in question's true identity has been deliberately disguised in another country as, for instance, appears to have been the case with the large numbers of plundered antiquities associated with the Medici Conspiracy.

At present, the available evidence suggests that there is scant use of these quite draconian but effective criminal law powers and sanctions in the arena of antiquities trafficking. We would contend that this is an arena where, because of the unique nature of the clientele involved and their status in many cases as social elites, some well-targeted and publicized prosecutions of prominent art dealers, auction houses and others involved in a trade which until now has been largely untouched or troubled by questionable dealings in cultural objects could have a strong deterrent effect. Already there would seem to be some signs that the ongoing and rippling international impact of the highly publicized prosecutions arising from the Medici Conspiracy has "named and shamed" some very prominent institutions. As noted earlier, over recent times this "outing" of past and flawed acquisition policies and

[1]We are indebted to a colleague, Professor John Broome of the Center for Transnational Crime Prevention at the University of Wollongong and an acknowledged international expert on AML and allied matters, for suggesting this possible application of AML and forfeiture laws to this area of criminality.

conduct has resulted in the return of numbers of looted objects to source countries like Italy (Gill 2009). There are now also encouraging signs that this impact may be extending to private collectors who at the very least should begin to recognize that much more probing questions need to be asked about the provenance of the objects they purchase if they are to avoid the risk of having them seized and returned to their country of origin.

Conclusion

We believe the steps we have outlined recognize the unique features of the antiquities trade, features which in fact make possible a much greater theoretical impact of deterrence than is likely to occur at the supply end of this market. In the demand environment, especially among social elites, there is some possibility of achieving the ideal conditions for a deterrence effect. That is, as deterrence theory would suggest, if the penalties are appropriately severe (and certainly the threat of jail itself for these individuals is likely to have an impact, as would the thought of a huge investment vanishing in an instant), and if there is enough publicity in the market about these activities, then the rational conditions of the deterrence model are achieved.

We stress, however, that consistent with the pyramid model of restorative justice, what we are proposing are strategies which mix mostly processes of persuasion and negotiation with a small amount of these deterrence mechanisms. Experience with such problems as the use of seat belts, the trade in furs, and cigarette smoking all suggest that change can be achieved, and that processes which mix a combination of education and punishment might bring about changes in behavior.

Like many other forms of organized crime, the illicit traffic in antiquities is a complex market involving the pull of consumers in market settings exerting a demand on those willing to take the risks of extracting the material from cultural heritage sites in order to provide the supply of illicit material. If nothing else, consideration of this activity as a form of "organized" crime gives emphasis to the complexity not only of the problem itself (in terms of its many constituent elements), but also how difficult it will be to bring any effective control to this traffic. Our argument here is that the unique aspects of this form of organized crime (in particular that it is legal in the market environment, and that it often involves social elites as consumers) have to be considered as we attempt to control this type of offending.

References

Alder, C., Polk, K. (2005). The illicit traffic in plundered antiquities. In Reichel, P. (ed.), *Handbook of Transnational Crime* (98–113). London: Sage.

Alder, C., Chappell, D., Polk, K. (2009). Perspectives on the organisation and control of the illicit traffic in antiquities in South East Asia. In Manacorda, S. (ed.), *Organized Crime in Art and Antiquities* (119–144). Milan: International Scientific and Professional Advisory Council of the United Nations Crime Prevention and Criminal Justice Programme.

Associated Press (2009). Thailand returns 7 ancient treasures to Cambodia. *Associated Press*, 12 June. http://www.msnbc.msn.com/id/31310821/ns/technology_and_science-science/. Accessed 22 September 2009.

Association for Research into Crimes Against Art – ARCA (2009). http://www.artcrime.info/. Accessed 22 September 2009.

Association of Art Museum Directors – AAMD (2001). A code of ethics for art museum directors. New York: AAMD. http://www.aamd.org/member/pdfs/ProPractices.pdf. Accessed 22 September 2009.

Association of Art Museum Directors – AAMD (2008). Report of the AAMD task force on the acquisition of archeological materials and ancient art (rev. 2008). New York: AAMD. http://www.aamd.org/newsroom/documents/2008ReportAndRelease.pdf. Accessed 22 September 2009.

Barnes, J. E. (2000). Alleging Theft, U.S. Demands Rare Sculpture Go Back to China. *The New York Times*, 30 March, 1.

Bowman, B. (2008). Transnational crimes against culture. *Journal of Contemporary Criminal Justice*, 24(3), 225–242.

Braithwaite, J. (1989). *Crime, Shame and Reintegration.* New York: Cambridge University Press.

Braithwaite, J. (1993). *Business Regulation and Australia's Future*. Canberra: Australian Institute of Criminology.

Braithwaite, J. (2002). *Restorative Justice and Responsive Regulation.* New York: Oxford University Press.

Broome, J. (2005). *Anti Money Laundering – International Practice and Policies*. Hong Kong: Sweet and Maxwell Asia.

Edwards, A., Levi, M. (2008). Researching the organization of serious crimes. *Criminology and Criminal Justice*, 8(4), 363–388.

Europol (2008). *EU Organized Crime Threat Assessment*. Europol: The Hague.

Felch, J. (2009). US Settles with Family of Southeast Asia Scholar. *Los Angeles Times*, 8 July. http://articles.latimes.com/2009/jul/08/local/me-roxanna8. Accessed 9 August 2009.

Felsen, D., Kalaitzidis, A. (2005). A historical overview of transnational crime. In Reichel, P. (ed.), *Handbook of Transnational Crime and Justice* (3–19). Thousand Oaks, CA: Sage.

Gerstenblith, P. (2002). United States v. Schultz. *Culture Without Context*, Spring(10), 27–32.

Gill, D. (2009). Looting matters: Are new museums acquisition policies having an impact on private collectors? Looting Matters. http://news.prnewswire.com/ViewContent.aspx?ACCT=109&STORY=/www/story/08-07-2009/0005073994&EDATE=. Accessed 22 September 2009.

ICOM (1997). *One Hundred Missing Objects: Looting in Angkor*. Paris: International Council of Museums.

Levi, M. (1998). Perspectives on organized crime: an overview. *The Howard Journal of Criminal Justice*, 37(4), 335–345.

Levi, M. (2007). Organized crime and terrorism. In Morgan, R., Reiner, R. (eds.), *The Oxford Handbook of Criminology*, 4th ed. Oxford: Oxford University Press.

Mackenzie, S. (2005). *Going, Going Gone: Regulating the Market in Illicit Antiquities*. Leicester: Institute of Art and Law.

Mackenzie, S. (2009). Identifying and preventing opportunities for organized crime in the international antiquities market. In Manacorda, S. (ed.), *Organized Crime in Art and Antiquities* (41–62). Milan: International Scientific and Professional Advisory Council of the United Nations Crime Prevention and Criminal Justice Programme.

Millington, T. (2007). *The Proceeds of Crime: Law and Practice of Restraint, Confiscation, Condemnation and Forfeiture*. New York: Oxford University Press.

Murphy, J. D. (1995). *Plunder and Preservation: Cultural Property Law and Practice in the People's Republic of China.* Oxford: Oxford University Press.

Nistri, G. (2009). The experience of the Italian Cultural Heritage Protection Unit. In Manacorda, S. (ed.), *Organized Crime in Art and Antiquities* (95–108, 100–101). Milan: International Scientific and Professional Advisory Council of the United Nations Crime Prevention and Criminal Justice Programme.

Russell, M. (2009). Intel Brief: Art theft and organized crime. Zurich: ISN Security Watch. http://www.isn.ethz.ch/isn/Communities-and-Partners/Partners/Detail/?lng=en&id=52001. Accessed 22 September 2009.

Scherer, S. (2009). Rome courtupholds conviction of antiquities dealer (update1). http://Bloomberg.com, 15 July 2009. http://www.culturalheritagelaw.org/news-issues/news-issues-in-cultural-heritage/rome-court-upholds-conviction-of-antiquities-dealer-update1/. Accessed 22 September 2009.

Serious Organized Crime Agency (2009). The United Kingdom Threat Assessment of Serious Organized Crime 2009/10. London: Serious Organized Crime Agency. http://www.soca.gov.uk/assessPublications/downloads/2009-10_UKTA_NPM.pdf. Accessed 22 September 2009.

Stead, I. M. (1998). *The Salisbury Hoard*. Brimscombe, Port Stroud, Gloucestershire: Tempus Publishing.

Tilley, N., Hopkins, M. (2008). Organized crime and local businesses. *Criminology and Criminal Justice*, 8(4), 443–459.

United Nations Office on Drugs and Crime (UNODC) (2004). *United Nations Convention Against Transnational Organized Crime and the Protocols Thereto*. Vienna: UNODC.

Watson, P. (1999). The lessons of Sipan: archaeologists and huaqueros. *Culture Without Context*, Spring (4), 15–20.

Watson, P., Todeschini, T. (2006). *The Medici Conspiracy*. Prahran, VIC: Hardie Great Books.

Wittman, R. (2009). United States vs art theft. In Manacorda, S. (ed.), *Organized Crime in Art and Antiquities* (115–119). Milan: International Scientific and Professional Advisory Council of the United Nations Crime Prevention and Criminal Justice Programme.

Wroe, D. (2009). German treasure hunters strike gold with English shipwreck. *Daily Telegraph*, 30 June.

Wyatt, E. (2008). Four California museums are raided. *New York Times*, 26 January, 3.

Part II
Case Studies

Chapter 7
The Market in Iraqi Antiquities 1980–2009 and Academic Involvement in the Marketing Process

Neil Brodie

Introduction

In the wake of the 1991 Gulf War, the large-scale looting of archaeological sites in Iraq started, and worsened around the time of the 2003 Coalition invasion, when the National Museum and other cultural institutions in Baghdad were also ransacked. These events were a source of public and political consternation, and prompted some legislative and law enforcement responses aimed at protecting Iraq's archaeological heritage (Emberling and Hanson 2008; Rothfield 2008; Stone and Farchakh Bajjaly 2008). Since 1974, it had been illegal under Iraqi domestic law to export archaeological artefacts from Iraq. Then, on August 6, 1990, the United Nations Security Council Resolution (UNSCR) 661 imposed a trade embargo, which made it illegal under international law to trade in archaeological artefacts exported from Iraq after that date. But despite the prohibitory intent of these laws, there continued and continues to be a healthy international (and illegal) market in Iraqi antiquities (Brodie 2006, 2008a, b). This paper offers an analysis of this market, with a view to (a) introducing some reliable, quantitative data into the public domain and (b) suggesting a new strategy of non-legislative interdiction.

The Market up to 2003

The state of the antiquities market from 1980, through August 1990 (when UNSCR 661 was adopted), to April 2003 (when the Iraq National Museum was attacked) can be gauged from statistics describing antiquities sales held at the major London

N. Brodie (✉)
Archaeology Center, Stanford University, 94305 Stanford, CA, USA
e-mail: njb1012@gmail.com

S. Manacorda and D. Chappell (eds.), *Crime in the Art and Antiquities World: Illegal Trafficking in Cultural Property*, DOI 10.1007/978-1-4419-7946-9_7,

and New York auction houses.[1] Christie's is used for the London part of this analysis because of the three major London auction houses that sell antiquities – Sotheby's, Christie's and Bonhams – only Christie's maintained sales through the period in question, holding major antiquities-only sales two or three times per year. Figure 7.1 shows the combined number of lots of unprovenanced Mesopotamian cylinder seals and cuneiform-inscribed objects consigned for sale at Christie's each year.[2] Both types of artefacts are found mainly in Iraq, and so the figures can be taken as indicators of the larger market in Iraqi antiquities. It is clear that during the period in question, the quantities of unprovenanced artefacts being offered for sale did not diminish; in fact, if anything they increased over the years running up to 2003, even though by 1994 notice of the trade embargo imposed by UNSCR 661 had been provided by the major London and New York auction houses in their relevant

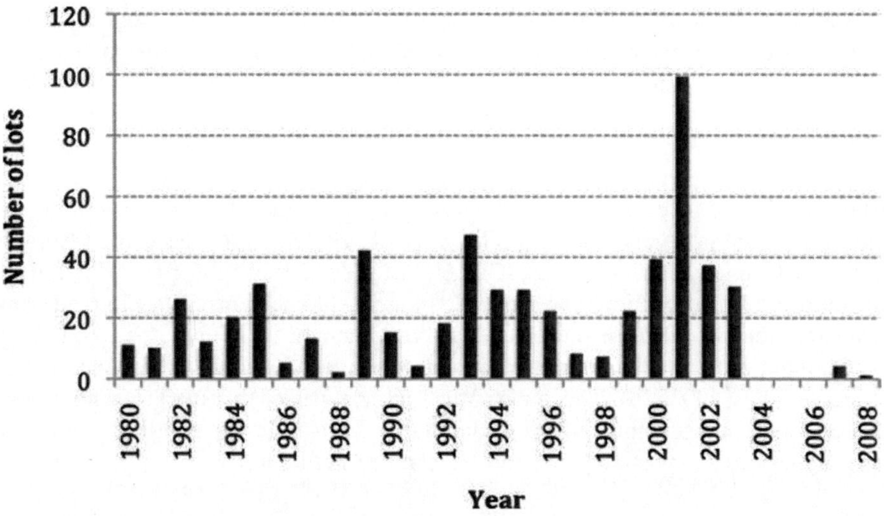

Fig. 7.1 Number of lots of unprovenanced cylinder seals and cuneiform objects offered annually at Christie's London 1980–2006

[1]Illustrated catalogues produced by the major auction houses are the only publicly accessible, long-term source of information about the antiquities market. The material appearing for auction can vary in quality, but is mainly middle to high range. Really expensive unprovenanced objects are traded outside the auction market in direct private transactions. Poorer quality material is nowadays traded mainly on the Internet.

[2]Cylinder seals are, as the name suggests, small cylinders engraved with a figurative or abstract design and sometimes with a short inscription. They were rolled on soft clay to create a reverse impression of their design which would function as a sign of ownership or authority. Cylinder seals were made from a variety of hard materials, and are usually in the range 2–4 cm long. Seal impressions were often made on clay tablets inscribed in the cuneiform script, which could be fired to produce a durable document. Cylinder seals and later cuneiform tablets underpinned the administrative systems of ancient Mesopotamia from about 3000 BC to 500 BC and today are found mainly, though not exclusively, in Iraq.

antiquities sales catalogues.[3] The increasing market volume suggests that new material was appearing, and new material could only have been moving out of Iraq through illegal means.

For New York, the largest data run available is for Sotheby's auction house, and the number of lots of unprovenanced Mesopotamian cylinder seals and cuneiform objects offered annually at Sotheby's are shown in Fig. 7.2. On average, fewer lots were offered at Sotheby's New York than at Christie's London. Auction statistics are not a straightforward reflection of the total antiquities market, but the ones presented here do suggest that for the period in question the New York market in unprovenanced Iraqi artefacts was smaller in volume than the London one. This observation is fully in accord with other evidence suggesting that much of the trade out of Iraq during the 1990s was passing through London (Brodie 2006: 214–222; Gibson 1997, 2008: 35–38).

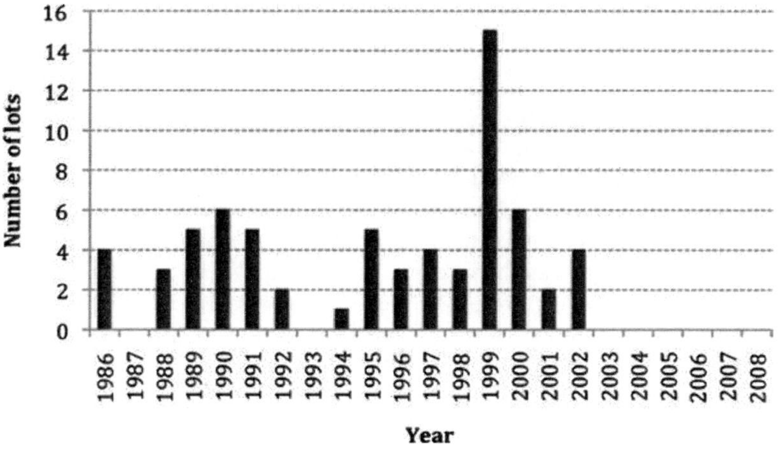

Fig. 7.2 Number of lots of unprovenanced cylinder seals and cuneiform objects offered annually at Sotheby's New York 1986–2006

[3]For example, the following statement appeared in the London Christie's catalogue of their December 12, 1990 Fine Antiquities sale: A recently imposed United Nations trade embargo prohibits us for accepting bids from any person in Iraq and/or Kuwait (including any body controlled by Iraq or Kuwait residents or companies, wherever carrying on business), or from any other person where we have reasonable cause to believe (a) that the Lots(s) will be supplied or delivered to or to the order of a person in either Iraq or Kuwait or (b) that the Lot(s) will be used for the purposes of any business carried on in or operated from Iraq or Kuwait.

Bonhams' first ever "Antiquities" sale catalogue of April 1991 contained a similar statement, and so too did comparable Sotheby's catalogues (for example, in the catalogue for the London December 1992 sale). These statements were aimed very much at potential buyers. There was no mention of potential consignors, and no overt prohibition on consignments originating in Iraq, even though Article 3(a) of UNSCR 661 stated specifically that States should prevent "The import into their territories of all commodities and products originating in Iraq or Kuwait exported there from after the date of the present resolution."

The issue of provenance is crucial here. Provenance is known ownership history, and so when an artefact is offered for sale with provenance, a potential purchaser can easily ascertain whether the piece is legally on the market, or not. For an unprovenanced artefact, however, it is harder if not impossible to establish its legitimacy. Thus, the unprovenanced Iraqi material being offered for auction between 1990 and 2003 might have been moved out of Iraq in part or in total before 1974, the date of the Iraqi domestic law prohibiting export, or before 1990, the date of international sanctions imposed by UNSCR 661. Equally, the material might all have been moved out of Iraq after those dates, and have entered the market illegally. The absence of provenance meant, however, that the auction houses would have had no necessary knowledge of that fact.

In May 2003, UNSCR 1483 lifted trade sanctions on Iraq, except for those on weapons and cultural objects. Article 7 of UNSCR 1483 specifically stated that the trade in Iraqi cultural objects would be prohibited when "reasonable suspicion exists that they have been illegally removed" from Iraq since the adoption of UNSCR 661, and that the return of any cultural objects stolen from cultural institutions or other locations in Iraq since that time should be facilitated. Since that date, the sale of unprovenanced Iraqi artefacts at public auction in New York and London has stopped almost entirely (Figs. 7.1 and 7.2), perhaps because of the widespread negative publicity that followed on from the break-in at the Iraq National Museum, or because of UNSCR 1483, though there might also have been a financial consideration, as discussed below. The fact that unprovenanced Iraqi artefacts suddenly disappeared from the auction market after 2003 is an important one as it reinforces the impression already formed that before 2003 a large part of the unprovenanced material on the market was there illegally. Otherwise, if it had been there legally, after 2003 it could have continued to have been consigned quite openly without any fear of criminal prosecution. Absence of provenance, it seems, is a good indicator of illegal trade.

The Sîn-iddinam Barrels

Some of the unprovenanced artefacts being sold at auction during this period were almost certainly looted. Between 1997 and 2002, for example, eight cuneiform inscribed clay barrels, dating to about 1900 BC and celebrating King Sîn-iddinam's dredging of the River Tigris, appeared for auction. Not one had any indication of provenance. The first to appear was at Sotheby's New York in May 1997. The catalogue entry stated correctly that at the time only three similarly inscribed barrels were known – one each at the Louvre, the Ashmolean Museum, and Chicago's Oriental Institute. The fact that the Sotheby's barrel was previously unknown might have raised questions about the legality or otherwise of its provenance, but, if it did, they were not enough to stop the sale. Nor were any questions asked over the following five years when a further seven unprovenanced barrels turned up at auction. It is hardly credible that so many of these barrels should have been in circulation since before 1974, eluding scholarly and public view, only to appear en masse at a time when there was widespread looting of archaeological sites in southern Iraq. A more parsimonious explanation for their sudden appearance is that, in fact, they were looted after 1990 and illegally traded.

Financial Considerations

The auction houses' decision in 2003 to stop offering unprovenanced Iraqi material might also have been influenced by the economic climate of the market. Economic analyses of the auction market in antiquities are in their infancy, yet it is clear that the value of the market in Iraqi antiquities started to increase in the late 1980s. Figure 7.3 shows the total annual value of all cylinder seal sales made at Christie's London over the period 1981–2008. These statistics are not derived from repeat sales and therefore do not chart the changing price of individual cylinder seals through time. Fluctuations in value might, for example, be due to variations in the quality and thus the price of seals being sold. What the statistics do reliably indicate, however, is the value of the market, and by extension the auction house's profit margins over the period in question (derived from buyer's and seller's premiums levied on the achieved price at auction). Thus the profits being made by Christie's from cylinder seal sales started increasing in the late 1980s, and stayed at a high level until 2002, when they declined sharply.

Not all lots offered for auction sell, and those that do not sell must constitute a loss for the auction house. The auction house devotes time and resources to their presentation, but receives no commission for a successful sale. Figure 7.4 attempts to place the cylinder seal sales in this broader market context. It shows the mean price per lot offered. Mean price per lot offered (as opposed to per lot sold) is intended to offer a composite measure of material profitability, offsetting the loss made from unsold lots against the profit made from sold lots. It is clear from Fig. 7.4 that the profits being made from cylinder seals sales started dropping after

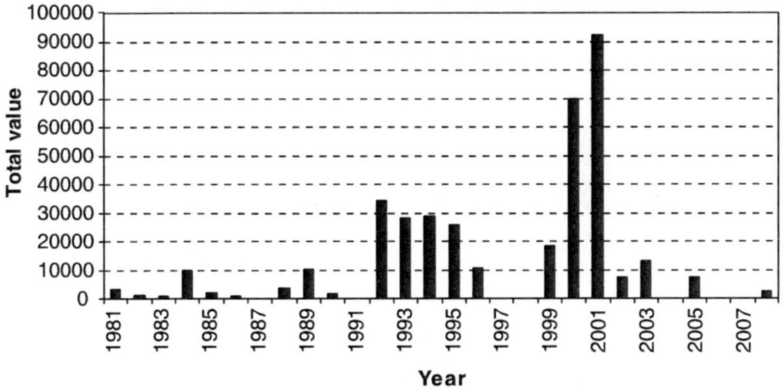

Fig. 7.3 Total annual value (£) of cylinder seal sales at Christie's London. Values deflated to 1975 using the Consumer Price Index

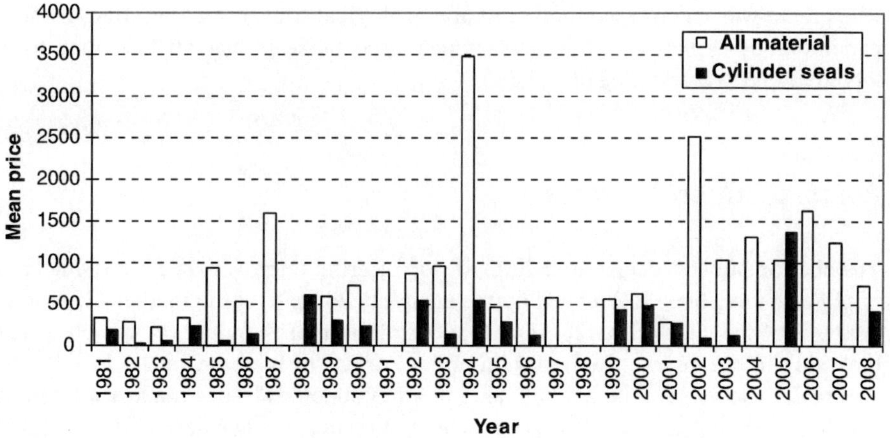

Fig. 7.4 Mean price per lot offered (£) of cylinder seal sales compared to sales of all other material at Christie's London. Values deflated to 1975 using the Consumer Price Index. For 1988 and 1998 there are no data for "all material" sales. The high mean prices for 2005 and 2007 are for good quality, well provenanced seals

2000, while from 2002 onwards profits from other types of material were increasing. This observation that cylinder seals were becoming less profitable in the run-up to the 2003 Coalition invasion seems confirmed by satellite and field surveys of southern Iraq that suggest looting intensified in the early 2000s, and diminished after 2003 (Curtis et al. 2008; Stone 2008). If more seals were reaching the market from Iraq, supply would have begun to outstrip demand.

Thus until 2002, Christie's clearly had a financial interest in maintaining sales of cylinder sales despite the UNSCR trade embargo. Once profits started declining, however, it might explain in part why Christie's and other auction houses were then less willing to shoulder the adverse publicity and possible risks involved in selling unprovenanced material. It might have proved expedient to stop offering artefacts of declining profitability and concentrate instead on selling more profitable and less controversial categories of material. Further research will establish whether the market fluctuations charted in Figs. 7.3 and 7.4 were characteristic of the market in Iraqi antiquities more generally, or specific to cylinder seal sales at Christie's. The facts that sales of unprovenanced cuneiform objects at Christie's stopped in 2003 along with those of cylinder seals, and that a similar situation prevailed at Sotheby's New York, suggest it was a more general phenomenon.

The Market in December 2006

Outside the auction market, after 2003 Iraqi artefacts continued and have continued to be openly traded on the Internet. On one day – 5 December 2006 – there were at least 55 Web sites offering antiquities for sale and that might have been expected to sell Iraqi objects.[4] In fact, 23 of those sites were offering for sale or had recently sold cylinder seals and/or cuneiform-inscribed objects. In total, there were 78 cylinder seals and 147 cuneiform objects listed (Table 7.1), but the real number might have been higher than the data suggest. There is no guarantee that what is openly offered for sale on a Web site represents the entire stock available for sale, and some Web sites specifically stated that this was in fact the case. Thus, there might have been more material available for sale than was advertised, potentially much more.

Hardly any of the cuneiform objects were advertised with a verifiable provenance. It is also instructive in this context to note the named findspots of the cuneiform objects (Table 7.2). It is suspicious that although the modern nation states of Iran, Israel, and Syria were identified as findspots, Iraq was not named once. Presumably, the term Mesopotamia was used instead. There was no evidence provided on any Web site to allow any of the findspots to be verified, and some of them, such as Mediterranean, seem unnecessarily vague. The reluctance of dealers to use the word "Iraq" as a geographical identifier suggests that even if they had no

Table 7.1 Iraqi artefacts for sale on the Internet in 2006 and 2008

	December 2006	September 2008
No. Web sites identified	55	72
No. Web sites offering cuneiform objects/ cylinder seals	23	32
No. cylinder seals offered	78	142
No. cuneiform objects offered	147	330
Total no. artefacts offered	225	472

Table 7.2 Provenance and findspot information for cuneiform objects available for sale on the Internet in 2006 and 2008

Provenance or findspot	Number of objects (2006)	Number of objects (2008)
Named previous owner	3	8
Mesopotamia	71	47
East Mediterranean	0	180
Mediterranean	12	9
Central Asia	0	4
Israel	8	6
Syria	8	10
Iran	1	0
Elam	1	0
Isin	1	1
Larsa	0	4
Lagash	1	0

[4]The search included Web sites selling ancient Mediterranean or "Classical" antiquities, either solely or in part, but excluded Web sites that specialise in, for example, Precolumbian or African artefacts.

specific knowledge of illegal provenance, they were well aware that many Iraqi objects were illegally on the market, and had also realised that specifying a findspot other than Iraq helps to reassure potential customers and confound police action. In fact, so long as care is taken when attributing findspot not to use the word "Iraq", it would appear possible to sell illegally exported Iraqi material with relative impunity. There was no real attempt to "launder" objects by providing them with a false provenance of a real or fictitious "old collection".

The Market in September 2008

In September 2008, the Internet survey conducted in 2006 was repeated, with the aim of establishing whether the market had changed over the intervening period. The results suggested that the market had actually increased in volume. There were more Web sites offering artefacts for sale, and the total number of available artefacts had more than doubled (Table 7.1). As in 2006, some sites were claiming a larger stock than advertised. The Royal-Athena Galleries Web site, for example, carried the following notice: "In addition to the pieces illustrated above, we have an extensive array of other cylinder seals ranging from $300 to $2,250 and cuneiform tablets and foundation cones ranging from $250 to $2,750 in price".[5] Also, and again as in 2006, there were no stated findspots of Iraq (Table 7.2). Two more things in particular stand out from the 2008 data. One is the appearance on the market of several "clay bricks" carrying an identical Neo-Babylonian inscription. The second is the prominence of the Barakat Gallery, offering 229 cuneiform pieces – 69% of all cuneiform material on offer. Both cases are discussed further below.

In August 2009, the sites identified in September 2008 were revisited to establish how many of the objects tabulated in 2008 had been sold, and to make an estimate of total annual sales values. Many of the objects tabulated in 2008 were still being advertised for sale, some were marked "sold", and many had been removed from display. The presumption here is that any object appearing in 2008 that had been removed by 2009 had been sold. (Another reason might be that it had been recognised as fake and quietly removed.) Leaving aside for the moment material on sale at the Barakat Gallery, about 75% of the objects offered for sale on other Web sites had been sold (and in most cases there was new material available). Not all objects sold had been advertised in 2008 with prices, but for those that were, the aggregate sales values are shown in Table 7.3. If these data are used to estimate mean prices, which are then multiplied by the total number of objects sold, then the total estimated value for the year of all cylinder seal sales would be $58,321[(38348/48)*73], and for cuneiform objects $78,530 [(42744/43)*79], or a combined value of $136,850.

---

[5] http://www.royalathena.com/PAGES/Under2500/neeastcat2500.html. Accessed 23 September 2008.

Table 7.3 Internet sales other than the Barakat Gallery, September 2008 to August 2009

Material	Number of objects for sale (September 2008)	Number of objects sold (August 2009)	Number of objects sold with price information	Total value of objects sold with price information
Cylinder seals	123	73	48	$38,348
Cuneiform objects	101	79	43	$42,744

The Nebuchadnezzar Larsa Bricks

In September 2008, six Web sites were displaying examples of what were said to be clay or cuneiform bricks from Larsa (Table 7.4), carrying an identical Neo-Babylonian inscription celebrating King Nebuchadnezzar's restoration of the temple of Shamash in Larsa. A Web site entry of LMLK Blogspot dated July 8, 2006[6] carried images of three more bricks said to be similarly inscribed that had appeared on eBay "over the past few years" (i.e. the few years before 2006). Brick no. 1 on the LMLK Web site was the same one as the September 2008 eBay brick, but otherwise the bricks are all different. Thus, there are at least eight examples of this inscribed brick that have been in circulation since 2003, and that do not seem to have been documented before that date.

There are 11 examples of this text on architectural blocks in the British Museum. The dimensions of the texts are in the approximate range 19×11 cm^2, while the dimensions of the blocks themselves are in the range $34 \times 33 \times 9$ cm^3 (Walker 1981: 90). It is notable that the dimensions of the "bricks" appearing on the Internet in 2008 closely approximate those of the texts on the British Museum blocks, and close inspection of images shows that in fact the recently appeared "bricks" had been cut down from larger blocks with the use of circular saws. Saw marks were clearly visible on the backs of several bricks, and the front view of one brick had what appeared to a horizontal saw-cut in its top edge. The saw marks constitute clear evidence that the "bricks" had been removed destructively from their architectural contexts and cut down in size to facilitate their illegal transport from Iraq. The question is, when? Larsa has suffered badly from illegal digging in recent years. The site guard was murdered in 1991 and the site was heavily looted in 2003. A National Geographic-sponsored team of archaeologists visited Larsa in the immediate aftermath of the 2003 Coalition invasion and reported severe damage to some large brick buildings of a type that often contained cuneiform archives. The situation seems to have improved by the time a British Museum team visited the site in 2008 and reported little evidence of recent looting (Wright et al. 2003; Stone 2008: 76; Curtis et al. 2008: 14, 17). Nevertheless, there is no concrete evidence at the moment to show that the sawn down Nebuchadnezzar bricks were

[6]http://lmlk.blogspot.com/; posted July 8, 2006. Accessed 23 September 2008.

Table 7.4 Websites showing Nebuchadnezzar Larsa bricks in September 2008

Dealer	Object as described	Dimensions (cm)	Price
Aweidah Gallery	Clay brick	21 × 13	Sold
Treasuregate Gallery	Clay brick	20 × 13	$2,000
BidAncient	Cuneiform brick	21.5 × 14 × 2.5	$1,100 – sold
Harlan Berk	Terracotta brick	21.3 × 13.3	$2,500 est.
eBay	Cuneiform brick		$1,450 res.
Ancient Resource	Brick inscription		Not for sale

removed from Larsa in 2003, though again, as for the Sîn-iddinam barrels, the most parsimonious explanation for their sudden appearance on the market after 2003 must be that they were looted.

The Barakat Cuneiform Objects

The Barakat Gallery (Los Angeles, London) had on offer 229 cuneiform inscribed objects in September 2008, almost all clay tablets or cones. Most of the objects were complete, though some had been reconstructed from two or more fragments. None had any provenance and the stated findspots are listed in Table 7.5. When approached, Barakat stated that the tablets had been in the gallery owner's family's possession since 1956, when they had been bought from a dealer in Jordan.

The major part of the cuneiform objects offered by Barakat (181 in total) comprised tablets dated to the first half of the twenty-first century BC. Their findspots are listed in Table 7.6. Included in this number was a quantity of the so-called messenger tablets – tablets recording the disbursement of rations to official messengers. At least 43 of these tablets dated to the year 2027 BC, and the same personal names could be found repeated on different tablets. Table 7.7 shows the names repeated on just four tablets, chosen at random. The fact that the same names appeared on these different messenger tablets shows that the tablets comprised an archive from a single archaeological site, and suggests that the larger twenty-first century corpus is part of the same archive. If that is in fact the case, then it is strange that according to Barakat some of the tablets had a findspot in Israel, others had a findspot in Syria, while the vast majority were said to come from the Eastern Mediterranean (Table 7.6).

The size distribution of the Barakat cuneiform tablets stands out from that of the tablets on other Web sites, with a modal maximum dimension in the range 6–8 cm, compared to a modal maximum dimension in the range 4–6 cm for all other Web sites (Fig. 7.5). The Barakat tablets were also being offered for prices far higher than those being asked by other Web sites. The price data of all Web sites other than Barakat show a general correlation between tablet size and price (Fig. 7.6). This correlation is to be expected, as tablet size is an indicator of inscription length, and the interest or importance of the inscription is a major determinant of price (though clearly there are other factors at work, such as wear,

Table 7.5 Stated place of origin for cuneiform objects offered by the Barakat Gallery in September 2008

Origin	Number
Mesopotamia	22
Syria	7
Israel	6
Mediterranean	9
East Mediterranean	180
Central Asia	4
None	1

Table 7.6 Stated place of origin for cuneiform tablets dating to the first half of the twenty-first century BC offered by the Barakat Gallery in September 2008

Origin	Number
Mesopotamia	0
Syria	6
Israel	5
Mediterranean	8
East Mediterranean	159
Central Asia	3
None	0

Table 7.7 Personal names repeated on four "messenger tablets"

AM0062	AM0063	AM0085	AM0103
Lu-dingirra		Lu-dingirra	
Shu-Adad	Shu-Adad		
Pululu	Pululu	Pululu	
Puzur-Sin			Puzur-Sin
Sharrum-bani		Sharrum-bani	Sharrum-bani
Shulgi-satuni		Shulgi-satuni	
		Hulal	Hulal

legibility, and breakage). About 50% of the Barakat tablets were offered "price on request", but the remainder were shown with a price, and they do not fit the correlation observed for all other Web sites. In general, the prices of the Barakat tablets were an order of magnitude greater than those of tablets offered on other Web sites. The reason for this large price difference is hard to explain, as it seems more than what the market bears. One explanation might be that Barakat is setting prices artificially high to deter the casual purchaser and attract "high-end" customers – wealthy institutions or private collectors. The actual sale prices negotiated with such customers might be much lower than the advertised ones. In similar fashion, the Barakat cylinder seals were being offered for prices an order of magnitude greater than those on other Web sites (Fig. 7.7), though for cylinder seals the correlation between size and price is not so marked.

By August 2009, 204 of the Barakat cuneiform objects had been sold, including all objects from the putative archive. Only one cylinder seal had been sold, for an unspecified price. The total sales value of the 132 cuneiform objects that had price

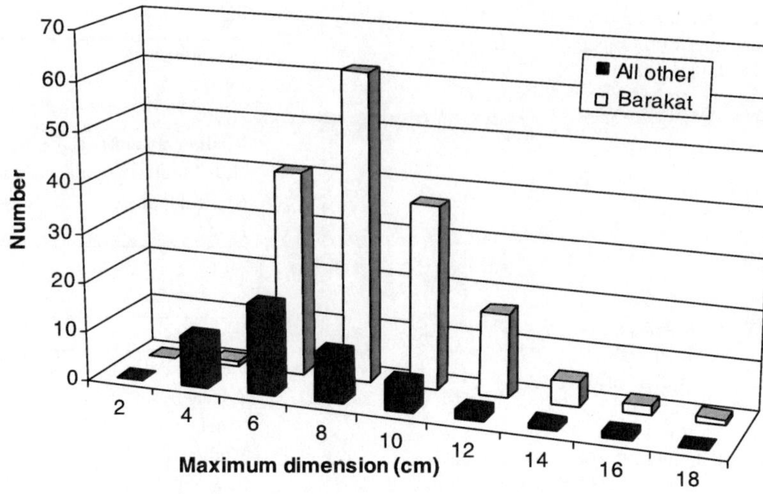

Fig. 7.5 Size distributions of cuneiform tablets offered for sale on the Internet in September 2008

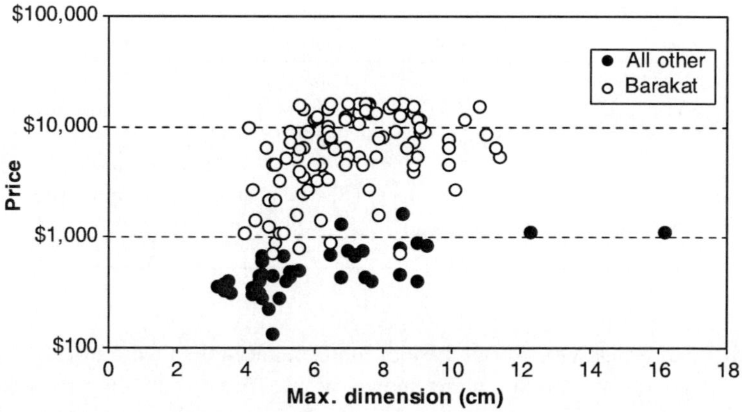

Fig. 7.6 Correlation between cuneiform tablet size and price in September 2008, also showing the high prices of Barakat tablets

data was $921,484, which multiplied up for the total 204 objects sold would be $1,424,112. Even if the real total is assumed to have been an order of magnitude less than this figure ($142,411), thus bringing the Barakat prices down into line with those for the rest of the market, it would still be substantial. When this downsized Barakat figure of $142,411 is added to the sales values from other Web sites, the total value for cuneiform object and cylinder seal sales for the period September 2008 to August 2009 was $279,262. This figure is almost certainly an underestimate, however, because it takes no account of objects that might have been offered and

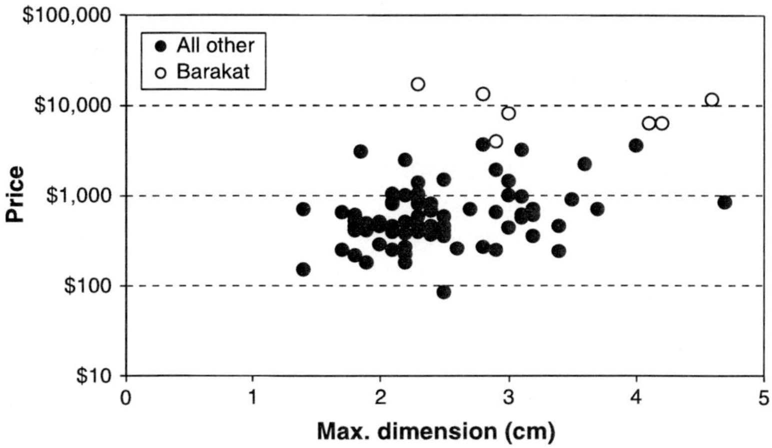

Fig. 7.7 Cylinder seal prices in September 2008

sold between the two study dates of September 2008 and August 2009, nor does it take any account of objects that might not have been advertised for sale on a Web site, but still sold by Internet dealers in direct transactions (as intimated by Web sites offering more material than advertised). It is important also to note that this figure of $279,262 does not describe the total value of all Iraqi objects sold on the Internet. There were many other types of object and material from Iraq being offered for sale, so the annual sales value for all Iraqi objects would be much higher.

Academic Involvement and the Problem of Fakes

Of the 142 cylinder seals offered for sale in 2008, 32 had been described by Wilfred Lambert, and he had also translated 211 of the 332 cuneiform objects on offer. Lambert is Professor Emeritus of Assyriology at Birmingham University and a Fellow of the British Academy. Lambert's identifications and authentications, and those of scholars like him, are of central importance for the antiquities market. They support a credible pricing regime by establishing the quality, interest and rarity of pieces on offer, and maintain customer confidence by keeping the market free of fakes. Most of the pieces that carry a Lambert authentication are unprovenanced, and Lambert himself seems unconcerned about provenance, or lack of it. When he was interviewed on the subject by the *New York Times* in April 2003, soon after the plunder of the Iraq National Museum, he admitted that he does not usually know the histories of objects he authenticates, and he suspected that the dealers who use him did not know either (Gottleib and Meier 2003). But Lambert cannot be alone. Translating cuneiform inscriptions and identifying cylinder seals are expert tasks, and clearly some unacknowledged expert had translated the texts of the Nebuchadnezzar Larsa bricks and the Sîn-iddinam barrels, for example, before they were offered for sale. The involvement of academics in the antiquities trade, and particularly the trade in ancient written materials, must be more pervasive than is generally recognised (Brodie 2009).

The importance of Lambert's work and that of other experts for the market is highlighted by the observation made by cuneiform expert David Owen, of Cornell University, that between 2003 and 2008 he identified fewer than 500 genuine cuneiform tablets on the Internet, but that he also observed fake tablets (Owen 2009: 131 note 3). The routine suppression of provenance that is a feature of the antiquities market is conducive for the entry into commerce of fakes because no checks can be made on their origin. But the Internet market is even more vulnerable to penetration by fakes than the more established antiquities market of auction houses and high street galleries, for two reasons. First, and Owen is unusual here, Internet sales are not routinely monitored by experts in the way that catalogues of the major auction houses are. Second, not all Internet vendors have a long-established reputation for good faith business to maintain. Thus, if they are caught selling fakes, they can simply change their name and address and start again. This option is not open to a major auction house like Christie's, for example, or even to some of the more established Internet dealers, who, like the auction houses, do regard and protect their reputation as a commercial asset. It is material sold on eBay in particular that has come in for a lot of criticism as regard fakes. Most Internet dealers, in fact, do seem to be concerned about the problem of fakes, presumably because if the public believes that the market is badly compromised by fakes, customer confidence will deteriorate and business will decline or collapse. Increasingly, Internet dealers are offering illustrated advice on how to recognise fakes. Even before the advent of the Internet market, authenticity was of greater concern than provenance to dealers, and most dealers, including Internet dealers, offer guarantees of authenticity.

The Internet antiquities market is still organising itself into a mature commercial institution. Establishing customer confidence is an important part of that process, and there are different strategies in play. One is the development of electronic marketplaces, which bring together on a single Web site and exert some quality assurance over a range of Internet dealers, or "members", offering closely related types of material. Trocadero, for example, links to the inventories of dealers in art and antiques, including antiquities. Customers visiting the Trocadero site can search according to material or browse according to vendor. By August 2009, there were more than 20 dealers listed as selling Mediterranean antiquities. Trocadero offers no guarantees to customers and accepts no liabilities as regards its members. It does, however, reserve the right to exclude members who are found misrepresenting material for sale, and it is probably in the interests of participating dealers for this to happen. VCoins offers a similar venue but with the emphasis more on coins than art. Absence of provenance, of course, is not misrepresentation, though passing off a forged piece as a genuine one is.

A second strategy used to guard against fakes is, as already described, the use of academics to authenticate material before sale. By September 2008, however, one Web site, the UK-based Collector Antiquities, had gone a step further and was offering a "cuneiform reading service".[7] Translations of cuneiform texts could be prepared for prices ranging between £30 and 105, depending upon the length and difficulty of the text. The service also stated that "If the piece is of academic importance and interest the translator requests that you would agree to allow the images/inscription to be recorded for eventual publication, so the new information is made available to scholars". Thus, the expert providing the service benefits twice over, first by receiving monetary payment, and second by receiving academic credit through publication. The translation can be made from a photograph, and there is no stated requirement to submit proof of legitimate title or evidence of legal export from Iraq. The service is available generally, and offers a good means of establishing the authenticity of objects bought from Collector Antiquities, or elsewhere. (And, in passing, also of transferring the cost of authentication from the vendor to the customer). The same Web site offers extensive discussion of fake cuneiform objects and cylinder seals, explaining how to recognise them, and includes a page advising on the perils of buying from eBay.

Conclusion

The data presented in this paper argue strongly for the existence of an illegal trade in Iraqi artefacts. When viewed in aggregate, the evidence that much of the material appearing on the market has been recently looted in Iraq appears overwhelming. The auction houses stopped selling unprovenanced material after 2003. Internet dealers never describe material as coming from Iraq. Large numbers of previously unknown but recognisable objects like the Sîn-iddinam barrels and the Nebuchadnezzar Larsa bricks appear, but with no explanation as to provenance or origin. These market observations mesh with information coming from within Iraq itself about the scale of archaeological looting. For any one individual object, however, it is difficult to prove that it was actually found in Iraq or to establish at what date it was taken out of Iraq. Dealers are always keen to emphasise that large quantities of material moved out of Iraq during the Ottoman period and under the British Mandate before the promulgation of the 1974 domestic law, and they are not always wrong (e.g. Eisenberg 2004). The market is a grey one, with dealers and collectors able to transact unprovenanced objects of unknown legitimacy, protected from certain knowledge that any material is stolen. There is little risk involved to dealers of being convicted for being selling stolen material.

The same market data reveal very little about the organisation of the trade. The degree and nature of the trade's organisation, and its possible links with other criminal trades or with terrorist groups, remain obscure. It is sometimes claimed that military or law enforcement agencies have intelligence about broader criminal articulations, and these claims might be true, but it is the nature of such intelligence that it cannot

[7] http://www.collector-antiquities.com/314/. Accessed 5 August 2009.

be made public. In its absence, the empirical assumption has to be made that although the illegal trade in Iraqi artefacts is likely to be organised, and is by definition transnational, it is organised within itself and not as part of a larger criminal enterprise.

Mackenzie (2009: 55) has drawn attention to the importance of "facilitators" at the interface of legitimate and illegitimate markets, and suggested that they can be protected by codes of conduct or licencing requirements. One group of facilitators in the market for Iraqi antiquities comprise the academics who describe and authenticate objects. Although professional codes of ethics proscribing such practices do exist, they have little normative force. One reason is that the academics concerned can defend their work to their peer professional community as "rescuing" historical documents for the public benefit. More research into the criminal structure of the trade and its negative social consequences might alter the ambivalent perceptions of peers and open academic involvement to closer scrutiny and more effective professional censure. If academics are abstracted from the antiquities market, it will diminish in profitability, size, and destructiveness.

References

Brodie, N. (2006). Iraq 1990–2004 and the London antiquities market. In Brodie, N., Kersel, M. M., Luke, C., Tubb, K. W. (eds.), *Archaeology, Cultural Heritage, and the Antiquities Trade* (206–226). Gainesville: University Press of Florida.

Brodie, N. (2008a). The Western market in Iraqi antiquities. In Rothfield, L. (ed.), *Antiquities Under Siege. Cultural Heritage Protection After the Iraq War* (63–74). Lanham MD: AltaMira.

Brodie, N. (2008b). The market background to the April 2003 plunder of the Iraq National Museum. In Stone, P. G., Farchakh Bajjaly, J. (eds.), *The Destruction of Cultural Heritage in Iraq* (41–54). Woodbridge: Boydell Press.

Brodie, N. (2009). Consensual relations? Academic involvement in the illegal trade in ancient manuscripts. In Green, P., Mackenzie, S. (eds.), *Criminology and Archaeology: Studies in Looted Antiquities* (Oñati International Series in Law and Society). Oxford: Hart.

Curtis, J. et al. (2008). An assessment of archaeological sites in June 2008: an Iraqi–British project. http://www.britishmuseum.org/PDF/Iraq%20Report_with%20images.pdf. Accessed 6 March 2009.

Eisenberg, J. (2004). The Mesopotamian antiquities trade and the looting of Iraq. *Minerva*, July–August, 41–44.

Emberling, G., Hanson, K. (2008) (eds.), *Catastrophe! The Looting and Destruction of Iraq's Past.* Chicago: University of Chicago.

Gibson, M. (1997). The loss of archaeological context and the illegal trade in Mesopotamian antiquities. *Culture Without Context*, Autumn, issue 1, 6–8.

Gibson, M. (2008). The acquisition of antiquities in Iraq, 19th Century to 2003, legal and illegal. In Stone, P. G., Farchakh Bajjaly, J. (eds.), *The Destruction of Cultural Heritage in Iraq* (31–40). Woodbridge: Boydell Press.

Gottleib, M., Meier, B. (2003). Of 2,000 treasures stolen in Gulf War of 1991, only 12 have been recovered. *New York Times*, 30 April.

Mackenzie, S. (2009). Identifying and preventing opportunities for organized crime in the international antiquities market. In Manacorda, S. (ed.), *Organised Crime in Art and Antiquities*

(41–62). Milan: International Scientific and Professional Advisory Council of the United Nations.

Owen, D. I. (2009). Censoring knowledge: the case for the publication of unprovenanced cuneiform tablets. In Cuno, J. (ed.), *Whose Culture? The Promise of Museums and the Debate Over Antiquities* (125–142). Princeton: Princeton University Press.

Rothfield, L. (2008) (ed.), *Antiquities Under Siege. Cultural Heritage Protection After the Iraq War.* Lanham, MD: AltaMira.

Stone, E. C. (2008). Archaeological site looting: the destruction of cultural heritage in southern Iraq. In Emberling, G., Hanson, K. (eds.), *Catastrophe! The looting and Destruction of Iraq's Past* (65–80). Chicago: University of Chicago Press.

Stone, P. G., Farchakh Bajjaly, J. (2008) (eds.), *The Destruction of Cultural Heritage in Iraq.* Woodbridge: Boydell Press.

Walker, C. B. F. (1981). *Cuneiform Brick Inscriptions.* London: British Museum.

Wright, H. T., Wilkinson, T. J., Gibson, M. (2003). The National Geographic Society's cultural assessment of Iraq. http://news.nationalgeographic.com/news/2003/06/0611_030611_iraqlootingreport.html. Accessed 1 September 2009.

Chapter 8
Looting and Illicit Traffic in Antiquities in Africa

Folarin Shyllon

Introduction

The looting of art and antiquities is an ancient practice. It is perhaps right to claim that in the twentieth century it grew exponentially. It may be claimed also that apart from countries like Italy, Greece, and Turkey, African countries suffered the most from unauthorised excavation of archaeological sites and trade in stolen antiquities in recent decades. In the 1960s and 1970s, the plundering of African cultural property assumed gigantic proportions. Michel Brent, who had devoted several years to cover the pillaging of terracotta statuettes from Mali, regretted that it was precisely "at the moment when the African peoples have begun to acquire their independence, during the 1960s and 1970s, and thus begun to hold their heads high, to hope for the future, that this clandestine traffic of antique objects developed and took on such huge proportions."[1] The relentless looting and illicit trafficking in the plastic arts of Africa continues to cause alarm in various concerned quarters.

In 1971, the Director of the then Antiquities Department of Nigeria warned that "unless the theft of Nigerian collections was arrested, nothing will be left of Nigerian antiquities in about ten years."[2] In 1996, while inaugurating an Inter-Ministerial Committee on the looting of Nigerian antiquities, the Minister of Culture said "we are losing our cultural heritage at such an alarming rate that unless the trend is arrested soon we may have no cultural artefacts to bequeath to our progeny."[3] The situation that gave rise to the comments of the Minister and director of antiquities is not unique to Nigeria. In this chapter, we shall see evidence of the looting of ancient sites and the illegal removal of antiquities and important cultural

[1]Brent (1996).

[2]Nigerian *Daily Times*, September 23, 1971.

[3]Address by the Honour Minister of Culture … at the Occasion of the Inaugural Meeting of the Inter-Ministerial Committee on the Looting of Nigeria's Cultural Property July 23, 1996. Mimeograph.

F. Shyllon (✉)
Olabisi Onabanjo University, Ago-Iwoye, Ogun State, Nigeria
e-mail: fshyllon@yahoo.co.uk

S. Manacorda and D. Chappell (eds.), *Crime in the Art and Antiquities World: Illegal Trafficking in Cultural Property*, DOI 10.1007/978-1-4419-7946-9_8,

objects from Africa. In 1996, in a general overview, Drewal urged that drastic steps be taken to curb the activities of those plundering Africa's past, otherwise Africa will soon have a "landscape barren of cultural heritage."[4] It is submitted, that if during the colonial encounter military force was used to take over land and resources of the people in the colonies, and if the missionaries destroyed and pillaged because their existence hindered the liberation of the African mind from demons, today the offer of hard currency by western collectors to thieves of art works encourages the plundering of African countries.

Country Surveys

By all accounts African countries are the most vulnerable to illegal activities in antiquities and cultural objects. Thus, the International Council of Museums (ICOM) series *One Hundred Missing Objects* started with *Looting in Africa* in 1994 to be followed by *Looting in America*, *Looting in Angkor*, and *Looting in Europe*. Similarly, ICOM's Red List began to address a specific African problem. From October 22 to 24, 1997 a group of African museums directors met with European and American professionals in Amsterdam to discuss ways and means of protecting Africa's cultural heritage. It is sufficient for our purpose here to note that the conference recommended the recognition of a periodically revised "Red List" of categories of objects that are presently particularly vulnerable to looting. Thus, the *Red List of African Cultural Objects at Risk* was inaugurated. It was followed subsequently by a *Red List of Latin-American Cultural Objects at Risk*, *Emergency Red List of Iraqi Antiquities at Risk*, and *Red List of Afghanistan Antiquities at Risk.*

Among African countries, Egypt is first in archaeological riches followed perhaps by Nigeria and Mali. It is proper therefore to examine the state of affairs in these countries.

Egypt

Over the centuries, Egypt has suffered grievously from the illegal antiquities trade and illicit excavation. In April 2002, one of the largest hauls of illicit antiquities ever found was impounded at Heathrow Airport, London. Egypt recovered 56,000 out of a total of 113,000 objects held at Heathrow. In order to combat the trade in illicit antiquities, aid the recovery of stolen artefacts and increase the protection of archaeological sites, Egypt had in 1983 enacted a Law on the Protection of Antiquities. Law 117 as it is often called, created, and declared state ownership of all antiquities. The Supreme Council of Antiquities (SCA) is the branch of the Egyptian Ministry of Culture responsible for enforcing Law 117. Zahi Hawass is the current Secretary General of SCA.

---

[4]Drewal (1996).

customs (the ivory headboard) and US Customs (the headless statue). The most recent recovery of an item stolen from the galleries that I can make public is that of the headless inscribed limestone statue from Lagash, from approximately 2450 BC. Of note is that before it was seized by US customs in 2006, it had traveled the time-tested classic route from Baghdad to Damascus to Beirut to Geneva.

With regard to the other two sets of thefts, the good news is that virtually all of the 3,138 pieces known to have been stolen from the aboveground storage rooms have been recovered through either the amnesty program or seizures – a startling testament to the courage and integrity of the Iraqi people. The bad news is that our efforts to recover antiquities stolen from the basement have proven less successful: of the 10,686 objects stolen from underground, fewer than 3,000 have been recovered worldwide. Part of the problem is that the entire haul from the basement could fit in one backpack.

Impressively, neighboring countries began making substantial recoveries of stolen Iraqi antiquities almost immediately after the looting – recoveries that continue to this day. Indeed, as of December 2008, eight countries have returned more than 5,200 stolen antiquities to Iraq.[23] Although when made, most authorities and media outlets invariably report all of these seized items as having come from the Iraq Museum – doubtless because of some perceived higher press value – in fact, most items that are claimed by recovering officials to have been stolen from the Iraq Museum were in fact stolen from archaeological sites.

Another 62,000 pieces that had been removed from the museum before 2003 were found in other locations in Iraq in 2003, including 8,366 display-case items found in a top-secret vault within the museum that a select group of museum staff had referred to as "the secret place," 39,453 ancient manuscripts found in a bomb shelter in Western Baghdad, 6,744 pieces from Iraq's royal family collection in the Central Bank's old building, and 7,360 exquisite ivories and pieces of jewelry from the royal tombs of Ur and Nimrud in the Central Bank's new building.[24]

Sadly, though, almost half of the stolen pieces – many of them truly priceless – are still missing. These include the nine Sumerian, Akkadian, and Babylonian cuneiform bricks, as well as a Babylonian boundary stone and five heads from Hatra: a copper head of winged victory, a stone head of a female deity, and marble heads of

[23] Jordan (2,450 items, see Mcelroy 2008); United States (1,046 items); Italy (833 items, see Reuters 2008 and Bogdanos 2005b); Syria (701 items, see Associated Press 2008); Dubai (100 items, see McClenaghan 2008); Lebanon (57 items, see Agence France-Presse 2008); Kuwait (38 items); and Saudi Arabia (18 items). Shockingly, no antiquities have been seized (or, to be more precise, acknowledged to have been seized) by the two border nations of Turkey and Iran. Nor have we ever been able to verify any seizures by French or Swiss authorities – despite reports of such seizures in 2005.

[24] From 1922 to 1934, Sir Leonard Woolley excavated approximately 1,850 graves near the Sumerian city of Ur, describing 16 of them (ca. 2600–2500) as "royal tombs" based on their wealth, architecture, and evidence of ritual, to include human sacrifice. Among the most spectacular was the so-called Great Death pit, containing 6 male and 68 female attendants. The treasure of Nimrud is a spectacular collection of more than 1,000 pieces of gold jewelry and precious stones from the eighth and ninth centuries BC that had been discovered between 1988 and 1990 by Iraqi archaeologist Muzahim Hussein Mahmud during his excavation of four royal tombs, and is considered by many to be one of the greatest archaeological finds of the last century. Both treasures had been removed from the museum by the Hussein regime in August of 1990 and not been seen publically since then.

Apollo, Poseidon, and Eros.[25] The list of missing pieces also includes the one that breaks my heart. It is the piece that is on the cover of *Thieves of Baghdad*: the Lioness attacking a Nubian Boy, an extraordinary eighth century BC chryselephantine ivory plaque inlaid with lapis and carnelian and overlaid with gold (see Fig. 9.1).

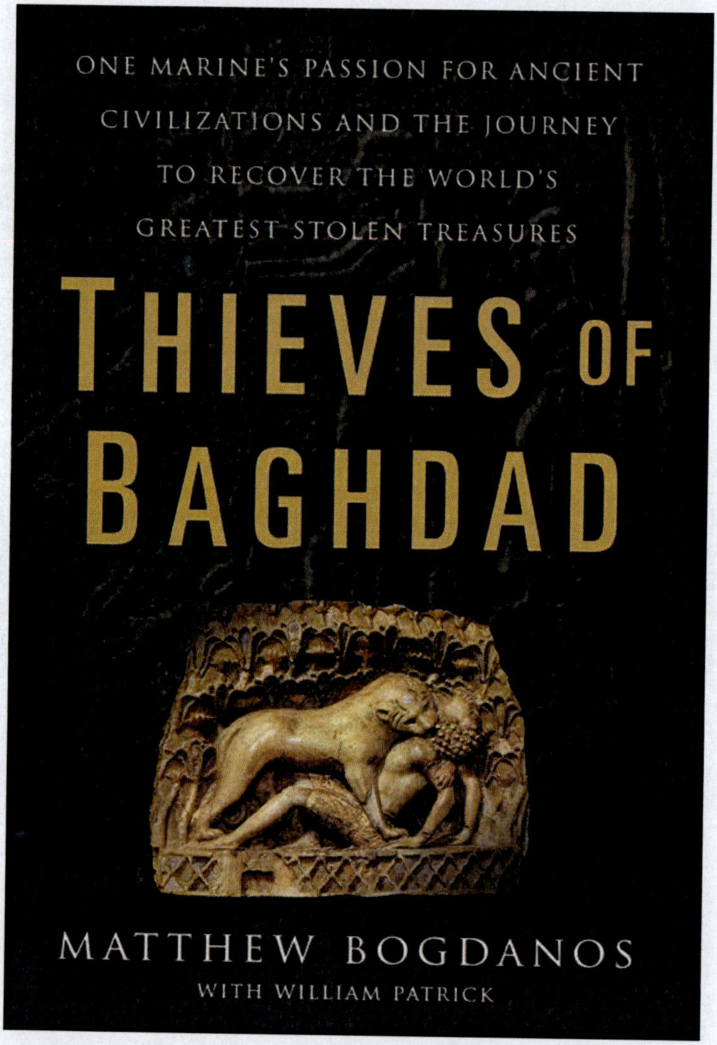

Fig. 9.1 The figure of a Lioness Attacking a Nubian Boy is shown on the cover of the hardcover edition of the book *Thieves of Baghdad* and one of the prominent plates of the soft cover edition. Colonel Bogdanos considers it the single most exquisite and historically significant piece that is still missing

[25]The female deity was the only statue whose head the thieves cut off. Discovered in a Hatrene temple dedicated to the worship of Hercules, it may, therefore, represent his wife (Basmachi 1975–1976: 309). The three heads of Poseidon, Apollo, and Eros were exquisite Roman copies of ca. A.D. 160 after Greek originals of the fourth century BC.

years, the plundering of archaeological sites affected the regions, where budding archaeology had brought terracotta statuettes into the lime light. Plundering occurred primarily in the Inland Niger Delta, and in the region of Djenne in particular where the first statue was discovered in 1941. Later, plundering affected the south of Mali, following the discovery of the statues known as Bankoni style on the commercial markets. The illegal excavation escalated partly due to subsistence digging by impoverished locals, and partly due to increasing demand by museums, galleries, and private collectors in Europe and America for ancient Malian arts. Whole villages and encampments of immigrant workers are mobilised for the open systematic excavation of very large sites, paid for and organised by dealers in the antiquarian trade.

Many actors are involved in the illicit market in Malian antiquities. At the top are local farmers, individual plunderers, or a network of pillagers organised by antique dealers or operating on their own. At the intermediary level are the antique dealers. They are located in the important suburbs at Bamako, at Mopti and at Djenne. These dealers connect with European and American markets through sales galleries, collectors, and museums to effect the distribution of the antiquities. Besides moving the items by air routes, a significant portion of the objects is illicitly exported by road or by rail to Cote d'Ivoire and Senegal. These two neighbouring countries of Mali have sales galleries operated by internationally connected Lebanese dealers.[11]

Mali has passed several laws to combat the plague of plundering of her cultural heritage. Four measures can be listed.

1. Law No 85-40 of 1985 relating to the protection and the promotion of national cultural heritage.
2. Decree No. 275 of 1985 regulating archaeological excavations.
3. Law No. 86-61 of 1986 relating to the profession of the traders in cultural possessions.
4. Decree No. 999 of 1986 relating to the commercialisation of cultural possessions.

At the International level, Mali in 1993 entered into a bilateral agreement with the USA to ban the import into the USA of broadly inclusive classes of Malian antiquities. The USA–Mali bilateral agreement covers a broad spectrum of archaeological materials from the Middle Niger and Dogon country. This import ban goes far beyond previous limited region or class of artefacts specific agreements with Bolivia, El Salvador Guatemala, and Peru. Mali is the first and so far the only African nation to have entered into this very useful import control agreement.

Tackling the Problems

The international market in illicitly acquired art and archaeological treasures is a huge business now running into billions of dollars. Many commentators have remarked on the similarity between the art trade and the hard drug trade. Coggins observes that the

[11] Sidibe (1996).

art market requires concealment at every level. She adds that "it operates more like the clandestine narcotics traffic".[12] McIntosh notes that the international structure of the illicit art trade and the illicit drug trade are remarkably similar.[13] While Gimbrere concludes that the trade in cultural property is the most important illegal trade after the drug trade, and moreover, "often carried out by the same people".[14] Regrettably, the stigma that attaches to dealers in hard drugs does not attach to traffickers in stolen antiquities and illegally excavated cultural property for which there are ready buyers. In Africa, the clandestine activities of the local agents are linked by a long international chain whose anchor is in Europe and North America. Tackling the activities of all involved in this chain should be a matter of high priority.

At the 1997 Amsterdam Conference on the Protection of African Cultural Heritage already alluded to, some Western experts demanded that Africa should first put her house in order. African countries must indeed do so. Let us first, however, note that even the richest countries, with state-of-the-art security, are seeing major thefts from the public museums and private collections as well as unauthorised digging at protected locations, doing irreparable damage to their archaeological sites. Nonetheless, there is scope for concerted efforts by African states. They should examine their legislations on the protection and preservation of cultural property and make sure they are adequate to deal with the current emergency. After such reviews, the laws should be upgraded in accordance with all international instruments for the protection of cultural property. In this connection, it is important to bear in mind that certain basic provisions are indispensable for the successful protection of Africa's antiquities and archaeological sites. It would be necessary to state that all archaeological objects belong to the state. It would also be expedient to prohibit the export of cultural objects unless the state's licence is given. The next stage should be the harmonisation of laws (through the African Union), as is being done in the EU, for example. There would be a need to establish joint border patrols. The "Red List" approved at the Amsterdam conference, for example, lists, Burkina Faso, Chad, Cameroon, Cote d'Ivoire, Ghana, Mali, Niger, and Nigeria. These countries, when linked in a chain, are neighbours. The feasibility and productivity of joint patrols is surely obvious. There is no reason why the respective police, customs, and immigration departments cannot have special units linked together under multilateral, mutually beneficial agreements. National budgets should provide for the expansion of preventive activities so that the cultural heritage can be passed on to future generations.

Earlier, it was urged that in our present predicament it is necessary to declare and create state ownership of all antiquities. Such a pivotal provision has been of immense help to Egypt whose Law 117 prohibits private ownership, possession, or trade in antiquities, and imposes sanctions for violations, including prison terms. In the celebrated Frederick Schultz case,[15] when asked who owns all recently discovered

---

[12]Coggins (1995).

[13]McIntosh (1996).

[14]Gimbrere (1995).

[15]*United States v. Schultz*, 178 F. Supp. 2d 445 (S.D.N.Y. 2002).

antiquities, one of the witnesses, Gaballa Ali Gaballa, then Secretary General of Egypt's Supreme Council of Antiquities, responded "the Egyptian government, of course", and said that a finder of an Egyptian antiquity could never legally keep it. The Federal District Court for the Southern District of New York held that a foreign law declaring state ownership of antiquities can make an object "stolen" for the purposes of the US law[16] – even if the object was not "stolen" in the traditional sense. The case is a first for New York in basing a criminal conviction on a foreign "patrimony" law claiming state ownership of antiquities. Accordingly, the court ordered the return to Egypt of an antiquity stolen from Saqqara, and the object was duly returned. On appeal, the US Court of Appeals for the Second Circuit affirming the decision concluded that Egyptian law is "clear and unambiguous" and that the objects Schultz received "were owned by the Egyptian government".[17]

It has long been argued by the art trade and many collectors that "nationalisation laws" are somehow not legal, and that the courts in the West, particularly those in the two main market countries, the USA and the UK should disregard them. The Schultz case and the conviction of Tokeley-Parry[18] appear to reject that thinking. The trial judge in the Schultz case opined that "Law 117 on its face vests with the state most, and perhaps all, the rights ordinarily associated with ownership of property, including title, possession, and right to transfer. This, on its face, is far more than a licencing scheme or export regulation". The judge went on to say : "In effectuating this policy, why should it make any difference that a foreign nation, in order to safeguard its precious cultural heritage, has chosen to assume ownership of those objects in its domain that have historical or archaeological importance, rather than leaving them in private hands". The Crown Court in London in the Tokeley-Parry case went further, and expressed its understanding of the scale of the problem for loser countries, and in sentencing Tokeley-Parry, the court stated that there had to be a deterrent factor in the length of sentence for this type of crime. The comments of the court and the length of sentence were later endorsed by the Court of Appeal.[19]

Another way of stemming the illicit trade in antiquities has been suggested to operate a licit trade. A licit trade could lead to African countries no longer losing valuable art objects without monetary compensation for them. As Gimbrere has pointed out, a normal international traffic of objects which are not of outstanding cultural importance to a particular culture is desirable. This has been going on for centuries.[20] A licit international trade will only be meaningful to Africans if it reverses the present derisory sums trickling into the local economy.

[16]National Stolen Property Act. 18 U.S.C. section, 18 U.S.C. section 2314.

[17]Frederick Schultz, the former President of the National Association of Dealers in Ancient, Oriental and Primitive Art, was jailed for 33 months for receiving stolen Egyptian antiquities.

[18]Jonathan Tokeley-Parry by his own admission had smuggled some 2,000 antiquities out of Egypt. He was found guilty at the Crown Court in England of dishonestly handling antiquities and another count of making a false statement to procure a passport. He was sent to jail for 6 years Watson (2002).

[19]Ellis (2002).

[20]Gimbrere (1995).

A Plea

The illicit traffic in African antiquities is a crime against a continent that has lost so much in the colonial period. The illicit traffic in African antiquities is as much a menace to her well-being as the illicit trade in drugs. Everything is done to combat the illicit drug trade, it is urged that the same intolerance and firmness should be extended to the fight against looting and illicit trade in antiquities. It is in this light that the convictions of Jonathan Tokeley-Parry and Frederick Schultz are most welcome.

References

Brent, M. (1996). A View Inside the Illicit Trade in African Antiquities. In *Plundering Africa's Past*, eds. Schmidt, P.R. and McIntosh, R.J., 63–78. Bloomington and Indianapolis: Indiana University Press.

Coggins, C.C. (1995). A Licit International Traffic in Ancient Art: Let There Be Light. *International Journal of Cultural Property*, 4, 61–79.

Drewal, H.J. (1996). Past as Prologues. In *Plundering Africa's Past*, eds. Schmidt, P.R. and McIntosh, R.J., 110–124. Bloomington and Indianapolis: Indiana University Press.

Ellis, R. (2002). "The Fred Schultz Case – An Example of International Cooperation Between Police, Archaeologists and Legal Experts." Paper presented at International Expert Meeting on the Return of Cultural Property and the Fight Against Its Illicit Trafficking, Korean National Commission for UNESCO and Cultural Properties Administration of the Republic of Korea, 30 September–3 October, pp. 161-165.

Fagg, W. (1963). *Nigerian Images*. London: Lund Humphries.

Gimbrere, S. (1995). Illicit Traffic in Cultural Property and National and International Law. In *Illicit Traffic in Cultural Property: Museums Against Pillage*, ed. Leyten, H. Amsterdam: Royal Tropical Institute.

McIntosh, R.J. (1996). Just Say Shame: Excising the Rot of Cultural Genocide. In *Plundering Africa's Past*, eds. Schmidt, P.R. and McIntosh, R.J., 45–62. Bloomington and Indianapolis: Indiana University Press.

Shyllon, F. (1998). One Hundred Years of Looting of Nigerian Art Treasures 1897–1996. *Art Antiquity and Law*, 3(3), 253–266.

Shyllon, F. (2003). Negotiation for the Return of Nok Sculptures from France to Nigeria: An Unrighteous Conclusion. *Art Antiquity and Law*, 8(2), 133–148.

Sidibe, S. (1996). The Fight Against the Plundering of Malian Cultural Heritage and Illicit Exportation: National Efforts and International Cooperation. In *Plundering Africa's Past*, eds. Schmidt, P.R. and McIntosh, R.J., 79–86. Bloomington and Indianapolis: Indiana University Press.

Watson, P. (2002). *The Investigation of Frederick Schultz. Culture without Context.* (10) Cambridge: McDonald Institute for Archaeological Research.

Chapter 9
Thieves of Baghdad: The Global Traffic in Stolen Iraqi Antiquities*

Mathew Bogdanos

Introduction

As the head of the investigation into one of the greatest art crimes in recent memory – the looting of the Iraq Museum in 2003 – I have spent more than 6 years attempting to recover and return to the Iraqi people their priceless heritage (Bogdanos 2005a, b). I have spent a significant amount of that time, however, attempting to correct the almost universal misconceptions about what happened at the museum in those fateful days in April 2003, to increase awareness of the continuing cultural catastrophe that is represented by the illegal trade in stolen antiquities, and to highlight the need for the concerted and cooperative efforts of the international community to preserve, protect, and recover the shared cultural heritage of all humanity.

Indeed, in 150 cities in 18 countries – in venues ranging from universities, museums, and governmental organizations to law-enforcement agencies, Interpol (the International Criminal Police Organization) and both houses of the British Parliament – I have urged a more active role for governments, international organizations, cultural organizations and foundations, and the art community.

I do so, knowing that most governments have their hands full combating terrorism, with few resources left to spare for tracking down stolen artifacts; that many

---

*Parts of the following chapter are adapted from *Thieves of Baghdad: One Marine's Passion to Recover the World's Greatest Stolen Treasures* (Bloomsbury 2005). Copyright © 2005 by Matthew Bogdanos. Reprinted by permission of Bloomsbury USA.

Colonel Bogdanos has been an assistant district attorney in New York City since 1988. A colonel in the US Marine Corps Reserves, middleweight boxer, author, and native New Yorker, he holds advanced degrees in law, classics, and military strategy. Recalled to active duty after September 11, 2001, he received a Bronze Star for counterterrorist operations in Afghanistan, served multiple tours in Iraq and the Horn of Africa, and received a 2005 National Humanities Medal for his work recovering Iraq's treasures, before deploying again to Afghanistan in 2009. He has returned to the DA's Office and continues the hunt for stolen antiquities. His royalties from his book, *Thieves of Baghdad*, are donated to the Iraq Museum.

M. Bogdanos (✉)
Colonel, US Marine Corps, New York, NY, USA
e-mail: mbogdanos@aol.com

S. Manacorda and D. Chappell (eds.), *Crime in the Art and Antiquities World: Illegal Trafficking in Cultural Property*, DOI 10.1007/978-1-4419-7946-9_9,

international organizations are content to issue proclamations, preferring to hit the conference center rather than the streets; and that many cultural organizations and foundations are equally content to issue a call for papers rather than a call to action. As for the art community, I have learnt that some members wash their hands of unpleasant realities and argue that, while technically illegal, the market in purloined antiquities is benign – victimless – as long as it brings the art to those who can properly protect it and appreciate it (namely, themselves).

All the while, the situation in Iraq after 2003 deteriorated dramatically, seemingly descending into chaos and causing most of the international community and many in the USA to call for drastic, if not complete, withdrawal of forces from Iraq. Even now – and despite the fact that most knowledgeable (read "nonpolitical") participants and observers have recognized significant advances in Iraq since the onset of the 2008 surge in US combat forces – a majority of the electorate in the USA and elsewhere seems increasingly reluctant to risk their own blood to save Iraqi lives. So it is a pretty tough sell to ask people to care about a bunch of old rocks with funny writing. Finding the political will to divert resources to save cultural artifacts, no matter how precious, seems like cutting funding for police and fire in order to expand the public library. There might be a case for it, but when? After all, looting has always been a cottage industry in Iraq, the region that gave birth not just to agriculture, cities, the wheel, and pottery, but to war and conquest as well.

The argument for protecting artifacts takes on added strength when we recognize that Iraq has been so bloody, not just because of the failure to provide sufficient security to overcome the long-festering tribal and religious animosities, but also, I submit, because of the continuing failure to appreciate the importance Iraqis place on the preservation of their history. This failure to protect a rich heritage going back to the dawn of civilization has convinced many in Iraq and the Middle East that we in the West do not care about any culture other than our own. Even today, more than 6 years after the initial looting, and despite having recovered more than half the antiquities stolen from the museum, we are hard-pressed to keep pace with the artifacts that are being looted from archaeological sites every day.

Before I address the current state of antiquities trafficking throughout the world, however, it is necessary to discuss first the tragedy of the looting of the Iraq Museum in 2003.

The Looting of the Iraq Museum

As word of the Iraq Museum's fate spread like wildfire throughout the world, US forces took a lot of heat. The "why didn't you prevent the looting?" – question emerged right from the start, during the period that British columnist David Aaronovitch summed up with "You cannot say anything too bad about the Yanks and not be believed" (2003).[1] So why had the USA not "done more" to protect the

[1]His full quote was more colorful: "And the only problem with reports that the museum was 'looted under the very noses of the Yanks, or by the Yanks themselves' is that it's nonsense. It isn't true. It's made up. It's bollocks" (Aaronovitch 2003).

museum? After hundreds of eyewitness interviews, and countless hours (and weeks) of forensic examinations of the entire museum compound – inside and out – here is what I learnt in 2003 about what actually occurred at the museum, and what US forces could and should have done.

Two months before the war began, in January 2003, a group of scholars, museum directors, and antiquities dealers met with Pentagon officials to discuss their fears about the threat to the museum's collection. McGuire Gibson of the University of Chicago's Oriental Institute went back twice more, and he and his colleagues continued to barrage defense department officials with e-mail reminders. Gibson and his colleagues were heard – but only partly. The Pentagon ordered the Iraq Museum placed on the coalition's no-strike list – in fact, it was to become #3 on that list. But the civilian leadership of the defense department at the Pentagon failed to disseminate those warnings to the military personnel who were planning for what became known as Operation Iraqi Freedom. Nor were the planners directed to protect the museum. Moreover, the planners themselves had no idea of the extent to which the average Iraqi viewed the museum, not as housing the priceless cultural heritage of their country, but as "Saddam's gift shop" – the phrase I heard used most often by neighborhood residents. As a result, planners did not understand that many Iraqis would equate stealing from the museum with stealing from Saddam Hussein and not with stealing from their own heritage. Even museum officials, who brought in sandbags and foam-rubber padding against possible bomb damage, were caught by surprise. The extraordinary Donny George Youkhanna, then the museum's Director of Antiquities and Research, told the *Wall Street Journal*, "We thought there would be some sort of bombing at the museum. We never thought it could be looted" (Trofimov 2003).[2]

Turning to the failure of coalition forces to secure the museum, it is clear that the law of armed conflict holds that cultural property should be protected against any act of hostility.[3] But the same international agreements that protect cultural property *absolutely prohibit* the military use of cultural sites, specifying that such sites lose their protections when so used. In clear violation of those provisions, the Iraqi Army had turned the museum and the surrounding 11-acre compound into a fortress and a very well-designed military position. Hussein's elite Special Republican Guard was stationed across the street. A firing position at the Children's Museum was aimed toward a traffic circle, offering an unobstructed field of fire on the high-speed avenue of approach that ran in front of the compound. That street,

---

[2]Ahmed Kamel, the museum's deputy director and head of the museum's cuneiform section, shared his surprise, remarking that "we didn't think anybody would come here and steal things because it has never happened before" (Harris 2004).

[3]See the "Protocol Additional to the Geneva Conventions" of August 12, 1949 (Protocol I), June 8, 1977; "Protocol Additional to the Geneva Conventions" of August 12, 1949 (Protocol II), June 8, 1977; "Convention for the Protection of Cultural Property in the Event of Armed Conflict," The Hague, May 14, 1954; "Protocol for the Protection of Cultural Property in the Event of Armed Conflict" (Protocol I), The Hague, May 14, 1954; "Second Protocol to the Hague Convention of 1954 for the Protection of Cultural Property in the Event of Armed Conflict" (Protocol II), The Hague, March 26, 1999.

running between the museum and the Special Republican Guard facility, led to the strategically important al-Ahrar Bridge across the Tigris, 900 m away. A sniper's position in one of the aboveground storage rooms provided a perfect flanking shot on any US forces moving through the marketplace to reinforce any battle in front of the museum. The sniper's window also overlooked the 10-ft. wall that protected soldiers running from the battle position in the back to the battle positions in the front courtyard. Each of those fighting holes, equipped with dirt ramparts and aiming sticks (used for machine gun positions), provided interlocking fire. All of this was run from the makeshift command post that had been set up in the back of the 11-acre museum compound.

On the morning of April 8, armed Iraqi soldiers took up their previously prepared firing positions in the museum compound. The museum staff, including all museum guards, had already left, decamping when US forces hit the outskirts of the city on April 5. The only exceptions were Jaber Ibrahim al-Tikriti (the Chairman of Iraq's State Board of Antiquities); Donny George; a driver; and an elderly archaeologist who lived in the rear of the museum compound. Bravely, they had planned to stay throughout the invasion, but decided to leave when they realized the level of violence that was imminent.

The violence in question was, in fact, part of a campaign to attack Baghdad from the inside out. With all the Iraqi defenses facing the perimeter, US Army General Tommy Franks opted for "thunder runs" into the center of the city with tanks and mechanized infantry. Crumbling from the inside out Baghdad fell in days instead of months. One of these "thunder runs" ran directly in front of the museum. And the intensity of fighting in the vicinity of the museum and the Special Republican Guard compound opposite it was directly proportional to this area's strategic importance.

At approximately 11:00 a.m. on April 8, before the first of those "thunder runs" and after ensuring that all of the doors to the museum and the storage rooms were locked, the four museum staffers left through the rear exit, locking it behind them. They then crossed the Tigris into eastern Baghdad, hoping to return later the same day. As they left, the nearest US forces were about 1,500 m west of the museum, receiving heavy mortar fire as they proceeded in the direction of the museum. When Donny George and his colleagues from the museum tried to come back several hours later, heavy fighting pinned them down on the other side of the river.

On April 9, a tank company from Task Force 1-64, the only US unit in that part of Baghdad, moved to an intersection about 500 m west and slightly south of the museum. Their orders were to keep that crossroads open as a lifeline to support US forces engaged in combat in the northern part of the city. Throughout that day, they took fire from the Children's Museum, the main building, the library, and the building to the rear of the museum that had previously been used as a police station. The tank company commander on the scene, US Army Captain Jason Conroy, reported that approximately 100–150 enemy fighters were within the museum compound firing on US forces. Some of these fighters were dressed in Special Republican Guard uniforms and some in civilian clothes. They were carrying RPGs (Soviet-designed, Iraqi-Army-issued rocket-propelled grenades)[4] and AK-47s.[5]

Later, many neighborhood residents told renowned combat journalist Roger Atwood that "the Americans had come under attack from inside the museum grounds and that fighting in the area was heavy" (2003).[6] The neighborhood residents told me the same story, but they were merely confirming what the museum grounds and its countless spent shell casings and dozens of RPGs had already told me: this was a fiercely contested battleground. Indeed, the fighting was so heavy that for 48 h, between April 8 and 10, some US soldiers in Task Force 1-64's C Company never left the inside of their tanks.

According to several accounts from nearby residents, it was during this time – on April 9 – that two Iraqi Army vehicles drove up to the back of the museum (near where the impromptu command post had been) and spent several hours loading boxes from the museum onto the vehicles before they left (Al-Radi 2009). On the following day, April 10, Second Lieutenant Erik Balascik's platoon received word of looting "in the area of the museum and the hospital." They passed this information up to the Task Force 1-64 commander, Lieutenant Colonel Eric Schwartz, who ordered them to move closer to investigate. As soon as they did so, they began receiving intense fire from the compound. This forced one of the tanks to fire a single round in return from its 120 mm main gun, which took out the RPG position, put a hole in the Children's Museum, captured the media's attention, and inflamed critics throughout the world.[7]

Because the Iraqi army had fortified this cultural site and people were firing from it, any forces would have been justified under international law in taking steps necessary to eliminate the threat, to include shooting back with ground – and air-based supporting fire – in which case there would have been nothing left of the museum either to save or to loot. Instead of conducting such an assault to "save"

[4]An RPG, or Raketniy Protivotankoviy Granatomet, is a shoulder-fired weapon, using an 85-mm armor-piercing shaped warhead capable of penetrating up to 35 cm of armor. The ubiquitous RPG-7 weighs 8.5 kg with its warhead and is devastatingly effective up to 500 m against a stationary target and 300 m against a moving target. An RPG-7 can penetrate the US Army's Bradley armored personnel carrier, and although it cannot penetrate the heavily armored portions of the US Army's main battle tank, the M1A1 Abrams, there are areas of the tank that are vulnerable.

[5]An AK-47, or Automat Kalashnikova Model 1947, is an assault rifle capable of firing up to 600 rounds per minute in its automatic fire mode. Its 7.62-by-39-mm bullet can penetrate US body armor and is lethal to 300 m.

[6]For this well-researched account, Roger Atwood interviewed approximately 30 neighborhood residents in addition to museum staff.

[7]When we had arrived 2 weeks earlier, and I had seen the infamous hole in the façade of the Children's Museum, I was furious and began to understand the world-wide condemnation. Then I saw the evidence. The tank gunner had fired only after someone had fired an RPG, rocket-propelled grenade, at him from that building. On the roof, we found a stash of RPGs and, inside, blood splatter whose pattern suggested that at least two shooters had been on the third floor when the round hit its mark(s).

the museum, the moment that Schwartz – a former high school teacher – was informed of the situation, he made the militarily wrong but culturally brilliant decision to pull those tanks back from the museum. This was the only way to avoid the Hobson's choice between endangering his men and destroying the institution.

Because of that fire, and because, from their position to the west, the Children's Museum blocked their view into the main compound, US forces never advanced close enough to determine what was actually going on within the compound, let alone within the galleries and the storage areas of the museum itself.

One of the residents we interviewed said that the looters – estimated by some witnesses to number between three or four hundred at their height – first appeared at the museum on the evening of April 10, entering through the back of the compound. If this single source was accurate, his account strongly suggests that the original fighters had left the museum by that date – April 10. There was, however, still intense fighting around the museum on the morning of April 11. It was on that day, at the intersection directly in front of the museum compound, that a US tank company destroyed an Iraqi Army truck and a Soviet-built armored fighting vehicle. This fighting in the front of the compound on the 11th prevented US forces from either approaching the museum or determining that enemy forces no longer occupied the museum itself. The 11th was, however, the last day that fighting was reported near the museum.

On the afternoon of April 12, the museum staff came back, courageously chasing looters from the museum, a moment famously captured by a German film crew. The soldiers had already left – but when? It is entirely possible, especially considering all the Iraqi Army uniforms we found lying around the compound, that some of the looters carrying out antiquities had been in uniform and carrying AK-47s only hours – or even minutes – earlier. We simply do not know. Regardless of when this retreat took place, however, it cannot be overstated how difficult it was for US forces on the ground to have known when the last fighter left, and whether it was safe to enter without a battle that would destroy the museum. I rarely knew what was happening 100 m away – let alone on the other side of an 11-acre compound.

Some critics have contended that if journalists were able to get into the museum on April 12, military forces should have been able to do the same on that day or even on April 11. With rare exceptions, however, journalists are not shot at simply because of who they are. Putting on a military uniform makes anyone a lawful target. Journalists, protected – officially at least – by their "noncombatant" status, are generally able to move more freely on the battlefield in order to report on the conflict. This is not to suggest that journalists are not vulnerable to random fire, or that being a combat journalist does not take guts, or that journalists are never targeted illegally. Rather, it is to point out that neither journalists nor uniformed combatants should be judged by the distinct restrictions placed on, or the distinct freedoms enjoyed by, the other.

The only way uniformed military could have entered a compound the size of the museum's was as part of a properly planned assault complete with supporting arms – tanks, mortars, and crew-served weapons – or by a "reconnaissance in force." This means having troops advance without supporting arms in the hope that they do not get shot. If no one shoots at them, it suggests that the buildings are clear. Either that or it is an ambush – with the risk that the football-field-sized open area between the compound wall and the buildings would become a killing ground.

Regardless of when the Iraqi fighters left the compound, however, it is clear that by April 12, the fighting in Baghdad had subsided, and the damage was done. Once the staff was back on-site to guard the museum, there was no more looting. On the afternoon of the 12th and then again on the 13th, with the compound no longer a battlefield, Donny George and others approached Task Force 1-64, the Army tank unit, and asked for help. But that unit did not move to the museum. So why did US forces not just move a tank closer to the museum at that point? All it would have required, the Monday morning field marshals said, was a single tank.[8]

First, you cannot just go hail a tank the way you hail a taxi. Unless you are requesting a suicide mission, you need a tank platoon. What those who have never been in combat do not understand is that a stationary tank is a death trap. While intimidating to look at, tanks are far from invulnerable – one well-placed round from an antitank weapon and you would need to use dog tags to identify the charred remains of the four men inside. The only way a tank can survive in combat, especially urban combat, is by virtue of speed and maneuverability, and by the firepower provided by other tanks. You have to have, at the least, tanks in pairs. You also need a squad of infantry alongside them because tanks have blind spots. But mostly, once you draw fire, you have to be able to return fire until you have eliminated the threat – demolishing whatever cover the enemy might be using – if that is what it takes to save the lives of those in your charge.

So it is not as simple as sending in a tank. Then, why not send in some ground troops instead? Committing "just" ground troops would have been criminally irresponsible on the part of the commander, whose obligation is to protect the lives of the men under his command. A proper military assault would have required supporting arms. And this once again brings us back to the specter of the museum reduced to rubble.[9]

---

[8]"All it would have taken was a tank parked at the gate," said Jane Waldbaum, president of the American Institute of Archaeology, in *USA Today*, April 14, 2003.

[9]In a similar vein, some critics complained about how coalition forces protected the oil ministry, but not the museum. What those critics failed to take into account is that to "secure" a building in combat, you usually have to physically occupy it, at least temporarily. If the building is fortified, that means a battle. In this comparison, there are three facts that such critics blithely ignore. First, the "securing" of the oil ministry began with US air strikes on April 9. It was a lawful target, and coalition forces dropped a bomb on it. No one was going to bomb the museum. Second, the oil ministry did not contain soldiers – it had not been turned into a fortress that housed armed combatants. The museum was filled with Republican Guards shooting at Americans with automatic weapons and tank-killer rocket-propelled grenades. Finally, the oil ministry is just one building – the coalition "secured" it in less than an hour. The museum was an 11-acre complex of interconnecting and overlapping buildings and courtyards. Securing it would have required a serious firefight that would likely have reduced the place to expensive rubble. Comparing the museum with the oil ministry, then, is more politics-based than fact-based.

Moreover, if the mere presence of uniformed military had not dispersed the crowd, what should these ground troops then have done – shoot the looters? Perhaps the critics would like to have been there with an M16, mowing down the local residents swarming through the museum. But people who know the law of war know that deadly force can only be used in response to a hostile act or a demonstration of hostile intent. Shooting unarmed looters in civilian clothes who were not presenting a risk to human life would have been a violation of the law of armed conflict and prosecutable for murder under Article 118 of the Uniform Code of Military Justice.[10]

Well, could not they have just fired some itsy-bitsy warning shots? Here, we see the influence of movies on assumptions about what is possible in a law-enforcement or military engagement. A warning shot only works if you are a member of the Screen Actors Guild. In real life, firing a weapon merely escalates the situation, usually causing unarmed participants to arm themselves, which once again means drawing return fire. Moreover, the bullets fired from the muzzle of a weapon – be they "warning shots" or shots aimed at center mass – do not just disappear into the ether. Eventually, they come back to earth and hit something – often with fatal effect – which happens all the time when revelers fire celebratory shots into the air during holidays and weddings.[11] For this reason, among others, the rules of engagement in effect in 2003 specifically instructed soldiers that if they must fire, they must "fire only aimed shots. NO WARNING SHOTS" (capitals in original).[12] Doubtless in recognition of the deteriorating security situation, by 2005, the rules had changed to permit warning shots to be fired as a last resort.[13]

---

[10] Although the use of nonlethal measures such as tear gas might have satisfied legal standards, several factors would have argued against their employment. First, even "nonlethal" measures sometimes result in death, particularly among the elderly and children. Second, there is the question of effectiveness. Nonlethal measures would have dispersed the looters (and have caused them to drop larger items). But most of the looted items were the smaller excavation-site pieces, and the use of tear gas, for example, would not necessarily have caused the looters to empty their pockets or drop their bags as they ran away. Finally, while it is easy to judge these events with the benefit of hindsight, any argument that US military should have used force, nonlethal or otherwise, to disperse a crowd at the museum, must first consider the extraordinarily negative reaction it would have been expected to cause among a people that in April 2003 believed that such governmental sponsored violence had ended with the fall of the Hussein regime.

[11] Both of the standard-issue rifles for US forces, the full-size M16A2 as well as the smaller M4 carbine, fire a NATO bullet that measures 5.56 mm in diameter and 45 mm in length, weighs 3.95 g, and leaves the muzzle at a velocity of 905.5 (M4) or 974.1 (M16A2) m per second. The bullets return to the ground at lethal terminal velocity.

[12] See, for example, Rule 4.1: "800th Military Police Brigade Rules of Engagement for Operations in Iraq," (declassified on November 1, 2003). As is standard procedure in all US military operations, all US forces deployed to Iraq were given a pocket card providing guidance for the use of force. Such rules of engagement were, as is usually the case, more restrictive than those permitted under international law.

[13] In 2005, Rule 4.1 was replaced by Rule 4.2 (b) (4), which permitted a warning shot under very specific circumstances.

The bottom line is that any suggestion that US forces could have done more than they did to secure the museum before the 12th is based on wishful thinking or political ideology rather than on any rational appreciation of military tactics, the reality of the conflict on the ground, the law of war, or the laws of physics. "If I'd raced up from south Baghdad to the museum, I'd have had a lot of dead soldiers outside the museum," the tank commander for this sector, Lieutenant Colonel Eric Schwartz, told the BBC. "It wasn't the museum anymore – it was a fighting position" (Cruickshank and Vincent 2003: 128).

The blame for the looting must lie squarely on the looters. But the blame for creating chaos at the museum from the 8th through the 11th of April that allowed the looting to occur must lie with the Iraqi Army. It was they who chose to take up fighting positions within the museum, they who chose to fire on the American tanks, and they who kept American forces from investigating the reports they had received of looting "in the area of the museum." After April 11, however, the blame clearly shifts to US forces.

The US Army finally showed up to secure the compound at 10:00 a.m. on the morning of the April 16. If critics want to question US reaction, the delay between the 12th and the 16th is fair game. In fact, this delay was inexcusable. Although nothing was taken during this period, that does not make the indictment any less valid – because the forces had no way of knowing that looters would not come back. You can thank the museum staff for guarding the compound for those 4 days and not the US military.

This leaves us with the more pointed question – the one that is never asked: Before the battle, why was no unit assigned the specific mission of moving in to protect the museum the moment Baghdad was secure?

There are two basic kinds of orders in the military. The first is the standard type that directs a unit to achieve a specific objective at a specific time. "At 08:00 tomorrow, you will seize the beachhead and advance to the cliff wall." Then, there are the kinds of orders that warn a unit that they will be expected to achieve a specific objective at a time yet to be determined. This is a be-prepared-to order, telling that unit to get ready to execute that mission, thereby enabling the commander on the ground to conduct proper reconnaissance, develop a tactical plan, and identify personnel and resources needed for the mission when it *is* ordered.

No such be-prepared-to-execute order was issued for the museum, and therefore no unit was either assigned or prepared to be assigned to secure it until the tank platoon showed up on the morning of the 16th. Why was not such an order issued? Why was there such a delay in responding to repeated requests for assistance on April 12 and 13? The answer is the same for both questions – and it is neither complicated nor entirely satisfactory.

Ultimately, the same "catastrophic success" on the battlefield that outstripped the ability of the Iraqi forces to react also outstripped the ability of coalition planners to anticipate security needs when Baghdad fell months sooner than originally expected. In the case of the museum, this was coupled with a lack of a sense of urgency on the part of military planners – which, in turn, was grounded in a failure to recognize the extent to which Iraqis identified the museum with the former regime.

Thus, despite the prior warnings, planners simply did not believe that the museum – unlike the presidential palaces and governmental buildings that were more overt manifestations of the regime – would be looted. To put it another way, planners naively thought that the recognition of the Iraqi people in their extraordinary heritage would deter them from looting the museum.

Further exacerbating the failure is that even if coalition forces had properly planned for the protection of the museum, there would have been no spare units to assign anyway given the lack of sufficient forces in country. As I said, the explanation is not at all satisfactory. But not sinister or callous either – just human error exacerbated by the speed of the fall of Baghdad and not enough boots on the ground.

Investigative Findings

The timeline for the fighting is a useful template to help explain the unfolding of what the evidence indicates are three distinct crimes: the thefts in the public galleries and restoration area, those in the aboveground storage area, and those in the basement storage area.[14]

It is crucial to note here that, in Baghdad in 2003, we did not have access to the kind of judicial and governmental apparatus that would have allowed us to determine precisely how many missing antiquities had been stolen in the years or even decades before the war – though sources told us the number was high. Because the museum had been open to the public only once since 1991 – on April 28, 2000, Saddam's birthday – and closed again shortly thereafter, we could not even turn to museum visitors for independent verification as to what had been in the museum just prior to the arrival of coalition forces. So even when we were able to determine what was missing, we were not always able to determine, independent of what the staff told us, when it was *first* missing – precluding, therefore, any definitive statement as to what was taken during those 4 days in April 2003. This did not affect our day-to-day operations, however, because our primary job was simply to get the stuff back.

In order to do *that*, though, we had to come up with three different investigative approaches to begin tracking down three different types of thieves – professionals, people off the street, and insiders. These three different categories of crooks had taken three different kinds of loot – marquee items from the galleries, random artifacts from the storage area, and high-value smaller pieces from the basement.

From the 28 galleries and landings on two floors, and from the nearby restoration room, thieves stole 40 of the museum's most treasured pieces. All evidence

[14] As will be made clear farther on, this tripartite scheme of criminality does not include tens of thousands of items that were removed from the museum in the weeks, months, years, and – in some cases – decades prior to the war, removal that was sometimes altruistic and sometimes not.

suggests that these marquee items were carefully chosen, implying that the thefts were professional. Whether or not these thieves were assisted by museum staff, the selection and removal of these items showed the mark of a professional. Likewise, the underworld connections necessary to move and sell these items required a level of professionalism beyond that of a low-level staff member or neighborhood looter. Indeed, we had been told that professionals had come in just before the war – possibly through Jordan – waiting for the fog of war and the opportunity of a lifetime.

One of the most telling clues to the professional eye of these thieves was that they passed right by the unmarked copies and lesser pieces and went straight for the highest-ticket items. There was one exhibit in particular that had 27 cuneiform bricks running from Sumerian through Akkadian and Old Babylonian to New Babylonian.[15] The nine most exquisite bricks were taken – selected from each time period – and all the others were left behind. That kind of selectivity happened repeatedly, also implying some measure of organization.

Of course, some observers have given credit where it was not due, citing, for instance, the fact that the stele containing Hammurabi's code was untouched. But it would not have required a master thief to read the large sign next to the display telling anyone in Arabic and English that this is a copy, and that the original is in the Louvre.

Others used the discovery of a pair of glass cutters as further evidence of professionalism and the advance planning that goes with it. But this tool was a rusty relic that should have been junked long ago, and it was never used on any of the glass inside the museum.[16] Moreover, why would a pro bother bringing along such a tool to a museum with neither a security system nor guards on the scene?

To me, the rusty glass cutters argued just the opposite – that while the professionals went about their business, they no doubt had to put up with any number of bumbling amateurs getting in their way. Would-be looters in off the street knocked over statues and, unsuccessfully, tried to drag them away on their foam-rubber padding. We could trace every single heavy piece that did leave the museum by following the trail of skid marks left in the floor. It is safe to say that these guys had never done this sort of thing before and had no idea what they were getting into. This is not to say that some random bumblers in the gallery area did not get lucky.

---

[15] The 27 bricks with royal inscriptions had been placed in chronological order from the cuneiform tablets of Eannatum I (ruler of Lagash, ca. 2470 BC), Naram-Sin (king of Akkad, ca. 2250 BC), and Hammurabi (king of Babylonia, 1792–1750 BC) to Assurnasirpal (ruler of Assyria, 885–858 BC), Nebuchadnezzar (king of Babylon, 605–562 BC), and – the most recent – a Latin-inscribed brick from a Roman barracks of the first century BC. The nine that were stolen were carefully selected.

[16] "Glass cutters left behind at the scene are viewed as another indication of professionals at work alongside the mob" (Rose 2003). Another popular claim is that these professionals "brought equipment to lift some of the heavier pieces" (Deblauwe, quoted in Elich 2004). No one brought any such equipment to the museum. At least, no one used any such equipment. In the case of the Bassetki Statue, we followed the cracks in the floor made by thieves who dropped it several times, and who certainly had no equipment at hand to assist them.

The guys who walked off with the Sacred Vase of Warka, for example, were nearby residents, not an experienced gang of thieves imported for the occasion.[17]

Altogether, in the galleries, corridors, and nearby restoration room, 25 pieces or exhibits were damaged by this sort of activity, including eight clay pots, four statues, three sarcophagi, three ivory reliefs, two rosettes, and what remained of the Golden Harp of Ur.[18] (Fortunately, the golden bull's head that was stolen from the harp while it lay in the restoration room was a modern replica. Unknown to most of the staff, the original had been removed to the Central Bank of Iraq before the 1991 Gulf War.) Sadly, one of the damaged statues was a 2-ft.-high terracotta lion from Tell Harmal dating from the Old Babylonian period of approximately 1800 BC.

It is also safe to say that some of the thievery in the galleries had been carried out by a third category of persons in addition to the professional and the neighborhood looters. That so many pieces originally missing from the galleries "miraculously" showed up on the restoration-room floor during the weeks and months we lived in the museum strongly suggests that they had been lifted by sticky-fingered staff who later chose to take advantage of our amnesty program by returning many dozens of antiquities to the room we had repeatedly and loudly announced that we would search last. Moreover, seven of the most precious items from the museum had been collected and left in the restoration room just days prior to the war: the Golden Harp of Ur, the Mask of Warka, the Lioness Attacking a Nubian, two plates inlaid with shell depicting ritual scenes from the royal tombs of Ur (2600–2500 BC), a large ninth century BC Assyrian ivory-relief headboard, and a ninth century BC wheeled wooden firebox from Nimrud.[19] Although the room itself had two small safes that could have housed the Mask, the Lioness, and the plates, none of the objects were secured. Instead, everything was left on a table and stolen, except for the wooden body of the harp, a reproduction that was severely damaged, the fragments of its intricate ivory inlay left scattered across the room.

From the two aboveground storage rooms, 3,138 excavation-site pieces (jars, vessels, pottery shards, etc.) were stolen – though I knew that number would surely

[17] The Sacred Vase of Warka, dating from ca. 3200 BC, depicts Sumerians offering gifts to Inanna, the patron goddess of Uruk (modern Warka, the biblical Erech). The 1.06-m alabaster vase was discovered by a German archaeological team in 1940 at Warka, near al-Samawa, in southern Iraq, and was justifiably the pride of the Iraq Museum.

[18] The gold bull's head that adorned Queen Puabi's Golden Harp of Ur, from the Early Dynastic III period (ca. 2600–2500 BC), was discovered in 1929 by a joint British–American archaeological team led by the archaeologist Sir Leonard Woolley.

[19] The Mask of Warka is an exquisite life-size limestone head from ca. 3100 BC. Unearthed by a German expedition in 1938 it possibly represents the goddess Inanna. The "Lioness Attacking a Nubian" is an extraordinary eighth century BC chryselephantine ivory plaque inlaid with lapis and carnelian and overlaid with gold. Joan Oates, a fellow at the McDonald Institute for Archaeological Research, recalled for me Sir Max Mallowan's 1951 discovery of the 10.4-by-9.8-cm plaque at the bottom of a well at Nimrud. Two such plaques are known to exist; the other is in the British Museum.

grow by another one to two thousand when inventories were finally completed.[20] Valuable in their own right, they were of significantly less value than the signature pieces that had been in the public galleries. This was largely the work of random looters – indiscriminate, or at least undiscerning. We saw traces in the dust where an arm had swept across an entire shelf, dragging anything and everything into a sack – and then dumping out the contents of the sack a few aisles away as if they had found something they liked better. Somebody took an entire shelf of fakes, leaving untouched an adjacent shelf containing pieces of infinitely greater value.

But these rookie mistakes do not rule out the possibility that our other bad actors made the amateur heist a lot easier. Neither of the two storage rooms that were looted showed any signs of forced entry on their exterior steel doors. One of the looted rooms was on the first floor, and the other was on the second, and both were connected by an interior stairwell – meaning that entry to one automatically enabled entry to the other. The second-floor room was where an Iraqi Army sniper team had been located. So our best judgment was that the looters gained access to both rooms when the sniper team decamped, leaving the door open behind them. But it was also possible that either the professionals who stole the high-end artifacts or the insider(s) with the keys to the basement may have left the doors open – intentionally. Crowds destroy evidence and help cover tracks.

As for the underground storage area, individuals with an intimate insider's knowledge of the museum and its storage practices breached a wall blocking entrance to the basement and walked past room upon room of tens of thousands of priceless antiquities until they got to the farthest corner of the farthest room of the most remote recesses of the sealed and secret basement to steal – our best count to date – 5,144 cylinder seals,[21] as well as 5,542 pins, glass bottles, beads, amulets, and other small items of jewelry. They knew how to get in, they knew where to find the keys, and they knew what they were looking for. Given this level of preparation, the loot from the basement was more likely to have a middleman buyer and make its way into the hands of organized smugglers able to move it out of Iraq and into the international market.

The most likely way of recovering loot from the museum, especially when the items in question were small and easily hidden, was at border crossings, where law and custom allow inspection of baggage on less than probable cause. As a result of Iraq's neighbors increasing the effectiveness of their border security and inspection programs to thwart terrorists, they were also intercepting many antiquities that would otherwise have slipped through. While relevant borders were far from airtight, and antiquities smuggling had become a quasi-cottage industry in many regions, the increased effectiveness of border inspections had probably discouraged many less

[20]In the absence of any master inventory, the numbers of missing items are based on the museum's staff's hand counting – shelf by shelf, aisle by aisle, room by room – those items still present and comparing those objects with the excavation catalogue for the particular site represented by that shelf and then writing out in longhand a list of the missing items by designation. Thus, the numbers will change as each shelf and box in each aisle in each room is inventoried and is likely to take many years.

[21]Altogether, the museum had approximately 15,000 cylinder seals in its collection in four different locations. One-third, then, was stolen by the insiders.

experienced smugglers from even making the attempt. Old hands, of course, would simply increase their patience and resourcefulness.

But increasing inspection rates is never enough to stop the traffic. A law-enforcement official must be able to articulate a rationale in order to seize an item in transit, and at a glance these smaller artifacts were not necessarily immediately recognizable as contraband. The key strategy at that point, then, was to educate law-enforcement authorities so that they could immediately recognize illicit antiquities and therefore be justified in seizing what they found.

As a result, we decided to treat recoveries inside Iraq and interdiction at the borders not as separate approaches, but as two prongs of the same pincer designed to work together to put the squeeze on the bad guys. Increased border inspections increase the risk of trying to move stolen goods out of the country – causing the thieves to keep the stuff in Iraq until the attention dies down. But the longer the goods stay in Iraq, the more likely they are to be seized through raids based on good intelligence inside the country. And the pressure of seizures inside Iraq pushes smugglers to risk export, which makes them more susceptible to interdiction at a border with improved inspection programs and better-educated guards. These actions were further enhanced by the increased scrutiny and investigative resources that resulted from heightened public interest and improved public awareness.

This pincer approach within Iraq, however, needed to be complemented by an international approach once the smaller basement and big-ticket gallery items left the country. My plan at that point depended on monitoring a rarefied group of known buyers and on developing confidential sources within the art community, most of whom would be museum employees and university professors. But because potential whistle-blowers risked losing their jobs, the challenge was, first, to find them, and, second, to protect their identities.

Six years later, I can offer some – albeit tentative – answers to the most basic questions: Of the 40 objects stolen from the public galleries and restoration rooms, 16 have been recovered, including six of the finest pieces the museum possessed: the Sacred Vase of Warka, the Mask of Warka, the Bassetki Statue, one of two Ninhursag Bulls, a ninth century BC Assyrian ivory headboard from Nimrud, and a headless inscribed limestone statue from Lagash.[22] The amnesty program we had established throughout Iraq with the assistance of sheikhs, imams, and local officials netted two pieces (the Ninhursag bull was returned when the thief simply walked in with it, and the vase was returned as a result of New York City Police Captain John Durkin's skilled negotiation with a neighborhood looter), while seizures accounted for the other four – two inside Iraq (the Warka mask and the Bassetki Statue) and two outside Iraq by Jordanian

[22]The Bassetki Statue, so called because it was discovered by a road construction crew in the 1960s near the town of Bassetki, in northern Iraq, dates to the Akkadian period (ca. 2250 BC). Cast in pure copper and weighing about 150 kg, it has three columns of text inscribed on the base that record the building of a temple and suggest that the statue once stood in the palace of Sargon's grandson, Naram-Sin, king of Akkad (ca. 2254 BC). The museum housed twin bulls from the façade of a temple in Tell al-Ubaid, in southern Iraq, built by Mesannipadda, king of Ur (ca. 2475 BC), and dedicated to the mother goddess Ninhursag. Among the oldest known bulls in relief, they were ripped from the wall in the Sumerian room on the second floor of the museum.

customs (the ivory headboard) and US Customs (the headless statue). The most recent recovery of an item stolen from the galleries that I can make public is that of the headless inscribed limestone statue from Lagash, from approximately 2450 BC. Of note is that before it was seized by US customs in 2006, it had traveled the time-tested classic route from Baghdad to Damascus to Beirut to Geneva.

With regard to the other two sets of thefts, the good news is that virtually all of the 3,138 pieces known to have been stolen from the aboveground storage rooms have been recovered through either the amnesty program or seizures – a startling testament to the courage and integrity of the Iraqi people. The bad news is that our efforts to recover antiquities stolen from the basement have proven less successful: of the 10,686 objects stolen from underground, fewer than 3,000 have been recovered worldwide. Part of the problem is that the entire haul from the basement could fit in one backpack.

Impressively, neighboring countries began making substantial recoveries of stolen Iraqi antiquities almost immediately after the looting – recoveries that continue to this day. Indeed, as of December 2008, eight countries have returned more than 5,200 stolen antiquities to Iraq.[23] Although when made, most authorities and media outlets invariably report all of these seized items as having come from the Iraq Museum – doubtless because of some perceived higher press value – in fact, most items that are claimed by recovering officials to have been stolen from the Iraq Museum were in fact stolen from archaeological sites.

Another 62,000 pieces that had been removed from the museum before 2003 were found in other locations in Iraq in 2003, including 8,366 display-case items found in a top-secret vault within the museum that a select group of museum staff had referred to as "the secret place," 39,453 ancient manuscripts found in a bomb shelter in Western Baghdad, 6,744 pieces from Iraq's royal family collection in the Central Bank's old building, and 7,360 exquisite ivories and pieces of jewelry from the royal tombs of Ur and Nimrud in the Central Bank's new building.[24]

Sadly, though, almost half of the stolen pieces – many of them truly priceless – are still missing. These include the nine Sumerian, Akkadian, and Babylonian cuneiform bricks, as well as a Babylonian boundary stone and five heads from Hatra: a copper head of winged victory, a stone head of a female deity, and marble heads of

---

[23] Jordan (2,450 items, see Mcelroy 2008); United States (1,046 items); Italy (833 items, see Reuters 2008 and Bogdanos 2005b); Syria (701 items, see Associated Press 2008); Dubai (100 items, see McClenaghan 2008); Lebanon (57 items, see Agence France-Presse 2008); Kuwait (38 items); and Saudi Arabia (18 items). Shockingly, no antiquities have been seized (or, to be more precise, acknowledged to have been seized) by the two border nations of Turkey and Iran. Nor have we ever been able to verify any seizures by French or Swiss authorities – despite reports of such seizures in 2005.

[24] From 1922 to 1934, Sir Leonard Woolley excavated approximately 1,850 graves near the Sumerian city of Ur, describing 16 of them (ca. 2600–2500) as "royal tombs" based on their wealth, architecture, and evidence of ritual, to include human sacrifice. Among the most spectacular was the so-called Great Death pit, containing 6 male and 68 female attendants. The treasure of Nimrud is a spectacular collection of more than 1,000 pieces of gold jewelry and precious stones from the eighth and ninth centuries BC that had been discovered between 1988 and 1990 by Iraqi archaeologist Muzahim Hussein Mahmud during his excavation of four royal tombs, and is considered by many to be one of the greatest archaeological finds of the last century. Both treasures had been removed from the museum by the Hussein regime in August of 1990 and not been seen publically since then.

Apollo, Poseidon, and Eros.[25] The list of missing pieces also includes the one that breaks my heart. It is the piece that is on the cover of *Thieves of Baghdad*: the Lioness attacking a Nubian Boy, an extraordinary eighth century BC chryselephantine ivory plaque inlaid with lapis and carnelian and overlaid with gold (see Fig. 9.1).

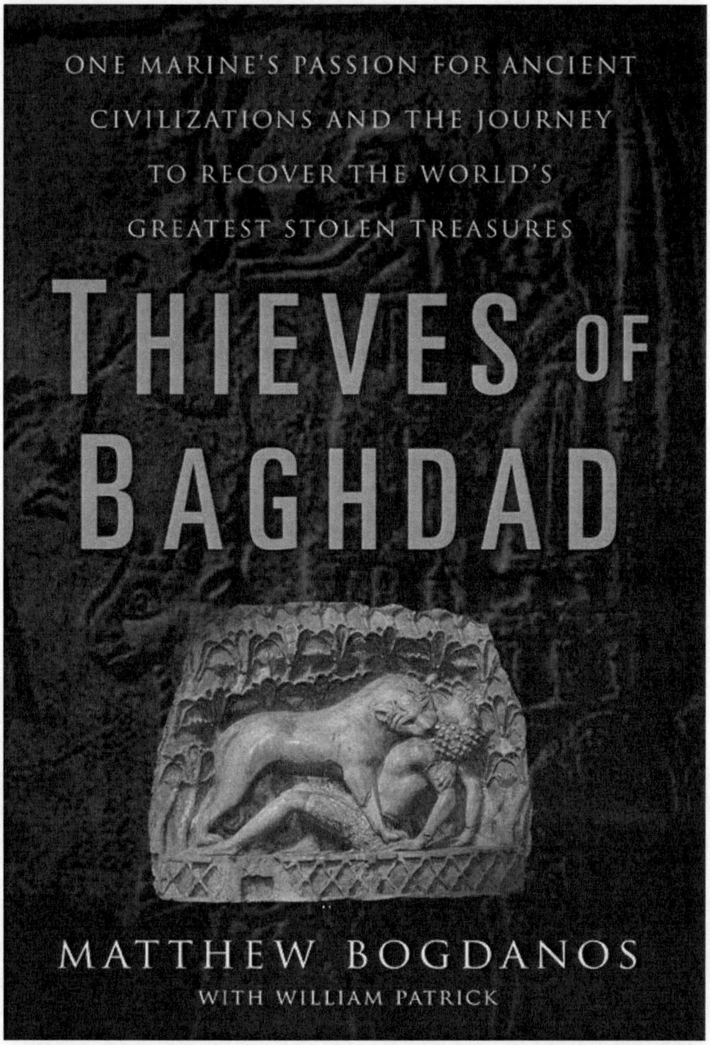

Fig. 9.1 The figure of a Lioness Attacking a Nubian Boy is shown on the cover of the hardcover edition of the book *Thieves of Baghdad* and one of the prominent plates of the soft cover edition. Colonel Bogdanos considers it the single most exquisite and historically significant piece that is still missing

[25] The female deity was the only statue whose head the thieves cut off. Discovered in a Hatrene temple dedicated to the worship of Hercules, it may, therefore, represent his wife (Basmachi 1975–1976: 309). The three heads of Poseidon, Apollo, and Eros were exquisite Roman copies of ca. A.D. 160 after Greek originals of the fourth century BC.

It is, in my view, the single most exquisite and historically significant piece that is still missing. This is why it is on the cover – a painful reminder to me that my journey has only just begun.

Global Criminal Enterprise

As the investigation continues, much has happened to reinforce the core lesson we learnt in the back alleys of Baghdad: that the genteel patina covering the world of antiquities rests atop a solid base of criminal activity. Witness the events taking place in the USA since 2003.

In New York, the Metropolitan Museum (the "Met") accepted what amounted to a plea bargain with Italian authorities – agreeing to return 21 separate antiquities the Italian government says were stolen, including one of the Met's most prized items: The Euphronios krater, a sixth century BC Greek vase (Kennedy and Eakin 2006a: A1). In Missouri, the St. Louis Art Museum is involved in a bitter dispute with Egypt over the museum's possession of a thirteenth century BC pharaonic mask that Egyptian authorities claim was stolen and smuggled out of their country (Gay 2006). In Ohio, the Cleveland Museum of Art agreed to return 13 antiquities that had been looted from Italy (David 2008). In California, the director of the J. Paul Getty Museum agreed to return antiquities the Greek government says were stolen, even as the Getty's longtime curator for ancient art resigned and is on trial in Rome against famed prosecutor Paolo Ferri on charges of conspiracy to receive a different set of stolen artifacts – the details of which are brilliantly documented by Peter Watson, and Cecilia Todeschini (Watson and Todeschini 2006; see also Reynolds 2005: E1). More trials are sure to follow.

I am delighted that nations are moving to reclaim their patrimony. I am also delighted to see media attention beginning to illuminate certain well-appointed shadows, where money changes hands and legitimate – but inconvenient – questions of the provenance (origin) of the object are too frequently considered outré. Many shadows remain.

In March 2006, for example, private collector Shelby White donated $200 million to New York University to establish an ancient studies institute, prompting one of the university's professors to resign in protest over what he considered the questionable acquisition practices of the donor (Povoledo 2006: E1). Ms. White and her late husband Leon Levy have generated considerable debate since at least 1990, when the Met (of which Ms. White is a Trustee) presented a major exhibition of 200 of their artifacts from Greece, Rome, and the Near East (ibidem). The Met did so despite the fact that a study later published in the *American Journal of Archaeology* determined that more than 90% of those artifacts had no known provenance whatsoever (Taylor 2007: 3; see generally Chippindale and David 2000: 463–511). As with the Euphronios krater, Italian authorities have consistently maintained that they can prove many of the antiquities in the Levy–White collection were illegally excavated (a.k.a., stolen) and smuggled out of their country (see Povoledo 2006: E1).

Not only did the Met proudly display that collection, dubious provenance notwithstanding, but it also (coincidentally?) celebrated the opening of its new Leon Levy and Shelby White Court for Hellenistic and Roman antiquities on April 15, 2007 (see Taylor 2007: 3). Other institutions continue to hold out one hand while covering their eyes with the other. In 2000, Cornell University accepted a gift from the well-known collector Jonathan Rosen of 1,679 cuneiform tablets from Ur (Gottlieb and Meier 2003: A1). They said, "Thank you very much," despite reports of widespread looting at Ur after the 1991 Persian Gulf War, and despite the fact that the provenance of 10% of the tablets consisted of the phrase "uncertain sites" (ibidem). Harvard University has done equally well in neglecting to ask awkward questions – witness its Shelby White–Leon Levy Program for Archaeological Publications (see Pogrebin 2006: A1).

But this is nothing new. In 1994, a decade before its current imbroglio, the Getty displayed a major exhibition of classical antiquities owned by Lawrence and Barbara Fleischman (see Felch and Frammolino 2007: A1). Like the Met, the Getty proudly held this exhibit despite the fact that 92% of the objects in the Fleischman collection had no provenance whatsoever, and the remaining 8% had questionable provenance at best (ibidem). To put it in starker terms, of 295 catalogued entries, not a single object had a declared archaeological find spot and only three (1%) were even described as coming from a specific location.

Sometimes, however, the questionable practices extend beyond merely willful ignorance. Consider the following. Prior to the exhibition in 1994, the Fleischman collection had never been published. Thus, the first catalogue for, and hence first publication of, the Fleischman exhibit was the Getty's – of which Ms. Fleischman was a trustee. Fewer than 2 years later, the Getty purchased part of that collection for US$20 million (ibidem). But the Getty had a stated policy of not purchasing objects unless they have been previously displayed in published collections. How, then, could they have justified the acquisition? Easy: the Getty was quick to point out that the collection had been published just 2 years earlier – as well it was – by themselves. Further sweetening the deal, while the collection had been purchased originally at a much lower price, it was valued at US$80 million at the time of the sale to the museum (ibidem). US tax laws use the fair market value at the time of the sale rather than the original purchase price in determining the value of a bequest. As a result, the difference between the 1996 valuation of US$80 million and the US$20 million sale price to the Getty would be deemed a gift of US$60 million, affording a $60 million tax deduction for the Fleischmans. Under these terms, the gift to the Getty, therefore, was actually financed by US taxpayers – a shell game of Homeric proportions.

In many respects, then, we have advanced very little since the imperial nineteenth century, when Lord Elgin could haul away the Parthenon Sculptures (now in the British Museum and commonly referred to as the "Elgin Marbles") and Henry Layard could haul away the Nineveh reliefs (now in the Met). Despite the hue and cry of the last several years, the Met's current policy is to require documentation covering only the last 10 years of an object's history.[26] This, even though most

[26] See generally The Metropolitan Museum of Art at http://www.metmuseum.org.

institutions view 1970 – the year of the landmark United Nations Educational, Scientific and Cultural Organization (UNESCO) Convention[27] to regulate the transfer of antiquities – as the cut-off date for requiring proof that an antiquity was not illegally looted (see Pogrebin 2006).

The imposition of a firm date (here 1970) is crucial in stopping the trade in illegal antiquities. As each year passes, it becomes less and less likely that a previously unpublished (and hence unknown) antiquity can appear on the market and be legal – either in the sense of having come from a properly sanctioned excavation or from some ancient collection that was assembled before the imposition of any requirement of documentation. To put it another way, as each year passes, it becomes increasingly certain that previously unpublished items are stolen.

Thus, the Met's policy of requiring documentation covering only the last 10 years of an object's history becomes more unsupportable as each year passes. Theoretically, in May of 2013, the Met could begin to buy items stolen from the Iraq Museum in April 2003 without violating its stated policy. All it need do is not ask where it comes from before the 10-year window. As if to flaunt the Met's policy of "see no evil," Philippe de Montebello, the museum's long-standing, but now-retired director, told the *New York Times* in February 2006 that the context in which an artifact is found is virtually meaningless; in his opinion, it accounts for less than 2% of what we can learn from antiquity (Kennedy and Eakin 2006b: E1). His position is as absurd as the equally unreasonable view of some purists that context is everything.

But far from this world of museum receptions and limos waiting at the curb, however, there has been an even more troubling development. In June 2005, US Marines in northwest Iraq arrested five insurgents holed up in underground bunkers filled with automatic weapons, ammunition stockpiles, black uniforms, ski masks, and night-vision goggles. Along with these tools of their trade, were 30 vases, cylinder seals, and statuettes that had been stolen from the Iraq Museum. Since then, the scenario has been repeated many times. It did not take a counterterrorism expert to detect the sinister adjustment that had taken place. In 2003, when pursuing leads to recover antiquities, we usually came across weapons and links to violent groups. Now, as security forces pursue leads for weapons and insurgents, they find antiquities.

In a modern-day version of the old "molasses to rum to slaves" triangle trade of pious New England ship captains and owners who sang hymns and offered prayers while getting rich off human misery, the cozy cabal of academics, dealers, and collectors who turn a blind eye to the illicit side of the trade is supporting the insurgents who are murdering innocent civilians in Iraq.

This is not surprising. As the National Commission on Terrorist Attacks Upon the United States ("The 9/11 Commission") noted, international law enforcement has aggressively attacked traditional means of terrorist financing by freezing assets and neutralizing charities that had previously served as fronts for jihadists (Bogdanos 2005c: A15). But terrorists are nothing if not adaptive. In late 2005, the German newspaper *Der Spiegel* reported that 9/11 conspirator Mohammed Atta had

[27] UNESCO's "Convention on the Means of Prohibiting and Preventing the Illicit Import, Export and Transfer of Ownership of Cultural Property," November 14, 1970, 823 U.N.T.S. 231.

approached a professor at the University of Goettingen trying to sell Afghan antiquities to raise money to buy an airplane (Der Spiegel 2005: 20). While nothing came of that inquiry, times have changed. Like the Taliban in Afghanistan who learnt to finance their activities through opium, insurgents in Iraq have discovered a new source of income in Iraq's cash crop: antiquities.

We do not have hard numbers – the traffic in art for arms is too recent and shadowy a phenomenon – and some of the investigations remain classified because of the connection to terrorists. But this illicit trade has become a growing source of revenue for the insurgents; ranking just below kidnappings for ransom and "protection" money from local residents and merchants. Among the most prized items are cylinder seals, intricately carved pieces of stone about the size of a piece of chalk that can sell for US$250,000, enabling an insurgent to smuggle millions of dollars in his pocket. Given this almost limitless supply of antiquities, the insurgency appears to have found an income stream sufficiently secure to make any chief financial officer sleep well at night. As a result, the desert night is filled with the roar of bulldozers ripping into the ancient mounds of clay that were once thriving cities.

Protect the Archaeological Sites

Based on my experience in both counterterrorism and law enforcement – and as a result of the years I have spent in Iraq and throughout the world in tracking down the stolen antiquities – I submit that the first order of business in addressing this catastrophe must be to protect the source: as the cradle of civilization, Iraq has more than 12,000 poorly guarded archaeological sites (Bogdanos 2005c: A15). Some of these, such as Babylon and Nimrud, require several hundred guards and support staff for protection around the clock. The math is daunting: country-wide more than 50,000 personnel are required, along with the necessary vehicles, radios, weapons, and logistical needs. But there is an immediate solution.

In other contexts, the UN and the North Atlantic Treaty Organisation (NATO) have acted to address catastrophic situations. In Bosnia, Cyprus, and Afghanistan, for example, many countries have provided contingents for specific missions under UN or NATO auspices – but not in Iraq. The reasons are much-argued, and I do not revisit them here. Recalling Voltaire's observation that "everyone is guilty of the good he didn't do," I focus instead on what we can do now.

So who might act? In the past, most archaeological digs in Iraq have had foreign sponsorship – the Germans at Babylon and Uruk, the British at Ur and Nimrud, the French at Kish and Lagash, the Italians at Hatra and Nimrud, the Americans at Nippur and Ur (Bogdanos 2007: A21). Leveraging this history, I have proposed that these (and eventually other) countries provide forces to protect Iraq's archaeological sites until a professional Iraqi security force dedicated to the sites can be recruited, equipped, and trained.

Under this proposal, with the permission of the Iraqi government, facilitated by the US military, and under the authority of the UN or NATO, each country would "adopt" a site. After sending an assessment team to the assigned sites to determine the precise numbers and type of personnel and equipment required, each donor nation would then draft and sign bilateral status of forces agreements with Iraq, outlining the rules of engagement, funding, billeting, and the standard logistical issues.

Then, each country would deploy its security forces (military, police, private contractors, or a combination of all three) to the agreed-upon archaeological sites around the perimeter and around the clock. Upon arrival, each country's contingent would also be assigned a group of Iraqi recruits (who would live and work with them) to train at their chosen site. Once those Iraqi security forces were fully trained – that ordinarily takes 6 months – the donor nation would recall (or reassign) its forces on a site-by-site basis. In half a year, every archaeological site of consequence in Iraq could be completely protected from the looters. Mesopotamia's cultural patrimony would be safe, Al-Jazeera would have to find other ways to show Western indifference to Arab culture, and the terrorists would have to find another income source.

Unfortunately, neither NATO nor the UN has ever shown the least inclination to protect the sites. NATO opened a training center in Iraq in 2005, but has trained only 1,500 Iraqi security personnel, none of whom have been assigned to archaeological sites. The UN has never trained guards for the sites. Even the UN's cultural arm, UNESCO has failed to act, claiming it has no such mandate from its member nations. Assuming that to be true, UNESCO ought to convince its member nations to support such an initiative. It is time for the UN to seize the mantle of international leadership and convince its members to support such a plan. As our best hope, UNESCO ought to step into the vacuum of international leadership, seize the bully pulpit, and become relevant again. "Man should share the action and passion of his time," former US Supreme Court justice Oliver Wendell Holmes once noted, "at peril of being judged never to have lived."

Individual countries are also slow to respond. Only the Italians, Danes, Dutch, and Poles have joined the Americans and British in protecting these sites – and the Danes, Dutch, and Italians have already left. Other countries have argued that the level of violence does not permit deployment of their forces. The circular nature of this rationalization is underscored by the fact that it is the failure to protect these sites that is partly funding those who are creating the unsafe environment. "If you were to take account of everything that could go wrong," Herodotus advised long ago, "you would never act." Of course there is risk. I know this firsthand. But the risks of the failure to act are far worse: more money for the insurgents, more propaganda for Al-Jazeera, and the loss of these extraordinary testaments to our common beginnings.

Equally risky are the politics: most elected officials view involvement in Iraq as political suicide. But an internationally coordinated contribution of personnel would not be a statement about the war or the Bush (or any) administration's policies in Iraq. It would be a humanitarian effort to protect a cultural heritage rich with a common ancestry that transcends the current violence. Real leaders should have no difficulty convincing their electorate of the distinction between politics and culture. It is, of course, the very definition of leadership to educate, inform, and motivate into action those who might otherwise be inclined to do nothing.

The Next Steps: A Five-Point Action Plan

The incomparable works of art unearthed in the land between the rivers predate the split between Sunni and Shiite. They predate the three competing traditions that have brought so much bloodshed to the Middle East – Islam, Christianity, and Judaism. Attending to this cultural heritage from the very dawn of civilization reminds us of our common humanity, our common aspiration to make sense of life on this planet. I have seen these pieces of alabaster and limestone – with funny writing on them – work their magic through a language that is immediate and universal, visceral and transcendent.

While protecting the archaeological sites in Iraq is a vital beginning, much more needs to be done. To stop the rampant looting and the black market that funnels money into terrorist hands, we must adopt a comprehensive global strategy using all of the elements of international power. Toward this end, I propose a five-step plan of action to combat the global traffic in antiquities.

Mount a Public Relations Campaign for Mainstream Society

The cornerstone to any comprehensive approach must take into account that real, measurable, and lasting progress in stopping the illegal trade depends on increasing public awareness of the importance of cultural property and of the magnitude of the current crisis. First, then, we must develop and communicate a message that resonates with mainstream society – not just with academics. We must create a climate of universal condemnation, rather than sophisticated indulgence, for trafficking in undocumented antiquities.

But this call to arms needs to avoid the sky-is-falling quotes so beloved by the media, while steering clear of the debilitating rhetoric of politics. It also has to keep the discussion of the illegal trade separate from broader issues such as repatriation of objects acquired prior to 1970 and whether there should be any trade in antiquities at all. The Parthenon Sculptures are in the British Museum, but their return is a diplomatic or public relations issue, not a matter for the criminal courts. Similarly, there is a legal trade in antiquities that is regulated and above board. It is simply unproven (and unfair) to argue that the legal trade somehow encourages an illegal trade. Most dealers and museums scrupulously do avoid trading in antiquities with a murky origin. Repatriation for pre-1970 transfers and the question of whether all trade in antiquities should be banned are legitimate issues, but they are not my issues. Every time the discussion about stopping the illegal trade in antiquities veers off into these broader realms we lose focus, we lose the attention of mainstream society, and it makes the job of recovering stolen antiquities that much harder.

Provide Funding to Establish or Upgrade Antiquities Task Forces

Second, although several countries – including the USA, Britain, Italy, and Japan – have pledged millions of dollars to upgrade the Iraq Museum, improve its conservation capacity, and enhance the training of the Iraq State Board of Antiquities and Heritage's archaeological staff, not a single government, international organization, or private foundation anywhere in the world has provided additional funding for investigative purposes. Reluctant to be seen cooperating with police and military forces, many cultural leaders and organizations seem oblivious to the fact that a stolen artifact cannot be *restored* until it has been *recovered*. To put it more clearly: money for conservators is pointless without first providing the money to track down the missing objects to be conserved.

This ivory-tower distortion of priorities affects investigative efforts worldwide. Interpol can afford to assign only two officers to its Iraqi Antiquities Tracking Task Force – and both have other responsibilities as well. Scotland Yard's art and antiquities squad has four officers covering the entire world – and in January of 2007, their budget was slashed in half. The US Federal Bureau of Investigation's (FBI) Rapid Deployment National Art Crime Team has eight people – and the head of that team, Special Agent Robert Whitman, retired earlier this year and has not been replaced. Regardless of the exceptional dedication and talent of these personnel, no law-enforcement agency can operate effectively at such pitiful levels.

Thus, as a second component, all countries – but most especially the countries of origin, transit, and destination – must establish robust, specialized art, and antiquities task forces, with particular attention paid to the borders and ports of entry. Where such forces already exist, we must increase their size and scope, with cultural foundations providing art-theft squads with vehicles, computers, communications equipment, and training.

Create a Coordinated International Law-Enforcement Response

Among the many dirty secrets of the looted antiquities market is that "open" borders are as profitable as they are dangerous. Many countries, especially those with free ports or free-trade zones, generate sizeable customs and excise fees from shipping and – despite their public protestations to the contrary – are not eager to impose any increase in inspection rates that might reduce such revenue. Even if willing, the sheer tonnage passing through international ports and free-trade zones makes 100% inspection rates impossible. Nor does the improved technology installed as a result of September 11 solve the problem: devices that detect weapons and explosives do not detect alabaster, lapis lazuli, and carnelian. Further exacerbating the problem, most high-end smugglers are simply too sophisticated, and the questionable acquisition practices of some dealers, collectors, and museums, too entrenched to be defeated by improved border inspections and heightened public consciousness alone.

The *sine qua non* for effective interdiction, then, is an organized, systematized, and seamlessly collaborative law-enforcement effort by the entire international community. We need coordinated simultaneous investigations of smugglers, sellers, and buyers in different countries. And – just as important – prosecution and incarceration need to be credible threats. Thus, as a third component, the UN, through UNESCO, should establish a commission to continue the Iraq Museum investigation, expanding it to include other pillaged countries as well. Interpol, the International Criminal Police Organization, must also become more active, entering into agreements with its 191 member nations stipulating that each country forward to them immediately, along a secure network (that already exists), a digital photograph and the particulars (who, what, when, and where) of all antiquities encountered by law enforcement or military forces anywhere in the world – including both those items that were seized and those that were inspected and not seized because there was insufficient evidence of criminality at the time of the inspection to hold the item.

The global criminal enterprise that is antiquities smuggling must be defeated globally through international cooperation (promoted by UNESCO) and real-time dissemination of information (enabled by INTERPOL). The consequent ability to conduct monitored deliveries of illegal shipments to their destinations (a tactic long used against drug smugglers) would enable legal authorities to incriminate and thereafter prosecute each culpable party along the trail. It would also serve as a deterrent to those collectors or curators who could never be sure that the next shipment was not being monitored by law-enforcement officials.

Establish a Code of Conduct for Trading in Antiquities

Fourth, museums, archaeologists, and dealers should establish a strict and uniform code of conduct. Similar to ethics rules for lawyers and doctors, this code of conduct would clarify the documentation and diligence required for an artifact to change hands legally. If they refuse such self-regulation, then Congress should impose regulation. Although many argue that the interests of dealers, collectors, museums, and archaeologists differ from each other so dramatically that any single code of conduct acceptable to all is impossible, I point out that the differences within the art world are no greater than those existing between prosecutors and criminal defense attorneys. Yet, the American Bar Association has adopted and actively enforces a single Code of Ethics applicable to every attorney admitted to the bar.[28] Until then, I continue to urge academics, curators, and dealers to abandon their self-serving complacency about – if not complicity in – irregularities of documentation.

[28] See, for example, ABA "Model Code of Professional Responsibility and Code of Judicial Conduct," adopted August 12, 1969, amended though August 1980, American Bar Association. Chicago, IL: National Center for Professional Responsibility, 1982, KF 305.A2 1986.

Increase Cooperation Between the Cultural Heritage Community and Law Enforcement

Finally, the art community must break down barriers and assist investigators by serving as the eyes and ears of law enforcement. We need scholars and knowledgeable dealers as on-call experts to identify and authenticate intercepted shipments, and to provide crucial in-court expert testimony. They should also request appropriate law-enforcement personnel (depending on country and focus) to provide detailed, factual briefings at every conference purporting to address art or antiquities smuggling. The call for up-to-date investigative facts should become as standard as the call for papers.

But the education and information exchange should run in both directions. In 2004, polymath C. Brian Rose, now President of the Archaeological Institute of America, developed and began conducting cultural-awareness training in half-a-dozen pilot locations around the USA for military personnel scheduled to deploy to Iraq or Afghanistan. Laurie Rush, a gifted archaeologist with the US Department of Defense's Legacy Heritage Management program, has also made significant strides in training military personnel, including creating the media-darling archaeological playing cards (Kaylan 2007: D7), establishing Web sites for Iraq and Afghanistan and disseminating pocket cards on the "Dos" and "Don'ts" for Military Operations concerning archaeological sites. A similar program should be offered on a regular basis to the FBI and the Department of Homeland Security within the USA and to similar law-enforcement agencies worldwide.

Internationally, there have been many significant advancements leading to enhanced cooperation between the cultural heritage and military communities since 2003. Three, however, are worthy of special mention. Peter Stone, Head of Newcastle University's School of Arts and Cultures and Chief Executive Officer of the World Archaeological Congress, has made exceptional progress in developing channels of communication between the archaeological and military communities – despite being the subject of ad hominem attacks from the more narrow-minded members of his own archaeological organization. Among the most promising of the countless nongovernmental organizations to arise in the aftermath of the looting of the Iraq Museum is WATCH, the World Association for the Protection of Tangible and Intangible Cultural Heritage in Times of Armed Conflicts. The brainchild of renowned professors Talal Akasheh from Jordan and Claudio Cimino from Italy, the goal of WATCH is to foster the safeguarding of cultural heritage by creating and maintaining contacts with military organizations throughout the world. Finally, the synthesizing activities of Joris Kila, an art historian and a lieutenant colonel in the Dutch Army, must be commended. As a community fellow with the University of Chicago's Cultural Policy Center and a board member for civil-military relations with WATCH, he has served in Iraq and as a lecturer at the Netherlands Defense Academy. Such cooperation between the art and archaeological communities and the law enforcement and military presents a real chance of winning a fight we cannot afford to lose.

Future Military Conflicts

The military of every nation has lessons to be learnt as well. It is, of course, axiomatic that in situations involving armed conflict, military forces will be present to a greater or lesser extent and, therefore, in a unique position to take steps to protect any sites of cultural significance at risk. Thus, and with the tragedy of the pillaging of Iraq's antiquities still fresh in our consciousness, it is incumbent on military forces around the globe to examine that tragedy and learn its lessons for the future. But, as Mark Twain once observed, "we should be careful to get out of an experience only the wisdom that is in it – and stop there; lest we be like the cat that sits down on a hot stove lid. She will never sit down on a hot stove lid again – and that is well; but also she will never sit down on a cold one anymore." In short, we must analyze those lessons dispassionately and nonpolitically to derive future strategies.

Using the USA as an example, but with the understanding that the lessons apply to all countries, the first lesson is that the USA must never again cede the moral high ground on issues of cultural sensitivity and national patrimony. Thus, before taking action in the future in any other country, the relevant military commanders must clearly articulate their recognition of the impacted country's proud cultural heritage and the intent to protect such property within its borders, to the extent possible, during the conflict and postconflict stage. Not just the message, but the actions that flow from it, must convince the world that the USA and, in particular, the US military are committed to honoring and preserving the heritage of all nations and religious traditions.

Second, and in order to fulfill such a commitment, military leaders must plan before any action for the protection of cultural property in the proposed area of operations. Such comprehensive planning, however, is dependent on – and indeed cannot be achieved without – the active cooperation from the archaeological community. Breaking down myopic and age-old barriers, the archaeological and academic communities must provide militaries in-depth and exhaustive information about any and all sites of cultural significance that might be at risk during any potential conflict in that area.

Such assistance would not be a statement about war, and it has absolutely nothing to do with "legitimizing" or "sanctioning" potential military action – the convenient, philosophically bankrupt excuse often used to justify inaction. Rather, it would be a courageous and humanitarian effort to protect cultural heritage (no matter where it is) that always transcends any current violence. And those who truly care about cultural heritage should have no difficulty finding the character to put aside political differences to try to do just that. Just as the information and guidance provided to the military by various humanitarian aid organizations, such as the International Committee of the Red Cross and others, does not represent any political statement about the imminent or ongoing military action, neither would the assistance or guidance of cultural heritage organizations make such a statement. In both cases, it is just about doing the right thing for humanity and culture.

Indeed, any blanket refusal of archaeologists to assist military forces is not only shortsighted; it also completely ignores issues of constitutional law. In virtually all western democracies, once the elected political leaders of a country have decided upon a military course of action and issue the necessary orders to effect that action, the military itself is legally bound to carry out those orders unless those orders are illegal. Political or philosophical disagreement is not a sufficient basis under the law to refuse to obey – in fact, failure to obey under such circumstances is actually criminal behavior: the orders must be prima facie illegal to warrant the failure to obey. Thus, the refusal to assist the military in advance of any action does not prevent the military action (it has already been decided upon), but does have one lasting result: the failure to protect sites of historical or cultural significance.

Third, once the sites have been identified with the active and enlightened assistance of the academic and archaeological communities, the military planners must ensure that their protection goes beyond merely putting each site on a no-strike list. It must also include the securing of significant sites (again, as identified by members of the archaeological community) and the immediate deployment, if needed, of on-call security forces upon reports of looting. In order to allow for their training, resourcing, and rapid deployment, such on-call forces must be identified in advance of the operation and given their assigned on-call mission in the planning phase.

Moreover, these security forces must be given, and trained in, explicit rules of engagement that provide for the escalating use of force and clearly delineate what levels of force they are permitted to use in preventing looting and, just as crucially, when they should desist from the use of force altogether. Where some security and policing forces already exist in the relevant country, US military forces should assist those units by providing them with vehicles, radios, and training. Where no such forces exist, the US military must protect the sites until trained forces are available.

Such preparation in advance of any action would also enable planners to identify shortfalls and, where appropriate, attempt to fill such needs from international organizations or coalition countries before the conflict. Thus, the identification of such additionally required resources might cause military commanders to broaden their coalition or international support for such actions in order to meet such shortfalls – a desirable result in and of itself.

Taken together, these steps offer measurable, realizable, and effective ways or preserving cultural heritage through the horrors of war and armed conflict and during the postconflict stabilization phase as well. Parenthetically, it is a small step to advance from the protection of cultural heritage during man-made disasters to their protection during natural disasters – after all, many of the challenges, dangers, and processes are the same. But that is a discussion for another day.

Conclusion

Diverting resources to save cultural artifacts during a time of war may seem trivial considering the human cost of war. But some of our best soldiers have seen the wisdom. “Inevitably, in the path of our advance will be found historical monuments and cultural centers which symbolize to the world all that we are fighting to preserve," said General Dwight D. Eisenhower, just before D-Day during the deadliest war of the last 100 years, one that threatened the very existence of the world as we know it. "It is the responsibility of every commander to protect and respect these symbols whenever possible."

Antiquities trafficking will never merit the same attention or resources as terrorism, drugs, human trafficking, or violent street crime. But, at the very least, it deserves to be on the same list. From government corridors, precinct headquarters, and media newsrooms to faculty lounges, museum boardrooms, and galleries on Madison Avenue, this cultural catastrophe must be confronted and debated. We must expose those who engage in the illegal trade for what they are: criminals.

On my first tour in Iraq, our mission was to track down illegal arms and terrorist networks. My decision to expand our mission to include investigating the looting of the Iraq Museum and tracking down the stolen artifacts was characterized by many as a distraction. I regret that I did not pursue that distraction even more.

References

Aaronovitch, D. (2003). Lost from the Baghdad Museum: Truth. *The Guardian* (London), 10 June.

Agence France-Presse (2008). Iraqi Antiquities Seized in Lebanon: Customs. *Middle East Times*, 26 October.

Al-Radi, S. (2009). War and Archaeological Heritage: Lessons from Lebanon, Kuwait, and Iraq.

Associated Press (2008). Syria Gives Iraq Back Treasure Seized at Border: 701 Artifacts Returned, But up to 7,000 Still Missing After Saddam Ouster, 27 April.

Atwood, R. (2003). Inside Iraq's National Museum. *Wall Street Journal*, July 17.

Basmachi, F. (1975–1976). *Treasures of the Iraq Museum*. Baghdad: Al-Jamahiriya Press.

Bogdanos, M. (2005a). *Thieves of Baghdad: One Marine's Passion to Recover the World's Greatest Stolen Treasures*. New York: Bloomsbury.

Bogdanos, M. (2005b). The Casualties of War: The Truth About the Iraq Museum. *American Journal of Archaeology*, 109(3), 477–526.

Bogdanos, M. (2005c) (op-ed.). The Terrorist in the Art Gallery. *New York Times*, 10 December.

Bogdanos, M. (2007) (op-ed.). Fighting for Iraq's Culture. *New York Times*, 6 March.

Chippindale, C., David, W. J. G. (2000). Material Consequences of Contemporary Classical Collecting. *American Journal of Archaeology*, 104(3), 463–511.

Cruickshank, D., Vincent, D. (2003). *People, Places, and Treasures Under Fire in Afghanistan, Iraq and Israel*. London: BBC Books.

David, A. (2008). Cleveland Museum of Art to Return Art to Italy. *Associated Press*, 19 November.

Der Spiegel (2005). Art for Financing Terrorism. *Der Spiegel* (F. R. G.), 18 July.

Elich, G. (2004). Spoils of War: The Antiquities Trade and the Looting of Iraq. *Center for Research on Globalisation*, 3 January.

Felch, J., Frammolino, R. (2007). The Return of Antiquities a Blow to Getty: Forty Disputed Artworks that Are Hallmarks of the Museum's Collection Will Be Returned to Italy in End to a Long Legal Fight. *Los Angeles Times*, 2 August.

Gay, M. (2006). Out of Egypt. *Riverfront Times* (St. Louis, MO), 15 February.

Gottlieb, M., Meier, B. (2003). Ancient Art at the Met Raises Old Ethical Questions. *New York Times*, 2 August.

Harris, T. (2004). Iraq Museum Still Counting the Cost of Invasion. *The Peninsula* (Qatar's Leading English Daily), 1 July.

Kaylan, M. (2007). U.S. to Troops: Play Cards Protect a Culture. *Wall Street Journal*, 7 October.

Kennedy, R., Eakin, H. (2006a). The Met, Ending 30-Year Stance Is Set to Yield Prized Vase to Italy. *New York Times*, 3 February.

Kennedy, R., Eakin, H. (2006b). Met Chief, Unbowed, Defends Museum's Role. *New York Times*, 28 February.

McClenaghan, G. (2008). Iraqi Antiquities Seized in Dubai. *The National*, 26 November.

Mcelroy, S. (2008). Looted Antiquities Returned to Iraq. *New York Times*, 23 June.

Pogrebin, R. (2006). US$200 Million Gift Prompts a Debate Over Antiquities. *New York Times*, 1 April.

Povoledo, E. (2006). Top Collector Is Asked to Relinquish Artifacts. *New York Times*, 29 November.

Reuters North American News Service (2008). Italy Returns Antiquities Looted from Iraq, 24 July.

Reynolds, C. (2005). The Puzzle of Marion True. *Los Angeles Times*, 31 October.

Rose, M. (2003). Taking Stock in Baghdad. *Archaeology: A Publication of the Archaeological Institute of America*, 15 April–11 July.

Taylor, K. (2007). Shelby White in Center Court at the Met. *New York Sun*, 1 May.

Trofimov, Y. (2003). Iraqis Say Museum Looting Wasn't as Bad as Feared. *Wall Street Journal*, 17 April.

Watson, P., Todeschini, C. (2006). *The Medici Conspiracy: The Illicit Journey of Looted Antiquities, from Italy's Tomb Raiders to the World's Greatest Museums*. New York: BBS Public Affairs.

Part III
Prevention and Control

Chapter 10
The Role of INTERPOL in the Fight Against the Illicit Trafficking in Cultural Property

Karl-Heinz Kind

Introduction

First of all, I would like to introduce myself. My name is Karl-Heinz Kind. I am a German police officer working at the International Criminal Police Organization (INTERPOL) General Secretariat where I am coordinating INTERPOL's activities related to cultural property crime. On INTERPOL's behalf, I would like to thank the International Scientific and Professional Advisory Council of the United Nations (ISPAC) for inviting me to attend this international workshop.

INTERPOL as an International Organization

To give you a better idea of what our Organization is and does, in a few words, I will present the structure of our Organization and I will develop the role of the INTERPOL General Secretariat in the fight against the illicit traffic in cultural property.

INTERPOL is an intergovernmental organization with 187 member countries. It is the second largest organization after the UN in terms of membership. The governing bodies of INTERPOL are the General Assembly and the Executive Committee. These are deliberative organs, with decision making and supervisory powers.

Approximately 150 police officers from about 75 countries representing all the regions of the world are working at the INTERPOL General Secretariat, which is located in Lyons, France. The composition of the staff ensures a sound knowledge and wide experience of both regional situations and the problems of international crime.

K.-H. Kind (✉)
INTERPOL General Secretariat, Lyons, France
e-mail: kh.kind@interpol.int

S. Manacorda and D. Chappell (eds.), *Crime in the Art and Antiquities World: Illegal Trafficking in Cultural Property*, DOI 10.1007/978-1-4419-7946-9_10,

The purpose of our Organization is:

- To ensure and promote the widest possible mutual assistance between all criminal police authorities, within the limits of the laws existing in different countries and in the spirit of the Universal Declaration of Human Rights.
- To establish and develop all institutions likely to contribute effectively to the prevention and suppression of ordinary law crimes.

It is strictly forbidden for the Organization to undertake any intervention or activities of a political, military, religious, or racial character.

Contrary to common belief, INTERPOL is not made up of international brigades of investigators. INTERPOL Police Officers cannot carry out investigations in the member countries. Instead, international investigations are conducted by the countries' national police forces.

The General Secretariat has no power to force a country to take action, or not to take action, in a specific police investigation.

In each INTERPOL member country, the task of cooperation is assigned to the National Central Bureau (NCB), usually located in the country's capital city.

The Tools Developed to Fight Against the Illicit Traffic in Cultural Property

Since 1947, INTERPOL has invested a lot of efforts in the fight against the criminality related to cultural property and various tools have been developed by the General Secretariat to assist its member countries. Some of the tools are also available to the public.

Telecommunications Network

For all operational activities by law enforcement agencies, the rapid, secure and reliable information exchange is crucial. INTERPOL's worldwide telecommunication network enables to circulate information among all the member countries within a few minutes. The ever-increasing number of messages, in particular of those containing images (photographs, fingerprints) presented a new challenge to INTERPOL. INTERPOL's response is a new telecommunications system based on the Internet technology, and which presents advantages in terms of speed and costs while maintaining the required high security standards. The system is called I-24/7, and meanwhile all member countries are connected.

To give you an idea, approximately 11 million messages transited the system in 2007, i.e., nearly 30,000 messages on a daily basis. That is three times of the amount we had in 2003. I-24/7 does not only enable a quick exchange of information among the NCBs and the General Secretariat, it also enables to connect more national law enforcement officers from other agencies and even to connect not only single users, but also entire local or national networks. It also gives access to a number of central databases, including the works of art database.

Poster of the Most Wanted Works of Art

Every 6 months we publish a poster showing the six most wanted works of art. It is the only paper publication remaining for the stolen works of art. On average, two out of six objects represented are recovered. As an exception, the poster issued in June 2003 has been entirely dedicated to objects looted from the Iraq Museum.

The "ASF: Works of Art" Computerized Database

In 1995, the General Secretariat developed a computerized database for stolen works of art, including descriptions and photographs. This database has been made for Police Officers and is based on a visual description of works of art, which is very easy to carry out.

End of October 2008, the database contained data of 32,573 individual objects. The majority of items have been reported by:

- European countries (24,350 or 74.7%), followed by
- America (4,222 or 12.9%)
- Middle East and North Africa (2,585 or 7.9%)
- Asia and South Pacific (1.254 or 3.9%) and
- Africa (162 or 0.5%).

Contrary to common belief, we do not keep information on all offenses committed anywhere in the world. We only record the crimes considered to have *international* ramifications and we only open files for *international* criminals.

Direct Access to the Database

Since January 1999, this database is available to all member countries by means of a specific computer program.

In an effort to increase both the speed and the user friendliness of our tools, in November 2005, we launched the access to INTERPOL's stolen art database through the new telecommunications system, and in September 2006, we added the French and Spanish versions.

Since, the number of remote queries has tremendously increased reaching approximately 7,000 queries this year.

The CD-ROM/DVD "INTERPOL: Stolen Works of Art"

With a view to enable the private sector to have access to information on stolen art, in cooperation with a private French company, the General Secretariat started in 1999 to produce and distribute a CD-ROM on stolen works of art.

On this CD-ROM, you had the possibility to select your working language: English, French, or Spanish. It contained not only information on stolen art, or art items found in suspicious circumstances, but also:

- The text of international Conventions of the UNESCO in 1970 and UNIDROIT in 1995
- The list of the member countries and their telephone numbers
- The OBJECT-ID developed by the Getty Information Institute (minimum description standard of a work of art) which was recognized by both UNESCO and ICOM
- A list of objects at risk (Red List of ICOM)

This CD-ROM can be considered as one of those registers mentioned in the UNIDROIT Convention of 1995 in its article 4§ 4, which a buyer should consult prior to the acquisition of a cultural good as a part of the due diligence process.

In August 2006, we switched from the CD-ROM to the DVD technology for an increased storage capacity and, as a result, a higher quality of the photographs.

All the NCBs continue to receive one DVD free of charge, whereas it is sold to other public and private institutions by annual subscription, including updates every 2 months (with a special price for law enforcement).

We are currently examining the possibility of granting access to the works of art database through INTERPOL's secure Web site.

Internet

In July 2000, the General Secretariat opened a specific section for the works of art on its Internet site (http://www.interpol.int).

This section, publicly accessible, contains information on:

- INTERPOL meetings and conferences, recommendations adopted
- Specific alerts in the event of important thefts (e.g., Munch's "The Scream" from the museum in Oslo, August 2004, and its recovery in 2006, the "Saliera" from the museum in Vienna, May 2003 and its recovery 3 years later)
- The most recent thefts of works of art. To ensure the continuity of information, stolen works of art reported to the General Secretariat between two updates of the DVD is published in this Web site section
- Items found by Police Officers who are trying to trace the legitimate owners
- The DVD (technical details and conditions of subscription)
- Frequently asked questions

In 2003, we created a specific Web site section for the cultural property stolen in Iraq holding all the information recorded in the General Secretariat's database (currently 2,283 items).

In 2004, we added a specific Web site section for cultural property stolen in the Kabul Museum, Afghanistan (including c. 670 items), where the entire information had been provided by the UNESCO. Later, data entry was amended with information from a publication, again provided by the UNESCO.

Success Stories

Various examples demonstrate the successful use of database information. They also illustrate the necessity to keep the information as long as possible, as well as the advantages of timely notification.

We have experience of cases where the stolen items were proposed for sale short time after the theft occurred. In other cases, it took decades before the objects were detected, and the database was the only remaining means allowing to identify the stolen property and to enable its restitution and the arrest of the offenders.

Organization of International Conferences

Every 3 years, the General Secretariat organizes an international symposium on the illicit traffic and theft of works of art, antiques, and cultural objects. This conference is held in Lyons. The last one took place in June 2008.

Since 1995, the General Secretariat has organized conferences in regions that are particularly affected by this type of criminality, in particular Europe and South America. In September 2007, in cooperation with the host country, we organized an international conference on cultural property stolen in Central and Eastern Europe in a former salt mine in Wielicka, Poland, a UNESCO cultural heritage site.

Since a couple of years, we are regularly organizing training courses in Latin America. Currently, such a training course is under preparation for Peruvian police, customs, and museums officials scheduled to take place in the first half of 2009.

Cooperation Problems

The key issue for INTERPOL has ever been and remains the international police cooperation. My previous statements demonstrate, however, that the tools already available to ensure this cooperation are greatly underutilized.

This seems not only to be the result of a lack of willingness or of practical means to cooperate, but also a deficit in an interagency cooperation at a national level. That is why it is of utmost importance to establish regular working relationships between police, customs, and the cultural authorities and to inform each other on important events.

Cooperation with Other International Organizations

INTERPOL signed Memoranda of Understanding with the World Customs Organization (WCO) in 1998, with the UNESCO in 1999 and with International Council of Museums (ICOM) in April 2000.

Since a couple of years, the General Secretariat has actively participated in regional workshops organized by UNESCO and ICOM where police and customs officers, and museum curators and representatives from cultural institutions have been invited.

We are glad to count on the strong support by the UNESCO and ICOM, which regularly send representatives to join INTERPOL's Experts Group on Cultural Property created in 2003. And we acknowledge the products put at the disposal of the international law enforcement community by the UNESCO, such as:

- The cultural heritage laws database
- The list of experts for Iraqi cultural heritage, and as a last result
- The common letter with basic recommendations concerning the sales of cultural property over the Internet, which was distributed to their respective membership by each of the Organizations (UNESCO, ICOM, INTERPOL)

Recently, the list of experts for Iraqi cultural heritage proved its usefulness. In the beginning of this year, the Peruvian National Institute for Culture informed us that a post mail parcel had been stopped at their borders. It contained ancient coins and three cuneiform tablets. Upon their request, we recommended a Spanish expert from the UNESCO list who stated that they were authentic and of Iraqi origin. The tablets were seized awaiting their restitution to Iraq.

Conclusion

In conclusion, I would like to reassert the intention of our Organization to cooperate closely in the fight against the illicit trafficking in stolen cultural property.

In order to make this fight effective, it is necessary to:

- Adopt appropriate laws for the protection of the cultural heritage
- Be party to the international conventions
- Establish and update the inventories of the collections

- Transmit any information concerning stolen works of art as rapidly as possible to the competent Police Services. A rapid and wide distribution of this information is an effective tool in the fight against this form of criminality
- Ensure the museum personnel participate in the police and customs training session
- Establish a good cooperation between the concerned ministries
- Adopt a specialized cultural property database

Thank you for your attention.

Chapter 11
The Experience of the Italian Cultural Heritage Protection Unit

Giovanni Nistri

The Carabinieri Headquarters for the Protection of Cultural Heritage

The Carabinieri Headquarters for the Protection of Cultural Heritage (Comando Carabinieri Tutela Patrimonio Culturale – TPC) was instituted in 1969, 1 year prior to the UNESCO Paris Convention in 1970, whereby all UNESCO member States were invited to institute specific services with a view to protecting the cultural heritage of the individual nations.

The TPC is a part of the Ministry of Culture and plays a role regarding the safety and protection of the national cultural heritage, through the prevention and repression of the multiple interrelated criminal activities.

In the particular sector of protection, the TPC has been identified as the center of information and analysis for all Italian law enforcement agencies.

The TPC is comprised at central level of a Centralized Staff Office and an Operational Department (split into three sections: Archeology, Antique, Modern Art, and Counterfeiting) and, on a territorial level, of 12 branches with regional or interregional jurisdiction, and of a section.

As regards its international scope, in addition to working in the sphere of international police cooperation through INTERPOL, the TPC has other responsibilities, such as providing specialized support to peace-keeping operations, such as in Iraq from 2003 to 2006; training of police officers and customs officials in countries that submit such a request; consulting to the Ministry of Cultural Heritage and Activities, in respect of activities centered on retrieving archeological relics belonging to the national heritage and exhibited in museums and private collections abroad.

Since the 1980s, the TPC has been using an auxiliary instrument in its investigations: the *Database of illegally removed cultural artifacts*, provided by Article 85 of the Legislative Decree No. 42 dated 22 January 2004 (Code of Cultural Heritage

G. Nistri (✉)
Heritage Protection Unit, Carabinieri Corps, Rome, Italy
e-mail: giovanni.nistri@carabinieri.it

S. Manacorda and D. Chappell (eds.), *Crime in the Art and Antiquities World: Illegal Trafficking in Cultural Property*, DOI 10.1007/978-1-4419-7946-9_11,

and Landscape), which contains information on the artifacts to recover, of Italian or foreign provenance, and on related criminal events. The database includes a record of 128,638 events, more than 3,297,608 objects, with more than 371,254 images.[1]

Furthermore, the use of sophisticated computer technology has made the database a reference point for the entire Headquarters and for the other Italian and foreign law-enforcement agencies; it also allows to conduct a careful analysis of criminal phenomenon concerning the illicit trafficking of cultural property.

The descriptive section of the database is now open to selective consultation by Associations of merchants working in the sector, with a view to improving market transparency, and is available on the Carabinieri's Web site http://www.carabinieri.it.

After this brief preamble, it is now possible to express some considerations about the developments of criminal events in this specific area occurred in Italy, on the basis of the activities carried out by the TPC, trying to underline the connections or, at least, the rising contiguities, resulting at the investigative level, between the common criminality in the sector and the organized crime, with particular attention to the last 3 years.

Organized Crime and Cultural Heritage

The countless objects which form part of the Italian cultural heritage and are located on the national territory, in many cases easily accessible (consider the easy access to art-filled churches, for example), the interest in them both in Italy and around the world, their great saleability through multiple channels that have also recently increased disproportionately with the explosion of "e-commerce," as well as the extremely high profits that can be made from these "goods," represent the most evident reasons for the enormous development of illegal trafficking in cultural artifacts (Just as an example, remember that in terms of annual income, in the year 2000, the volume of business relating to works of art and artifacts, according to estimates made by the international organizations, was valued at around two billion dollars a year, second only to drugs and weapons trafficking). Consequently, it is obvious that the sector also is of interest to organized crime. In fact, only in the 3-year period from 2007 to 2009 (in the first 6 months), the TPC headquarters has made 23 arrests for criminal association, with a total of 328 people referred to the judicial authorities.

It should, however, be specified that the term "organized" refers largely to networks whose task is to handle the numerous changes of hand that take place from the time of the theft (or the clandestine excavation) to the time the objects reach the final users (major collectors, museums, art institutions, etc.); while these networks have coordinated activities and even use the same channels, this does not necessarily denote the involvement of "traditional" criminal associations and even less so the presence of a "Mafia."

We should also underline, at least as regards our own experience, that no evidence has ever been found at judicial level of an involvement of Mafia-type

[1] Statistical data referred at June 2009.

organizations in the direct and continuing organization of the activities related to the traffic of cultural artifacts, despite the fact that investigations have often demonstrated, as was told, a link between Mafia organizations and the specific criminal sector regarding both the monitoring of the territory and the selection of objectives, i.e., in some cases the involvement – either directly or on behalf of third parties – of individuals affiliated with local Mafia-type clans was demonstrated or suspected.

An example of this can be found in the results of the investigations relating to the theft of the "Nativity" by Caravaggio from the Oratory of San Lorenzo in Palermo in 1969, which was never recovered. In fact, according to legal records, a prominent member of the Sicilian clan who turned an informant to the police attested to his involvement in organizing the theft of the masterpiece.

In the same way, major investigative leads have led to a justified belief that members of the Neapolitan Camorra were involved in the theft and subsequent possession of two paintings by Van Gogh ("View of the Sea at Scheveningen" and "Congregation Leaving the Reformed Church at Nuenen") taken from the Van Gogh museum in Amsterdam in 2002.

Having said this, we now examine some recently conducted investigations, listed by type of crime and/or by type of cultural artifact, which were found to be the work of organized crime (including in the broad definition illustrated here). The differentiation was made only for the purpose of clarity, since experience shows that some groups commit a string of crimes which often involve multiple types of objects and offenses.

Clandestine Excavations

These criminal events represent one of the greatest blights that afflict Italy and many other countries with a wealth of historic relics. In this forum, we do not discuss the incalculable damage that clandestine excavations can bring to the scientific, historic, and cultural area of reference. We only state that, in the Italian legislative framework, anybody who takes possession of any archeological material in a clandestine excavation site can be charged with the crime set forth and punished by the regulation on the protection of cultural artifacts (Article 176 of the Legislative Decree No. 42/2004), while anybody who purchases such objects can be charged with receiving stolen goods (Article 648 of the Penal Code) or with purchase or acquisition of objects of uncertain provenance (Article 712 of the Penal Code).

Clandestine excavation is not a crime that can be quantified in absolute terms, just as it is impossible to pinpoint exactly which and how many ancient relics are removed from sites each year. However, a general idea might be given by the numerous relics recovered by the TPC Unit and other law enforcement agencies.

There has been a gradual decrease in the number of clandestine excavations discovered, whose numbers have dwindled from a peak of more than 1,000 per year, identified in the 1980s and 1990s, to 103 in 2008. Despite this good news, the fact remains that this type of crime continues to be serious and the sector is still "at risk," as it can rely on a significant internal demand and a flourishing international market, albeit with very different quantity and quality characteristics compared to the past.

The circuit of clandestine excavations is complicated and varies according to the geographical area in question, but chiefly involves the zones with a rich ancient history (Lazio, Puglia and Basilicata, Campania, Calabria and Sicily).

Clandestine excavations are defined as occasional when they are the work of local farmers or land owners whose land is involved in building works, or take place sporadically by individuals in digs; in these cases, the person who has found the relic decides to keep it for himself or resell it rather than deliver it to the competent authorities.

Another story is the problem of systematic pillaging, which is much more destructive and is carried out by "tomb raiders" who frequently work in organized groups and use heavy machinery in their digs. They set up local "collection centers" which are controlled by one or more individuals, which in turn report to a local "collector" in the area. The collector is generally a seasoned professional in the rules of the black market and knows exactly the best time to place the relic on the black market. He is therefore also the reference person for export and sale abroad.

One of the investigations conducted by the TPC that has brought to light these dynamics was the "Ghelas" operation (from the ancient name of Gela, from where the intercepted team of tomb raiders originated). The operation was conducted between late 2003 and April 2007 and made it possible to dismantle an organized crime racket dedicated to international trafficking of archeological relics excavated clandestinely from major digs in Sicily and in Spain.

The organization was founded on a rudimentary and at the same time complex structure in which every player performed specific tasks. Indeed, the association – which was modeled on the Mafia clans, despite not having their "technical" attributes – could rely on various trusted members of local groups in the areas of interest whose job was to organize and control the numerous phases of the illegal activity, including research, collection and distribution of relics, preparing them for sale, and making reproductions of pieces of highest value; assessing the value of the pieces, organizing their transfer to potential markets, and searching for buyers and contacts abroad, this latter job assigned to a very well-known local delinquent.

The "bosses" of the various groups provided each other with their expertise on the territory, including the tools needed for clandestine excavations and the knowledge for receiving the stolen artifacts, and even traded among themselves authentic material to use as templates to create counterfeit works for sale.

Theft of Cultural Heritage

This type of criminal activity comprises a diversity of illegal actions and *modus operandi* as well as objectives, which we generally group together in the antiques sector, of sacred art and other genres. Even in this framework, it should be noted that over the past few years there has been a slight but gradual decline in the phenomenon (4.5% in 2008 vs. 2007, a trend confirmed in the first 6 months of 2009), which is closely related to the more general trends of the specific crime. This is true especially for thefts from museums and art galleries while the trend is the reverse for libraries and archives (it is difficult to make an exact assessment of the materials stolen except by indirect estimates based on the materials recovered, since the theft is frequently only discovered after the material is recovered).

In general, the authors of these crimes can be split into three categories:

- Criminal groups, primarily specialized in the theft of church objects, which work in numerous regions and hide the booty in warehouses close to the place of origin awaiting its subsequent sale, or the booty might be resold immediately in localities far from the place of the theft
- Individuals who occasionally steal objects to get money to fuel their drug addiction or are engaged specifically by unscrupulous merchants and/or collectors
- Foreign nationals who make their living off illegal activities

It is important to remember that theft "on commission" generally displays very particular characteristics and that, as such, represents a very limited, niche type of crime. If we leave aside the crimes committed by petty criminals living on the fringes of society, those who commit crimes of theft of cultural heritage usually move in specific spheres of criminal activity, where criminal organizations are involved in every stage of the operation, from the actual theft to the subsequent sale of the stolen goods.

The special nature of the theft often requires a certain skill and specialization by the "thieves" and the receivers of the stolen property, since both must have the ability to recognize the value of the artifact to steal and, often, also a knowledge of the export techniques, in order to avoid damaging the object, and its restoration, to make it easier to sell on the market. The scope of this activity extends beyond the national territory especially for higher value artifacts or for niche articles (ancient books).

An investigation was conducted between 2002 and 2004 in Calabria, code-named "Arberia," which allowed the TPC investigators to dismantle a criminal association involved in the theft and misappropriation of cultural artifacts which acted on behalf of third parties. Under this scheme, the organization was required to obtain authorization from the head of the local "ndrina" to commit criminal acts in a certain territory and pay a 5% commission on the total profits.

The operation code-named "Arte protetta" ended in 2007 and made it possible to dismantle a criminal organization based in the Marche, specialized in the theft and subsequent introduction onto the black market of works of seventeenth and eighteenth century art, as well as in the falsification and subsequent sale of the counterfeit works of art, falsely attributed by experts to major names in contemporary art. Among other things, the investigation also discovered the foundry, where members of the association had been fabricating fake bronze artifacts. The investigators seized the molds used to reproduce them.

The investigation code-named "Tarlo," conducted between 2006 and 2009, made it possible to identify and define operating strategies of a criminal organization centered on thefts perpetrated in homes and places of worship, made up of well-defined "batteries" of parties entrenched in the outlying areas of Naples and operating across the country, especially in central and southern Italy. These batteries used local base units to which they would deliver part of the stolen property for broader sale on the antiques market, using a well-established circuit of receivers. In total, 20 criminals were arrested and other 10 were referred to the judicial authority.

Counterfeiting

The statistical data in the possession of the Office and the information acquired lead to believe that this particular criminal activity is in constant expansion, since it is very remunerative and, on the whole, not very risky. The operating results, aside from the quantity figures on the seizures and confiscations made, in many cases have made it possible to stop particularly prolific production chains with confiscation of the molds. The results have also given a more precise indication of the breadth of the problem as regards the diverse artistic expressions (sculpture, graphics, painting) and the methods of execution and the parties involved. In particular, *approximately 70% of the crimes discovered involve contemporary art*, for obvious reasons of organizational and executive simplicity.

According to prevailing legislation, counterfeiting of cultural artifacts can be effected in different ways, all carried out with a view to making a profit (Article 178 Legislative Decree No. 42/2004).[2]

Since there is no absolute list of the ways to counterfeit art, an act is considered a crime when there is the knowledge of the falsity of the work by the person involved.

The significant differentiation and specialization of the acts that comprise the crime in question means, therefore, that counterfeiting can be carried out by persons who "deal" with works of art in a professional way (consider gallery owners or art merchants) as well as by official actions or private agreements, by collectors and art lovers who sell or trade works of art.

However, the division of tasks and responsibilities necessary to reach the illegal profit, on certain levels, makes it essential to create specialized organizational chains in the particular area of falsified cultural artifacts.

For example, an investigation conducted in 2007–2008 in Northern Italy in cooperation with the FBI and the Spanish police, directed by the anti-Mafia District Attorney in Milan, revealed the existence of a close relationship between Italian organized crime and certain Spanish citizens. With the assistance of scores of complicit galleries in California and Florida, they were able to export counterfeit works of art produced illegally in Italy and Spain, forging a trail of counterfeiting that

[2]In particular:

- Counterfeiting, which is defined as meticulously imitating a work of art in order to sell it as if it were the original.
- Alteration, which means changing the essence of an original work by tampering with it (which can include sectioned paintings, those in which details have been added or removed or those which, by making certain modifications, are dated back to a certain author, while they were really executed by someone else).
- Reproduction, which entails the mechanical multiplication of copies of an original work which is then sold as the original: this is used in lithographs, etchings, xylographs, silk screens, and multiples of sculptures in excess of the number originally authorized by the artist.

Other activities which can be considered criminal and concerned more specifically the commercial world include: circulation or possession of counterfeited works with the intention of selling them despite not actually being involved in or contributing to the actual act of counterfeiting; authentication of a work known to be false; accreditation as authentic of a work known to be false.

stretched from Italy to Spain to the USA. Under those circumstances, the judicial authority, for the first time in Italy and in the particular sector, considered it necessary to apply the specific legislation concerning transnational crime under Law 146/2006, in respect of the 2000 ONU Convention of Palermo principles.

Laundering and Use of Dirty Money, Artifacts, or Black Market Objects

The crimes under Article 648-bis and 648-ter of the Penal Code, namely, introduction on the legal market of monies from black market transactions or illegal activities, are "intrinsic" with the growth of criminal associations, which conceal and recycle illicit capital to avoid taxation and to evade investigative activities that use the artifacts to trace back to the organizations themselves.

While this conduct has always been examined as a part of "traditional" criminal investigations, it is important to underscore the rising importance of money laundering that involves the reinvestment of profits from the black market traffic of cultural artifacts.[3] This finding arises from the increasingly widespread occurrence of this type of crime and the increasing awareness of the investigators, judges, and police.

In this context, I should make mention of the supporting activities supplied by the TPC to the anti-Mafia investigative Unit of Milan in the operation code-named "Metallica," which began in February 2007 and is still in progress. The investigation tracked down criminals based in Lombardy and members of Mafia-like criminal associations. The investigation was launched pursuant to specific leads and in

---

[3]Works of art are often the objects of both real and fictitious operations finalized to hide their (having a) criminal provenance as well as their illicit exportation, such facts may be considered, exactly, a laundering crime.

As a matter of fact, most of triangulations by means of which a work of art is physically transferred abroad just in order to hide its real provenance should be punished as a laundering crime. Such triangulations are acted to place cultural objects in foreign countries whose legislation is more permissive in order to render their sale easier and more convenient in other foreign markets. For instance, during an investigation we noticed illegal exports of cultural goods from Italy to foreign countries which have not signed UNESCO Conventions, so that, in such a way, the same works of art are also sent, in a second time, to other country signatory of UNESCO Conventions, without checks and limitations prescribed by such Conventions for the specific import–export operation among signatory countries. We have to underline another insidious conduct, unfortunately very common: it consists in breaking voluntarily an archeological item illicitly excavated, even if ungrounded integral, in order to make its "laundering" in the black market easier. In fact, in such a way, fragments can be hidden more easily during customs checks. In addition, fragments are used to be shared out among the individuals belonging to the same criminal group in order to split the booty, to strengthen the ties among companions, and, last but not least, to obtain more economical profits, creating a sort of long lasting blackmail with the buyers.

Moreover, the same criminal behavior is often acted, where the illicit market regards a painting, especially a big size one, for instance a triptych or an altar-piece, which sometimes can be cut to obtain different and split works of art. Each of these split parts can be sold autonomously, increasing gains as well as obstructing the identification and recovery of the whole painting.

fact revealed an international racket involving counterfeit works and original works procured on the black market from foreign countries, introduced onto the legal market in order to launder money obtained from other crimes committed by members of Mafia-like associations. Furthermore, the specialized involvement of this unit in the investigation, vital to accomplishing the verifications and providing technical and operating support, represents another confirmation of the success of the existing model of coordination, which assigns the execution of specialized activities to the national unit most competent in the relevant sector. Another operation that shed light on money laundering activities centered on cultural objects ended by the TPC in 2008 is the one code-named "Boucher," which was conducted in close association with another investigation by the Unit's French counterparts OCBC and the French financial police (OCRGDF).

The investigative activities have revealed a criminal organization comprising several groups of tomb raiders working in Apulian and Lucano territories, with ramifications in France. The groups cooperated with each other, despite belonging to different realities, thus forming a dense network of contacts in order to conceal black market trade. The investigation revealed a money laundering activity, already under examination by the French investigators, which consisted in depositing monies in a French bank in exchange for archeological relics taken from Southern Italy, relics that were sold by complicit "front men" in public auctions and in art galleries, and in reinvesting the large sums of money obtained in real estate.

Illegal Export

This type of crime is much more common than one might believe and involves cultural artifacts traded on the black market as well as artworks whose export is restricted due to their historic and artistic value. It is facilitated by a diversity of strategies that can be implemented to avoid checks[4] and is "stimulated" by the differences between laws on a European level and the fact that the market outside of

[4]In looking at the various cases under examination, we find that black market export takes place through the use of:

- International shipping companies (many times unaware of the illicit merchandise they are carrying) with the use of lorries and refrigerated trucks for road traffic or in containers for shipping by sea, with merchandise hidden among other completely unrelated goods.
- Leisure craft, taking advantage of the characteristic geography of Italy's coastline, which is a destination for tourists from around the world.
- Hollow spaces in campers and mobile homes.
- International trains, with goods held in luggage or bags located in compartments far away from the person transporting them.
- Hand luggage, in air traffic.

Furthermore, in the illicit export of particularly valuable paintings, one technique involves painting a contemporary design over the original painting in order to more easily obtain the necessary permits for export, as well as other fraudulent methods.

Italy promises much higher profits that what could be obtained in this country. This crime is committed generally by professional art traders and by individual collectors, in addition to receivers of stolen property, experts on foreign markets.

The investigation code-named "Guardinghi," launched in 2008 and still in progress, has shed light on numerous criminal activities undertaken by the same criminal group, which submitted major paintings to the Export Offices, falsifying the attribution and painting quality in order to deceive the officials in charge of issuing certification, or to illegally move them out of the country (onto European markets and on other continents). Once exported, they would be sold by several select auction houses, purchased directly by individuals and shell companies, only to be temporarily reimported back to Italy after having falsified their origin so as to significantly raise their value.

Conclusions

From all the information above, it is clear how crimes involving cultural artifacts are no longer, admitting they ever were, crimes only concerning the intellectual elite or wealthy billionaires with a weakness for art or narrow circles of professionals in the sector. On the contrary, they have become the basis for a considerable business that requires the use of sophisticated tools and highly developed organizations to earn increasingly greater profits. These organizations – even if they are not Mafia-style in the traditional sense of the word – use operating methods very similar to these organized crime rackets and are developing multinational characteristics.

As a result, the instruments that law enforcement agencies require, especially specialized corps such as the TPC, must be adapted to the rapid evolution of the threat. This is also true for international legislation.

Among the other possible solutions, which are not necessarily disjoined the one with the others, I will only comment on a few proposals that could represent an excellent starting point and which are already included in a legislative proposal which was brought to the attention of the parliamentary committees in the former legislature. Some of the operating instruments are already available in our system because they are applicable in other criminal sectors and because they are already included in international regulations that have been implemented in Italy or are awaiting implementation. The measure was made with a view to modernize the current system of criminal protection of the cultural artifact, which considers the cultural value as an ancillary quality of the object and as a result, sets forth an indirect protection, solely by adding aggravating circumstances to the key crime. It included strong direct criminal protection of cultural artifacts, based on a legal concept of the cultural object as distinct from the material object underlying it, and therefore, worthy of protection in its own right.

In this perspective, criminal protection of the cultural heritage might be achieved through a modification of the sanctions contained in the prevailing "Code of the Cultural and Landscape Heritage" (Legislative Decree No. 42/2004) by setting forth that theft and receiving of stolen cultural artifacts are separate offenses, by making illegal export of cultural artifacts a permanent offense, by specifically mentioning the offense of receiving counterfeit objects, by instituting a special charge for money laundering when the activity centers on counterfeited cultural artifacts and by shoring up the investigative instruments. In particular, more specifically:

- The inability to punish officials and law enforcement agents in carrying out undercover investigative activities, modeled as narcotics trafficking laws and transnational crimes laws as well.
- The ability to proceed with simulated purchase of cultural artifacts; on par with the matters indicated above, this instrument is already used in relation to cultural artifacts by the Naples II Convention, based on Article k3 of the Treaty of the European Union regarding mutual assistance and cooperation between customs agencies, signed in Brussels in 1997.
- The ability to make delayed arrests for justifiable reasons, here also, implementing measures already set forth in narcotics trafficking laws as well as the legal procedure concerning the transnational crime, in accordance with the 2000 Palermo Convention.
- Use of undercover operations, including setting up Web sites, to create or manage areas of communication or exchanges online if the crimes are committed by the use of computerized or other electronic means, modeled after the laws counteracting child pornography.
- Seizure of real estate, property and sums of money which are instrumental to perpetrating crimes on cultural artifacts, requiring seized assets to be surrendered to the Ministry for Culture or to the legal custody of the police if they require them to stop activities in the specific sector.
- Applying preventive and prohibitive measures (concerning the issue of licenses, permits, registrations, authorizations, etc.) in relation to individuals considered a danger to the community, when the criminal activity is believed to center on cultural artifacts.

Also as regards the illustrated evolution of the trend, as mentioned above, it would be appropriate to cooperate with other nations. This could be achieved by strengthening the relationship already in place between the various national law-enforcement agencies and evaluating the feasibility of direct relationships between specialized data bases, as already suggested in the European Union ambit. At the same time, it would be necessary to review European legislation (e.g., EEC Directive 93/7) and harmonizing relevant national legislation, so as to extend the tools already available in civil law to the area of criminal law and facilitate the legal procedures between countries.

Finally, it would be useful to reconsider the regulations in some important sectors on the art market, such as the auction houses and specialized Web sites, in the first case by passing laws that implement the codes of ethics established by international organizations, such as UNESCO and ICOM, and in the second, by setting up standard agreements aimed at a faster acquisition of information on users and a better regulation of the individual "virtual markets," as it has been realized, for instance, by an agreement between the Swiss Federal Office of Culture and eBay Switzerland.

Appendix 1

Convention for the Protection of Cultural Property in the Event of Armed Conflict with Regulations for the Execution of the Convention 1954

The High Contracting Parties,

Recognizing that cultural property has suffered grave damage during recent armed conflicts and that, by reason of the developments in the technique of warfare, it is in increasing danger of destruction;

Being convinced that damage to cultural property belonging to any people whatsoever means damage to the cultural heritage of all mankind, since each people makes its contribution to the culture of the world;

Considering that the preservation of the cultural heritage is of great importance for all peoples of the world and that it is important that this heritage should receive international protection;

Guided by the principles concerning the protection of cultural property during armed conflict, as established in the Conventions of The Hague of 1899 and of 1907 and in the Washington Pact of 15 April, 1935;

Being of the opinion that such protection cannot be effective unless both national and international measures have been taken to organize it in time of peace;

Being determined to take all possible steps to protect cultural property; have agreed upon the following provisions.

Chapter I. General provisions regarding protection

Article 1. Definition of cultural property

For the purposes of the present Convention, the term "cultural property" shall cover, irrespective of origin or ownership:

a. movable or immovable property of great importance to the cultural heritage of every people, such as monuments of architecture, art or history, whether religious

S. Manacorda and D. Chappell (eds.), *Crime in the Art and Antiquities World: Illegal Trafficking in Cultural Property*, DOI 10.1007/978-1-4419-7946-9, or secular; archaeological sites; groups of buildings which, as a whole, are of historical or artistic interest; works of art; manuscripts, books and other objects of artistic, historical or archaeological interest; as well as scientific collections and important collections of books or archives or of reproductions of the property defined above;

b. buildings whose main and effective purpose is to preserve or exhibit the movable cultural property defined in sub-paragraph (a) such as museums, large libraries and depositories of archives, and refuges intended to shelter, in the event of armed conflict, the movable cultural property defined in sub-paragraph (a); and
c. centers containing a large amount of cultural property as defined in sub-paragraphs (a) and (b), to be known as "centers containing monuments."

Article 2. Protection of cultural property

For the purposes of the present Convention, the protection of cultural property shall comprise the safeguarding of and respect for such property.

Article 3. Safeguarding of cultural property

The High Contracting Parties undertake to prepare in time of peace for the safeguarding of cultural property situated within their own territory against the foreseeable effects of an armed conflict, by taking such measures as they consider appropriate.

Article 4. Respect for cultural property

1. The High Contracting Parties undertake to respect cultural property situated within their own territory as well as within the territory of other High Contracting Parties by refraining from any use of the property and its immediate surroundings or of the appliances in use for its protection for purposes which are likely to expose it to destruction or damage in the event of armed conflict; and by refraining from any act of hostility directed against such property.
2. The obligations mentioned in paragraph 1 of the present Article may be waived only in cases where military necessity imperatively requires such a waiver.
3. The High Contracting Parties further undertake to prohibit, prevent and, if necessary, put a stop to any form of theft, pillage or misappropriation of, and any acts of vandalism directed against, cultural property. They shall refrain from requisitioning movable cultural property situated in the territory of another High Contracting Party.
4. They shall refrain from any act directed by way of reprisals against cultural property.
5. No High Contracting Party may evade the obligations incumbent upon it under the present Article, in respect of another High Contracting Party, by reason of the fact that the latter has not applied the measures of safeguard referred to in Article 3.

Article 5. Occupation

1. Any High Contracting Party in occupation of the whole or part of the territory of another High Contracting Party shall as far as possible support the competent national authorities of the occupied country in safeguarding and preserving its cultural property.
2. Should it prove necessary to take measures to preserve cultural property situated in occupied territory and damaged by military operations, and should the competent national authorities be unable to take such measures, the Occupying Power shall, as far as possible, and in close co-operation with such authorities, take the most necessary measures of preservation.
3. Any High Contracting Party whose government is considered their legitimate government by members of a resistance movement, shall, if possible, draw their attention to the obligation to comply with those provisions of the Convention dealing with respect for cultural property.

Article 6. Distinctive marking of cultural property

In accordance with the provisions of Article 16, cultural property may bear a distinctive emblem so as to facilitate its recognition.

Article 7. Military measures

1. The High Contracting Parties undertake to introduce in time of peace into their military regulations or instructions such provisions as may ensure observance of the present Convention and to foster in the members of their armed forces a spirit of respect for the culture and cultural property of all peoples.
2. The High Contracting Parties undertake to plan or establish in peace-time, within their armed forces, services or specialist personnel whose purpose will be to secure respect for cultural property and to co-operate with the civilian authorities responsible for safeguarding it.

Chapter II. Special protection

Article 8. Granting of special protection

1. There may be placed under special protection a limited number of refuges intended to shelter movable cultural property in the event of armed conflict, of centers containing monuments and other immovable cultural property of very great importance, provided that they:

   a. are situated at an adequate distance from any large industrial center or from any important military objective constituting a vulnerable point, such as, for example, an aerodrome, broadcasting station, establishment engaged upon work of national defense, a port or railway station of relative importance or a main line of communication;

b. are not used for military purposes.

2. A refuge for movable cultural property may also be placed under special protection, whatever its location, if it is so constructed that, in all probability, it will not be damaged by bombs.
3. A center containing monuments shall be deemed to be used for military purposes whenever it is used for the movement of military personnel or material, even in transit. The same shall apply whenever activities directly connected with military operations, the stationing of military personnel, or the production of war material are carried on within the center.
4. The guarding of cultural property mentioned in paragraph I above by armed custodians specially empowered to do so, or the presence, in the vicinity of such cultural property, of police forces normally responsible for the maintenance of public order shall not be deemed to be used for military purposes.
5. If any cultural property mentioned in paragraph 1 of the present Article is situated near an important military objective as defined in the said paragraph, it may nevertheless be placed under special protection if the High Contracting Party asking for that protection undertakes, in the event of armed conflict, to make no use of the objective and particularly, in the case of a port, railway station or aerodrome, to divert all traffic there from. In that event, such diversion shall be prepared in time of peace.
6. Special protection is granted to cultural property by its entry in the "International Register of Cultural Property under Special Protection." This entry shall only be made, in accordance with the provisions of the present Convention and under the conditions provided for in the Regulations for the execution of the Convention.

Article 9. Immunity of cultural property under special protection

The High Contracting Parties undertake to ensure the immunity of cultural property under special protection by refraining, from the time of entry in the International Register, from any act of hostility directed against such property and, except for the cases provided for in paragraph 5 of Article 8, from any use of such property or its surroundings for military purposes.

Article 10. Identification and control

During an armed conflict, cultural property under special protection shall be marked with the distinctive emblem described in Article 16 and shall be open to international control as provided for in the Regulations for the execution of the Convention.

Article 11. Withdrawal of immunity

1. If one of the High Contracting Parties commits, in respect of any item of cultural property under special protection, a violation of the obligations under Article 9, the opposing Party shall, so long as this violation persists, be released from the obligation to ensure the immunity of the property concerned. Nevertheless, whenever possible, the latter Party shall first request the cessation of such violation within a reasonable time.
2. Apart from the case provided for in paragraph 1 of the present Article, immunity shall be withdrawn from cultural property under special protection only in exceptional cases of unavoidable military necessity, and only for such time as that necessity continues. Such necessity can be established only by the officer commanding a force the equivalent of a division in size or larger. Whenever circumstances permit, the opposing Party shall be notified, a reasonable time in advance, of the decision to withdraw immunity.
3. The Party withdrawing immunity shall, as soon as possible, so inform the Commissioner-General for cultural property provided for in the Regulations for the execution of the Convention, in writing, stating the reasons.

Chapter III. Transport of cultural property

Article 12. Transport under special protection

1. Transport exclusively engaged in the transfer of cultural property, whether within a territory or to another territory, may, at the request of the High Contracting Party concerned, take place under special protection in accordance with the conditions specified in the Regulations for the execution of the Convention.
2. Transport under special protection shall take place under the international supervision provided for in the aforesaid Regulations and shall display the distinctive emblem described in Article 16.
3. The High Contracting Parties shall refrain from any act of hostility directed against transport under special protection.

Article 13. Transport in urgent cases

1. If a High Contracting Party considers that the safety of certain cultural property requires its transfer and that the matter is of such urgency that the procedure laid down in Article 12 cannot be followed, especially at the beginning of an armed conflict, the transport may display the distinctive emblem described in Article 16, provided that an application for immunity referred to in Article 12 has not

already been made and refused. As far as possible, notification of transfer should be made to the opposing Parties. Nevertheless, transport conveying cultural property to the territory of another country may not display the distinctive emblem unless immunity has been expressly granted to it.

2. The High Contracting Parties shall take, so far as possible, the necessary precautions to avoid acts of hostility directed against the transport described in paragraph 1 of the present Article and displaying the distinctive emblem.

Article 14. Immunity from seizure, capture and prize

1. Immunity from seizure, placing in prize, or capture shall be granted to:
   a. cultural property enjoying the protection provided for in Article 12 or that provided for in Article 13;
   b. the means of transport exclusively engaged in the transfer of such cultural property.
2. Nothing in the present Article shall limit the right of visit and search.

Chapter IV. Personnel

Article 15. Personnel

As far as is consistent with the interests of security, personnel engaged in the protection of cultural property shall, in the interests of such property, be respected and, if they fall into the hands of the opposing Party, shall be allowed to continue to carry out their duties whenever the cultural property for which they are responsible has also fallen into the hands of the opposing Party.

Chapter V. The distinctive emblem

Article 16. Emblem of the convention

1. The distinctive emblem of the Convention shall take the form of a shield, pointed below, per saltire blue and white (a shield consisting of a royal-blue square, one of the angles of which forms the point of the shield, and of a royal-blue triangle above the square, the space on either side being taken up by a white triangle).
2. The emblem shall be used alone, or repeated three times in a triangular formation (one shield below), under the conditions provided for in Article 17.

Article 17. Use of the emblem

1. The distinctive emblem repeated three times may be used only as a means of identification of:

   a. immovable cultural property under special protection:
   b. the transport of cultural property under the conditions provided for in Articles 12 and 13;
   c. improvised refuges, under the conditions provided for in the Regulations for the execution of the Convention.

2. The distinctive emblem may be used alone only as a means of identification of:

   a. cultural property not under special protection;
   b. the persons responsible for the duties of control in accordance with the Regulations for the execution of the Convention;
   c. the personnel engaged in the protection of cultural property;
   d. the identity cards mentioned in the Regulations for the execution of the Convention.

3. During an armed conflict, the use of the distinctive emblem in any other cases than those mentioned in the preceding paragraphs of the present Article, and the use for any purpose whatever of a sign resembling the distinctive emblem, shall be forbidden.
4. The distinctive emblem may not be placed on any immovable cultural property unless at the same time there is displayed an authorization duly dated and signed by the competent authority of the High Contracting Party.

Chapter VI. Scope of application of the Convention

Article 18. Application of the Convention

1. Apart from the provisions which shall take effect in time of peace, the present Convention shall apply in the event of declared war or of any other armed conflict which may arise between two or more of the High Contracting Parties, even if the state of war is not recognized by, one or more of them.
2. The Convention shall also apply to all cases of partial or total occupation of the territory of a High Contracting Party, even if the said occupation meets with no armed resistance.
3. If one of the Powers in conflict is not a Party to the present Convention, the Powers which are Parties thereto shall nevertheless remain bound by it in their mutual relations. They shall furthermore be bound by the Convention, in relation to the said Power, if the latter has declared, that it accepts the provisions thereof and so long as it applies them.

Article 19. Conflicts not of an international character

1. In the event of an armed conflict not of an international character occurring within the territory of one of the High Contracting Parties, each party to the conflict shall be bound to apply, as, a minimum, the provisions of the present Convention which relate to respect for cultural property.
2. The parties to the conflict shall endeavour to bring into force, by means of special agreements, all or part of the other provisions of the present Convention.
3. The United Nations Educational, Scientific and Cultural Organization may offer its services to the parties to the conflict.
4. The application of the preceding provisions shall not affect the legal status of the parties to the conflict.

Chapter VII. Execution of the Convention

Article 20. Regulations for the execution of the Convention

The procedure by which the present Convention is to be applied is defined in the Regulations for its execution, which constitute an integral part thereof.

Article 21. Protecting powers

The present Convention and the Regulations for its execution shall be applied with the co-operation of the Protecting Powers responsible for safeguarding the interests of the Parties to the conflict.

Article 22. Conciliation procedure

1. The Protecting Powers shall lend their good offices in all cases where they may deem it useful in the interests of cultural property, particularly if there is disagreement between the Parties to the conflict as to the application or interpretation of the provisions of the present Convention or the Regulations for its execution.
2. For this purpose, each of the Protecting Powers may, either at the invitation of one Party, of the Director-General of the United Nations Educational, Scientific and Cultural Organization, or on its own initiative, propose to the Parties to the conflict a meeting of their representatives, and in particular of the authorities responsible for the protection of cultural property, if considered appropriate on suitably chosen neutral territory. The Parties to the conflict shall be bound to give effect to the proposals for meeting made to them. The Protecting Powers shall propose for approval by the Parties to the conflict a person belonging to a neutral

Power or a person presented by the Director-General of the United Nations Educational, Scientific and Cultural Organization, which person shall be invited to take part in such a meeting in the capacity of Chairman.

Article 23. Assistance of UNESCO

1. The High Contracting Parties may call upon the United Nations Educational, Scientific and Cultural Organization for technical assistance in organizing the protection of their cultural property, or in connexion with any other problem arising out of the application of the present Convention or the Regulations for its execution. The Organization shall accord such assistance within the limits fixed by its programme and by its resources.
2. The Organization is authorized to make, on its own initiative, proposals on this matter to the High Contracting Parties.

Article 24. Special agreements

1. The High Contracting Parties may conclude special agreements for all matters concerning which they deem it suitable to make separate provision.
2. No special agreement may be concluded which would diminish the protection afforded by the present Convention to cultural property and to the personnel engaged in its protection.

Article 25. Dissemination of the Convention

The High Contracting Parties undertake, in time of peace as in time of armed conflict, to disseminate the text of the present Convention and the Regulations for its execution as widely as possible in their respective countries. They undertake, in particular, to include the study thereof in their programmes of military and, if possible, civilian training, so that its principles are made known to the whole population, especially the armed forces and personnel engaged in the protection of cultural property.

Article 26. Translations reports

1. The High Contracting Parties shall communicate to one another, through the Director-General of the United Nations Educational, Scientific and Cultural Organization, the official translations of the present Convention and of the Regulations for its execution.
2. Furthermore, at least once every 4 years, they shall forward to the Director-General a report giving whatever information they think suitable concerning

any measures being taken, prepared or contemplated by their respective administrations in fulfillment of the present Convention and of the Regulations for its execution.

Article 27. Meetings

1. The Director-General of the United Nations Educational, Scientific and Cultural Organization may, with the approval of the Executive Board, convene meetings of representatives of the High Contracting Parties. He must convene such a meeting if at least one-fifth of the High Contracting Parties so request.
2. Without prejudice to any other functions which have been conferred on it by the present Convention or the Regulations for its execution, the purpose of the meeting will be to study problems concerning the application of the Convention and of the Regulations for its execution, and to formulate recommendations in respect thereof.
3. The meeting may further undertake a revision of the Convention or the Regulations for its execution if the majority of the High Contracting Parties are represented, and in accordance with the provisions of Article 39.

Article 28. Sanctions

The High Contracting Parties undertake to take, within the framework of their ordinary criminal jurisdiction, all necessary steps to prosecute and impose penal or disciplinary sanctions upon those persons, of whatever nationality, who commit or order to be committed a breach of the present Convention.

Final provisions

Article 29. Languages

1. The present Convention is drawn up in English, French, Russian and Spanish, the four texts being equally authoritative.
2. The United Nations Educational, Scientific and Cultural Organization shall arrange for translations of the Convention into the other official languages of its General Conference.

Article 30. Signature

The present Convention shall bear the date of 14 May, 1954 and, until the date of 31 December, 1954, shall remain open for signature by all States invited to the Conference which met at The Hague from 21 April, 1954 to 14 May, 1954.

Article 31. Ratification

1. The present Convention shall be subject to ratification by signatory States in accordance with their respective constitutional procedures.
2. The instruments of ratification shall be deposited with the Director-General of the United Nations Educational, Scientific and Cultural Organization.

Article 32. Accession

From the date of its entry into force, the present Convention shall be open for accession by all States mentioned in Article 30 which have not signed it, as well as any other State invited to accede by the Executive Board of the United Nations Educational, Scientific and Cultural Organization. Accession shall be effected by the deposit of an instrument of accession with the Director-General of the United Nations Educational, Scientific and Cultural Organization.

Article 33. Entry into force

1. The present Convention shall enter into force 3 months after five instruments of ratification have been deposited.
2. Thereafter, it shall enter into force, for each High Contracting Party, 3 months after the deposit of its instrument of ratification or accession.
3. The situations referred to in Articles 18 and 19 shall give immediate effect to ratifications or accessions deposited by the Parties to the conflict either before or after the beginning of hostilities or occupation. In such cases, the Director-General of the United Nations Educational, Scientific and Cultural Organization shall transmit the communications referred to in Article 38 by the speediest method.

Article 34. Effective application

1. Each State Party to the Convention on the date of its entry into force shall take all necessary measures to ensure its effective application within a period of 6 months after such entry into force.
2. This period shall be 6 months from the date of deposit of the instruments of ratification or accession for any State which deposits its instrument of ratification or accession after the date of the entry into force of the Convention.

Article 35. Territorial extension of the Convention

Any High Contracting Party may, at the time of ratification or accession, or at any time thereafter, declare by notification addressed to the Director-General of the United Nations Educational, Scientific and Cultural Organization, that the present

Convention shall extend to all or any of the territories for whose international relations it is responsible. The said notification shall take effect 3 months after the date of its receipt.

Article 36. Relation to previous conventions

1. In the relations between Powers which are bound by the Conventions of The Hague concerning the Laws and Customs of War on Land (IV) and concerning Naval Bombardment in Time of War (IX), whether those of 29 July, 1899 or those of 18 October, 1907, and which are Parties to the present Convention, this last Convention shall be supplementary to the aforementioned Convention (IX) and to the Regulations annexed to the aforementioned Convention (IV) and shall substitute for the emblem described in Article 5 of the aforementioned Convention (IX) the emblem described in Article 16 of the present Convention, in cases in which the present Convention and the Regulations for its execution provide for the use of this distinctive emblem.
2. In the relations between Powers which are bound by the Washington Pact of 15 April, 1935 for the Protection of Artistic and Scientific Institutions and of Historic Monuments (Roerich Pact) and which are Parties to the present Convention, the latter Convention shall be supplementary to the Roerich Pact and shall substitute for the distinguishing flag described in Article III of the Pact the emblem defined in Article 16 of the present Convention, in cases in which the present Convention and the Regulations for its execution provide for the use of this distinctive emblem.

Article 37. Denunciation

1. Each High Contracting Party may denounce the present Convention, on its own behalf, or on behalf of any territory for whose international relations it is responsible.
2. The denunciation shall be notified by an instrument in writing, deposited with the Director-General of the United Nations Educational, Scientific and Cultural Organization.
3. The denunciation shall take effect 1 year after the receipt of the instrument of denunciation. However, if, on the expiry of this period, the denouncing Party is involved in an armed conflict, the denunciation shall not take effect until the end of hostilities, or until the operations of repatriating cultural property are completed, whichever is the later.

Article 38. Notifications

The Director-General of the United Nations Educational, Scientific and Cultural Organization shall inform the States referred to in Articles 30 and 32, as well as the United Nations, of the deposit of all the instruments of ratification, accession or acceptance provided for in Articles 31, 32 and 39 and of the notifications and denunciations provided for respectively in Articles 35, 37 and 39.

Article 39. Revision of the Convention and of the Regulations for its execution

1. Any High Contracting Party may propose amendments to the present Convention or the Regulations for its execution. The text of any proposed amendment shall be communicated to the Director-General of the United Nations Educational, Scientific and Cultural Organization who shall transmit it to each High Contracting Party with the request that such Party reply within 4 months stating whether it:

   a. desires that a Conference be convened to consider the proposed amendment;
   b. favours the acceptance of the proposed amendment without a Conference;
   c. favours the rejection of the proposed amendment without a Conference.

2. The Director-General shall transmit the replies, received under paragraph 1 of the present Article, to all High Contracting Parties.
3. If all the High Contracting Parties which have, within the prescribed time limit, stated their views to the Director-General of the United Nations Educational, Scientific and Cultural Organization, pursuant to paragraph 1(b) of this Article, inform him that they favour acceptance of the amendment without a Conference, notification of their decision shall be made by the Director-General in accordance with Article 38. The amendment shall become effective for all the High Contracting Parties on the expiry of 90 days from the date of such notification.
4. The Director-General shall convene a Conference of the High Contracting Parties to consider the proposed amendment if requested to do so by more than one-third of the High Contracting Parties.
5. Amendments to the Convention or to the Regulations for its execution, dealt with under the provisions of the preceding paragraph, shall enter into force only after they have been unanimously adopted by the High Contracting Parties represented at the Conference and accepted by each of the High Contracting Parties.
6. Acceptance by the High Contracting Parties of amendments to, the Convention or to the Regulations for its execution, which have been adopted by the Conference mentioned in paragraphs 4 and 5, shall be effected by the deposit of a formal instrument with the Director-General of the United Nations Educational, Scientific and Cultural Organization.
7. After the entry into force of amendments to the present Convention or to the Regulations for its execution, only the text of the Convention or of the Regulations for its execution thus amended shall remain open for ratification or accession.

Article 40. Registration

In accordance with Article 102 of the Charter of the United Nations, the present Convention shall be registered with the Secretariat of the United Nations at the request of the Director-General of the United Nations Educational, Scientific and Cultural Organization.

IN FAITH WHEREOF the undersigned, duly authorized, have signed the present Convention.

Done at The Hague, this 14th day of May, 1954, in a single copy which shall be deposited in the archives of the United Nations Educational, Scientific and Cultural Organization, and certified true copies of which shall be delivered to all the States referred to in Articles 30 and 32 as well as to the United Nations.

Regulations for the Execution of the Convention for the Protection of Cultural Property in the Event of Armed Conflict

Chapter I. Control

Article 1. International list of persons

On the entry into force of the Convention, the Director-General of the United Nations Educational, Scientific and Cultural Organization shall compile an international list consisting of all persons nominated by the High Contracting Parties as qualified to carry out the functions of Commissioner-General for Cultural Property. On the initiative of the Director-General of the United Nations Educational, Scientific and Cultural Organization, this list shall be periodically revised on the basis of requests formulated by the High Contracting Parties.

Article 2. Organization of control

As soon as any High Contracting Party is engaged in an armed conflict to which Article 18 of the Convention applies:

a. It shall appoint a representative for cultural property situated in its territory; if it is in occupation of another territory, it shall appoint a special representative for cultural property situated in that territory;
b. The Protecting Power acting for each of the Parties in conflict with such High Contracting Party shall appoint delegates accredited to the latter in conformity with Article 3 below;
c. A Commissioner-General for Cultural Property shall be appointed to such High Contracting Party in accordance with Article 4.

Article 3. Appointment of delegates of Protecting Powers

The Protecting Power shall appoint its delegates from among the members of its diplomatic or consular staff or, with the approval of the Party to which they will be accredited, from among other persons.

Article 4. Appointment of Commissioner-General

1. The Commissioner-General for Cultural Property shall be chosen from the international list of persons by joint agreement between the Party to which he will be accredited and the Protecting Powers acting on behalf of the opposing Parties.
2. Should the Parties fail to reach agreement within 3 weeks from the beginning of their discussions on this point, they shall request the President of the International Court of Justice to appoint the Commissioner-General, who shall not take up his duties until the Party to which he is accredited has approved his appointment.

Article 5. Functions of delegates

The delegates of the Protecting Powers shall take note of violations of the Convention, investigate, with the approval of the Party to which they are accredited, the circumstances in which they have occurred, make representations locally to secure their cessation and, if necessary, notify the Commissioner-General of such violations. They shall keep him informed of their activities.

Article 6. Functions of the Commissioner-General

1. The Commissioner-General for Cultural Property shall deal with all matters referred to him in connexion with the application of the Convention, in conjunction with the representative of the Party to which he is accredited and with the delegates concerned.
2. He shall have powers of decision and appointment in the cases specified in the present Regulations.
3. With the agreement of the Party to which he is accredited, he shall have the right to order an investigation or to, conduct it himself.
4. He shall make any representations to the Parties to the conflict or to their Protecting Powers which he deems useful for the application of the Convention.
5. He shall draw up such reports as may be necessary on the application of the Convention and communicate them to the Parties concerned and to their Protecting Powers. He shall send copies to the Director-General of the United Nations Educational, Scientific and Cultural Organization, who may make use only of their technical contents.
6. If there is no Protecting Power, the Commissioner-General shall exercise the functions of the Protecting Power as laid down in Articles 21 and 22 of the Convention.

Article 7. Inspectors and experts

1. Whenever the Commissioner-General for Cultural Property considers it necessary, either at the request of the delegates concerned or after consultation with them, he shall propose, for the approval of the Party to which he is accredited,

an inspector of cultural property to be charged with a specific mission. An inspector shall be responsible only to the Commissioner-General.

2. The Commissioner-General, delegates and inspectors may have recourse to the services of experts, who will also be proposed for the approval of the Party mentioned in the preceding paragraph.

Article 8. Discharge of the mission of control

The Commissioners-General for Cultural Property, delegates of the Protecting Powers, inspectors and experts shall in no case exceed their mandates. In particular, they shall take account of the security needs of the High Contracting Party to which they are accredited and shall in all circumstances act in accordance with the requirements of the military situation as communicated to them by that High Contracting Party.

Article 9. Substitutes for Protecting Powers

If a Party to the conflict does not benefit or ceases to benefit from the activities of a Protecting Power, a neutral State may be asked to undertake those functions of a Protecting Power which concern the appointment of a Commissioner-General for Cultural Property in accordance with the procedure laid down in Article 4 above. The Commissioner-General thus appointed shall, if need be, entrust to inspectors the functions of delegates of Protecting Powers as specified in the present Regulations.

Article 10. Expenses

The remuneration and expenses of the Commissioner-General for Cultural Property, inspectors and experts shall be met by the Party to which they are accredited. Remuneration and expenses of delegates of the Protecting Powers shall be subject to agreement between those Powers and the States whose interests they are safeguarding.

Chapter II. Special protection

Article 11. Improvised refuges

1. If, during an armed conflict, any High Contracting Party is induced by unforeseen circumstances to set up an improvised refuge and desires that it should be placed under special protection, it shall communicate this fact forthwith to the Commissioner-General accredited to that Party.

2. If the Commissioner-General considers that such a measure is justified by the circumstances and by the importance of the cultural property sheltered in this improvised refuge, he may authorize the High Contracting Party to display on such refuge the distinctive emblem defined in Article 16 of the Convention. He shall communicate his decision without delay to the delegates of the Protecting Powers who are concerned, each of whom may, within a time limit of 30 days, order the immediate withdrawal of the emblem.
3. As soon as such delegates have signified their agreement or if the time limit of 30 days has passed without any of the delegates concerned having made an objection, and if, in the view of the Commissioner-General, the refuge fulfils the conditions laid down in Article 8 of the Convention, the Commissioner-General shall request the Director-General of the United Nations Educational, Scientific and Cultural Organization to enter the refuge in the Register of Cultural Property under Special Protection.

Article 12. International Register of Cultural Property under Special Protection

1. An "International Register of Cultural Property under Special Protection" shall be prepared.
2. The Director-General of the United Nations Educational, Scientific and Cultural Organization shall maintain this Register. He shall furnish copies to the Secretary-General of the United Nations and to the High Contracting Parties.
3. The Register shall be divided into sections, each in the name of a High Contracting Party. Each section shall be subdivided into three paragraphs, headed: Refuges, Centers containing Monuments, Other Immovable Cultural Property. The Director-General shall determine what details each section shall contain.

Article 13. Requests for registration

1. Any High Contracting Party may submit to the Director-General of the United Nations Educational, Scientific and Cultural Organization an application for the entry in the Register of certain refuges, centers containing monuments or other immovable cultural property situated within its territory. Such application shall contain a description of the location of such property and shall certify that the property complies with the provisions of Article 8 of the Convention.
2. In the event of occupation, the Occupying Power shall be competent to make such application.
3. The Director-General of the United Nations Educational, Scientific and Cultural Organization shall, without delay, send copies of applications for registration to each of the High Contracting Parties.

Article 14. Objections

1. Any High Contracting Party may, by letter addressed to the Director-General of the United Nations Educational, Scientific and Cultural Organization, lodge an objection to the registration of cultural property. This letter must be received by him within 4 months of the day on which he sent a copy of the application for registration.
2. Such objection shall state the reasons giving rise to it, the only, valid grounds being that:

   a. the property is not cultural property;
   b. the property does not comply with the conditions mentioned in Article 8 of the Convention.

3. The Director-General shall send a copy of the letter of objection to the High Contracting Parties without delay. He shall, if necessary, seek the advice of the International Committee on Monuments, Artistic and Historical Sites and Archaeological Excavations and also, if he thinks fit, of any other competent organization or person.
4. The Director-General, or the High Contracting Party requesting registration, may make whatever representations they deem necessary to the High Contracting Parties which lodged the objection, with a view to causing the objection to be withdrawn.
5. If a High Contracting Party which has made an application for registration in time of peace becomes involved in an armed conflict before the entry has been made, the cultural property concerned shall at once be provisionally entered in the Register, by the Director-General, pending the confirmation, withdrawal or cancellation of any objection that may be, or may have been, made.
6. If, within a period of 6 months from the date of receipt of the letter of objection, the Director-General has not received from the High Contracting Party lodging the objection a communication stating that it has been withdrawn, the High Contracting Party applying for registration may request arbitration in accordance with the procedure in the following paragraph.
7. The request for arbitration shall not be made more than 1 year after the date of receipt by the Director-General of the letter of objection. Each of the two Parties to the dispute shall appoint an arbitrator. When more than one objection has been lodged against an application for registration, the High Contracting Parties which have lodged the objections shall, by common consent, appoint a single arbitrator. These two arbitrators shall select a chief arbitrator from the international list mentioned in Article 1 of the present Regulations. If such arbitrators cannot agree upon their choice, they shall ask the President of the International Court of Justice to appoint a chief arbitrator who need not necessarily be chosen from the international list. The arbitral tribunal thus constituted shall fix its own procedure. There shall be no appeal from its decisions.
8. Each of the High Contracting Parties may declare, whenever a dispute to which it is a Party arises, that it does not wish to apply the arbitration procedure provided

for in the preceding paragraph. In such cases, the objection to an application for registration shall be submitted by the Director-General to the High Contracting Parties. The objection will be confirmed only if the High Contracting Parties so decide by a two-third majority of the High Contracting Parties voting. The vote shall be taken by correspondence, unless the Directory-General of the United Nations Educational, Scientific and Cultural Organization deems it essential to convene a meeting under the powers conferred upon him by Article 27 of the Convention. If the Director-General decides to proceed with the vote by correspondence, he shall invite the High Contracting Parties to transmit their votes by sealed letter within 6 months from the day on which they were invited to do so.

Article 15. Registration

1. The Director-General of the United Nations Educational, Scientific and Cultural Organization shall cause to be entered in the Register, under a serial number, each item of property for which application for registration is made, provided that he has not received an objection within the time limit prescribed in paragraph 1 of Article 14.
2. If an objection has been lodged, and without prejudice to the provision of paragraph 5 of Article 14, the Director-General shall enter property in the Register only if the objection has been withdrawn or has failed to be confirmed following the procedures laid down in either paragraph 7 or paragraph 8 of Article 14.
3. Whenever paragraph 3 of Article 11 applies, the Director-General shall enter property in the Register if so requested by the Commissioner-General for Cultural Property.
4. The Director-General shall send without delay to the Secretary-General of the United Nations, to the High Contracting Parties, and, at the request of the Party applying for registration, to all other States referred to in Articles 30 and 32 of the Convention, a certified copy of each entry in the Register. Entries shall become effective 30 days after despatch of such copies.

Article 16. Cancellation

1. The Director-General of the United Nations Educational, Scientific and Cultural Organization shall cause the registration of any property to be cancelled:

    a. at the request of the High Contracting Party within whose territory the cultural property is situated;
    b. if the High Contracting Party which requested registration has denounced the Convention, and when that denunciation has taken effect;
    c. in the special case provided for in Article 14, paragraph 5, when an objection has been confirmed following the procedures mentioned either in paragraph 7 or in paragraph 8 or Article 14.

2. The Director-General shall send without delay, to the Secretary-General of the United Nations and to all States which received a copy of the entry in the Register, a certified copy of its cancellation. Cancellation shall take effect 30 days after the despatch of such copies.

Chapter III. Transport of cultural property

Article 17. Procedure to obtain immunity

1. The request mentioned in paragraph I of Article 12 of the Convention shall be addressed to the Commissioner-General for Cultural Property. It shall mention the reasons on which it is based and specify the approximate number and the importance of the objects-to be transferred, their present location, the location now envisaged, the means of transport to be used, the route to be followed, the date proposed for the transfer, and any other relevant information.
2. If the Commissioner-General, after taking such opinions as he deems fit, considers that such transfer is justified, he shall consult those delegates of the Protecting Powers who are concerned, on the measures proposed for carrying it out. Following such consultation, he shall notify the Parties to the conflict concerned of the transfer, including in such notification all useful information.
3. The Commissioner-General shall appoint one or more inspectors, who shall satisfy themselves that only the property stated in the request is to be transferred and that the transport is to be by the approved methods and bears the distinctive emblem. The inspector or inspectors shall accompany the property to its destination.

Article 18. Transport abroad

Where the transfer under special protection is to the territory of another country, it shall be governed not only by Article 12 of the Convention and by Article 17 of the present Regulations, but by the following further provisions:

a. while the cultural property remains on the territory of another State, that State shall be its depositary and shall extend to it as great a measure of care as that which it bestows upon its own cultural property of comparable importance;
b. the depositary State shall return the property only on the cessation of the conflict; such return shall be effected within 6 months from the date on which it was requested;
c. during the various transfer operations, and while it remains on the territory of another State, the cultural property shall be exempt from confiscation and may not be disposed of either by the depositor or by the depositary. Nevertheless, when the safety of the property requires it, the depositary may, with the assent of

the depositor, have the property transported to the territory of a third country, under the conditions laid down in the present article;

d. the request for special protection shall indicate that the State to whose territory the property is to be transferred accepts the provisions of the present Article.

Article 19. Occupied territory

Whenever a High Contracting Party occupying territory of another High Contracting Party transfers cultural property to a refuge situated elsewhere in that territory, without being able to follow the procedure provided for in Article 17 of the Regulations, the transfer in question shall not be regarded as misappropriation within the meaning of Article 4 of the Convention, provided that the Commissioner-General for Cultural Property certifies in writing, after having consulted the usual custodians, that such transfer was rendered necessary by circumstances.

Chapter IV. The distinctive emblem

Article 20. Affixing of the emblem

1. The placing of the distinctive emblem and its degree of visibility shall be left to the discretion of the competent authorities of each High Contracting Party. It may be displayed on flags or armlets; it may be painted on an object or represented in any other appropriate form.
2. However, without prejudice to any possible fuller markings, the emblem shall, in the event of armed conflict and in the cases mentioned in Articles 12 and 13 of the Convention, be placed on the vehicles of transport so as to be clearly visible in daylight from the air as well as from the ground. The emblem shall be visible from the ground:

   a. at regular intervals sufficient to indicate clearly the perimeter of a centre containing monuments under special protection;
   b. at the entrance to other immovable cultural property under special protection.

Article 21. Identification of persons

1. The persons mentioned in Article 17, paragraph 2(b) and (c) of the Convention may wear an armlet bearing the distinctive emblem, issued and stamped by the competent authorities.
2. Such persons shall carry a special identity card bearing the distinctive emblem. This card shall mention at least the surname and first names, the date of birth, the title or rank, and the function of the holder. The card shall bear the photograph of

the holder as well as his signature or his fingerprints, or both. It shall bear the embossed stamp of the competent authorities.

3. Each High Contracting Party shall make out its own type of identity card, guided by the model annexed, by way of example, to the present Regulations. The High Contracting Parties shall transmit to each other a specimen of the model they are using. Identity cards shall be made out, if possible, at least in duplicate, one copy being kept by the issuing Power.
4. The said persons may not, without legitimate reason, be deprived of their identity card or of the right to wear the armlet.

Appendix II

Protocol to the Convention for the Protection of Cultural Property in the Event of Armed Conflict 1954

The High Contracting Parties are agreed as follows:

I

1. Each High Contracting Party undertakes to prevent the exportation, from a territory occupied by it during an armed conflict, of cultural property as defined in Article 1 of the Convention for the Protection of Cultural Property in the Event of Armed Conflict, signed at The Hague on 14 May, 1954.
2. Each High Contracting Party undertakes to take into its custody cultural property imported into its territory either directly or indirectly from any occupied territory. This shall either be effected automatically upon the importation of the property or, failing this, at the request of the authorities of that territory.
3. Each High Contracting Party undertakes to return, at the close of hostilities, to the competent authorities of the territory previously occupied, cultural property which is in its territory, if such property has been exported in contravention of the principle laid down in the first paragraph. Such property shall never be retained as war reparations.
4. The High Contracting Party whose obligation it was to prevent the exportation of cultural property from the territory occupied by it, shall pay an indemnity to the holders in good faith of any cultural property which has to be returned in accordance with the preceding paragraph.

II

5. Cultural property coming from the territory of a High Contracting Party and deposited by it in the territory of another High Contracting Party for the purpose

of protecting such property against the dangers of an armed conflict, shall be returned by the latter, at the end of hostilities, to the competent authorities of the territory from which it came.

III

6. The present Protocol shall bear the date of 14 May, 1954 and, until the date of 31 December, 1954, shall remain open for signature by all States invited to the Conference which met at The Hague from 21 April, 1954 to 14 May, 1954.
7.
   a. The present Protocol shall be subject to ratification by signatory States in accordance with their respective constitutional procedures.
   b. The instruments of ratification shall be deposited with the Director-General of the United Nations Educational, Scientific and Cultural Organization.
8. From the date of its entry into force, the present Protocol shall be open for accession by all States mentioned in paragraph 6 which have not signed it as well as any other State invited to accede by the Executive Board of the United Nations Educational, Scientific and Cultural Organization. Accession shall be effected by the deposit of an instrument of accession with the Director-General of the United Nations Educational, Scientific and Cultural Organization.
9. The States referred to in paragraphs 6 and 8 may declare, at the time of signature, ratification or accession, that they will not be bound by the provisions of Section I or by those of Section II of the present Protocol.
10.
    a. The present Protocol shall enter into force 3 months after five instruments of ratification have been deposited.
    b. Thereafter, it shall enter into force, for each High Contracting Party, 3 months after the deposit of its instrument of ratification or accession.
    c. The situations referred to in Articles 18 and 19 of the Convention for the Protection of Cultural Property in the Event of Armed Conflict, signed at The Hague on 14 May, 1954, shall give immediate effect to ratifications and accessions deposited by the Parties to the conflict either before or after the beginning of hostilities or occupation. In such cases, the Director-General of the United Nations Educational, Scientific and Cultural Organization shall transmit the communications' referred to in paragraph 14 by the speediest method.
11.
    a. Each State Party to the Protocol on the date of its entry into force shall take all necessary measures to ensure its effective application within a period of 6 months after such entry into force.

b. This period shall be 6 months from the date of deposit of the instruments of ratification or accession for any State which deposits its instrument of ratification or accession after the date of the entry into force of the Protocol.

12. Any High Contracting Party may, at the time of ratification or accession, or at any time thereafter, declare by notification addressed to the Director-General of the United Nations Educational, Scientific and Cultural Organization that the present Protocol shall extend to all or any of the territories for whose international relations it is responsible. The said notification shall take effect 3 months after the date of its receipt.
13.
    a. Each High Contracting Party may denounce the present Protocol, on its own behalf, or on behalf of any territory for whose international relations it is responsible.
    b. The denunciation shall be notified by an instrument in writing, deposited with the Director-General of the United Nations Educational, Scientific and Cultural Organization.
    c. The denunciation shall take effect 1 year after receipt of the instrument of denunciation. However, if, on the expiry of this period, the denouncing Party is involved in an armed conflict, the denunciation shall not take effect until the end of hostilities, or until the operations of repatriating cultural property are completed, whichever is the later.
14. The Director-General of the United Nations Educational, Scientific and Cultural Organization shall inform the States referred to in paragraphs 6 and 8, as well as the United Nations, of the deposit of all the instruments of ratification, accession or acceptance provided for in paragraphs 7, 8 and 15 and the notifications and denunciations provided for, respectively, in paragraphs 12 and 13.
15.
    a. The present Protocol may be revised if revision is requested by more than one-third of the High Contracting Parties.
    b. The Director-General of the United Nations Educational, Scientific and Cultural Organization shall convene a Conference for this purpose.
    c. Amendments to the present Protocol shall enter into force only after they have been unanimously adopted by the High Contracting Parties represented at the Conference and accepted by each of the High Contracting Parties.
    d. Acceptance by the High Contracting Parties of amendments to the present Protocol, which have been adopted by the Conference mentioned in subparagraphs (b) and (c), shall be effected by the deposit of a formal instrument with the Director-General of the United Nations Educational, Scientific and Cultural Organization.
    e. After the entry into force of amendments to the present Protocol, only the text of the said Protocol thus amended shall remain open for ratification or accession.

In accordance with Article 102 of the Charter of the United Nations, the present Protocol shall be registered with the Secretariat of the United Nations at the request of the Director-General of the United Nations Educational, Scientific and Cultural Organization.

In faith whereof the undersigned, duly authorized, have signed the present Protocol.

Done at The Hague, this 14th day of May, 1954, in English, French, Russian and Spanish, the four texts being equally authoritative, in a single copy which shall be deposited in the archives of the United Nations Educational, Scientific and Cultural Organization, and certified true copies of which shall be delivered to all the States referred to in paragraphs 6 and 8 as well as to the United Nations.

Appendix III

Second Protocol to The Hague Convention of 1954 for the Protection of Cultural Property in the Event of Armed Conflict 1999

The Parties,

Conscious of the need to improve the protection of cultural property in the event of armed conflict and to establish an enhanced system of protection for specifically designated cultural property;

Reaffirming the importance of the provisions of the Convention for the Protection of Cultural Property in the Event of Armed Conflict, done at the Hague on 14 May 1954, and emphasizing the necessity to supplement these provisions through measures to reinforce their implementation;

Desiring to provide the High Contracting Parties to the Convention with a means of being more closely involved in the protection of cultural property in the event of armed conflict by establishing appropriate procedures; therefore, considering that the rules governing the protection of cultural property in the event of armed conflict should reflect developments in international law;

Affirming that the rules of customary international law will continue to govern questions not regulated by the provisions of this Protocol;

Have agreed as follows:

Chapter 1 Introduction

Article 1 Definitions

For the purposes of this Protocol:

a. "Party" means a State Party to this Protocol;
b. "cultural property" means cultural property as defined in Article 1 of the Convention;

c. "Convention" means the Convention for the Protection of Cultural Property in the Event of Armed Conflict, done at The Hague on 14 May 1954;
d. "High Contracting Party" means a State Party to the Convention;
e. "enhanced protection" means the system of enhanced protection established by Articles 10 and 11;
f. "military objective" means an object which by its nature, location, purpose, or use makes an effective contribution to military action and whose total or partial destruction, capture or neutralisation, in the circumstances ruling at the time, offers a definite military advantage;
g. "illicit" means under compulsion or otherwise in violation of the applicable rules of the domestic law of the occupied territory or of international law.
h. "List" means the International List of Cultural Property under Enhanced Protection established in accordance with Article 27, sub-paragraph 1(b);
i. "Director-General" means the Director-General of UNESCO;
j. "UNESCO" means the United Nations Educational, Scientific and Cultural Organization;
k. "First Protocol" means the Protocol for the Protection of Cultural Property in the Event of Armed Conflict done at The Hague on 14 May 1954;

Article 2 Relation to the Convention

This Protocol supplements the Convention in relations between the Parties.

Article 3 Scope of application

1. In addition to the provisions which shall apply in time of peace, this Protocol shall apply in situations referred to in Article 18 paragraphs 1 and 2 of the Convention and in Article 22 paragraph 1.
2. When one of the parties to an armed conflict is not bound by this Protocol, the Parties to this Protocol shall remain bound by it in their mutual relations. They shall furthermore be bound by this Protocol in relation to a State party to the conflict which is not bound by it, if the latter accepts the provisions of this Protocol and so long as it applies them.

Article 4 Relationship between Chapter 3 and other provisions of the Convention and this Protocol

The application of the provisions of Chapter 3 of this Protocol is without prejudice to:
a. the application of the provisions of Chapter I of the Convention and of Chapter 2 of this Protocol;

b. the application of the provisions of Chapter II of the Convention save that, as between Parties to this Protocol or as between a Party and a State which accepts and applies this Protocol in accordance with Article 3 paragraph 2, where cultural property has been granted both special protection and enhanced protection, only the provisions of enhanced protection shall apply.

Chapter 2 General provisions regarding protection

Article 5 Safeguarding of cultural property

Preparatory measures taken in time of peace for the safeguarding of cultural property against the foreseeable effects of an armed conflict pursuant to Article 3 of the Convention shall include, as appropriate, the preparation of inventories, the planning of emergency measures for protection against fire or structural collapse, the preparation for the removal of movable cultural property or the provision for adequate in situ protection of such property, and the designation of competent authorities responsible for the safeguarding of cultural property.

Article 6 Respect for cultural property

With the goal of ensuring respect for cultural property in accordance with Article 4 of the Convention:

a. a waiver on the basis of imperative military necessity pursuant to Article 4 paragraph 2 of the Convention may only be invoked to direct an act of hostility against cultural property when and for as long as:

   i. that cultural property has, by its function, been made into a military objective and
   ii. there is no feasible alternative available to obtain a similar military advantage to that offered by directing an act of hostility against that objective;

b. a waiver on the basis of imperative military necessity pursuant to Article 4 paragraph 2 of the Convention may only be invoked to use cultural property for purposes which are likely to expose it to destruction or damage when and for as long as no choice is possible between such use of the cultural property and another feasible method for obtaining a similar military advantage;
c. the decision to invoke imperative military necessity shall only be taken by an officer commanding a force the equivalent of a battalion in size or larger, or a force smaller in size where circumstances do not permit otherwise;
d. in case of an attack based on a decision taken in accordance with sub-paragraph (a), an effective advance warning shall be given whenever circumstances permit.

Article 7 Precautions in attack

Without prejudice to other precautions required by international humanitarian law in the conduct of military operations, each Party to the conflict shall:

a. do everything feasible to verify that the objectives to be attacked are not cultural property protected under Article 4 of the Convention;
b. take all feasible precautions in the choice of means and methods of attack with a view to avoiding, and in any event to minimizing, incidental damage to cultural property protected under Article 4 of the Convention;
c. refrain from deciding to launch any attack which may be expected to cause incidental damage to cultural property protected under Article 4 of the Convention which would be excessive in relation to the concrete and direct military advantage anticipated; and
d. cancel or suspend an attack if it becomes apparent:
    i. that the objective is cultural property protected under Article 4 of the Convention;
    ii. that the attack may be expected to cause incidental damage to cultural property protected under Article 4 of the Convention which would be excessive in relation to the concrete and direct military advantage anticipated.

Article 8 Precautions against the effects of hostilities

The Parties to the conflict shall, to the maximum extent feasible:

a. remove movable cultural property from the vicinity of military objectives or provide for adequate in situ protection;
b. avoid locating military objectives near cultural property.

Article 9 Protection of cultural property in occupied territory

1. Without prejudice to the provisions of Articles 4 and 5 of the Convention, a Party in occupation of the whole or part of the territory of another Party shall prohibit and prevent in relation to the occupied territory:
    a. any illicit export, other removal or transfer of ownership of cultural property;
    b. any archaeological excavation, save where this is strictly required to safeguard, record or preserve cultural property;
    c. any alteration to, or change of use of, cultural property which is intended to conceal or destroy cultural, historical or scientific evidence.
2. Any archaeological excavation of, alteration to, or change of use of, cultural property in occupied territory shall, unless circumstances do not permit, be carried out in close co-operation with the competent national authorities of the occupied territory.

Chapter 3 Enhanced Protection

Article 10 Enhanced protection

Cultural property may be placed under enhanced protection provided that it meets the following three conditions:

a. it is cultural heritage of the greatest importance for humanity;
b. it is protected by adequate domestic legal and administrative measures recognising its exceptional cultural and historic value and ensuring the highest level of protection;
c. it is not used for military purposes or to shield military sites and a declaration has been made by the Party which has control over the cultural property, confirming that it will not be so used.

Article 11 The granting of enhanced protection

1. Each Party should submit to the Committee a list of cultural property for which it intends to request the granting of enhanced protection.
2. The Party which has jurisdiction or control over the cultural property may request that it be included in the List to be established in accordance with Article 27 sub-paragraph 1(b). This request shall include all necessary information related to the criteria mentioned in Article 10. The Committee may invite a Party to request that cultural property be included in the List.
3. Other Parties, the International Committee of the Blue Shield and other non-governmental organisations with relevant expertise may recommend specific cultural property to the Committee. In such cases, the Committee may decide to invite a Party to request inclusion of that cultural property in the List.
4. Neither the request for inclusion of cultural property situated in a territory, sovereignty or jurisdiction over which is claimed by more than one State, nor its inclusion, shall in any way prejudice the rights of the parties to the dispute.
5. Upon receipt of a request for inclusion in the List, the Committee shall inform all Parties of the request. Parties may submit representations regarding such a request to the Committee within 60 days. These representations shall be made only on the basis of the criteria mentioned in Article 10. They shall be specific and related to facts. The Committee shall consider the representations, providing the Party requesting inclusion with a reasonable opportunity to respond before taking the decision. When such representations are before the Committee, decisions for inclusion in the List shall be taken, notwithstanding Article 26, by a majority of four-fifths of its members present and voting.
6. In deciding upon a request, the Committee should ask the advice of governmental and non-governmental organisations, as well as of individual experts.
7. A decision to grant or deny enhanced protection may only be made on the basis of the criteria mentioned in Article 10.

8. In exceptional cases, when the Committee has concluded that the Party requesting inclusion of cultural property in the List cannot fulfil the criteria of Article 10 sub-paragraph (b), the Committee may decide to grant enhanced protection, provided that the requesting Party submits a request for international assistance under Article 32.
9. Upon the outbreak of hostilities, a Party to the conflict may request, on an emergency basis, enhanced protection of cultural property under its jurisdiction or control by communicating this request to the Committee. The Committee shall transmit this request immediately to all Parties to the conflict. In such cases, the Committee will consider representations from the Parties concerned on an expedited basis. The decision to grant provisional enhanced protection shall be taken as soon as possible and, notwithstanding Article 26, by a majority of four-fifths of its members present and voting. Provisional enhanced protection may be granted by the Committee pending the outcome of the regular procedure for the granting of enhanced protection, provided that the provisions of Article 10 sub-paragraphs (a) and (c) are met.
10. Enhanced protection shall be granted to cultural property by the Committee from the moment of its entry in the List.
11. The Director-General shall, without delay, send to the Secretary-General of the United Nations and to all Parties notification of any decision of the Committee to include cultural property on the List.

Article 12 Immunity of cultural property under enhanced protection

The Parties to a conflict shall ensure the immunity of cultural property under enhanced protection by refraining from making such property the object of attack or from any use of the property or its immediate surroundings in support of military action.

Article 13 Loss of enhanced protection

1. Cultural property under enhanced protection shall only lose such protection:
   a. if such protection is suspended or cancelled in accordance with Article 14; or
   b. if, and for as long as, the property has, by its use, become a military objective.
2. In the circumstances of sub-paragraph 1(b), such property may only be the object of attack if:
   a. the attack is the only feasible means of terminating the use of the property referred to in sub-paragraph 1(b);
   b. all feasible precautions are taken in the choice of means and methods of attack, with a view to terminating such use and avoiding, or in any event minimising, damage to the cultural property;

c. unless circumstances do not permit, due to requirements of immediate self-defence:

   i. the attack is ordered at the highest operational level of command;
   ii. effective advance warning is issued to the opposing forces requiring the termination of the use referred to in sub-paragraph 1(b);
   iii. Reasonable time is given to the opposing forces to redress the situation.

Article 14 Suspension and cancellation of enhanced protection

a. Where cultural property no longer meets any one of the criteria in Article 10 of this Protocol, the Committee may suspend its enhanced protection status or cancel that status by removing that cultural property from the List.
b. In the case of a serious violation of Article 12 in relation to cultural property under enhanced protection arising from its use in support of military action, the Committee may suspend its enhanced protection status. Where such violations are continuous, the Committee may exceptionally cancel the enhanced protection status by removing the cultural property from the List.
c. The Director-General shall, without delay, send to the Secretary-General of the United Nations and to all Parties to this Protocol notification of any decision of the Committee to suspend or cancel the enhanced protection of cultural property.
d. Before taking such a decision, the Committee shall afford an opportunity to the Parties to make their views known.

Chapter 4 Criminal responsibility and jurisdiction

Article 15 Serious violations of this Protocol

1. Any person commits an offence within the meaning of this Protocol if that person intentionally and in violation of the Convention or this Protocol commits any of the following acts:

   a. making cultural property under enhanced protection the object of attack;
   b. using cultural property under enhanced protection or its immediate surroundings in support of military action;
   c. extensive destruction or appropriation of cultural property protected under the Convention and this Protocol;
   d. making cultural property protected under the Convention and this Protocol the object of attack;
   e. theft, pillage or misappropriation of, or acts of vandalism directed against cultural property protected under the Convention.

2. Each Party shall adopt such measures as may be necessary to establish as criminal offences under its domestic law the offences set forth in this Article and to make such offences punishable by appropriate penalties. When doing so, Parties shall comply with general principles of law and international law, including the rules extending individual criminal responsibility to persons other than those who directly commit the act.

Article 16 Jurisdiction

1. Without prejudice to paragraph 2, each Party shall take the necessary legislative measures to establish its jurisdiction over offences set forth in Article 15 in the following cases:
   a. when such an offence is committed in the territory of that State;
   b. when the alleged offender is a national of that State;
   c. in the case of offences set forth in Article 15 sub-paragraphs (a) to (c), when the alleged offender is present in its territory.
2. With respect to the exercise of jurisdiction and without prejudice to Article 28 of the Convention:
   a. this Protocol does not preclude the incurring of individual criminal responsibility or the exercise of jurisdiction under national and international law that may be applicable, or affect the exercise of jurisdiction under customary international law;
   b. except in so far as a State which is not Party to this Protocol may accept and apply its provisions in accordance with Article 3 paragraph 2, members of the armed forces and nationals of a State which is not Party to this Protocol, except for those nationals serving in the armed forces of a State which is a Party to this Protocol, do not incur individual criminal responsibility by virtue of this Protocol, nor does this Protocol impose an obligation to establish jurisdiction over such persons or to extradite them.

Article 17 Prosecution

1. The Party in whose territory the alleged offender of an offence set forth in Article 15 sub-paragraphs 1 (a) to (c) is found to be present shall, if it does not extradite that person, submit, without exception whatsoever and without undue delay, the case to its competent authorities, for the purpose of prosecution, through proceedings in accordance with its domestic law or with, if applicable, the relevant rules of international law.
2. Without prejudice to, if applicable, the relevant rules of international law, any person regarding whom proceedings are being carried out in connection with the Convention or this Protocol shall be guaranteed fair treatment and a fair trial in

accordance with domestic law and international law at all stages of the proceedings, and in no cases shall be provided guarantees less favorable to such person than those provided by international law.

Article 18 Extradition

1. The offences set forth in Article 15 sub-paragraphs 1 (a) to (c) shall be deemed to be included as extraditable offences in any extradition treaty existing between any of the Parties before the entry into force of this Protocol. Parties undertake to include such offences in every extradition treaty to be subsequently concluded between them.
2. When a Party which makes extradition conditional on the existence of a treaty receives a request for extradition from another Party with which it has no extradition treaty, the requested Party may, at its option, consider the present Protocol as the legal basis for extradition in respect of offences as set forth in Article 15 sub-paragraphs 1 (a) to (c).
3. Parties which do not make extradition conditional on the existence of a treaty shall recognise the offences set forth in Article 15 sub-paragraphs 1 (a) to (c) as extraditable offences between them, subject to the conditions provided by the law of the requested Party.
4. If necessary, offences set forth in Article 15 sub-paragraphs 1 (a) to (c) shall be treated, for the purposes of extradition between Parties, as if they had been committed not only in the place in which they occurred but also in the territory of the Parties that have established jurisdiction in accordance with Article 16 paragraph 1.

Article 19 Mutual legal assistance

1. Parties shall afford one another the greatest measure of assistance in connection with investigations or criminal or extradition proceedings brought in respect of the offences set forth in Article 15, including assistance in obtaining evidence at their disposal necessary for the proceedings.
2. Parties shall carry out their obligations under paragraph 1 in conformity with any treaties or other arrangements on mutual legal assistance that may exist between them. In the absence of such treaties or arrangements, Parties shall afford one another assistance in accordance with their domestic law.

Article 20 Grounds for refusal

1. For the purpose of extradition, offences set forth in Article 15 sub-paragraphs 1 (a) to (c), and for the purpose of mutual legal assistance, offences set forth in Article 15 shall not be regarded as political offences nor as offences connected with political offences nor as offences inspired by political motives. Accordingly, a request for extradition or for mutual legal assistance based on such offences may

not be refused on the sole ground that it concerns a political offence or an offence connected with a political offence or an offence inspired by political motives.

2. Nothing in this Protocol shall be interpreted as imposing an obligation to extradite or to afford mutual legal assistance if the requested Party has substantial grounds for believing that the request for extradition for offences set forth in Article 15 sub-paragraphs 1 (a) to (c) or for mutual legal assistance with respect to offences set forth in Article 15 has been made for the purpose of prosecuting or punishing a person on account of that person's race, religion, nationality, ethnic origin or political opinion or that compliance with the request would cause prejudice to that person's position for any of these reasons.

Article 21 Measures regarding other violations

Without prejudice to Article 28 of the Convention, each Party shall adopt such legislative, administrative or disciplinary measures as may be necessary to suppress the following acts when committed intentionally:

a. any use of cultural property in violation of the Convention or this Protocol;
b. any illicit export, other removal or transfer of ownership of cultural property from occupied territory in violation of the Convention or this Protocol.

Chapter 5 The protection of cultural property in armed conflicts not of an international character

Article 22 Armed conflicts not of an international character

1. This Protocol shall apply in the event of an armed conflict not of an international character, occurring within the territory of one of the Parties.
2. This Protocol shall not apply to situations of internal disturbances and tensions, such as riots, isolated and sporadic acts of violence and other acts of a similar nature.
3. Nothing in this Protocol shall be invoked for the purpose of affecting the sovereignty of a State or the responsibility of the government, by all legitimate means, to maintain or re-establish law and order in the State or to defend the national unity and territorial integrity of the State.
4. Nothing in this Protocol shall prejudice the primary jurisdiction of a Party in whose territory an armed conflict not of an international character occurs over the violations set forth in Article 15.
5. Nothing in this Protocol shall be invoked as a justification for intervening, directly or indirectly, for any reason whatever, in the armed conflict or in the internal or external affairs of the Party in the territory of which that conflict occurs.
6. The application of this Protocol to the situation referred to in paragraph 1 shall not affect the legal status of the parties to the conflict.
7. UNESCO may offer its services to the parties to the conflict.

Chapter 6 Institutional Issues

Article 23 Meeting of the Parties

1. The Meeting of the Parties shall be convened at the same time as the General Conference of UNESCO, and in co-ordination with the Meeting of the High Contracting Parties, if such a meeting has been called by the Director-General.
2. The Meeting of the Parties shall adopt its Rules of Procedure.
3. The Meeting of the Parties shall have the following functions:

    a. to elect the Members of the Committee, in accordance with Article 24 paragraph 1;
    b. to endorse the Guidelines developed by the Committee in accordance with Article 27 sub-paragraph 1(a);
    c. to provide guidelines for, and to supervise the use of the Fund by the Committee;
    d. to consider the report submitted by the Committee in accordance with Article 27 sub-paragraph 1(d);
    e. to discuss any problem related to the application of this Protocol, and to make recommendations, as appropriate.

4. At the request of at least one-fifth of the Parties, the Director-General shall convene an Extraordinary Meeting of the Parties.

Article 24 Committee for the Protection of Cultural Property in the Event of Armed Conflict

1. The Committee for the Protection of Cultural Property in the Event of Armed Conflict is hereby established. It shall be composed of 12 Parties which shall be elected by the Meeting of the Parties.
2. The Committee shall meet once a year in ordinary session and in extraordinary sessions whenever it deems necessary.
3. In determining membership of the Committee, Parties shall seek to ensure an equitable representation of the different regions and cultures of the world.
4. Parties that are members of the Committee shall choose as their representatives persons qualified in the fields of cultural heritage, defence or international law, and they shall endeavour, in consultation with one another, to ensure that the Committee as a whole contains adequate expertise in all these fields.

Article 25 Term of office

1. A Party shall be elected to the Committee for 4 years and shall be eligible for immediate re-election only once.

2. Notwithstanding the provisions of paragraph 1, the term of office of half of the members chosen at the time of the first election shall cease at the end of the first ordinary session of the Meeting of the Parties following that at which they were elected. These members shall be chosen by lot by the President of this Meeting after the first election.

Article 26 Rules of procedure

1. The Committee shall adopt its Rules of Procedure.
2. A majority of the members shall constitute a quorum. Decisions of the Committee shall be taken by a majority of two-thirds of its members voting.
3. Members shall not participate in the voting on any decisions relating to cultural property affected by an armed conflict to which they are parties.

Article 27 Functions

1. The Committee shall have the following functions:
   a. to develop Guidelines for the implementation of this Protocol;
   b. to grant, suspend or cancel enhanced protection for cultural property and to establish, maintain and promote the List of Cultural Property under Enhanced Protection;
   c. to monitor and supervise the implementation of this Protocol and promote the identification of cultural property under enhanced protection;
   d. to consider and comment on reports of the Parties, to seek clarifications as required, and prepare its own report on the implementation of this Protocol for the Meeting of the Parties;
   e. to receive and consider requests for international assistance under Article 32;
   f. to determine the use of the Fund;
   g. to perform any other function which may be assigned to it by the Meeting of the Parties.
2. The functions of the Committee shall be performed in co-operation with the Director-General.
3. The Committee shall co-operate with international and national governmental and non-governmental organizations having objectives similar to those of the Convention, its First Protocol and this Protocol. To assist in the implementation of its functions, the Committee may invite to its meetings, in an advisory capacity, eminent professional organizations such as those which have formal relations with UNESCO, including the International Committee of the Blue Shield (ICBS) and its constituent bodies. Representatives of the International Centre for the Study of the Preservation and Restoration of Cultural Property (Rome Centre)

(ICCROM) and of the International Committee of the Red Cross (ICRC) may also be invited to attend in an advisory capacity.

Article 28 Secretariat

The Committee shall be assisted by the Secretariat of UNESCO which shall prepare the Committee's documentation and the agenda for its meetings and shall have the responsibility for the implementation of its decisions.

Article 29 The Fund for the Protection of Cultural Property in the Event of Armed Conflict

1. A Fund is hereby established for the following purposes:
   a. to provide financial or other assistance in support of preparatory or other measures to be taken in peacetime in accordance with, inter alia, Article 5, Article 10 sub-paragraph (b) and Article 30;
   b. to provide financial or other assistance in relation to emergency, provisional or other measures to be taken in order to protect cultural property during periods of armed conflict or of immediate recovery after the end of hostilities in accordance with, inter alia, Article 8 sub-paragraph (a).
2. The Fund shall constitute a trust fund, in conformity with the provisions of the financial regulations of UNESCO.
3. Disbursements from the Fund shall be used only for such purposes as the Committee shall decide in accordance with the guidelines as defined in Article 23 sub-paragraph 3(c). The Committee may accept contributions to be used only for a certain programme or project, provided that the Committee shall have decided on the implementation of such programme or project.
4. The resources of the Fund shall consist of:
   a. voluntary contributions made by the Parties;
   b. contributions, gifts or bequests made by:
      i. other States;
      ii. UNESCO or other organizations of the United Nations system;
      iii. other intergovernmental or non-governmental organizations; and
      iv. public or private bodies or individuals;
   c. any interest accruing on the Fund;
   d. funds raised by collections and receipts from events organized for the benefit of the Fund; and
   e. all other resources authorized by the guidelines applicable to the Fund.

Chapter 7 Dissemination of Information and International Assistance

Article 30 Dissemination

1. The Parties shall endeavour by appropriate means, and in particular by educational and information programmes, to strengthen appreciation and respect for cultural property by their entire population.
2. The Parties shall disseminate this Protocol as widely as possible, both in time of peace and in time of armed conflict.
3. Any military or civilian authorities who, in time of armed conflict, assume responsibilities with respect to the application of this Protocol, shall be fully acquainted with the text thereof. To this end the Parties shall, as appropriate:

   a. incorporate guidelines and instructions on the protection of cultural property in their military regulations;
   b. develop and implement, in cooperation with UNESCO and relevant governmental and non-governmental organizations, peacetime training and educational programmes;
   c. communicate to one another, through the Director-General, information on the laws, administrative provisions and measures taken under sub-paragraphs (a) and (b);
   d. communicate to one another, as soon as possible, through the Director-General, the laws and administrative provisions which they may adopt to ensure the application of this Protocol.

Article 31 International cooperation

In situations of serious violations of this Protocol, the Parties undertake to act, jointly through the Committee, or individually, in cooperation with UNESCO and the United Nations and in conformity with the Charter of the United Nations.

Article 32 International assistance

1. A Party may request from the Committee international assistance for cultural property under enhanced protection as well as assistance with respect to the preparation, development or implementation of the laws, administrative provisions and measures referred to in Article 10.
2. A party to the conflict, which is not a Party to this Protocol but which accepts and applies provisions in accordance with Article 3, paragraph 2, may request appropriate international assistance from the Committee.

3. The Committee shall adopt rules for the submission of requests for international assistance and shall define the forms the international assistance may take.
4. Parties are encouraged to give technical assistance of all kinds, through the Committee, to those Parties or parties to the conflict who request it.

Article 33 Assistance of UNESCO

1. A Party may call upon UNESCO for technical assistance in organizing the protection of its cultural property, such as preparatory action to safeguard cultural property, preventive and organizational measures for emergency situations and compilation of national inventories of cultural property, or in connection with any other problem arising out of the application of this Protocol. UNESCO shall accord such assistance within the limits fixed by its programme and by its resources.
2. Parties are encouraged to provide technical assistance at bilateral or multilateral level.
3. UNESCO is authorized to make, on its own initiative, proposals on these matters to the Parties.

Chapter 8 Execution of this Protocol

Article 34 Protecting Powers

This Protocol shall be applied with the co-operation of the Protecting Powers responsible for safeguarding the interests of the Parties to the conflict.

Article 35 Conciliation procedure

1. The Protecting Powers shall lend their good offices in all cases where they may deem it useful in the interests of cultural property, particularly if there is disagreement between the Parties to the conflict as to the application or interpretation of the provisions of this Protocol.
2. For this purpose, each of the Protecting Powers may, either at the invitation of one Party, of the Director-General, or on its own initiative, propose to the Parties to the conflict a meeting of their representatives, and in particular of the authorities responsible for the protection of cultural property, if considered appropriate, on the territory of a State not party to the conflict. The Parties to the conflict shall be bound to give effect to the proposals for meeting made to them. The Protecting Powers shall propose for approval by the Parties to the conflict a person belonging to a State not party to the conflict or a person presented by the Director-General, which person shall be invited to take part in such a meeting in the capacity of Chairman.

Article 36 Conciliation in absence of Protecting Powers

1. In a conflict where no Protecting Powers are appointed the Director-General may lend good offices or act by any other form of conciliation or mediation, with a view to settling the disagreement.
2. At the invitation of one Party or of the Director-General, the Chairman of the Committee may propose to the Parties to the conflict a meeting of their representatives, and in particular of the authorities responsible for the protection of cultural property, if considered appropriate, on the territory of a State not party to the conflict.

Article 37 Translations and reports

1. The Parties shall translate this Protocol into their official languages and shall communicate these official translations to the Director-General.
2. The Parties shall submit to the Committee, every 4 years, a report on the implementation of this Protocol.

Article 38 State responsibility

No provision in this Protocol relating to individual criminal responsibility shall affect the responsibility of States under international law, including the duty to provide reparation.

Chapter 9 Final Clauses

Article 39 Languages

This Protocol is drawn up in Arabic, Chinese, English, French, Russian and Spanish, the six texts being equally authentic.

Article 40 Signature

This Protocol shall bear the date of 26 March 1999. It shall be opened for signature by all High Contracting Parties at The Hague from 17 May 1999 until 31 December 1999.

Article 41 Ratification, acceptance or approval

1. This Protocol shall be subject to ratification, acceptance or approval by High Contracting Parties which have signed this Protocol, in accordance with their respective constitutional procedures.

2. The instruments of ratification, acceptance or approval shall be deposited with the Director-General.

Article 42 Accession

1. This Protocol shall be open for accession by other High Contracting Parties from 1 January 2000.
2. Accession shall be effected by the deposit of an instrument of accession with the Director-General.

Article 43 Entry into force

1. This Protocol shall enter into force 3 months after 20 instruments of ratification, acceptance, approval or accession have been deposited.
2. Thereafter, it shall enter into force, for each Party, 3 months after the deposit of its instrument of ratification, acceptance, approval or accession.

Article 44 Entry into force in situations of armed conflict

The situations referred to in Articles 18 and 19 of the Convention shall give immediate effect to ratifications, acceptances or approvals of or accessions to this Protocol deposited by the parties to the conflict either before or after the beginning of hostilities or occupation. In such cases the Director-General shall transmit the communications referred to in Article 46 by the speediest method.

Article 45 Denunciation

1. Each Party may denounce this Protocol.
2. The denunciation shall be notified by an instrument in writing, deposited with the Director-General.
3. The denunciation shall take effect 1 year after the receipt of the instrument of denunciation. However, if, on the expiry of this period, the denouncing Party is involved in an armed conflict, the denunciation shall not take effect until the end of hostilities, or until the operations of repatriating cultural property are completed, whichever is the later.

Article 46 Notifications

The Director-General shall inform all High Contracting Parties as well as the United Nations, of the deposit of all the instruments of ratification, acceptance, approval or accession provided for in Articles 41 and 42 and of denunciations provided for Article 45.

Article 47 Registration with the United Nations

In conformity with Article 102 of the Charter of the United Nations, this Protocol shall be registered with the Secretariat of the United Nations at the request of the Director-General.

IN FAITH WHEREOF the undersigned, duly authorized, have signed the present Protocol.

DONE at The Hague, this 26th day of March 1999, in a single copy which shall be deposited in the archives of the UNESCO, and certified true copies of which shall be delivered to all the High Contracting Parties.

Appendix IV

Model Treaty for the Prevention of Crimes that Infringe on the Cultural Heritage of Peoples in the Form of Movable Property[1,2]

The________________________ and the ___________________________

Conscious of the need to cooperate in the field of criminal justice,

Wishing to add to the effectiveness of the cooperation between their two countries in combating criminal activities which involve movable cultural property through the introduction of measures for impeding illicit transnational trafficking in movable cultural property whether or not it has been stolen, the imposition of appropriate and effective administrative and penal sanctions and the provision of a means for restitution,

Have agreed as follows:

[1] Eighth United Nations Congress on the Prevention of Crime and the Treatment of Offenders, Havana, 27 August–7 September 1990: report prepared by the Secretariat (United Nations publication, Sales No. E.91.IV.2), chapter I, section B.1, annex.

[2] An alternative title could be "Model treaty concerning crimes relating to the restitution of movable cultural property."

Article 1

Scope of application and definition[3]

1. For the purposes of this treaty, movable cultural property[4] shall be understood as referring to property which, on religious or secular grounds, is specifically designated by a State Party as being subject to export control by reason of its importance for archaeology, prehistory, history, literature, art or science, and as belonging to one or more of the following categories:

   a. Rare collections and specimens of fauna, flora, minerals and anatomy, and objects of paleontological interest;
   b. Property relating to history, including the history of science and technology, military history, and the history of societies and religions, as well as to the lives of leaders, thinkers, scientists and artists and other national figures, and to events of national importance;
   c. Products of archaeological excavations or discoveries, including clandestine excavations or discoveries, whether on land or under water;
   d. Elements of artistic or historical monuments or archaeological sites which have been dismantled;
   e. Antiquities, including tools, ceramics, ornaments, musical instruments, pottery, inscriptions of all kinds, coins, engraved seals, jewels, weapons and funerary remains of any description;
   f. Materials of anthropological, historical or ethnological interest;
   g. Property of artistic interest, such as:

      i. Pictures, paintings and drawings produced entirely by hand on any support and in any material excluding industrial designs and manufactured articles decorated by hand);
      ii. Original works of statuary art and sculpture in any material;
      iii. Original engravings, prints, lithographs and art photographs;
      iv. Original artistic assemblages and montages in any material;

   h. Rare manuscripts and incunabula, old books, documents and publications of special historical, artistic, scientific, literary or other interest, singly or in collections;
   i. Postage, revenue and similar stamps, either singly or in collections;

---

[3] Suggested alternatives to article 1, paragraph 1, are: (i) "This treaty covers all items of movable cultural property specifically designated as such by a State Party, and subject to export control by that State Party." or (ii) "This treaty covers those items of movable cultural property specifically agreed to between the States Parties as being subject to export control."

[4] The categories follow closely the list contained in article 1 of the UNESCO Convention on the Means of Prohibiting and Preventing the Illicit Import, Export and Transfer of Ownership of Cultural Property, of 1970. However, this list may not be exhaustive, and States Parties may wish to add other categories.

j. Archives, including phonographic, photographic and cinematographic archives;
k. Articles of furniture, furnishings and musical instruments of more than 100 years of age.

2. This treaty applies to movable cultural property stolen in or illicitly exported from the other State Party after the coming into force of the treaty.[5]

Article 2

General principles

1. Each State Party undertakes:

   a. To take the necessary measures to prohibit the import and export of movable cultural property

      i. which has been stolen in the other State Party or
      ii. which has been illicitly exported from the other State Party;

   b. To take the necessary measures to prohibit the acquisition of, and dealing within its territory with, movable cultural property which has been imported contrary to the prohibitions resulting from the implementation of subparagraph (a) above;
   c. To legislate in order to prevent persons and institutions within its territory from entering into international conspiracies with respect to movable cultural property;
   d. To provide information concerning its stolen movable cultural property to an international database agreed upon between the States Parties;[6]
   e. To take the measures necessary to ensure that the purchaser of stolen movable cultural property which is listed on the international database is not considered to be a purchaser who has acquired such property in good faith;[7]
   f. To introduce a system whereby the export of movable cultural property is authorized by the issue of an export certificate;[8]

---

[5] States Parties may wish to consider providing for a period of limitation after which the right to request recovery of stolen or illicitly exported movable cultural property will be extinguished.

[6] Further developments in this field will provide the international community, particularly potential States Parties, with an opportunity to implement this method of crime prevention. (See *Eighth United Nations Congress...*, chapter I, section C.6.) The United Nations Congresses on the Prevention of Crime and the Treatment of Offenders may wish to develop initiatives in this direction.

[7] This provision is intended to supplement, and not be in substitution for, the normal rules relating to good faith acquisition.

[8] This procedure is consistent with the validation procedure described in article 6 of the Convention on the Means of Prohibiting and Preventing the Illicit Import, Export and Transfer of Ownership of Cultural Property.

g. To take the measures necessary to ensure that a purchaser of imported movable cultural property which is not accompanied by an export certificate issued by the other State Party and who did not acquire the movable cultural property prior to the entry into force of this treaty shall not be considered to be a person who has acquired the movable cultural property in good faith;[9]
h. To use all the means at its disposal, including the fostering of public awareness, to combat the illicit import and export, theft, illicit excavation and illicit dealing in movable cultural property.

2. Each State Party undertakes to take the necessary measures to recover and return, at the request of the other State Party, any movable cultural property which is covered by subparagraph (a) above.

Article 3

Sanctions[9]

Each State Party undertakes to impose sanctions[10] upon:

a. Persons or institutions responsible for the illicit import or export of movable cultural property;
b. Persons or institutions that knowingly acquire or deal in stolen or illicitly imported movable cultural property;
c. Persons or institutions that enter into international conspiracies to obtain, export or import movable cultural property by illicit means.

Article 4

Procedures

1. Requests for recovery and return shall be made through diplomatic channels. The requesting State Party shall furnish, at its expense, the documentation and other evidence, including the date of export, necessary to establish its claim for recovery and return.
2. All expenses incidental to the return and delivery of the movable cultural property shall be borne by the requesting State Party,[11] and no person or institution

[9] States Parties may wish to consider adding certain types of offences against movable cultural property to the list of extraditable offences covered by an extradition treaty. (See also General Assembly resolution 45/166, annex.)

[10] States Parties may wish to consider establishing minimum penalties for certain offences.

[11] States Parties may wish to consider whether the expenses and/or the expense of providing compensation should be shared between them.

shall be entitled to claim any form of compensation from the State Party returning the property claimed. Neither shall the requesting State Party be required to compensate in any way such persons or institutions as may have participated in illegally sending abroad the property in question, although it must pay fair compensation to any person or institution that in good faith acquired or was in legal possession of the property.[12]

3. Both parties agree not to levy any customs or other duties on such movable property as may be discovered and returned in accordance with the present treaty.
4. The States Parties agree to make available to each other such information as will assist in combating crimes against movable cultural property.[13]
5. Each State Party shall provide information concerning laws which protect its movable cultural property to an international database agreed upon between the States Parties.[14]

Article 5

Final provisions[15]

1. This treaty is subject to (ratification, acceptance or approval). The instruments of (ratification, acceptance or approval) shall be exchanged as soon as possible, through diplomatic channels.
2. This treaty shall come into force on the 30th day after the day on which the instruments of (ratification, acceptance or approval) are exchanged.
3. Either State Party may denounce this treaty by giving notice in writing to the other State Party. Such denunciation shall take effect 6 months after the date on which such notice is received by the other State Party.

---

[12] States Parties may wish to consider the position of a blameless possessor who has inherited or otherwise gratuitously acquired a cultural object which had been previously dealt with in bad faith.

[13] Some States Parties may wish to preface article 4, paragraph 3, by the following: "Subject to domestic laws, particularly those concerning access to information and the protection of privacy,...."

[14] It should be noted that General Assembly resolution 44/18 of November 6, 1989 and quite a number of resolutions of the General Conference of UNESCO have invited member States to establish, with the assistance of UNESCO, national inventories of cultural property. At the date of the drafting of this treaty, national legislative texts on the protection of cultural movable property from 76 countries have been collected, published and disseminated by UNESCO.

[15] States Parties may wish to consider providing for a process for the resolution of disputes concerning the treaty.

4. This treaty is intended to be complementary to, and does not in any way exclude, participation in other international arrangements.

In witness where of the undersigned, being duly authorized thereto by their respective Governments, have signed this treaty.

Done at...................... on..

in the................ and....................................... languages, [both/all] texts being equally authentic.

Appendix V

Draft Resolution VI

Prevention of Crimes that Infringe on the Cultural Heritage of Peoples in the Form of Movable Property

The Economic and Social Council,
Aware of the serious harm done to States and to the objects themselves by the theft and illicit export of objects regarded as part of States' cultural heritage, in particular as a result of the plundering of archaeological sites and of other sites of historical and cultural value,

Recognizing the importance for States of protecting and preserving their cultural heritage in accordance with the Convention on the Means of Prohibiting and Preventing the Illicit Import, Export and Transfer of Ownership of Cultural Property, adopted by the United Nations Educational, Scientific and Cultural Organization on 14 November 1970,[16] the preamble to which refers, inter alia, to the duty of every State to protect the cultural property existing within its territory against the dangers of theft, clandestine excavation and illicit export, and also the commitment by States and relevant international organizations to combat such practices with all the means at their disposal, in particular with regard to international cooperation on the return of such property,

Wishing to promote mutual cooperation in preventing illegal acts against the historical and cultural legacy of peoples,

Aware of the urgent need to establish standards for the restitution and return of movable property forming part of the cultural heritage of peoples after it has been stolen or illicitly exported, and for its protection and preservation,

Recognizing that one of the main objectives of the United Nations in the field of crime prevention and criminal justice is the promotion and strengthening of international cooperation in the fight against transnational organized crime,

---

[16] United Nations, *Treaty Series*, vol. 823, No. 11806.

Recalling General Assembly resolution 45/121 of 14 December 1990 on the Eighth United Nations Congress on the Prevention of Crime and the Treatment of Offenders, held in Havana from 27 August to 7 September 1990,

Recalling also the Model Treaty for the Prevention of Crimes that Infringe on the Cultural Heritage of Peoples in the Form of Movable Property, adopted by the Eighth Congress,[17]

Welcoming the organization by the Andean Community of Nations and the Government of France of a regional workshop on theft and illicit trafficking of cultural property, held in Lima from 14 to 16 May 2003,

1. Encourages Member States to consider, where appropriate and in accordance with national law, when concluding relevant agreements with other States, the Model Treaty for the Prevention of Crimes that Infringe on the Cultural Heritage of Peoples in the Form of Movable Property, adopted by the Eighth United Nations Congress on the Prevention of Crime and the Treatment of Offenders, held in Havana from 27 August to 7 September 1990;[2]
2. Calls upon all Member States to continue to strengthen international cooperation and mutual assistance in the prevention and prosecution of crimes against movable property that forms part of the cultural heritage of peoples;
3. Requests the Secretary-General to report to the Commission on Crime Prevention and Criminal Justice at its 13th session on the implementation of the present resolution.

---

[17] See *Eighth United Nations Congress on the Prevention of Crime and the Treatment of Offenders, Havana, 27August–7 September 1990: report prepared by the Secretariat* (United Nations publication, Sales No. E.91.IV.2), chapter I, section B, paragraph 2.

Appendix VI

Resolution 1483 (2003)

Adopted by the Security Council at its 4761st meeting, on 22 May 2003

The Security Council,
Recalling all its previous relevant resolutions,

Reaffirming the sovereignty and territorial integrity of Iraq,

Reaffirming also the importance of the disarmament of Iraqi weapons of mass destruction and of eventual confirmation of the disarmament of Iraq,

Stressing the right of the Iraqi people freely to determine their own political future and control their own natural resources, *welcoming* the commitment of all parties concerned to support the creation of an environment in which they may do so as soon as possible, and *expressing* resolve that the day when Iraqis govern themselves must come quickly,

Encouraging efforts by the people of Iraq to form a representative government based on the rule of law that affords equal rights and justice to all Iraqi citizens without regard to ethnicity, religion, or gender, and, in this connection, *recalls* resolution 1325 (2000) of 31 October 2000,

Welcoming the first steps of the Iraqi people in this regard, and *noting* in this connection the 15 April 2003 Nasiriyah statement and the 28 April 2003 Baghdad statement,

Resolved that the United Nations should play a vital role in humanitarian relief, the reconstruction of Iraq, and the restoration and establishment of national and local institutions for representative governance,

Noting the statement of 12 April 2003 by the Ministers of Finance and Central Bank Governors of the Group of Seven Industrialized Nations in which the member recognized the need for a multilateral effort to help rebuild and develop Iraq and for the need for assistance from the International Monetary Fund and the World Bank in these efforts,

Welcoming also the resumption of humanitarian assistance and the continuing efforts of the Secretary-General and the specialized agencies to provide food and medicine to the people of Iraq,

Welcoming the appointment by the Secretary-General of his Special Adviser on Iraq,

Affirming the need for accountability for crimes and atrocities committed by the previous Iraqi regime,

Stressing the need for respect for the archaeological, historical, cultural, and religious heritage of Iraq, and for the continued protection of archaeological, historical, cultural, and religious sites, museums, libraries, and monuments,

Noting the letter of 8 May 2003 from the Permanent Representatives of the United States of America and the United Kingdom of Great Britain and Northern Ireland to the President of the Security Council (S/2003/538) and recognizing the specific authorities, responsibilities, and obligations under applicable international law of these states as occupying powers under unified command (the "Authority"),

Noting further that other States that are not occupying powers are working now or in the future may work under the Authority,

Welcoming further the willingness of Member States to contribute to stability and security in Iraq by contributing personnel, equipment, and other resources under the Authority,

Concerned that many Kuwaitis and Third-State Nationals still are not accounted for since 2 August 1990,

Determining that the situation in Iraq, although improved, continues to constitute a threat to international peace and security,

Acting under Chapter VII of the Charter of the United Nations,

1. *Appeals* to Member States and concerned organizations to assist the people of Iraq in their efforts to reform their institutions and rebuild their country, and to contribute to conditions of stability and security in Iraq in accordance with this resolution;
2. *Calls upon* all Member States in a position to do so to respond immediately to the humanitarian appeals of the United Nations and other international organizations for Iraq and to help meet the humanitarian and other needs of the Iraqi people by providing food, medical supplies, and resources necessary for reconstruction and rehabilitation of Iraq's economic infrastructure;
3. *Appeals* to Member States to deny safe haven to those members of the previous Iraqi regime who are alleged to be responsible for crimes and atrocities and to support actions to bring them to justice;
4. *Calls upon* the Authority, consistent with the Charter of the United Nations and other relevant international law, to promote the welfare of the Iraqi people through the effective administration of the territory, including in particular working towards the restoration of conditions of security and stability and the creation of conditions in which the Iraqi people can freely determine their own political future;

5. *Calls upon* all concerned to comply fully with their obligations under international law including in particular the Geneva Conventions of 1949 and the Hague Regulations of 1907;
6. *Calls upon* the Authority and relevant organizations and individuals to continue efforts to locate, identify, and repatriate all Kuwaiti and Third-State Nationals or the remains of those present in Iraq on or after 2 August 1990, as well as the Kuwaiti archives, that the previous Iraqi regime failed to undertake, and, in this regard, directs the High-Level Coordinator, in consultation with the International Committee of the Red Cross and the Tripartite Commission and with the appropriate support of the people of Iraq and in coordination with the Authority, to take steps to fulfil his mandate with respect to the fate of Kuwaiti and Third-State National missing persons and property;
7. *Decides* that all Member States shall take appropriate steps to facilitate the safe return to Iraqi institutions of Iraqi cultural property and other items of archaeological, historical, cultural, rare scientific, and religious importance illegally removed from the Iraq National Museum, the National Library, and other locations in Iraq since the adoption of resolution 661 (1990) of 6 August 1990, including by establishing a prohibition on trade in or transfer of such items and items with respect to which reasonable suspicion exists that they have been illegally removed, and calls upon the United Nations Educational, Scientific, and Cultural Organization, Interpol, and other international organizations, as appropriate, to assist in the implementation of this paragraph;
8. *Requests* the Secretary-General to appoint a Special Representative for Iraq whose independent responsibilities shall involve reporting regularly to the Council on his activities under this resolution, coordinating activities of the United Nations in post-conflict processes in Iraq, coordinating among United Nations and international agencies engaged in humanitarian assistance and reconstruction activities in Iraq, and, in coordination with the Authority, assisting the people of Iraq through:

    a. coordinating humanitarian and reconstruction assistance by United Nations agencies and between United Nations agencies and non-governmental organizations;
    b. promoting the safe, orderly, and voluntary return of refugees and displaced persons;
    c. working intensively with the Authority, the people of Iraq, and others concerned to advance efforts to restore and establish national and local institutions for representative governance, including by working together to facilitate a process leading to an internationally recognized, representative government of Iraq;
    d. facilitating the reconstruction of key infrastructure, in cooperation with other international organizations;
    e. promoting economic reconstruction and the conditions for sustainable development, including through coordination with national and regional organizations, as appropriate, civil society, donors, and the international financial institutions;

f. encouraging international efforts to contribute to basic civilian administration functions;
g. promoting the protection of human rights;
h. encouraging international efforts to rebuild the capacity of the Iraqi civilian police force; and
i. encouraging international efforts to promote legal and judicial reform;

9. *Supports* the formation, by the people of Iraq with the help of the Authority and working with the Special Representative, of an Iraqi interim administration as a transitional administration run by Iraqis, until an internationally recognized, representative government is established by the people of Iraq and assumes the responsibilities of the Authority;
10. *Decides* that, with the exception of prohibitions related to the sale or supply to Iraq of arms and related materiel other than those arms and related materiel required by the Authority to serve the purposes of this and other related resolutions, all prohibitions related to trade with Iraq and the provision of financial or economic resources to Iraq established by resolution 661 (1990) and subsequent relevant resolutions, including resolution 778 (1992) of 2 October 1992, shall no longer apply;
11. *Reaffirms* that Iraq must meet its disarmament obligations, encourages the United Kingdom of Great Britain and Northern Ireland and the United States of America to keep the Council informed of their activities in this regard, and underlines the intention of the Council to revisit the mandates of the United Nations Monitoring, Verification, and Inspection Commission and the International Atomic Energy Agency as set forth in resolutions 687 (1991) of 3 April 1991, 1284 (1999) of 17 December 1999, and 1441 (2002) of 8 November 2002;
12. *Notes* the establishment of a Development Fund for Iraq to be held by the Central Bank of Iraq and to be audited by independent public accountants approved by the International Advisory and Monitoring Board of the Development Fund for Iraq and looks forward to the early meeting of that International Advisory and Monitoring Board, whose members shall include duly qualified representatives of the Secretary-General, of the Managing Director of the International Monetary Fund, of the Director-General of the Arab Fund for Social and Economic Development, and of the President of the World Bank;
13. *Notes further* that the funds in the Development Fund for Iraq shall be disbursed at the direction of the Authority, in consultation with the Iraqi interim administration, for the purposes set out in paragraph 14 below;
14. *Underlines* that the Development Fund for Iraq shall be used in a transparent manner to meet the humanitarian needs of the Iraqi people, for the economic reconstruction and repair of Iraq's infrastructure, for the continued disarmament of Iraq, and for the costs of Iraqi civilian administration, and for other purposes benefiting the people of Iraq;

15. *Calls upon* the international financial institutions to assist the people of Iraq in the reconstruction and development of their economy and to facilitate assistance by the broader donor community, and welcomes the readiness of creditors, including those of the Paris Club, to seek a solution to Iraq's sovereign debt problems;
16. *Requests* also that the Secretary-General, in coordination with the Authority, continue the exercise of his responsibilities under Security Council resolution 1472 (2003) of 28 March 2003 and 1476 (2003) of 24 April 2003, for a period of 6 months following the adoption of this resolution, and terminate within this time period, in the most cost effective manner, the ongoing operations of the "Oil-for-Food" Programme (the "Programme"), both at headquarters level and in the field, transferring responsibility for the administration of any remaining activity under the Programme to the Authority, including by taking the following necessary measures:

    a. to facilitate as soon as possible the shipment and authenticated delivery of priority civilian goods as identified by the Secretary-General and representatives designated by him, in coordination with the Authority and the Iraqi interim administration, under approved and funded contracts previously concluded by the previous Government of Iraq, for the humanitarian relief of the people of Iraq, including, as necessary, negotiating adjustments in the terms or conditions of these contracts and respective letters of credit as set forth in paragraph 4 (d) of resolution 1472 (2003);
    b. to review, in light of changed circumstances, in coordination with the Authority and the Iraqi interim administration, the relative utility of each approved and funded contract with a view to determining whether such contracts contain items required to meet the needs of the people of Iraq both now and during reconstruction, and to postpone action on those contracts determined to be of questionable utility and the respective letters of credit until an internationally recognized, representative government of Iraq is in a position to make its own determination as to whether such contracts shall be fulfilled;
    c. (c) to provide the Security Council within 21 days following the adoption of this resolution, for the Security Council's review and consideration, an estimated operating budget based on funds already set aside in the account established pursuant to paragraph 8 (d) of resolution 986 (1995) of 14 April 1995, identifying:

        i. all known and projected costs to the United Nations required to ensure the continued functioning of the activities associated with implementation of the present resolution, including operating and administrative expenses associated with the relevant United Nations agencies and programmes responsible for the implementation of the Programme both at Headquarters and in the field;
        ii. all known and projected costs associated with termination of the Programme;

   iii. all known and projected costs associated with restoring Government of Iraq funds that were provided by Member States to the Secretary-General as requested in paragraph 1 of resolution 778 (1992); and
   iv. all known and projected costs associated with the Special Representative and the qualified representative of the Secretary-General identified to serve on the International Advisory and Monitoring Board, for the 6-month time period defined above, following which these costs shall be borne by the United Nations;

d. to consolidate into a single fund the accounts established pursuant to paragraphs 8 (a) and 8 (b) of resolution 986 (1995);
e. to fulfil all remaining obligations related to the termination of the Programme, including negotiating, in the most cost effective manner, any necessary settlement payments, which shall be made from the escrow accounts established pursuant to paragraphs 8 (a) and 8 (b) of resolution 986 (1995), with those parties that previously have entered into contractual obligations with the Secretary-General under the Programme, and to determine, in coordination with the Authority and the Iraqi interim administration, the future status of contracts undertaken by the United Nations and related United Nations agencies under the accounts established pursuant to paragraphs 8 (b) and 8 (d) of resolution 986 (1995);
f. to provide the Security Council, 30 days prior to the termination of the Programme, with a comprehensive strategy developed in close coordination with the Authority and the Iraqi interim administration that would lead to the delivery of all relevant documentation and the transfer of all operational responsibility of the Programme to the Authority;

17. *Requests further* that the Secretary-General transfer as soon as possible to the Development Fund for Iraq 1 billion United States dollars from unencumbered funds in the accounts established pursuant to paragraphs 8 (a) and 8 (b) of resolution 986 (1995), restore Government of Iraq funds that were provided by Member States to the Secretary-General as requested in paragraph 1 of resolution 778 (1992), and decides that, after deducting all relevant United Nations expenses associated with the shipment of authorized contracts and costs to the Programme outlined in paragraph 16 (c) above, including residual obligations, all surplus funds in the escrow accounts established pursuant to paragraphs 8 (a), 8 (b), 8 (d), and 8 (f) of resolution 986 (1995) shall be transferred at the earliest possible time to the Development Fund for Iraq;
18. *Decides* to terminate effective on the adoption of this resolution the functions related to the observation and monitoring activities undertaken by the Secretary-General under the Programme, including the monitoring of the export of petroleum and petroleum products from Iraq;
19. *Decides* to terminate the Committee established pursuant to paragraph 6 of resolution 661 (1990) at the conclusion of the 6-month period called for in paragraph 16 above and further decides that the Committee shall identify individuals and entities referred to in paragraph 23 below;

20. *Decides* that all export sales of petroleum, petroleum products, and natural gas from Iraq following the date of the adoption of this resolution shall be made consistent with prevailing international market best practices, to be audited by independent public accountants reporting to the International Advisory and Monitoring Board referred to in paragraph 12 above in order to ensure transparency, and decides further that, except as provided in paragraph 21 below, all proceeds from such sales shall be deposited into the Development Fund for Iraq until such time as an internationally recognized representative government of Iraq is properly constituted;
21. *Decides further* that 5% of the proceeds referred to in paragraph 20 above shall be deposited into the Compensation Fund established in accordance with resolution 687 (1991) and subsequent relevant resolutions and that, unless an internationally recognized, representative government of Iraq and the Governing Council of the United Nations Compensation Commission, in the exercise of its authority over methods of ensuring that payments are made into the Compensation Fund, decide otherwise, this requirement shall be binding on a properly constituted, internationally recognized, representative government of Iraq and any successor thereto;
22. *Noting* the relevance of the establishment of an internationally recognized, representative government of Iraq and the desirability of prompt completion of the restructuring of Iraq's debt as referred to in paragraph 15 above, further decides that, until December 31, 2007, unless the Council decides otherwise, petroleum, petroleum products, and natural gas originating in Iraq shall be immune, until title passes to the initial purchaser from legal proceedings against them and not be subject to any form of attachment, garnishment, or execution, and that all States shall take any steps that may be necessary under their respective domestic legal systems to assure this protection, and that proceeds and obligations arising from sales thereof, as well as the Development Fund for Iraq, shall enjoy privileges and immunities equivalent to those enjoyed by the United Nations except that the abovementioned privileges and immunities will not apply with respect to any legal proceeding in which recourse to such proceeds or obligations is necessary to satisfy liability for damages assessed in connection with an ecological accident, including an oil spill, that occurs after the date of adoption of this resolution;
23. *Decides* that all Member States in which there are:

    a. funds or other financial assets or economic resources of the previous Government of Iraq or its state bodies, corporations, or agencies, located outside Iraq as of the date of this resolution, or
    b. funds or other financial assets or economic resources that have been removed from Iraq, or acquired, by Saddam Hussein or other senior officials of the former Iraqi regime and their immediate family members, including entities owned or controlled, directly or indirectly, by them or by persons acting on their behalf or at their direction, shall freeze without delay those funds or other financial assets or economic resources and,

unless these funds or other financial assets or economic resources are themselves the subject of a prior judicial, administrative, or arbitral lien or judgement, immediately shall cause their transfer to the Development Fund for Iraq, it being understood that, unless otherwise addressed, claims made by private individuals or non-government entities on those transferred funds or other financial assets may be presented to the internationally recognized, representative government of Iraq; and decides further that all such funds or other financial assets or economic resources shall enjoy the same privileges, immunities, and protections as provided under paragraph 22;

24. *Requests* the Secretary-General to report to the Council at regular intervals on the work of the Special Representative with respect to the implementation of this resolution and on the work of the International Advisory and Monitoring Board and encourages the United Kingdom of Great Britain and Northern Ireland and the United States of America to inform the Council at regular intervals of their efforts under this resolution; 25.
25. *Decides* to review the implementation of this resolution within 12 months of adoption and to consider further steps that might be necessary;
26. *Calls upon* Member States and international and regional organizations to contribute to the implementation of this resolution;
27. *Decides* to remain seized of this matter.

Appendix VII

ECOSOC Resolution 2004/34

Protection Against Trafficking in Cultural Property

The Economic and Social Council,

Emphasizing the importance for States of protecting and preserving their cultural heritage in accordance with the Convention on the Means of Prohibiting and Preventing the Illicit Import, Export and Transfer of Ownership of Cultural Property, adopted by the United Nations Educational, Scientific and Cultural Organization on 14 November 1970,[18] and other relevant instruments such as the 1995 Unidroit Convention on Stolen or Illegally Exported Cultural Objects[19] and the 1954 Convention for the Protection of Cultural Property in the Event of Armed Conflict[20] and its two Protocols,

Reaffirming its resolution 2003/29 of 22 July 2003, entitled "Prevention of crimes that infringe on the cultural heritage of peoples in the form of movable property",

Recalling General Assembly resolution 58/17 of 3 December 2003, entitled "Return or restitution of cultural property to the countries of origin",

Recalling also the model treaty for the prevention of crimes that infringe on the cultural heritage of peoples in the form of movable property, adopted by the Eighth United Nations Congress on the Prevention of Crime and the Treatment of Offenders, which was welcomed by the General Assembly in its resolution 45/121 of 14 December 1990,

Noting with appreciation the Cairo Declaration on the Protection of Cultural Property, made at the international conference celebrating the 5th anniversary of the 1954 Convention for the Protection of Cultural Property in the Event of Armed Conflict, held in Cairo from 14 to 16 February 2004, as well as its relevant recommendations,

---

[18] United Nations, *Treaty Series*, vol. 823, No. 11806.

[19] See http://www.unidroit.org.

[20] United Nations, *Treaty Series*, vol. 249, No. 3511.

Alarmed that organized criminal groups are involved in trafficking in stolen cultural property and that the international trade in looted, stolen or smuggled cultural property is estimated at several billion United States dollars per year,

Stressing that the entry into force of the United Nations Convention against Transnational Organized Crime[21] is expected to create a new impetus in international cooperation to counter and curb transnational organized crime, which will in turn lead to innovative and broader approaches to dealing with the various manifestations of such crime, including trafficking in movable cultural property,

Expressing the need to enhance or to establish, as appropriate, standards for the restitution and return of movable property forming part of the cultural heritage of peoples after it has been stolen or trafficked and for its protection and preservation,

1. *Takes note with appreciation* of the report of the Secretary-General on the prevention of crimes that infringe on the cultural heritage of peoples in the form of movable property;[22]
2. *Welcomes* international, regional and national initiatives for the protection of cultural property, in particular the work of the United Nations Educational, Scientific and Cultural Organization and its Intergovernmental Committee for Promoting the Return of Cultural Property to its Countries of Origin or its Restitution in Case of Illicit Appropriation;
3. *Requests* the Secretary-General to direct the United Nations Office on Drugs and Crime, in close cooperation with the United Nations Educational, Scientific and Cultural Organization and subject to the availability of extrabudgetary resources, to convene an expert group meeting to submit relevant recommendations to the Commission on Crime Prevention and Criminal Justice at its 15th session on protection against trafficking in cultural property, including ways of making more effective the model treaty for the prevention of crimes that infringe on the cultural heritage of peoples in the form of movable property;
4. *Encourages* Member States asserting state ownership of cultural property to consider means of issuing statements of such ownership with a view to facilitating the enforcement of property claims in other States;
5. *Urges* Member States to continue to strengthen international cooperation and mutual assistance in the prevention and prosecution of crime against movable property that forms part of the cultural heritage of peoples, as well as to ratify and implement the Convention on the Means of Prohibiting and Preventing the Illicit Import, Export and Transfer of Ownership of Cultural Property and the other relevant conventions;
6. *Requests* the Secretary-General to report to the Commission on Crime Prevention and Criminal Justice at its 15th session on the implementation of the present resolution.

47th plenary meeting
21 July 2004

---

[21] General Assembly resolution 55/25, annex I.

[22] E/CN.15/2004/10 and Add.1.

Appendix VIII

Commission on Crime Prevention and Criminal Justice

15th session
Vienna, 24–28 April 2006
Item 8 (b) of the provisional agenda
Use and application of United Nations standards and norms in crime prevention and criminal justice: protection against trafficking in cultural property
Protection against trafficking in cultural property
Report of the Secretary-General
E/CN.15/2006/14

I. Introduction

1. In its resolution 56/8 of 21 November 2001, the General Assembly proclaimed 2002 as the United Nations Year for Cultural Heritage.
2. In its resolution 58/17 of 3 December 2003, on the return or restitution of cultural property to the countries of origin, the General Assembly, recalling the Convention for the Protection of Cultural Property in the Event of Armed Conflict, adopted at The Hague on 14 May 1954,[23] and the two Protocols thereto, adopted in 1954 and 1999; the Convention on the Means of Prohibiting and Preventing the Illicit Import, Export and Transfer of Ownership of Cultural Property, adopted on 14 November 1970 by the General Conference of the United Nations Educational, Scientific and Cultural Organization (UNESCO);[24] the Convention for the Protection of the World Cultural and Natural Heritage, adopted on 16 November 1972 by the General Conference of UNESCO;[25] and

[23] United Nations, *Treaty Series*, vol. 249, No. 3511.

[24] United Nations, *Treaty Series*, vol. 823, No. 11806.

[25] United Nations, *Treaty Series*, vol. 1037, No. 15511.

the Convention on Stolen or Illegally Exported Cultural Objects, adopted in Rome on 24 June 1995 by the International Institute for the Unification of Private Law (Unidroit) (see http://www.unidroit.org); taking note of the adoption of the Convention on the Protection of the Underwater Cultural Heritage by the General Conference of UNESCO on 2 November 2001;[26] recalling the Medellin Declaration for Cultural Diversity and Tolerance and the Plan of Action on Cultural Cooperation, adopted at the first Meeting of the Ministers of Culture of the Movement of Non-Aligned Countries, held in Medellin, Colombia, on 4 and 5 September 1997 (A/52/432, annexes I and II); and noting the adoption of the Universal Declaration on Cultural Diversity and the action plan for its implementation, adopted by the General Conference of UNESCO on 2 November 2001;[27] welcomed the adoption of the Declaration concerning the Intentional Destruction of Cultural Heritage, adopted by the General Conference of UNESCO on 17 October 2003;[28] invited Member States to consider adopting and implementing the Convention on the Means of Prohibiting and Preventing the Illicit Import, Export and Transfer of Ownership of Cultural Property; also welcomed the adoption of the International Code of Ethics for Dealers in Cultural Property by the General Conference of UNESCO on 16 November 1999,[29] and invited those who dealt with trade in cultural property and their associations, where they existed, to encourage the implementation of the Code; and urged Member States to introduce effective national and international measures to prevent and combat illicit trafficking in cultural property, including special training for police, customs and border services.

3. In its resolution 2003/29 of 22 July 2003, entitled "Prevention of crimes that infringe on the cultural heritage of peoples in the form of movable property," the Economic and Social Council encouraged Member States to consider, where appropriate and in accordance with national law, when concluding relevant agreements with other States, the model treaty for the prevention of crimes that infringe on the cultural heritage of peoples in the form of movable property;[30] and called upon all Member States to continue to strengthen international cooperation and mutual assistance in the prevention and prosecution of

---

[26] See United Nations Educational, Scientific and Cultural Organization, *Records of the General Conference, Thirty-first Session, Paris, 15 October–3 November 2001*, vol. 1: and corrigendum: *Resolutions*, resolution 24.

[27] *United Nations Educational, Scientific and Cultural Organization, Records of the General Conference, Thirty-first Session, Paris, 15 October–3 November 2001*, vol. 1: *Resolutions*, resolution 25, annex I and II.

[28] Ibidem, *Thirty-second Session, Paris, 29 September–17 October 2003*, vol. 1: *Resolutions*, resolution 33, annex.

[29] Ibidem, *Thirty-Session, Paris, 26 October–17 November 1999*, vol. 1: Resolutions.

[30] *Eighth United Nations Congress on the Prevention of Crime and the Treatment of Offenders, Havana, 27 August–7 September 1990: report prepared by the Secretariat* (United Nations publication, Sales No. E.91.IV.2), chapter I, section B.1, annex.

crimes against movable property forming part of the cultural heritage of peoples. Pursuant to that resolution, the Secretary-General reported on its implementation to the Commission on Crime Prevention and Criminal Justice at its 13th session (E/CN.15/2004/10 and Add. 1).

4. In its resolution 2004/34 of 21 July 2004, entitled "Protection against trafficking in cultural property," the Economic and Social Council, noting with appreciation the Cairo Declaration on the Protection of Cultural Property, made at the international conference celebrating the 50th anniversary of the 1954 Convention for the Protection of Cultural Property in the Event of Armed Conflict, held in Cairo from 14 to 16 February 2004, as well as its relevant recommendations, alarmed that organized criminal groups were involved in trafficking in stolen cultural property and that the international trade in looted, stolen or smuggled cultural property was estimated at several billion dollars per year, stressing that the entry into force of the United Nations Convention against Transnational Organized Crime (General Assembly resolution 55/25, annex I) was expected to create a new impetus in international cooperation to counter and curb transnational organized crime, which would in turn lead to innovative and broader approaches to dealing with the various manifestations of such crime, including trafficking in movable cultural property, expressing the need to enhance or to establish, as appropriate, standards for the restitution and return of movable property forming part of the cultural heritage of peoples after it had been stolen or trafficked and for its protection and preservation, welcomed international, regional and national initiatives for the protection of cultural property, in particular the work of UNESCO and its Intergovernmental Committee for Promoting the Return of Cultural Property to its Countries of Origin or its Restitution in Case of Illicit Appropriation; requested the Secretary-General to direct the United Nations Office on Drugs and Crime (UNODC), in close cooperation with UNESCO and subject to the availability of extrabudgetary resources, to convene an expert group meeting to submit relevant recommendations to the Commission on Crime Prevention and Criminal Justice at its 15th session on protection against trafficking in cultural property, including ways of making more effective the model treaty for the prevention of crimes that infringe on the cultural heritage of peoples in the form of movable property; encouraged Member States asserting state ownership of cultural property to consider means of issuing statements of such ownership with a view to facilitating the enforcement of property claims in other States; urged Member States to continue to strengthen international cooperation and mutual assistance in the prevention and prosecution of crime against movable property forming part of the cultural heritage of peoples, as well as to ratify and implement the Convention on the Means of Prohibiting and Preventing the Illicit Import, Export and Transfer of Ownership of Cultural Property and the other relevant conventions; and requested the Secretary-General to report to the Commission on Crime Prevention and Criminal Justice at its 15th session on the implementation of the resolution.

5. The present report is submitted to the Commission on Crime Prevention and Criminal Justice pursuant to Economic and Social Council resolution 2004/34. It provides a brief overview and analysis of the replies received from Member States on their efforts to implement that resolution. UNODC is consulting with interested Governments to secure funding to convene an expert group meeting on protection against trafficking in cultural property.

II. Brief overview and analysis of replies received from Governments

6. In response to a note verbale sent to Member States by the Secretariat on 25 February 2005, the following 19 Member States provided comments and information on the implementation of Economic and Social Council resolution 2004/34: Austria, Belarus, Bolivia, Costa Rica, Czech Republic, Italy, Kuwait, Latvia, Mauritius, Mexico, Netherlands, Oman, Peru, Romania, Spain, Switzerland, Turkey, Ukraine and United States of America.
7. Austria reported on the strict criteria applied by the Austrian Federal Museums and the Austrian National Library in scrutinizing the origin of acquired cultural property. Austria also stressed the improvement of safety and security measures for permanent collections, as well as for special exhibitions, including by resorting to external expertise. As far as financial expenditures were concerned, the competent Federal Ministry for Education, Science and Culture had invested 10 million euros with a view to reinforcing the safety and security of art collections in the years 2005 and 2006. Austria also referred to the practice of registering the inventory of art collections in databases, taking into account in particular the origin and the type of acquisition of the cultural property, with a view to facilitating the object identification requirements of the International Criminal Police Organization (Interpol).
8. With regard to international cooperation in the area of protection against trafficking in cultural property, Austria referred to an international forum for discussion and consultations between museums, which served the exchange of information and views on all relevant areas of modern museum management, including those highlighted in resolution 2004/34. The Austrian National Library was also a member of an international security network among libraries, which had been set up in 2002 within the framework of the Ligue des bibliothèques européennes de recherche (LIBER) and aimed at facilitating the exchange of confidential security information between European research libraries with valuable inventories. Furthermore, the Austrian Federal Museums were members of the International Committee for Museum Security (ICMS), which formed part of the International Council of Museums (ICOM) and was assigned to improve security and safety measures in museums, including by developing common security and safety standards.

9. Belarus provided in its response an overview of the legal framework regulating the ownership of the material or intellectual property of the nation of Belarus and briefly described the rights and obligations, including regarding registration and preservation, of owners of such property, who could be the State itself, legal entities or individuals. It was stressed, inter alia, that any change of owner of material or intellectual property or transfer of a part of the copyright to a work of value was subject to mandatory registration with the Ministry of Culture and that the deed of transfer of ownership of such property had to be notarized. Belarus also reported that it was party to the Convention on the Means of Prohibiting and Preventing the Illicit Import, Export and Transfer of Ownership of Cultural Property, as well as the Convention for the Protection of Cultural Property in the Event of Armed Conflict and its two Protocols. In addition, Belarus was party to a number of agreements among member States of the Commonwealth of Independent States. The Ministry of Internal Affairs had endorsed a draft law on accession to the Unidroit Convention on Stolen or Illegally Exported Cultural Objects.
10. The Ministry of Internal Affairs of Belarus had participated in an international conference on international cooperation between police, border and customs services in fighting crime and trafficking in property of historical and cultural value, held in Szczytno, Poland, from 3 to 5 November 2004. Some 160 representatives from 20 countries had attended the Conference, organized by Poland's Interdepartmental Centre for Combating Organized Crime and International Terrorism in conjunction with the National Police Academy.
11. Belarus also referred to ongoing work in implementing measures to combat trafficking in property of cultural and/or historical value, including the creation of a database of objects of historical and cultural value.
12. Bolivia presented statistical data from the Ministry of Economic Development, Vice-Ministry of Culture, demonstrating an increase of 145% in the number of cultural objects that had been catalogued in different areas of the country during the period 1975–2004. In addition, whereas the average of catalogued cultural objects was 310 items per year for the period 1975–2000, it had been multiplied by almost 10 in the period 2001–2004 (2,800 items catalogued per year). Moreover, there was a decrease in theft of objects of cultural heritage: 20 incidents had been reported in 1999 and only 1 in 2004.
13. Bolivia's response provided a brief overview of the measures taken to control the export of works of art and included information on the ongoing efforts to create a database that would make it possible to register cultural objects in digital format. Reference was also made to the organization of events aiming at raising public awareness about the importance of preserving the national cultural heritage, as well as the concerted national efforts for the development of a national plan for the prevention of trafficking in cultural property.
14. Costa Rica stated that experts in archaeology, anthropology and history from institutions and departments involved in the protection of cultural heritage, including officers from the National Museum, had provided technical assistance

to the Attorney General's Office and, where necessary, to the judicial and law enforcement authorities, especially by participating in criminal proceedings to assess the damage caused to national archaeological sites and other cultural treasures. Similar assistance could also be provided in the context of operational activities of the police or the customs officers, in particular in terms of assessing confiscated objects or acting as depositaries.

15. Costa Rica reported on its domestic legal framework regulating issues related to the national archaeological heritage and provided information on the coordination between national authorities in cases of transfer of cultural goods to and from the country. Additional information was provided regarding the inventories of cultural heritage collections and archaeological sites that had been created to ensure further protection of national cultural property. In some cases, public and private entities provided assistance and consultancy services for making stock lists or for the storage, preservation or restoration of cultural objects.
16. Costa Rica was party to most of the international instruments relating to the protection of cultural property. An initiative had been taken by the Vice-Ministry of Culture, Youth and Sports to draft a law on the protection of national cultural heritage.
17. The Czech Republic pointed out that after 1989 there had been an increase in crimes related to cultural heritage and in the unlawful export of parts of that heritage from the country. While before 1989 there had been on average 35 cases of theft and burglary per year, in 1990 the number of such cases had risen to 611 and in 1991 to almost 1,000. The actual number of stolen objects was often higher, since in some cases the criminals had stolen the complete interior furnishings of churches.
18. The Czech Republic indicated that the Board of National Police had set up a database of stolen cultural property that was based on similar principles to those of the Interpol database and was available in the Web site of the Ministry of the Interior in English and German. It was also reported that, since 1992, the Ministry of Culture had financed from the state budget the registration and documentation of cultural property owned by the Roman Catholic Church, which had been and still was the most frequent target of thieves.
19. The Czech Republic also referred to the national legislation on the protection of cultural heritage. Specific reference was made to the law on the sale and export of objects of cultural value, which also had a screening function enabling the National Heritage Institute, authorized to issue licences for the export of objects of a religious nature, to identify and locate a number of stolen religious objects. Other laws mentioned by the Czech Republic dealt with the export of national cultural monuments, the export of museum-type collections and the export of registered archival materials. Cultural property whose circulation was subject to those laws might be exported from the territory of the country only for a fixed period of time.
20. Additional information was provided on the Czech Law on the Restitution of Unlawfully Exported Cultural Property, which had entered into force on the day of the accession of the country to the European Union, implementing the Council

of the European Communities directive 93/7/EEC of 15 March 1993 on the return of cultural objects unlawfully removed from the territory of a member State.[31] In the recent years, the Ministry of Culture, in cooperation with the National Heritage Institute, had been making random surveys of the market in antiquities in neighbouring countries, especially Austria and Germany. In that context, the location and restitution of a number of objects stolen from churches in the country and unlawfully exported had been ensured by means of police cooperation. A recent case involving requests to Austria and Germany for the restitution of stolen and illegally exported objects listed in ecclesiastical inventories was also reported.

21. The Czech Republic referred to national legislation enacted in 2002, which had set additional conditions for the export of cultural property from the customs territory of the European Communities and designated the competent authorities to grant export licences for cultural objects and archival materials. In addition, the law set conditions for granting export licences on the basis of permits and certificates issued under national regulations and provided for appropriate sanctions.
22. Furthermore, according to the statistical data reported, the Ministry of Culture had granted a total of 37 standard export licences from 1 May 2004 to 13 May 2005. Of those licences, 36 were for export for exhibition purposes (to Japan, Switzerland and the United States of America) and one licence had concerned export for restoration (Switzerland). Information on the procedure followed for the issuance of the export licences was provided.
23. Moreover, the Czech Republic noted that, after its accession to the European Union, its customs authorities had terminated most of their activities at the borders, with the exception of international airports, and moved their activities inland. For that purpose, mobile customs units had been established to carry out their duties throughout the national territory, including random checks near borders. The customs authorities also cooperated closely with the Ministry of Culture in the control of trafficking in cultural property.
24. The Czech Republic reported that it was party to the Convention on the Means of Prohibiting and Preventing the Illicit Import, Export and Transfer of Ownership of Cultural Property.
25. Italy noted that Economic and Social Council resolution 2004/34 could be more adequately considered in relation to the model treaty for the prevention of crimes that infringe on the cultural heritage of peoples in the form of movable property. In addition, Italy referred to the European Convention on Mutual Assistance in Criminal Matters of 1959,[32] as well as the Council of Europe Convention on Laundering, Search, Seizure and Confiscation of the Proceeds from Crime of 1990,[33] as substantial tools for the promotion of international cooperation to combat crime and achieve concrete results, in particular in the fight against organized crime.

---

[31] *Official Journal of the European Communities*, No. L 74, March 27, 1993.

[32] United Nations, *Treaty Series*, vol. 472, No. 6841.

[33] United Nations, *Treaty Series*, vol. 1862, No. 31704.

26. Italy stressed the importance of fostering international law enforcement cooperation to combat trafficking in cultural property and in particular the need to exchange intelligence data in order to operate in a more effective way. As far as the involvement of organized crime in trafficking in cultural property was concerned, reference was made to the analysis of results of investigations carried out in the country showing that only in a few limited circumstances were mafia-type organizations involved in that specific field. Such trafficking was more often organized by individuals or criminal groups that utilized international contacts consolidated over the years and managed to set up illicit markets abroad. Italy highlighted the existence of the Carabinieri Unit for the Protection of Cultural Property, a specialized unit dealing with the prevention of and fight against trafficking in cultural property. It noted that the Unit had become an international point of reference for the development of projects aimed at assisting foreign police forces in the fight against illicit trafficking in cultural property.
27. Kuwait reported no incidents of stolen movable cultural objects, either local or imported, that would fall under the terms of the Unidroit Convention on Stolen or Illegally Exported Cultural Objects or under the Convention for the Protection of Cultural Property in the Event of Armed Conflict and its two Protocols.
28. Latvia reported on its regulation 526, adopted by the Cabinet of Ministers on 16 January 2003, on the procedure for the return of illegally exported art and antique articles, applying to relations with countries with which Latvia had signed relevant agreements. The regulation referred to the procedures followed for the search and return to the country of origin or to Latvia of illegally imported or exported cultural property, respectively. In that connection, Latvia also mentioned that Council of the European Communities directive 93/7/EEC on the return of cultural objects unlawfully removed from the territory of a member State had entered into force in its domestic legal order on 1 May 2004.
29. Mauritius reported on the purpose and activities of the National Heritage Fund, initially established in 1997 with the task of preserving, protecting, developing and improving the aesthetic and architectural quality of buildings, structures and antiques that were of historical importance or of public interest, as well as of educating the public in geography and natural history. Under the new legislation of 2003, the objectives of the Fund had been expanded to cover the safeguard, management and promotion of the national heritage of Mauritius. The Fund was also responsible for the preservation of national heritage sites as source material for scientific and cultural investigation and as an enduring basis for purposes of development, leisure and tourism. The Fund was administered and managed by a Board with the following functions: identifying sites, monuments, structures, intangible heritage or such other objects of cultural significance to be designated as national heritage; regulating and authorizing activities pertaining to the exploration, excavation and salvage of national heritage or any object or structure of cultural significance; taking the necessary measures to maintain, protect and promote national heritage and attain the objects of the Fund; and working in collaboration with the international community to trace

and recover any national heritage that might be outside the country or to restore foreign heritage or to jointly manage shared heritage. In addition, the prior approval of the Board was necessary, according to the legislation, for exporting, or causing to export, objects of national heritage.

30. Mauritius expressed its readiness and commitment to strengthen international cooperation and mutual assistance in the prevention and prosecution of crimes against movable property, although no incidents of looted, stolen or smuggled cultural property or related activities of organized criminal groups had been reported in the country. In that connection, it was reported that Mauritius had since 1978 been a party to the Convention on the Means of Prohibiting and Preventing the Illicit Import, Export and Transfer of Ownership of Cultural Property of 1970.
31. Mexico reported no precedent of indictments against persons involved in trafficking in cultural property. It provided information on the special unit designated to deal with related crimes and made a brief reference to the legal framework (constitutional provisions and ad hoc legislation) providing for the investigation and prosecution of such crimes.
32. The Netherlands stated that it considered UNESCO and Unidroit the core bodies to report to on issues related to cultural property. However, it pointed out that the United Nations Convention against Transnational Organized Crime could serve as the basis for the promotion of international law enforcement cooperation in the area. The Netherlands also reported on its preparations to sign and ratify the Convention on the Means of Prohibiting and Preventing the Illicit Import, Export and Transfer of Ownership of Cultural Property.
33. Oman indicated that it had taken action to accede to the international conventions related to the prohibition and prevention of the illicit importation and transport of cultural property, by virtue of royal decree 69/77, issued on 25 October 1977, in addition to national laws governing the protection of such property. Oman also stated that its Ministry of Heritage and Culture had consistently coordinated in a direct manner with law enforcement authorities to prevent the importation and exportation of cultural property through any of the country's border points.
34. Peru provided information on the legislative and administrative measures taken at the national level in relation to the import and export of cultural objects and made extensive reference to the provisions of the basic domestic legislation for the protection of cultural heritage (general law 28296, in force since July 2004). Peru also presented an overview of the organizational structure and functions of the National Institute of Culture, which was entrusted with the preparation, execution and supervision of plans of action for the protection of national cultural heritage.
35. With regard to cooperation with foreign countries for the protection of cultural property and the restitution of cultural objects, Peru referred to the memorandum of understanding between its Government and the Government of the United States, which provided for the protection of archaeological treasures and ethnographic colonial heritage in a broader and more detailed manner than existing conventions or agreements and extended the bilateral cooperation until 2007.

36. Peru reported on measures taken to prevent illicit trafficking in cultural objects, including the monitoring of auctions and the establishment of an institutional unit at Jorge Chávez International Airport to detect possible illicit export of cultural objects. Additional information was provided on cases of repatriation of cultural objects discovered in foreign countries.
37. Peru's response also included information on the competent authorities for the control of the export and import of cultural objects, as well as the institutions involved in the protection of cultural heritage. Efforts to strengthen the effectiveness of the national judicial system in dealing with crimes related to cultural property were also highlighted. Specific and extensive reference was made to training and educational activities at the national and local levels geared towards raising awareness and sensitivity about the negative effects of crimes against national cultural heritage.
38. Romania provided information on its existing national legislation to prevent and combat trafficking in mobile cultural property. It was noted that the legislation was analogous to the relevant European legislation, in particular the Council of the European Communities regulation 3911/92 of 9 December 1992 on the export of cultural goods[34] and the 1993 Council directive 93/7/EEC on the return of cultural objects unlawfully removed from the territory of a member State. Comprehensive information was also provided on the most significant provisions of the national legislation that governed the specific circumstances and conditions under which the lending, public sale, temporary or permanent export of listed mobile cultural objects might be allowed. Legislative requirements and conditions were also presented in relation to the location, preservation and recovery of cultural assets taken from the territory of a European Union member State and found in Romanian territory. Romania's response also included a list of acts relating to the export or import of cultural assets that were treated as criminal offences in its national legislation, as well as information on the sanctions prescribed for such crimes.
39. Furthermore, Romania noted that national law enforcement authorities had undertaken action geared towards strengthening cooperation with cultural institutions and creating an interdisciplinary team with the purpose of improving the protection of cultural heritage and the efficiency of related recovery mechanisms, including information exchange. Moreover, the Romanian police systematically transmitted information to Interpol on theft of and trafficking in cultural property, the involvement of criminal networks and the means used by traffickers, and shared information on cases involving theft or forgery of art objects. Other action at the national level included monitoring the market in art objects and increased sales on the Internet and intensifying security measures for museums, public collections and churches in order to prevent theft, as well as encouraging the photographic inventory of objects in public or private collections, attracting public attention through media campaigns and educational

[34] *Official Journal of the European Communities*, No. L 395, December 31, 1992.

programmes and offering specific training to law enforcement personnel. National action also focused on the establishment of communication networks and data systems facilitating the rapid exchange of information on cultural objects declared national treasures that might not be taken out of the country, as well as on stolen or missing objects.

40. Spain listed its laws protecting cultural property and provided further information on the relevant international instruments, which were already in force in its domestic legal order or were in the process of ratification. Spain also highlighted the competence of the regional authorities (*comunidades autónomas*) to regulate issues related to the protection of cultural property. Additional reference was made to the particular nature of cultural goods, which justified the existence of cautions, restricting measures or limitations to the freedom of movement of goods among member States of the European Union.
41. Spain made specific mention of the Treaty on the Protection of Artistic and Scientific Institutions and Historical Monuments of 1935,[35] which was broadly used for the protection of cultural property in wartime. In addition, Spain referred to the Intergovernmental Committee for Promoting the Return of Cultural Property to its Countries of Origin or its Restitution in Case of Illicit Appropriation, a consultative body, composed of 22 member States, that had been established by the General Conference of UNESCO in 1980 and had convened its 13th session in February 2005.
42. Switzerland reported on its Federal Act on the International Transfer of Cultural Property, adopted in June 2003, as well as on the ratification in October 2003 of the Convention on the Means of Prohibiting and Preventing the Illicit Import, Export and Transfer of Ownership of Cultural Property. The Federal Act covered, inter alia, the following areas: protection of national cultural heritage; contribution to the protection of the cultural heritage of other States and conclusion of bilateral treaties to that effect; encouragement of international exchange of cultural objects between museums and guarantees of restitution; and promotion of diligence in trading cultural objects.
43. Switzerland provided information on its Federal Office of Culture, the administrative authority in charge of implementing the above-mentioned Federal Act. The theft of cultural property fell under the competence of the regional authorities, while the Federal Department of Justice and Police and its art experts ensured coordination and communication between the regions and foreign authorities.
44. Switzerland stressed the importance of information exchange at the national and international levels in dealing effectively with trafficking in cultural property and highlighted, in that connection, the cooperation of its national authorities with Interpol. Switzerland participated in a group of experts established by the Interpol General Secretariat for the revision of the structure of its international database on stolen art objects. Switzerland also supported the joint activities

[35] League of Nations, *Treaty Series*, vol. 167, No. 3874.

of Interpol and UNESCO to control trafficking in cultural property and participated in the group established by Interpol to do research on the cultural property stolen during the conflict in Iraq. In addition, Switzerland attended international conferences and training workshops organized by UNESCO, Interpol and the International Council of Museums for countries whose national heritage was under particular threat.

45. Turkey made reference to the information that its competent national authorities had provided in relation to the implementation of Economic and Social Council resolution 2003/29 and also reported on the ratification on 6 October 2004 of the Council of Europe Convention on Laundering, Search, Seizure and Confiscation of the Proceeds from Crime. Moreover, the new Penal Code, which entered into force on 1 June 2005, introduced the offence of laundering of property derived from crime, punishable by imprisonment of at least 1 year.
46. Ukraine reported that it had been party to the Convention on the Means of Prohibiting and Preventing the Illicit Import, Export and Transfer of Ownership of Cultural Property since 1988. It also referred to its law of 1999 on the export, import and return of cultural property, as well as the decree of 2002 that described the procedure for formulating a law on the export or temporary export of cultural property and control over its transfer beyond the State boundaries. Information was also provided on the establishment of mechanisms dealing with the listing of items that belonged to the property of the Ukrainian State and should not be exported from its territory. Ukraine also mentioned the legislative initiatives taken in order to streamline the national legislation and prepare new laws that would increase the penalties for offences relating to the protection of the State's cultural heritage.
47. Furthermore, Ukraine provided statistical data on offences involving cultural property. It was noted that more than 2,000 crimes related to the acquisition of antiques and works of art had been committed in the country over the last 12 years, of which almost half had been successfully encountered. Many of the offences involving cultural property had been committed in 1993 and 1994, when the average was between 300 and 350 crimes per year, while in the following years the average dropped to 200–250 offences per year. However, 378 crimes involving cultural property or antiques were recorded throughout the country in 2004. Of that number, 93% were thefts, while an alarming increase in the use of violence to acquire historical and cultural property (robberies, armed robberies) was also recorded in 2004. In the first quarter of 2005, there was a sharp drop in the number of crimes related to attempts to acquire cultural property: 89 crimes were recorded, compared with 122 crimes committed in the same period in 2004, and 28 of the perpetrators were identified.
48. Ukraine also reported on the efforts of its Ministry of Internal Affairs to set up an antiques database. It was noted that the database currently covered 986 objects, 333 of which were accompanied by a digital image. The number of stolen antiques found in searches or confiscated by departments of the Ministry of Internal Affairs was 834 (813 stolen, 168 of which were accompanied by a digital image, and 21 confiscated, 17 with images). Of these, 449 were icons or

holy vessels (36 with images), 9 were weapons (7 with images), 133 were paintings (57 with images), 52 were sets of coins (47 with images) and 6 were sculptures (all 6 with images). The total number of registered objects stolen from State institutions was 498. Of the latter, a weakness of the system reported in Ukraine's response was that 77.8% of the stolen objects were not accompanied by a digital image, which made it impossible to carry out an expert appraisal when they were registered and, thus, much more difficult to identify them when searching the antiques database.

49. Ukraine indicated that its law enforcement authorities were involved in international cooperation efforts to combat the crimes concerned by exchanging information through Interpol. In that connection, it was reported that an international search was under way for 96 cultural objects (works of art and antiques) stolen from Ukraine. Since it began its operations, the National Central Bureau of Interpol had dealt with over 1,600 enquiries about stolen cultural objects, including over 90 in 2004 and over 20 in the first 3 months of 2005. As a result of those enquiries, more than 170 cultural objects and works of art stolen from Ukraine had been located in the territory of other countries.

50. In addition, Ukraine referred to the Interpol General Secretariat's initiative to give the law enforcement authorities of all its member States the opportunity to make use of the information in its international database on stolen cultural property. In that context, the full version of the database, stored on magnetic and optical media and comprising over 27,000 records, was sent regularly to the competent national authorities of Ukraine. The National Central Bureau of Interpol had also introduced the Interpol standardized registration document for stolen cultural property into the work of the national law enforcement authorities.

51. The United States of America stressed that a number of measures had been taken to stop trafficking in illicit cultural property. It was reported that, in order to fulfil its obligations as a State party to the Convention on the Means of Prohibiting and Preventing the Illicit Import, Export and Transfer of Ownership of Cultural Property, the United States had entered into bilateral agreements with other States parties with a view to restricting the import of certain categories of archaeological and ethnological objects into the country, as well as thwarting the looting and trafficking of illicit objects by reducing the incentive to pillage sites. Currently, the United States had agreements with Bolivia, Cambodia, Cyprus, El Salvador, Guatemala, Honduras, Italy, Mali, Nicaragua and Peru. Similar agreements with China and Colombia were pending. In addition, import restrictions on cultural property existed outside of these bilateral agreements. Under the 1973 pre-Columbian monumental or architectural sculpture or murals statute, for example, such objects could be imported into the United States territory only with an export licence issued by the country of origin or verifiable documentation that they had left the country of origin prior to 1 June 1973.

52. Additional information was also provided on the United States authorities involved, and the progress made, in the fight against trafficking in cultural property at the operational level, as well as the relevant legislation that such authorities applied to that effect. It was pointed out that the Department of

State worked in cooperation with the Department of Homeland Security to enforce restrictions imposed under the relevant bilateral agreements in force. Furthermore, cases of recovery and repatriation of cultural property by the United States Immigration and Customs Enforcement, the largest investigative branch of the Department of Homeland Security, were reported, including the return of two 2,000-year-old coins to Afghanistan in May 2005. Reference was also made to the provisions of the National Stolen Property Act, which made it possible to prosecute a person who knowingly transferred, received or sold stolen goods of more than $5,000 in interstate or foreign commerce. The application of those provisions in the case of prosecution of a prominent dealer who had imported Egyptian antiquities into the United States in violation of Egypt's national ownership law was also highlighted.

53. The United States reported that in 2004 Congress had mandated the creation within the Department of State of an inter-agency group, the Cultural Antiquities Task Force, with the task of promoting international efforts to preserve the cultural heritage of all countries and combating trafficking in illegal antiquities and looting of archaeological sites by identifying and carrying out effective law enforcement, as well as diplomatic and other programmatic measures. On 25 and 26 May 2005, the Task Force had hosted a workshop for law enforcement experts from the United States, Europe and the Middle East to discuss ways to better coordinate transnational law enforcement efforts, the link between organized crime and trafficking in movable cultural property, and the investigation and prosecution of cases involving illicit cultural property in the United States. During the workshop, law enforcement officials spoke of their particular experiences relating to the recovery and restitution of looted and stolen material illicitly removed from Iraq.

III. Concluding remarks

54. The harm to a nation's heritage resulting from theft of and trafficking in cultural property, as well as the dire need to take effective measures at the national level to combat these criminal activities were discussed during the Eleventh United Nations Congress on Crime Prevention and Criminal Justice, held in Bangkok, from 18 to 25 April 2005. In the Bangkok Declaration on Synergies and Responses: Strategic Alliances in Crime Prevention and Criminal Justice,[36] the Congress took note of the increased involvement of organized criminal groups in the theft of and trafficking in cultural property and reaffirmed the fundamental importance of implementation of existing instruments and the further development of national measures and international cooperation in criminal matters, calling upon Member States to take effective action to that effect.

[36] A/CONF.203/18, chapter I, resolution 1.

55. Moreover, the United Nations System Chief Executives Board for Coordination, in addressing the issue of curbing transnational organized crime at its session held in April 2004, identified specific areas on which joint work of the concerned United Nations organizations should focus and agreed on a series of measures for immediate implementation that would promote concerted action of the members organizations, in accordance with their respective mandates, and build an effective inter-agency response to curbing transnational organized crime and its specific manifestations. One of these measures was the launch of multi-agency assessments to determine the extent of involvement of organized criminal activity in various forms of trafficking, including trafficking in cultural property (see E/2004/67, paragraph 21).
56. In view of the above, UNODC stands ready to convene, in cooperation with UNESCO and subject to the availability of extrabudgetary resources, an expert group meeting that would explore and assess the challenges posed and the difficulties encountered in the fight against trafficking in cultural property. The Commission on Crime Prevention and Criminal Justice may therefore wish to renew its appeal to Member States to consider making voluntary contributions towards the organization of such a meeting.

Appendix IX

ECOSOC Resolution 2008/23

Protection Against Trafficking in Cultural Property

The Economic and Social Council,
Recalling General Assembly resolution 56/8 of 21 November 2001, in which the Assembly proclaimed 2002 the United Nations Year for Cultural Heritage, and resolutions 58/17 of 3 December 2003 and 61/52 of 4 December 2006, on the return or restitution of cultural property to the countries of origin,

Recalling also the model treaty for the prevention of crimes that infringe on the cultural heritage of peoples in the form of movable property,[37] which was adopted by the Eighth United Nations Congress on the Prevention of Crime and the Treatment of Offenders and welcomed by the General Assembly in its resolution 45/121 of 14 December 1990,

Emphasizing the importance for States of protecting and preserving their cultural heritage in accordance with relevant international instruments such as the Convention on the Means of Prohibiting and Preventing the Illicit Import, Export and Transfer of Ownership of Cultural Property, adopted by the United Nations Educational, Scientific and Cultural Organization on 14 November 1970,[38] the Convention on Stolen or Illegally Exported Cultural Objects, adopted at Rome on 24 June 1995 by the International Institute for the Unification of Private Law,[39] and the Convention for the Protection of Cultural Property in the Event of Armed Conflict, adopted at The Hague on 14 May 1954,[40] and the two Protocols thereto of 14 May 1954 and 26 March 1999,

---

[37] *Eighth United Nations Congress on the Prevention of Crime and the Treatment of Offenders, Havana, 27 August-7 September 1990: report prepared by the Secretariat* (United Nations publication, Sales No. E.91.IV.2), chapter I, section B.1.

[38] United Nations, *Treaty Series*, vol. 823, No. 11806.

[39] Available from www.unidriot.org.

[40] United Nations, *Treaty Series*, vol. 249, No. 3511.

Reiterating the significance of cultural property as part of the common heritage of humankind and as unique and important testimony of the culture and identity of peoples and the necessity of protecting it,

Reaffirming the necessity of international cooperation in preventing and combating all aspects of trafficking in cultural property,[41] and noting that such cultural property is especially transferred through licit markets, such as auctions, including through the Internet,

Reaffirming also its resolutions 2004/34 of 21 July 2004, entitled "Protection against trafficking in cultural property," and 2003/29 of 22 July 2003, entitled "Prevention of crimes that infringe on the cultural heritage of peoples in the form of movable property,"

Recalling the deliberations of the Eleventh United Nations Congress on Crime Prevention and Criminal Justice, and the Bangkok Declaration on Synergies and Responses: Strategic Alliances in Crime Prevention and Criminal Justice,[42] in which the Congress took note of the increased involvement of organized criminal groups in the theft of and trafficking in cultural property and reaffirmed the fundamental importance of implementation of existing instruments and the further development of national measures and international cooperation in criminal matters, calling upon Member States to take effective action to that end,

Expressing concern about the demand for cultural property, which leads to its loss, destruction, removal, theft and trafficking,

Alarmed at the growing involvement of organized criminal groups in all aspects of trafficking in cultural property,

Expressing regret that the United Nations Office on Drugs and Crime could not convene the expert group meeting envisaged in Economic and Social Council resolution 2004/34, mainly because of the lack of extrabudgetary resources,

Stressing the importance of fostering international law enforcement cooperation to combat trafficking in cultural property and, in particular, the need to increase the exchange of information and experiences in order for competent authorities to operate in a more effective manner,

Stressing also that the entry into force of the United Nations Convention against Transnational Organized Crime[43] has created a new impetus to international cooperation in countering and curbing transnational organized crime, which will in turn lead to innovative and broader approaches to dealing with the various manifestations of such crime, including trafficking in cultural property,

---

[41] It is understood that the expression "trafficking in cultural property" shall be interpreted in conformity with the relevant international instruments, including the Convention on the Means of Prohibiting and Preventing the Illicit Import, Export and Transfer of Ownership of Cultural Property.

[42] *Eleventh United Nations Congress on Crime Prevention and Criminal Justice, Bangkok, 18–25 April 2005: report prepared by the Secretariat* (United Nations publication, Sales No. E.05.IV.7), chapter I, resolution 1; subsequently endorsed by the General Assembly in its resolution 60/177 of 16 December 2005, and contained in the annex thereto.

[43] United Nations, *Treaty Series*, vol. 2225, No. 39574.

Expressing the need, where appropriate, to strengthen and fully implement mechanisms for the return or restitution of cultural property after it has been stolen or trafficked and for its protection and preservation,

1. *Takes note with appreciation* of the report of the Secretary-General on protection against trafficking in cultural property;[80]
2. *Welcomes* national, regional and international initiatives for the protection of cultural property, in particular the work of the United Nations Educational, Scientific and Cultural Organization and its Intergovernmental Committee for Promoting the Return of Cultural Property to its Countries of Origin or its Restitution in Case of Illicit Appropriation;
3. *Reiterates its request* that the United Nations Office on Drugs and Crime, in close cooperation with the United Nations Educational, Scientific and Cultural Organization, convene an open-ended intergovernmental expert group meeting, with interpretation in all the official languages of the United Nations, to submit to the Commission on Crime Prevention and Criminal Justice at its 18th session relevant recommendations on protection against trafficking in cultural property, including ways of making more effective the model treaty for the prevention of crimes that infringe on the cultural heritage of peoples in the form of movable property, and invites Member States and other donors to provide extrabudgetary contributions for those purposes in accordance with the rules and procedures of the United Nations;
4. *Encourages* Member States asserting State ownership of cultural property to consider means of issuing statements of such ownership with a view to facilitating the enforcement of property claims in other States;
5. *Urges* Member States and relevant institutions, as appropriate, to strengthen and fully implement mechanisms to strengthen international cooperation, including mutual legal assistance, in order to combat trafficking in cultural property, including trafficking committed through the use of the Internet, and to facilitate the recovery, return or restitution of cultural property;
6. *Urges* Member States to protect cultural property and prevent trafficking in such property by introducing appropriate legislation, including, in particular, procedures for the seizure, return or restitution of cultural property, promoting education, launching awareness-raising campaigns, mapping and carrying out inventories of cultural property, providing adequate security measures, developing the capacities and human resources of monitoring institutions such as the police, customs services and the tourism sector, involving the media and disseminating information on the theft and pillaging of cultural property;
7. *Also urges* Member States to take effective measures to prevent the transfer of illicitly acquired or illegally obtained cultural property, especially through auctions, including through the Internet, and to effect its return or restitution to its rightful owners;

[80] E/CN.15/2006/14.

8. *Further urges* Member States to continue to strengthen international cooperation and mutual assistance for the prevention and prosecution of crime against cultural property that forms part of the cultural heritage of peoples, and to ratify and implement the Convention on the Means of Prohibiting and Preventing the Illicit Import, Export and Transfer of Ownership of Cultural Property and other relevant international instruments;
9. *Requests* the United Nations Office on Drugs and Crime to develop its relations with the cooperative network established among the United Nations Educational, Scientific and Cultural Organization, the International Council of Museums, the International Criminal Police Organization (INTERPOL), the International Institute for the Unification of Private Law and the World Customs Organization in the areas of trafficking in cultural property and its return or restitution;
10. *Requests* the Secretary-General to report to the Commission on Crime Prevention and Criminal Justice at its 19th session on the implementation of the present resolution.

42nd plenary meeting
24 July

Appendix X

UNESCO Convention on the Means of Prohibiting and Preventing the Illicit Import, Export and Transfer of Ownership of Cultural Property 1970

Paris, 14 November 1970

The General Conference of the United Nations Educational, Scientific and Cultural Organization, meeting in Paris from 12 October to 14 November 1970, at its 16th session,

Recalling the importance of the provisions contained in the Declaration of the Principles of International Cultural Co-operation, adopted by the General Conference at its 14th session,

Considering that the interchange of cultural property among nations for scientific, cultural and educational purposes increases the knowledge of the civilization of Man, enriches the cultural life of all peoples and inspires mutual respect and appreciation among nations,

Considering that cultural property constitutes one of the basic elements of civilization and national culture, and that its true value can be appreciated only in relation to the fullest possible information regarding is origin, history and traditional setting,

Considering that it is incumbent upon every State to protect the cultural property existing within its territory against the dangers of theft, clandestine excavation, and illicit export,

Considering that, to avert these dangers, it is essential for every State to become increasingly alive to the moral obligations to respect its own cultural heritage and that of all nations,

Considering that, as cultural institutions, museums, libraries and archives should ensure that their collections are built up in accordance with universally recognized moral principles,

Considering that the illicit import, export and transfer of ownership of cultural property is an obstacle to that understanding between nations which it is part of UNESCO's mission to promote by recommending to interested States, international conventions to this end,

Considering that the protection of cultural heritage can be effective only if organized both nationally and internationally among States working in close co-operation,

Considering that the UNESCO General Conference adopted a Recommendation to this effect in 1964,

Having before It further proposals on the means of prohibiting and preventing the illicit import, export and transfer of ownership of cultural property, a question which is on the agenda for the session as item 19,

Having decided, at its 15th session, that this question should be made the subject of an international convention,

Adopts this Convention on the 14th day of November 1970.

Article 1

For the purposes of this Convention, the term "cultural property" means property which, on religious or secular grounds, is specifically designated by each State as being of importance for archaeology, prehistory, history, literature, art or science and which belongs to the following categories:

a. Rare collections and specimens of fauna, flora, minerals and anatomy, and objects of palaeontological interest;
b. property relating to history, including the history of science and technology and military and social history, to the life of national leaders, thinkers, scientists and artist and to events of national importance;
c. products of archaeological excavations (including regular and clandestine) or of archaeological discoveries;
d. elements of artistic or historical monuments or archaeological sites which have been dismembered;
e. antiquities more than 100 years old, such as inscriptions, coins and engraved seals;
f. objects of ethnological interest;
g. property of artistic interest, such as:
    i. pictures, paintings and drawings produced entirely by hand on any support and in any material (excluding industrial designs and manufactured articles decorated by hand);
    ii. original works of statuary art and sculpture in any material;
    iii. original engravings, prints and lithographs;
    iv. original artistic assemblages and montages in any material;

h. rare manuscripts and incunabula, old books, documents and publications of special interest (historical, artistic, scientific, literary, etc.) singly or in collections;
i. postage, revenue and similar stamps, singly or in collections;
j. archives, including sound, photographic and cinematographic archives;
k. articles of furniture more than 100 years old and old musical instruments.

Article 2

1. The States Parties to this Convention recognize that the illicit import, export and transfer of ownership of cultural property is one of the main causes of the impoverishment of the cultural heritage of the countries of origin of such property and that international co-operation constitutes one of the most efficient means of protecting each country's cultural property against all the dangers resulting there from.
2. To this end, the States Parties undertake to oppose such practices with the means at their disposal, and particularly by removing their causes, putting a stop to current practices, and by helping to make the necessary reparations.

Article 3

The import, export or transfer of ownership of cultural property effected contrary to the provisions adopted under this Convention by the States Parties thereto, shall be illicit.

Article 4

The States Parties to this Convention recognize that for the purpose of the Convention property which belongs to the following categories forms part of the cultural heritage of each State:

a. Cultural property created by the individual or collective genius of nationals of the State concerned, and cultural property of importance to the State concerned created within the territory of that State by foreign nationals or stateless persons resident within such territory;
b. cultural property found within the national territory;
c. cultural property acquired by archaeological, ethnological or natural science missions, with the consent of the competent authorities of the country of origin of such property;
d. cultural property which has been the subject of a freely agreed exchange;
e. cultural property received as a gift or purchased legally with the consent of the competent authorities of the country of origin of such property.

Article 5

To ensure the protection of their cultural property against illicit import; export and transfer of ownership, the States Parties to this Convention undertake, as appropriate for each country, to set up within their territories one or more national services, where such services do not already exist, for the protection of the cultural heritage, with a qualified staff sufficient in number for the effective carrying out of the following functions:

a. contributing to the formation of draft laws and regulations designed to secure the protection of the cultural heritage and particularly prevention of the illicit import, export and transfer of ownership of important cultural property;
b. establishing and keeping up to date, on the basis of a national inventory of protected property, a list of important public and private cultural property whose export would constitute an appreciable impoverishment of the national cultural heritage;
c. promoting the development or the establishment of scientific and technical institutions (museums, libraries, archives, laboratories, workshops…) required to ensure the preservation and presentation of cultural property;
d. organizing the supervision of archaeological excavations, ensuring the preservation "in situation" of certain cultural property, and protecting certain areas reserved for future archaeological research;
e. establishing, for the benefit of those concerned (curators, collectors, antique dealers, etc.) rules in conformity with the ethical principles set forth in this Convention; and taking steps to ensure the observance of those rules;
f. taking educational measures to stimulate and develop respect for the cultural heritage of all States, and spreading knowledge of the provisions of this Convention;
g. seeing that appropriate publicity is given to the disappearance of any items of cultural property.

Article 6

The States Parties to this Convention undertake:

a. To introduce an appropriate certificate in which the exporting State would specify that the export of the cultural property in question is authorized. The certificate should accompany all items of cultural property exported in accordance with the regulations;
b. to prohibit the exportation of cultural property from their territory unless accompanied by the above-mentioned export certificate;
c. to publicize this prohibition by appropriate means, particularly among persons likely to export or import cultural property.

Article 7

The States Parties to this Convention undertake:

a. To take the necessary measures, consistent with national legislation, to prevent museums and similar institutions within their territories from acquiring cultural property originating in another State Party which has been illegally exported after entry into force of this Convention, in the States concerned. Whenever possible, to inform a State of origin Party to this Convention of an offer of such cultural property illegally removed from that State after the entry into force of this Convention in both States;

b.

  i. to prohibit the import of cultural property stolen from a museum or a religious or secular public monument or similar institution in another State Party to this Convention after the entry into force of this Convention for the States concerned, provided that such property is documented as appertaining to the inventory of that institution;
  ii. at the request of the State Party of origin, to take appropriate steps to recover and return any such cultural property imported after the entry into force of this Convention in both States concerned, provided, however, that the requesting State shall pay just compensation to an innocent purchaser or to a person who has valid title to that property. Requests for recovery and return shall be made through diplomatic offices. The requesting Party shall furnish, at its expense, the documentation and other evidence necessary to establish its claim for recovery and return. The Parties shall impose no customs duties or other charges upon cultural property returned pursuant to this Article. All expenses incident to the return and delivery of the cultural property shall be borne by the requesting Party.

Article 8

The States Parties to this Convention undertake to impose penalties or administrative sanctions on any person responsible for infringing the prohibitions referred to under Articles 6(b) and 7(b) above.

Article 9

Any State Party to this Convention whose cultural patrimony is in jeopardy from pillage of archaeological or ethnological materials may call upon other States Parties who are affected. The States Parties to this Convention undertake, in these circumstances, to participate in a concerted international effort to determine and to carry out the necessary concrete measures, including the control of exports and imports and international commerce in the specific materials concerned. Pending agreement each State concerned shall take provisional measures to the extent feasible to prevent irremediable injury to the cultural heritage of the requesting State.

Article 10

The States Parties to this Convention undertake:

a. To restrict by education, information and vigilance, movement of cultural property illegally removed from any State Party to this Convention and, as appropriate for each country, oblige antique dealers, subject to penal or administrative sanctions, to maintain a register recording the origin of each item of cultural property, names and addresses of the supplier, description and price of each item sold and to inform the purchaser of the cultural property of the export prohibition to which such property may be subject;
b. to endeavour by educational means to create and develop in the public mind a realization of the value of cultural property and the threat to the cultural heritage created by theft, clandestine excavations and illicit exports.

Article 11

The export and transfer of ownership of cultural property under compulsion arising directly or indirectly from the occupation of a country by a foreign power shall be regarded as illicit.

Article 12

The States Parties to this Convention shall respect the cultural heritage within the territories for the international relations of which they are responsible, and shall take all appropriate measures to prohibit and prevent the illicit import, export and transfer of ownership of cultural property in such territories.

Article 13

The States Parties to this Convention also undertake, consistent with the laws of each State:

a. To prevent by all appropriate means transfers of ownership of cultural property likely to promote the illicit import or export of such property;

b. to ensure that their competent services co-operate in facilitating the earliest possible restitution of illicitly exported cultural property to its rightful owner;
c. to admit actions for recovery of lost or stolen items of cultural property brought by or on behalf of the rightful owners;
d. to recognize the indefeasible right of each State Party to this Convention to classify and declare certain cultural property as inalienable which should therefore ipso facto not be exported, and to facilitate recovery of such property by the State concerned in cases where it has been exported.

Article 14

In order to prevent illicit export and to meet the obligations arising from the implementation of this Convention, each State Party to the Convention should, as far as it is able, provide the national services responsible for the protection of its cultural heritage with an adequate budget and, if necessary, should set up a fund for this purpose.

Article 15

Nothing in this Convention shall prevent States Parties thereto from concluding special agreements among themselves or from continuing to implement agreements already concluded regarding the restitution of cultural property removed, whatever the reason, from its territory of origin, before the entry into force of this Convention for the States concerned.

Article 16

The States Parties to this Convention shall in their periodic reports submitted to the General Conference of the United Nations Educational, Scientific and Cultural Organization on dates and in a manner to be determined by it, give information on the legislative and administrative provisions which they have adopted and other action which they have taken for the application of this Convention, together with details of the experience acquired in this field.

Article 17

1. The States Parties to this Convention may call on the technical assistance of the United Nations Educational, Scientific and Cultural Organization, particularly as regards:

   a. Information and education;

b. consultation and expert advice;
c. co-ordination and good offices.

2. The United Nations Educational, Scientific and Cultural Organization may, on its own initiative conduct research and publish studies on matters relevant to the illicit movement of cultural property.
3. To this end, the United Nations Educational, Scientific and Cultural Organization may also call on the co-operation of any competent non-governmental organization.
4. The United Nations Educational, Scientific and Cultural Organization may, on its own initiative, make proposals to States Parties to this Convention for its implementation.
5. At the request of at least two States Parties to this Convention which are engaged in a dispute over its implementation, UNESCO may extend its good offices to reach a settlement between them.

Article 18

This Convention is drawn up in English, French, Russian and Spanish, the four texts being equally authoritative.

Article 19

1. This Convention shall be subject to ratification or acceptance by States members of the United Nations Educational, Scientific and Cultural Organization in accordance with their respective constitutional procedures.
2. The instruments of ratification or acceptance shall be deposited with the Director-General of the United Nations Educational, Scientific and Cultural Organization.

Article 20

1. This Convention shall be open to accession by all States not members of the United Nations Educational, Scientific and Cultural Organization which are invited to accede to it by the Executive Board of the Organization.
2. Accession shall be effected by the deposit of an instrument of accession with the Director-General of the United Nations Educational, Scientific and Cultural Organization.

Article 21

This Convention shall enter into force 3 months after the date of the deposit of the third instrument of ratification, acceptance or accession, but only with respect to those States which have deposited their respective instruments on or before that date. It shall enter into force with respect to any other State 3 months after the deposit of its instrument of ratification, acceptance or accession.

Article 22

The States Parties to this Convention recognize that the Convention is applicable not only to their metropolitan territories but also to all territories for the international relations of which they are responsible; they undertake to consult, if necessary, the governments or other competent authorities of these territories on or before ratification, acceptance or accession with a view to securing the application of the Convention to those territories, and to notify the Director-General of the United Nations Educational, Scientific and cultural Organization of the territories to which it is applied, the notification to take effect 3 months after the date of its receipt.

Article 23

1. Each State Party to this Convention may denounce the Convention on its own behalf or on behalf of any territory for whose international relations it is responsible.
2. The denunciation shall be notified by an instrument in writing, deposited with the Director-General of the United Nations Educational, Scientific and Cultural Organization.
3. The denunciation shall take effect 12 months after the receipt of the instrument of denunciation.

Article 24

The Director-General of the United Nations Educational, Scientific and Cultural Organization shall inform the States members of the Organization, the States not members of the Organization which are referred to in Article 20, as well as the United Nations, of the deposit of all the instruments of ratification, acceptance and accession provided for in Articles 19 and 20, and of the notifications and denunciations provided for in Articles 22 and 23, respectively.

Article 25

1. This Convention may be revised by the General Conference of the United Nations Educational, Scientific and Cultural Organization. Any such revision shall, however, bind only the States which shall become Parties to the revising convention.
2. If the General Conference should adopt a new convention revising this Convention in whole or in part, then, unless the new convention otherwise provides, this Convention shall cease to be open to ratification, acceptance or accession, as from the date on which the new revising convention enters into force.

Article 26

In conformity with Article 102 of the Charter of the United Nations, this Convention shall be registered with the Secretariat of the United Nations at the request of the Director-General of the United Nations Educational, Scientific and Cultural Organization.

Done in Paris this 17th day of November 1970, in two authentic copies bearing the signature of the President of the 16th session of the General Conference and of the Director-General of the United Nations Educational, Scientific and Cultural Organization, which shall be deposited in the archives of the United Nations Educational, Scientific and Cultural Organization, and certified true copies of which shall be delivered to all the States referred to in Articles 19 and 20 as well as to the United Nations.

Declarations and Reservations:

Australia [at time of acceptance]

"The Government of Australia declares that Australia is not at present in a position to oblige antique dealers, subject to penal or administrative sanctions, to maintain a register recording the origin of each item of cultural property, names and addresses of the supplier, description and price of each item sold and to inform the purchaser of the cultural property of the export prohibition to which such property may be subject. Australia therefore accepts the Convention subject to a reservation as to Article 10, to the extent that it is unable to comply with the obligations imposed by that Article." (See letter LA/Depositary/1989/20 of 10 January 1990)

Byelorussian Soviet Socialist Republic [at time of ratification]

"The Byelorussian Soviet Socialist Republic declares that the provisions of Articles 12, 22 and 23 of the Convention on the Means of Prohibiting and Preventing the Illicit Import, Export and Transfer of Ownership of Cultural Property, providing for the possibility for the contracting parties to extend its application to the territories for the international relations of which they are responsible, are outdated and contrary to the Declaration of the United Nations General Assembly on the Granting of Independence to Colonial Countries and Peoples (Resolution 1514/XV of 14 December 1960)." (See letter LA/Depositary/1988/11 of 15 September 1988)

Cuba

"The Government of the Republic of Cuba considers that the implementation of the provisions contained in Articles 22 and 23 of the Convention is contrary to the Declaration on Granting Independence to Colonial Countries and Peoples (Resolution 1514) adopted by the United Nations General Assembly on 14 December 1960, which proclaims the necessity of bringing to a speedy and unconditional end colonialization in all its forms and manifestations." (See letter LA/Depositary/1980/7 of 11 March 1980)

Czechoslovakia

"Accepting the Convention, the Government of the Czechoslovak Socialist Republic wishes to declare that preservation of the state of dependence of certain countries from which the provisions of Articles 12, 22, and 23 proceed is in contradiction with the contents and objective of the Declaration of the United Nations General Assembly No. 1514 on the granting of independence to colonial countries and nations of 14 December 1960. The Government of the Czechoslovak Socialist Republic further declares in connection with Article 20 that the Convention, according to the problems it regulates, should be open also to non-Member States of the United Nations Educational, Scientific and Cultural Organization without the need of invitation by the Executive Council of the United Nations Educational, Scientific and Cultural Organization." (See letter LA/Depositary/1977/6 of 8 April 1977)

Denmark [at the time of ratification]

The instrument contained the following temporary reservation: "... until further decision, the Convention will apply neither to the Feroe Islands nor to Groenland" [original: French], and was accompanied by the following declaration: The property designated as "of importance for archaeology, prehistory, history, literature, art or science", in accordance with Article 1 of the Convention, are the properties covered by the Danish legislation concerning protection of cultural assets and the Danish Museum Act. Act on Protection of Cultural Assets in Denmark The Act on Protection of Cultural Assets in Denmark came into force on 1 January 1987. According to section 2[44] in the Act on Protection of Cultural Assets in Denmark the Act applies to the following cultural assets which are not publicly owned:

- cultural objects of the period before 1660;
- cultural objects older than 100 years and valued at DKK 100,000 or more;
- photographs (regardless of age) if they have a value of DKK 30,000 or more.

"In exceptional cases the Minister of Culture can decide that the Act is also applicable to other objects of cultural interest. Coins and medals are the only cultural objects explicitly exempted from the regulations of the Act. The above-mentioned assets must not be exported from Denmark without permission from the Commission on Export of Cultural Assets. Museum Act According to section 28 of the Museum Act, any person who finds an ancient relic or monument, including shipwrecks, cargo or parts of such wrecks, which at any time must be assumed lost more than 100 years ago, in watercourses, in lakes, in territorial waters or on the continental shelf, but not beyond 24 nautical miles from the base lines from which the width of outer territorial waters is measured, shall immediately notify the Minister of Culture. Such objects shall belong to the State, unless any person proves that he or she is the rightful owner. Any person who gathers up an object belonging to the State, and any person who gains possession of such an object, shall immediately deliver it to the Minister of Culture. According to section 30 of the Museum Act objects of the past, including coins found in Denmark, of which no one can prove to be the rightful owner, shall be treasure trove (danefæ) if made of valuable material or being of a special cultural heritage value. Treasure trove shall belong to the State. Any person who finds treasure trove, and any person who gains possession of treasure trove, shall immediately deliver it to the National Museum of Denmark. According to section 31 of the Museum Act, a geological object or a botanical or zoological object of a fossil or sub-fossil nature or a meteorite found in Denmark is fossil trove (danekræ) if the object is of unique scientific or exhibitional value. Fossil trove shall belong to the State. Any person who finds fossil trove, and any person, who gains possession of fossil trove, shall immediately deliver it to the Danish Museum of Natural History." (See letter LA/Depositary/2003/12)

[44] More than 50 years old and not belonging to their creators.

Finland [at the time of ratification]

"The Government of Finland declares that it will implement the provisions of Article 7(b) (ii) of this Convention in accordance with its obligations under Unidroit Convention on Stolen or Illegally Exported Cultural Objects done at Rome on 24 June 1995."

France [at the time of ratification]

"The property designated as 'of importance for archaeology, prehistory, history, literature, art, or science,' in accordance with Article 1 of the Convention, are the following properties whose value exceeds the thresholds indicated opposite:

Thresholds (in ECUs)[45]

1. Archaeological objects more than 100 years old originating from:
   - terrestrial and submarine excavations and discoveries,
   - archaeological sites, archaeological collections

   0
2. Elements more than 100 years old that form an integral part of artistic, historical or religious monuments which have been dismembered
   0
3. Pictures and paintings produced entirely by hand on any support and in any material (see note 1)
   150.000
4. Mosaics, other than those included in categories 1 or 2, and drawings produced entirely by hand on any support and in any material (see note 1)
   15.000
5. Original engravings, prints, serigraphs et lithographs and their respective matrices, and original posters (see note 1)
   15.000
6. Original works of statuary art or sculpture and copies obtained by the same means as the original (see note 1), other than items included in category
   150.000

---

[45] The conversion value in national currencies of the amounts in ECUs is that in force on January 1, 1993.

7. Photographs, films and their negatives (see note 1)
   15.000

8. Incunabula and manuscripts, including geographical maps and musical scores, singly or in collections (see note 1)
   0

9. Books more than 100 years old, singly or in collections
   50.000

10. Printed geographical maps more than 200 years old
    15.000

11. Archives of any sort comprising elements more than 50 years old, whatever their medium
    0

12.

    a. Collections[46] and specimens from collections of fauna, flora, minerals, and anatomy
       50.000

    b. Collections (see note 3) of a historical, palaeontological, ethnographic or numismatic interest
       50.000

13. Means of transport over 75 years old
    50.000

14. Any other ancient object not included in categories 1–13 between 50 and 100 years old

    a.

       - toys or games,
       - glassware,
       - objects made of precious metals,
       - furniture and furnishings,
       - optical, photographic or de cinematographic instruments,
       - musical instruments,

[46] Objects for collections are objects that posses the necessary qualities for admission to a collection, that is to say, objects that are relatively rare, not normally used for their original purpose, are the subject of special transactions distinct from the normal trade in usable objects of a similar nature, and have a high value.

- timepieces,
- objects made of wood,
- pottery,
- tapestries,
- carpets,
- wallpapers,
- weapons

50.000

b. More than 100 years old

50.000

This list is in conformity with rules in force in France and subject to modification. The government of the French Republic will make known any modifications to it that may be made at a future date." (See LA/DEP/1997/1)

Guatemala

"The Republic of Guatemala, mindful that, in conformity with the Fundamental Statute of Government, monuments and archaeological vestiges are the property of the nation and that, furthermore, national law prohibits the unauthorized export of property constituting its cultural wealth, makes an express reservation concerning paragraph (b) (ii) of Article 7 of the Convention to the effect that it does not consider itself obliged to pay any compensation to any person or persons holding cultural property that has been looted or stolen in Guatemala or exported illicitly to another State Party and that, at the request of the Government of Guatemala, has been the subject of appropriate steps for its confiscation and/or restitution by that other State Party. In any case, the Republic of Guatemala does not consider that the purchase of property forming part of its cultural wealth is in good faith solely through having been made in ignorance of the law. Concerning Article 3 of the Convention, the Republic of Guatemala shall also consider to be illicit the import and transfer of ownership of cultural property effected contrary to the national provisions in force that are not in conflict with the provisions of the Convention." (See letter LA/Depositary/1985/1)

Hungary

"Articles 12, 22 and 23 of the Convention contradict United Nations General Assembly Resolution 1514(XV) of 14 December 1960, which proclaimed the necessity of bringing to a speedy and unconditional end colonialism in all its forms and manifestations. Article 20 of the Convention is not in conformity with the principle of the sovereign equality of States; in view of the matters it regulates, the

Convention should be open to all States without restriction." (See letter LA/Depositary/1978/17 of 12 December 1978)

Mexico

"The Government of the United Mexican States has studied the text of the comments and reservations on the convention on the means of prohibiting and preventing the illicit import, export and transfer of ownership of cultural property made by the United States of America on 20 June 1983. It has reached the conclusion that these comments and reservations are not compatible with the purposes and aims of the Convention, and that their application would have the regrettable result of permitting the import into the United States of America of cultural property and its re-export to other countries, with the possibility that the cultural heritage of Mexico might be affected." (See letter LA/Depositary/1985/40 of 3 March 1986)

New Zealand

"AND DECLARES that, consistent with the constitutional status of Tokelau and taking into account the commitment of the Government of New Zealand to the development of self-government for Tokelau through an act of self-determination under the Charter of the United Nations, this acceptance shall not extend to Tokelau unless and until a Declaration to this effect is lodged by the Government of New Zealand with the Depositary on the basis of appropriate consultation with that territory."

Republique of Moldova

"Until the full re-establishment of the territorial integrity of the Republic of Moldova, the provisions of the convention shall be applied only on the territory controlled effectively by the authorities of the Republic of Moldova."

Sweden

The property designated as "of importance for archaeology, prehistory, history, literature, art or science," in accordance with Article 1 of the Convention, are the following properties:

1. Archaeological objects – Swedish archaeological objects, regardless of material or value, dating from 1650 or before and not belonging to the State.

2. Pictures and paintings
   a. Swedish paintings more than 100 years old and worth more than SEK 50,000,
   b. portraits picturing a Swede or other persons who were active in Sweden, which are more than 100 years old and worth more than SEK 20,000,
   c. foreign paintings worth more than SEK 50,000.
3. Drawings
   a. Swedish drawings, water-colours, gouaches and pastels more than 100 years old and worth more than SEK 50,000,
   b. portraits picturing a Swede or other persons who were active in Sweden, in the form of water-colours, gouaches and pastels more than 100 years old and worth more than SEK 20,000,
   c. foreign drawings, water-colours, gouaches and pastels worth more than SEK 50,000.
4. Original engravings – Swedish woodcut and copperplate engraving, made before 1650, regardless of value.
5. Original sculptures
   a. Swedish original sculptures and copies produced by the same process as the original, regardless of material, which are more than 100 years old and worth more than SEK 50,000,
   b. foreign original sculptures and copies produced by the same process as the original, regardless of material, which are worth more than SEK 50,000.
6. Incunabula and manuscripts
   a. Swedish incunabula, regardless of value,
   b. Swedish manuscripts on parchment or paper produced before 1650, regardless of value,
   c. Swedish unprinted minutes, letters, diaries, manuscripts, music, accounts, hand-drawn maps and drawings, which are more than 50 years old and worth more than SEK 2,000,
   d. collections of foreign incunabula and Swedish unprinted material in category (b) and (c), which are older than 50 years and are worth more than SEK 50,000.
7. Books
   a. Swedish books printed before 1600, regardless of value;
   b. other Swedish books, which are older than 100 years and are worth more than SEK 10,000;
   c. foreign books worth more than SEK 10,000.
8. Printed maps
   a. Swedish printed maps, which are older than 100 years and worth more than SEK 10,000;
   b. foreign printed maps, worth more than SEK 10,000.

9. Archives – Swedish unprinted minutes, letters, diaries, manuscripts, music, accounts, hand-drawn maps and drawings, which are more than 50 years and are worth more than SEK 2,000.
10. Means of transport
    a. Swedish means of transport which are older than 100 years and are worth more than SEK 50,000;
    b. foreign means of transport worth more than SEK 50,000.
11. Any other antique item not included in categories 1–10:
    a. Swedish items of wood, bone, pottery, metal or textile which are produced before 1650, regardless of value;
    b. Swedish furniture, mirrors and boxes which are made before 1860, regardless of value,
    c. Swedish drinking-vessels, harness and textile implements if they are made of wood and have painted or carved decorations, folk costumes and embroidered or pattern-woven traditional textiles, tapestry paintings, long-case clocks, wall clocks and brackets clocks, signed faience, firearms, edged weapons and defensive weapons and musical instruments, which are more than 100 years old, regardless of value;
    d. Swedish items of pottery, glass, porphyry, gold, silver or bronze, with exception of coins and medals, chandeliers, woven tapestries and tiled stoves, which are older than 100 years and worth more than SEK 50,000;
    e. Swedish technical models and prototypes and scientific instruments, which are older than 50 years and worth more than SEK 2,000;
    f. foreign furniture, mirrors, boxes, long-case clocks, wall clocks and brackets clocks, musical instruments, firearms, edged weapons and defensive weapons, items of pottery, glass, ivory, gold, silver or bronze, with exception of coins and medals, chandeliers and woven tapestries, which are worth more than SEK 50,000.
12. Lapp (Sami) items which are more than 50 years and worth more than SEK 2,000. The term Swedish items of historic interest refers to items which were actually or presumably made in Sweden or in some other country by a Swede. The term foreign items of historic interest refers to items made in another country by a non-Swede. This list is in conformity with rules in force in Sweden at present.

Ukrainian Soviet Socialist Republic [at time of ratification]

"The Ukrainian Soviet Socialist Republic declares that the provisions of Articles 12, 22 and 23 of the Convention on the Means of Prohibiting and Preventing the Illicit Import, Export and Transfer of Ownership of Cultural Property, providing for the possibility for the contracting parties to extend its application to the territories for the international relations of which they are responsible, are outdated and contrary to the Declaration of the United Nations General Assembly on the Granting of Independence to Colonial Countries and Peoples (Resolution 1514/XV of 14 December 1960)." (See letter LA/Depositary/1988/12 of 15 September 1988)

Union of Soviet Socialist Republics [at time of ratification]

"The Union of Soviet Socialist Republics declares that the provisions of Articles 12, 22 and 23 of the Convention on the Means of Prohibiting and Preventing the Illicit Import, Export and Transfer of Ownership of Cultural Property, providing for the possibility for the contracting parties to extend its application to the territories for the international relations of which they are responsible, are outdated and contrary to the Declaration of the United Nations General Assembly on the Granting of Independence to Colonial Countries and Peoples (resolution 1514/XV of 14 December 1960)." (See letter LA/Depositary/1988/13 of 15 September 1988)

United Kingdom of Great Britain and Northern Ireland (see letter LA/Depositary/2002/31)

a. The United Kingdom interprets the term "cultural property" as confined to those objects listed in the Annex to Council Regulation (EEC) N° 3911/1992 of 9 December 1992, as amended, on the export of cultural goods and in the Annex to Council Directive 1993/EEC of 15 March 1993, as amended, on the return of cultural objects unlawfully removed from the territory of a Member State;
b. As between EC member states, the United Kingdom shall apply the relevant EC legislation to the extent that that legislation covers matters to which the Convention applies; and
c. The United Kingdom interprets Article 7(b) (ii) to the effect that it may continue to apply its existing rules on limitation to claims made under this Article for the recovery and return of cultural objects.

United States of America [at the time of ratification]

"United States reserves the right to determine whether or not to impose export controls over cultural property."

The United States understands the provisions of the Convention to be neither self-executing nor retroactive.

The United States understands Article 3 not to modify property interests in cultural property under the laws of the States parties.

The United States understands Article 7(a) to apply to institutions whose acquisition policy is subject to national control under existing domestic legislation and not to require the enactment of new legislation to establish national control over other institutions.

The United States understands that Article 7(b) is without prejudice to other remedies, civil or penal, available under the laws of the States parties for the recovery of stolen cultural property to the rightful owner without payment of compensation.

The United States is further prepared to take the additional steps contemplated by Article 7(b) (ii) for the return of covered stolen cultural property without payment of compensation, except to the extent required by the Constitution of the United States, for those states parties that agree to do the same for the United States institutions.

The United States understands the words "as appropriate for each country" in Article 10(a) as permitting each state party to determine the extent of regulation, if any, of antique dealers and declares that in the United States that determination would be made by the appropriate authorities of state and municipal governments.

The United States understands Article 13(d) as applying to objects removed from the country of origin after the entry into force of this Convention for the states concerned, and, as stated by the Chairman of the Special Committee of Governmental Experts that prepared the text, and reported in paragraph 28 of the Report of that Committee, the means of recovery of cultural property under subparagraph(d) are the judicial actions referred to in subparagraph(c) of Article 13, and that such actions are controlled by the law of the requested State, the requesting State having to submit necessary proofs."

Territorial Application:

Notification by

Date of receipt of notification
Extension to>
Denmark
27 May 2004
Greenland (see letter LA/DEP/2004/014)
17 April 2008
Faroes
Norway
16 February 2007

Territory of the Kingdom of Norway and the Norwegian dependencies Bouvet Island, Peter I's Island and Queen Maud Land

Appendix XI

UNESCO Convention on the Protection of the Underwater Cultural Heritage

Paris, 2 November 2001

The General Conference of the United Nations Educational, Scientific and Cultural Organization, meeting in Paris from 15 October to 3 November 2001, at its 31st session,

Acknowledging the importance of underwater cultural heritage as an integral part of the cultural heritage of humanity and a particularly important element in the history of peoples, nations, and their relations with each other concerning their common heritage,

Realizing the importance of protecting and preserving the underwater cultural heritage and that responsibility therefor rests with all States,

Noting growing public interest in and public appreciation of underwater cultural heritage,

Convinced of the importance of research, information and education to the protection and preservation of underwater cultural heritage,

Convinced of the public's right to enjoy the educational and recreational benefits of responsible non-intrusive access to in situ underwater cultural heritage, and of the value of public education to contribute to awareness, appreciation and protection of that heritage,

Aware of the fact that underwater cultural heritage is threatened by unauthorized activities directed at it, and of the need for stronger measures to prevent such activities,

Conscious of the need to respond appropriately to the possible negative impact on underwater cultural heritage of legitimate activities that may incidentally affect it,

Deeply concerned by the increasing commercial exploitation of underwater cultural heritage, and in particular by certain activities aimed at the sale, acquisition or barter of underwater cultural heritage,

Aware of the availability of advanced technology that enhances discovery of and access to underwater cultural heritage,

Believing that cooperation among States, international organizations, scientific institutions, professional organizations, archaeologists, divers, other interested parties and the public at large is essential for the protection of underwater cultural heritage,

Considering that survey, excavation and protection of underwater cultural heritage necessitate the availability and application of special scientific methods and the use of suitable techniques and equipment as well as a high degree of professional specialization, all of which indicate a need for uniform governing criteria,

Realizing the need to codify and progressively develop rules relating to the protection and preservation of underwater cultural heritage in conformity with international law and practice, including the UNESCO Convention on the Means of Prohibiting and Preventing the Illicit Import, Export and Transfer of Ownership of Cultural Property of 14 November 1970, the UNESCO Convention for the Protection of the World Cultural and Natural Heritage of 16 November 1972 and the United Nations Convention on the Law of the Sea of 10 December 1982,

Committed to improving the effectiveness of measures at international, regional and national levels for the preservation in situ or, if necessary for scientific or protective purposes, the careful recovery of underwater cultural heritage,

Having decided at its 29th session that this question should be made the subject of an international convention,

Adopts this 2nd day of November 2001 this Convention.

Article 1: Definitions

For the purposes of this Convention:

1.

a. "Underwater cultural heritage" means all traces of human existence having a cultural, historical or archaeological character which have been partially or totally under water, periodically or continuously, for at least 100 years such as:

   i. sites, structures, buildings, artefacts and human remains, together with their archaeological and natural context;
   ii. vessels, aircraft, other vehicles or any part thereof, their cargo or other contents, together with their archaeological and natural context; and
   iii. objects of prehistoric character.

b. Pipelines and cables placed on the seabed shall not be considered as underwater cultural heritage.

c. Installations other than pipelines and cables, placed on the seabed and still in use, shall not be considered as underwater cultural heritage.

2.

   a. "States Parties" means States which have consented to be bound by this Convention and for which this Convention is in force.
   b. This Convention applies *mutatis mutandis* to those territories referred to in Article 26, paragraph b. which become Parties to this Convention in accordance with the conditions set out in that paragraph, and to that extent "States Parties" refers to those territories.

3. "UNESCO" means the United Nations Educational, Scientific and Cultural Organization.
4. "Director-General" means the Director-General of UNESCO.
5. "Area" means the seabed and ocean floor and subsoil thereof, beyond the limits of national jurisdiction.
6. "Activities directed at underwater cultural heritage" means activities having underwater cultural heritage as their primary object and which may, directly or indirectly, physically disturb or otherwise damage underwater cultural heritage.
7. "Activities incidentally affecting underwater cultural heritage" means activities which, despite not having underwater cultural heritage as their primary object or one of their objects, may physically disturb or otherwise damage underwater cultural heritage.
8. "State vessels and aircraft" means warships, and other vessels or aircraft that were owned or operated by a State and used, at the time of sinking, only for government non-commercial purposes, that are identified as such and that meet the definition of underwater cultural heritage.
9. "Rules" means the Rules concerning activities directed at underwater cultural heritage, as referred to in Article 33 of this Convention.

Article 2: Objectives and general principles

1. This Convention aims to ensure and strengthen the protection of underwater cultural heritage.
2. States Parties shall cooperate in the protection of underwater cultural heritage.
3. States Parties shall preserve underwater cultural heritage for the benefit of humanity in conformity with the provisions of this Convention.
4. States Parties shall, individually or jointly as appropriate, take all appropriate measures in conformity with this Convention and with international law that are necessary to protect underwater cultural heritage, using for this purpose the best practicable means at their disposal and in accordance with their capabilities.
5. The preservation in situ of underwater cultural heritage shall be considered as the first option before allowing or engaging in any activities directed at this heritage.
6. Recovered underwater cultural heritage shall be deposited, conserved and managed in a manner that ensures its long-term preservation.
7. Underwater cultural heritage shall not be commercially exploited.

8. Consistent with State practice and international law, including the United Nations Convention on the Law of the Sea, nothing in this Convention shall be interpreted as modifying the rules of international law and State practice pertaining to sovereign immunities, nor any State's rights with respect to its State vessels and aircraft.
9. States Parties shall ensure that proper respect is given to all human remains located in maritime waters.
10. Responsible non-intrusive access to observe or document in situ underwater cultural heritage shall be encouraged to create public awareness, appreciation, and protection of the heritage except where such access is incompatible with its protection and management.
11. No act or activity undertaken on the basis of this Convention shall constitute grounds for claiming, contending or disputing any claim to national sovereignty or jurisdiction.

Article 3: Relationship between this Convention and the United Nations Convention on the Law of the Sea

Nothing in this Convention shall prejudice the rights, jurisdiction and duties of States under international law, including the United Nations Convention on the Law of the Sea. This Convention shall be interpreted and applied in the context of and in a manner consistent with international law, including the United Nations Convention on the Law of the Sea.

Article 4: Relationship to law of salvage and law of finds

Any activity relating to underwater cultural heritage to which this Convention applies shall not be subject to the law of salvage or law of finds, unless it:

a. is authorized by the competent authorities, and
b. is in full conformity with this Convention, and
c. ensures that any recovery of the underwater cultural heritage achieves its maximum protection.

Article 5: Activities incidentally affecting underwater cultural heritage

Each State Party shall use the best practicable means at its disposal to prevent or mitigate any adverse effects that might arise from activities under its jurisdiction incidentally affecting underwater cultural heritage.

Article 6: Bilateral, regional or other multilateral agreements

1. States Parties are encouraged to enter into bilateral, regional or other multilateral agreements or develop existing agreements, for the preservation of underwater cultural heritage. All such agreements shall be in full conformity with the provisions of this Convention and shall not dilute its universal character. States may, in such agreements, adopt rules and regulations which would ensure better protection of underwater cultural heritage than those adopted in this Convention.
2. The Parties to such bilateral, regional or other multilateral agreements may invite States with a verifiable link, especially a cultural, historical or archaeological link, to the underwater cultural heritage concerned to join such agreements.
3. This Convention shall not alter the rights and obligations of States Parties regarding the protection of sunken vessels, arising from other bilateral, regional or other multilateral agreements concluded before its adoption, and, in particular, those that are in conformity with the purposes of this Convention.

Article 7: Underwater cultural heritage in internal waters, archipelagic waters and territorial sea

1. States Parties, in the exercise of their sovereignty, have the exclusive right to regulate and authorize activities directed at underwater cultural heritage in their internal waters, archipelagic waters and territorial sea.
2. Without prejudice to other international agreements and rules of international law regarding the protection of underwater cultural heritage, States Parties shall require that the Rules be applied to activities directed at underwater cultural heritage in their internal waters, archipelagic waters and territorial sea.
3. Within their archipelagic waters and territorial sea, in the exercise of their sovereignty and in recognition of general practice among States, States Parties, with a view to cooperating on the best methods of protecting State vessels and aircraft, should inform the flag State Party to this Convention and, if applicable, other States with a verifiable link, especially a cultural, historical or archaeological link, with respect to the discovery of such identifiable State vessels and aircraft.

Article 8: Underwater cultural heritage in the contiguous zone

Without prejudice to and in addition to Articles 9 and 10, and in accordance with Article 303, paragraph 2, of the United Nations Convention on the Law of the Sea, States Parties may regulate and authorize activities directed at underwater cultural heritage within their contiguous zone. In so doing, they shall require that the Rules be applied.

Article 9: Reporting and notification in the exclusive economic zone and on the continental shelf

1. All States Parties have a responsibility to protect underwater cultural heritage in the exclusive economic zone and on the continental shelf in conformity with this Convention. Accordingly:
   a. a State Party shall require that when its national, or a vessel flying its flag, discovers or intends to engage in activities directed at underwater cultural heritage located in its exclusive economic zone or on its continental shelf, the national or the master of the vessel shall report such discovery or activity to it;
   b. in the exclusive economic zone or on the continental shelf of another State Party:
      i. States Parties shall require the national or the master of the vessel to report such discovery or activity to them and to that other State Party;
      ii. alternatively, a State Party shall require the national or master of the vessel to report such discovery or activity to it and shall ensure the rapid and effective transmission of such reports to all other States Parties.
2. On depositing its instrument of ratification, acceptance, approval or accession, a State Party shall declare the manner in which reports will be transmitted under paragraph 1(b) of this Article.
3. A State Party shall notify the Director-General of discoveries or activities reported to it under paragraph 1 of this Article.
4. The Director-General shall promptly make available to all States Parties any information notified to him under paragraph 3 of this Article.
5. Any State Party may declare to the State Party in whose exclusive economic zone or on whose continental shelf the underwater cultural heritage is located its interest in being consulted on how to ensure the effective protection of that underwater cultural heritage. Such declaration shall be based on a verifiable link, especially a cultural, historical or archaeological link, to the underwater cultural heritage concerned.

Article 10: Protection of underwater cultural heritage in the exclusive economic zone and on the continental shelf

1. No authorization shall be granted for an activity directed at underwater cultural heritage located in the exclusive economic zone or on the continental shelf except in conformity with the provisions of this Article.
2. A State Party in whose exclusive economic zone or on whose continental shelf underwater cultural heritage is located has the right to prohibit or authorize any

activity directed at such heritage to prevent interference with its sovereign rights or jurisdiction as provided for by international law including the United Nations Convention on the Law of the Sea.

3. Where there is a discovery of underwater cultural heritage or it is intended that activity shall be directed at underwater cultural heritage in a State Party's exclusive economic zone or on its continental shelf, that State Party shall:

   a. consult all other States Parties which have declared an interest under Article 9, paragraph 5, on how best to protect the underwater cultural heritage;
   b. coordinate such consultations as "Coordinating State," unless it expressly declares that it does not wish to do so, in which case the States Parties which have declared an interest under Article 9, paragraph 5, shall appoint a Coordinating State.

4. Without prejudice to the duty of all States Parties to protect underwater cultural heritage by way of all practicable measures taken in accordance with international law to prevent immediate danger to the underwater cultural heritage, including looting, the Coordinating State may take all practicable measures, and/or issue any necessary authorizations in conformity with this Convention and, if necessary prior to consultations, to prevent any immediate danger to the underwater cultural heritage, whether arising from human activities or any other cause, including looting. In taking such measures assistance may be requested from other States Parties.
5. The Coordinating State:

   a. shall implement measures of protection which have been agreed by the consulting States, which include the Coordinating State, unless the consulting States, which include the Coordinating State, agree that another State Party shall implement those measures;
   b. shall issue all necessary authorizations for such agreed measures in conformity with the Rules, unless the consulting States, which include the Coordinating State, agree that another State Party shall issue those authorizations;
   c. may conduct any necessary preliminary research on the underwater cultural heritage and shall issue all necessary authorizations therefor, and shall promptly inform the Director-General of the results, who in turn will make such information promptly available to other States Parties.

6. In coordinating consultations, taking measures, conducting preliminary research and/or issuing authorizations pursuant to this Article, the Coordinating State shall act on behalf of the States Parties as a whole and not in its own interest. Any such action shall not in itself constitute a basis for the assertion of any preferential or jurisdictional rights not provided for in international law, including the United Nations Convention on the Law of the Sea.
7. Subject to the provisions of paragraphs 2 and 4 of this Article, no activity directed at State vessels and aircraft shall be conducted without the agreement of the flag State and the collaboration of the Coordinating State.

Article 11: Reporting and notification in the Area

1. States Parties have a responsibility to protect underwater cultural heritage in the Area in conformity with this Convention and Article 149 of the United Nations Convention on the Law of the Sea. Accordingly when a national, or a vessel flying the flag of a State Party, discovers or intends to engage in activities directed at underwater cultural heritage located in the Area, that State Party shall require its national, or the master of the vessel, to report such discovery or activity to it.
2. States Parties shall notify the Director-General and the Secretary-General of the International Seabed Authority of such discoveries or activities reported to them.
3. The Director-General shall promptly make available to all States Parties any such information supplied by States Parties.
4. Any State Party may declare to the Director-General its interest in being consulted on how to ensure the effective protection of that underwater cultural heritage. Such declaration shall be based on a verifiable link to the underwater cultural heritage concerned, particular regard being paid to the preferential rights of States of cultural, historical or archaeological origin.

Article 12: Protection of underwater cultural heritage in the Area

1. No authorization shall be granted for any activity directed at underwater cultural heritage located in the Area except in conformity with the provisions of this Article.
2. The Director-General shall invite all States Parties which have declared an interest under Article 11, paragraph 4, to consult on how best to protect the underwater cultural heritage, and to appoint a State Party to coordinate such consultations as the "Coordinating State." The Director-General shall also invite the International Seabed Authority to participate in such consultations.
3. All States Parties may take all practicable measures in conformity with this Convention, if necessary prior to consultations, to prevent any immediate danger to the underwater cultural heritage, whether arising from human activity or any other cause including looting.
4. The Coordinating State shall:
   a. implement measures of protection which have been agreed by the consulting States, which include the Coordinating State, unless the consulting States, which include the Coordinating State, agree that another State Party shall implement those measures; and
   b. issue all necessary authorizations for such agreed measures, in conformity with this Convention, unless the consulting States, which include the Coordinating State, agree that another State Party shall issue those authorizations.

5. The Coordinating State may conduct any necessary preliminary research on the underwater cultural heritage and shall issue all necessary authorizations therefore, and shall promptly inform the Director-General of the results, who in turn shall make such information available to other States Parties.
6. In coordinating consultations, taking measures, conducting preliminary research, and/or issuing authorizations pursuant to this Article, the Coordinating State shall act for the benefit of humanity as a whole, on behalf of all States Parties. Particular regard shall be paid to the preferential rights of States of cultural, historical or archaeological origin in respect of the underwater cultural heritage concerned.
7. No State Party shall undertake or authorize activities directed at State vessels and aircraft in the Area without the consent of the flag State.

Article 13: Sovereign immunity

Warships and other government ships or military aircraft with sovereign immunity, operated for non-commercial purposes, undertaking their normal mode of operations, and not engaged in activities directed at underwater cultural heritage, shall not be obliged to report discoveries of underwater cultural heritage under Articles 9, 10, 11 and 12 of this Convention. However, States Parties shall ensure, by the adoption of appropriate measures not impairing the operations or operational capabilities of their warships or other government ships or military aircraft with sovereign immunity operated for non-commercial purposes, that they comply, as far as is reasonable and practicable, with Articles 9, 10, 11 and 12 of this Convention.

Article 14: Control of entry into the territory, dealing and possession

States Parties shall take measures to prevent the entry into their territory, the dealing in, or the possession of, underwater cultural heritage illicitly exported and/or recovered, where recovery was contrary to this Convention.

Article 15: Non-use of areas under the jurisdiction of States Parties

States Parties shall take measures to prohibit the use of their territory, including their maritime ports, as well as artificial islands, installations and structures under their exclusive jurisdiction or control, in support of any activity directed at underwater cultural heritage which is not in conformity with this Convention.

Article 16: Measures relating to nationals and vessels

States Parties shall take all practicable measures to ensure that their nationals and vessels flying their flag do not engage in any activity directed at underwater cultural heritage in a manner not in conformity with this Convention.

Article 17: Sanctions

1. Each State Party shall impose sanctions for violations of measures it has taken to implement this Convention.
2. Sanctions applicable in respect of violations shall be adequate in severity to be effective in securing compliance with this Convention and to discourage violations wherever they occur and shall deprive offenders of the benefit deriving from their illegal activities.
3. States Parties shall cooperate to ensure enforcement of sanctions imposed under this Article.

Article 18: Seizure and disposition of underwater cultural heritage

1. Each State Party shall take measures providing for the seizure of underwater cultural heritage in its territory that has been recovered in a manner not in conformity with this Convention.
2. Each State Party shall record, protect and take all reasonable measures to stabilize underwater cultural heritage seized under this Convention.
3. Each State Party shall notify the Director-General and any other State with a verifiable link, especially a cultural, historical or archaeological link, to the underwater cultural heritage concerned of any seizure of underwater cultural heritage that it has made under this Convention.
4. A State Party which has seized underwater cultural heritage shall ensure that its disposition be for the public benefit, taking into account the need for conservation and research; the need for reassembly of a dispersed collection; the need for public access, exhibition and education; and the interests of any State with a verifiable link, especially a cultural, historical or archaeological link, in respect of the underwater cultural heritage concerned.

Article 19: Cooperation and information-sharing

1. States Parties shall cooperate and assist each other in the protection and management of underwater cultural heritage under this Convention, including, where practicable, collaborating in the investigation, excavation, documentation, conservation, study and presentation of such heritage.

2. To the extent compatible with the purposes of this Convention, each State Party undertakes to share information with other States Parties concerning underwater cultural heritage, including discovery of heritage, location of heritage, heritage excavated or recovered contrary to this Convention or otherwise in violation of international law, pertinent scientific methodology and technology, and legal developments relating to such heritage.
3. Information shared between States Parties, or between UNESCO and States Parties, regarding the discovery or location of underwater cultural heritage shall, to the extent compatible with their national legislation, be kept confidential and reserved to competent authorities of States Parties as long as the disclosure of such information might endanger or otherwise put at risk the preservation of such underwater cultural heritage.
4. Each State Party shall take all practicable measures to disseminate information, including where feasible through appropriate international databases, about underwater cultural heritage excavated or recovered contrary to this Convention or otherwise in violation of international law.

Article 20: Public awareness

Each State Party shall take all practicable measures to raise public awareness regarding the value and significance of underwater cultural heritage and the importance of protecting it under this Convention.

Article 21: Training in underwater archaeology

States Parties shall cooperate in the provision of training in underwater archaeology, in techniques for the conservation of underwater cultural heritage and, on agreed terms, in the transfer of technology relating to underwater cultural heritage.

Article 22: Competent authorities

1. In order to ensure the proper implementation of this Convention, States Parties shall establish competent authorities or reinforce the existing ones where appropriate, with the aim of providing for the establishment, maintenance and updating of an inventory of underwater cultural heritage, the effective protection, conservation, presentation and management of underwater cultural heritage, as well as research and education.
2. States Parties shall communicate to the Director-General the names and addresses of their competent authorities relating to underwater cultural heritage.

Article 23: Meetings of States Parties

1. The Director-General shall convene a Meeting of States Parties within 1 year of the entry into force of this Convention and thereafter at least once every 2 years. At the request of a majority of States Parties, the Director-General shall convene an Extraordinary Meeting of States Parties.
2. The Meeting of States Parties shall decide on its functions and responsibilities.
3. The Meeting of States Parties shall adopt its own Rules of Procedure.
4. The Meeting of States Parties may establish a Scientific and Technical Advisory Body composed of experts nominated by the States Parties with due regard to the principle of equitable geographical distribution and the desirability of a gender balance.
5. The Scientific and Technical Advisory Body shall appropriately assist the Meeting of States Parties in questions of a scientific or technical nature regarding the implementation of the Rules.

Article 24: Secretariat for this Convention

1. The Director-General shall be responsible for the functions of the Secretariat for this Convention.
2. The duties of the Secretariat shall include:

   a. organizing Meetings of States Parties as provided for in Article 23, paragraph 1; and
   b. assisting States Parties in implementing the decisions of the Meetings of States Parties.

Article 25: Peaceful settlement of disputes

1. Any dispute between two or more States Parties concerning the interpretation or application of this Convention shall be subject to negotiations in good faith or other peaceful means of settlement of their own choice.
2. If those negotiations do not settle the dispute within a reasonable period of time, it may be submitted to UNESCO for mediation, by agreement between the States Parties concerned.
3. If mediation is not undertaken or if there is no settlement by mediation, the provisions relating to the settlement of disputes set out in Part XV of the United Nations Convention on the Law of the Sea apply *mutatis mutandis* to any dispute between States Parties to this Convention concerning the interpretation or application of this Convention, whether or not they are also Parties to the United Nations Convention on the Law of the Sea.
4. Any procedure chosen by a State Party to this Convention and to the United Nations Convention on the Law of the Sea pursuant to Article 287 of the latter

shall apply to the settlement of disputes under this Article, unless that State Party, when ratifying, accepting, approving or acceding to this Convention, or at any time thereafter, chooses another procedure pursuant to Article 287 for the purpose of the settlement of disputes arising out of this Convention.

5. A State Party to this Convention which is not a Party to the United Nations Convention on the Law of the Sea, when ratifying, accepting, approving or acceding to this Convention or at any time thereafter shall be free to choose, by means of a written declaration, one or more of the means set out in Article 287, paragraph 1, of the United Nations Convention on the Law of the Sea for the purpose of settlement of disputes under this Article. Article 287 shall apply to such a declaration, as well as to any dispute to which such State is party, which is not covered by a declaration in force. For the purpose of conciliation and arbitration, in accordance with Annexes V and VII of the United Nations Convention on the Law of the Sea, such State shall be entitled to nominate conciliators and arbitrators to be included in the lists referred to in Annex V, Article 2, and Annex VII, Article 2, for the settlement of disputes arising out of this Convention.

Article 26: Ratification, acceptance, approval or accession

1. This Convention shall be subject to ratification, acceptance or approval by Member States of UNESCO.
2. This Convention shall be subject to accession:
    a. by States that are not members of UNESCO but are members of the United Nations or of a specialized agency within the United Nations system or of the International Atomic Energy Agency, as well as by States Parties to the Statute of the International Court of Justice and any other State invited to accede to this Convention by the General Conference of UNESCO;
    b. by territories which enjoy full internal self-government, recognized as such by the United Nations, but have not attained full independence in accordance with General Assembly resolution 1514 (XV) and which have competence over the matters governed by this Convention, including the competence to enter into treaties in respect of those matters.
3. The instruments of ratification, acceptance, approval or accession shall be deposited with the Director-General.

Article 27: Entry into force

This Convention shall enter into force 3 months after the date of the deposit of the 20th instrument referred to in Article 26, but solely with respect to the 20 States or territories that have so deposited their instruments. It shall enter into force for each other State or territory 3 months after the date on which that State or territory has deposited its instrument.

Article 28: Declaration as to inland waters

When ratifying, accepting, approving or acceding to this Convention or at any time thereafter, any State or territory may declare that the Rules shall apply to inland waters not of a maritime character.

Article 29: Limitations to geographical scope

At the time of ratifying, accepting, approving or acceding to this Convention, a State or territory may make a declaration to the depositary that this Convention shall not be applicable to specific parts of its territory, internal waters, archipelagic waters or territorial sea, and shall identify therein the reasons for such declaration. Such State shall, to the extent practicable and as quickly as possible, promote conditions under which this Convention will apply to the areas specified in its declaration, and to that end shall also withdraw its declaration in whole or in part as soon as that has been achieved.

Article 30: Reservations

With the exception of Article 29, no reservations may be made to this Convention.

Article 31: Amendments

1. A State Party may, by written communication addressed to the Director-General, propose amendments to this Convention. The Director-General shall circulate such communication to all States Parties. If, within 6 months from the date of the circulation of the communication, not less than one half of the States Parties reply favourably to the request, the Director-General shall present such proposal to the next Meeting of States Parties for discussion and possible adoption.
2. Amendments shall be adopted by a two-thirds majority of States Parties present and voting.
3. Once adopted, amendments to this Convention shall be subject to ratification, acceptance, approval or accession by the States Parties.
4. Amendments shall enter into force, but solely with respect to the States Parties that have ratified, accepted, approved or acceded to them, 3 months after the

deposit of the instruments referred to in paragraph 3 of this Article by two-thirds of the States Parties. Thereafter, for each State or territory that ratifies, accepts, approves or accedes to it, the amendment shall enter into force 3 months after the date of deposit by that Party of its instrument of ratification, acceptance, approval or accession.

5. A State or territory which becomes a Party to this Convention after the entry into force of amendments in conformity with paragraph 4 of this Article shall, failing an expression of different intention by that State or territory, be considered:

   a. as a Party to this Convention as so amended; and
   b. as a Party to the unamended Convention in relation to any State Party not bound by the amendment.

Article 32: Denunciation

1. A State Party may, by written notification addressed to the Director-General, denounce this Convention.
2. The denunciation shall take effect 12 months after the date of receipt of the notification, unless the notification specifies a later date.
3. The denunciation shall not in any way affect the duty of any State Party to fulfil any obligation embodied in this Convention to which it would be subject under international law independently of this Convention.

Article 33: The Rules

The Rules annexed to this Convention form an integral part of it and, unless expressly provided otherwise, a reference to this Convention includes a reference to the Rules.

Article 34: Registration with the United Nations

In conformity with Article 102 of the Charter of the United Nations, this Convention shall be registered with the Secretariat of the United Nations at the request of the Director-General.

Article 35: Authoritative texts

This Convention has been drawn up in Arabic, Chinese, English, French, Russian and Spanish, the six texts being equally authoritative.

Annex

Rules concerning activities directed at underwater cultural heritage

I. General principles

Rule 1. The protection of underwater cultural heritage through in situ preservation shall be considered as the first option. Accordingly, activities directed at underwater cultural heritage shall be authorized in a manner consistent with the protection of that heritage, and subject to that requirement may be authorized for the purpose of making a significant contribution to protection or knowledge or enhancement of underwater cultural heritage.

Rule 2. The commercial exploitation of underwater cultural heritage for trade or speculation or its irretrievable dispersal is fundamentally incompatible with the protection and proper management of underwater cultural heritage. Underwater cultural heritage shall not be traded, sold, bought or bartered as commercial goods. This Rule cannot be interpreted as preventing:

a. the provision of professional archaeological services or necessary services incidental thereto whose nature and purpose are in full conformity with this Convention and are subject to the authorization of the competent authorities;
b. the deposition of underwater cultural heritage, recovered in the course of a research project in conformity with this Convention, provided such deposition does not prejudice the scientific or cultural interest or integrity of the recovered material or result in its irretrievable dispersal; is in accordance with the provisions of Rules 33 and 34; and is subject to the authorization of the competent authorities.

Rule 3. Activities directed at underwater cultural heritage shall not adversely affect the underwater cultural heritage more than is necessary for the objectives of the project.

Rule 4. Activities directed at underwater cultural heritage must use non-destructive techniques and survey methods in preference to recovery of objects. If excavation or recovery is necessary for the purpose of scientific studies or for the ultimate protection of the underwater cultural heritage, the methods and techniques used must be as non-destructive as possible and contribute to the preservation of the remains.

Rule 5. Activities directed at underwater cultural heritage shall avoid the unnecessary disturbance of human remains or venerated sites.

Rule 6. Activities directed at underwater cultural heritage shall be strictly regulated to ensure proper recording of cultural, historical and archaeological information.

Rule 7. Public access to in situ underwater cultural heritage shall be promoted, except where such access is incompatible with protection and management.

Rule 8. International cooperation in the conduct of activities directed at underwater cultural heritage shall be encouraged in order to further the effective exchange or use of archaeologists and other relevant professionals.

II. Project design

Rule 9. Prior to any activity directed at underwater cultural heritage, a project design for the activity shall be developed and submitted to the competent authorities for authorization and appropriate peer review.

Rule 10. The project design shall include:

a. an evaluation of previous or preliminary studies;
b. the project statement and objectives;
c. the methodology to be used and the techniques to be employed;
d. the anticipated funding;
e. an expected timetable for completion of the project;
f. the composition of the team and the qualifications, responsibilities and experience of each team member;
g. plans for post-fieldwork analysis and other activities;
h. a conservation programme for artefacts and the site in close cooperation with the competent authorities;
i. a site management and maintenance policy for the whole duration of the project;
j. a documentation programme;
k. a safety policy;
l. an environmental policy;
m. arrangements for collaboration with museums and other institutions, in particular scientific institutions;
n. report preparation;
o. deposition of archives, including underwater cultural heritage removed; and
p. a programme for publication.

Rule 11. Activities directed at underwater cultural heritage shall be carried out in accordance with the project design approved by the competent authorities.

Rule 12. Where unexpected discoveries are made or circumstances change, the project design shall be reviewed and amended with the approval of the competent authorities.

Rule 13. In cases of urgency or chance discoveries, activities directed at the underwater cultural heritage, including conservation measures or activities for a period of short duration, in particular site stabilization, may be authorized in the absence of a project design in order to protect the underwater cultural heritage.

III. Preliminary work

Rule 14. The preliminary work referred to in Rule 10 (a) shall include an assessment that evaluates the significance and vulnerability of the underwater cultural heritage and the surrounding natural environment to damage by the proposed project, and the potential to obtain data that would meet the project objectives.

Rule 15. The assessment shall also include background studies of available historical and archaeological evidence, the archaeological and environmental characteristics of the site, and the consequences of any potential intrusion for the long-term stability of the underwater cultural heritage affected by the activities.

IV. Project objective, methodology and techniques

Rule 16. The methodology shall comply with the project objectives, and the techniques employed shall be as non-intrusive as possible.

V. Funding

Rule 17. Except in cases of emergency to protect underwater cultural heritage, an adequate funding base shall be assured in advance of any activity, sufficient to complete all stages of the project design, including conservation, documentation and curation of recovered artefacts, and report preparation and dissemination.

Rule 18. The project design shall demonstrate an ability, such as by securing a bond, to fund the project through to completion.

Rule 19. The project design shall include a contingency plan that will ensure conservation of underwater cultural heritage and supporting documentation in the event of any interruption of anticipated funding.

VI. Project duration: timetable

Rule 20. An adequate timetable shall be developed to assure in advance of any activity directed at underwater cultural heritage the completion of all stages of the project design, including conservation, documentation and curation of recovered underwater cultural heritage, as well as report preparation and dissemination.

Rule 21. The project design shall include a contingency plan that will ensure conservation of underwater cultural heritage and supporting documentation in the event of any interruption or termination of the project.

VII. Competence and qualifications

Rule 22. Activities directed at underwater cultural heritage shall only be undertaken under the direction and control of, and in the regular presence of, a qualified underwater archaeologist with scientific competence appropriate to the project.

Rule 23. All persons on the project team shall be qualified and have demonstrated competence appropriate to their roles in the project.

VIII. Conservation and site management

Rule 24. The conservation programme shall provide for the treatment of the archaeological remains during the activities directed at underwater cultural heritage, during transit and in the long term. Conservation shall be carried out in accordance with current professional standards.

Rule 25. The site management programme shall provide for the protection and management in situ of underwater cultural heritage, in the course of and upon termination of fieldwork. The programme shall include public information, reasonable provision for site stabilization, monitoring, and protection against interference.

IX. Documentation

Rule 26. The documentation programme shall set out thorough documentation including a progress report of activities directed at underwater cultural heritage, in accordance with current professional standards of archaeological documentation.

Rule 27. Documentation shall include, at a minimum, a comprehensive record of the site, including the provenance of underwater cultural heritage moved or removed in the course of the activities directed at underwater cultural heritage, field notes, plans, drawings, sections, and photographs or recording in other media.

X. Safety

Rule 28. A safety policy shall be prepared that is adequate to ensure the safety and health of the project team and third parties and that is in conformity with any applicable statutory and professional requirements.

XI. Environment

Rule 29. An environmental policy shall be prepared that is adequate to ensure that the seabed and marine life are not unduly disturbed.

XII. Reporting

Rule 30. Interim and final reports shall be made available according to the timetable set out in the project design, and deposited in relevant public records.

Rule 31. Reports shall include:

a. an account of the objectives;
b. an account of the methods and techniques employed;
c. an account of the results achieved;
d. basic graphic and photographic documentation on all phases of the activity;
e. recommendations concerning conservation and curation of the site and of any underwater cultural heritage removed; and
f. recommendations for future activities.

XIII. Curation of project archives

Rule 32. Arrangements for curation of the project archives shall be agreed to before any activity commences, and shall be set out in the project design.

Rule 33. The project archives, including any underwater cultural heritage removed and a copy of all supporting documentation shall, as far as possible, be kept together and intact as a collection in a manner that is available for professional and public access as well as for the curation of the archives. This should be done as rapidly as possible and in any case not later than 10 years from the completion of the project, in so far as may be compatible with conservation of the underwater cultural heritage.

Rule 34. The project archives shall be managed according to international professional standards, and subject to the authorization of the competent authorities.

XIV. Dissemination

Rule 35. Projects shall provide for public education and popular presentation of the project results where appropriate.

Rule 36. A final synthesis of a project shall be:

a. made public as soon as possible, having regard to the complexity of the project and the confidential or sensitive nature of the information; and
b. deposited in relevant public records.

The foregoing is the authentic text of the Convention duly adopted by the General Conference of the United Nations Educational, Scientific and Cultural Organization during its 31st session, which was held in Paris and declared closed the 3rd day of November 2001.

Appendix XII

UNIDROIT Convention on Stolen or Illegally Exported Cultural Objects

Rome, 24 June 1995

The states parties to this convention,

Assembled in Rome at the invitation of the Government of the Italian Republic from 7 to 24 June 1995 for a Diplomatic Conference for the adoption of the draft Unidroit Convention on the International Return of Stolen or Illegally Exported Cultural Objects,

Convinced of the fundamental importance of the protection of cultural heritage and of cultural exchanges for promoting understanding between peoples, and the dissemination of culture for the well-being of humanity and the progress of civilisation,

Deeply concerned by the illicit trade in cultural objects and the irreparable damage frequently caused by it, both to these objects themselves and to the cultural heritage of national, tribal, indigenous or other communities, and also to the heritage of all peoples, and in particular by the pillage of archaeological sites and the resulting loss of irreplaceable archaeological, historical and scientific information,

Determined to contribute effectively to the fight against illicit trade in cultural objects by taking the important step of establishing common, minimal legal rules for the restitution and return of cultural objects between Contracting States, with the objective of improving the preservation and protection of the cultural heritage in the interest of all,

Emphasising that this Convention is intended to facilitate the restitution and return of cultural objects, and that the provision of any remedies, such as compensation, needed to effect restitution and return in some States, does not imply that such remedies should be adopted in other States,

Affirming that the adoption of the provisions of this Convention for the future in no way confers any approval or legitimacy upon illegal transactions of whatever kind which may have taken place before the entry into force of the Convention,

Conscious that this Convention will not by itself provide a solution to the problems raised by illicit trade, but that it initiates a process that will enhance international cultural co-operation and maintain a proper role for legal trading and inter-State agreements for cultural exchanges,

Acknowledging that implementation of this Convention should be accompanied by other effective measures for protecting cultural objects, such as the development and use of registers, the physical protection of archaeological sites and technical co-operation,

Recognising the work of various bodies to protect cultural property, particularly the 1970 UNESCO Convention on illicit traffic and the development of codes of conduct in the private sector,

Have agreed as follows:

Chapter 1: Scope of application and definition

Article 1

This Convention applies to claims of an international character for:

a. the restitution of stolen cultural objects;
b. the return of cultural objects removed from the territory of a Contracting State contrary to its law regulating the export of cultural objects for the purpose of protecting its cultural heritage (hereinafter "illegally exported cultural objects").

Article 2

For the purposes of this Convention, cultural objects are those which, on religious or secular grounds, are of importance for archaeology, prehistory, history, literature, art or science and belong to one of the categories listed in the Annex to this Convention.

Chapter 2: Restitution of stolen cultural objects

Article 3

1. The possessor of a cultural object which has been stolen shall return it.
2. For the purposes of this Convention, a cultural object which has been unlawfully excavated or lawfully excavated but unlawfully retained shall be considered stolen, when consistent with the law of the State where the excavation took place.

3. Any claim for restitution shall be brought within a period of 3 years from the time when the claimant knew the location of the cultural object and the identity of its possessor, and in any case within a period of 50 years from the time of the theft.
4. However, a claim for restitution of a cultural object forming an integral part of an identified monument or archaeological site, or belonging to a public collection, shall not be subject to time limitations other than a period of 3 years from the time when the claimant knew the location of the cultural object and the identity of its possessor.
5. Notwithstanding the provisions of the preceding paragraph, any Contracting State may declare that a claim is subject to a time limitation of 75 years or such longer period as is provided in its law. A claim made in another Contracting State for restitution of a cultural object displaced from a monument, archaeological site or public collection in a Contracting State making such a declaration shall also be subject to that time limitation.
6. A declaration referred to in the preceding paragraph shall be made at the time of signature, ratification, acceptance, approval or accession.
7. For the purposes of this Convention, a "public collection," consists of a group of inventoried or otherwise identified cultural objects owned by:

   a. a Contracting State
   b. a regional or local authority of a Contracting State;
   c. a religious institution in a Contracting State; or
   d. an institution that is established for an essentially cultural, educational or scientific purpose in a Contracting State and is recognised in that State as serving the public interest.

8. In addition, a claim for restitution of a sacred or communally important cultural object belonging to and used by a tribal or indigenous community in a Contracting State as part of that community's traditional or ritual use, shall be subject to the time limitation applicable to public collections.

Article 4

1. The possessor of a stolen cultural object required to return it shall be entitled, at the time of its restitution, to payment of fair and reasonable compensation provided that the possessor neither knew nor ought reasonably to have known that the object was stolen and can prove that it exercised due diligence when acquiring the object.
2. Without prejudice to the right of the possessor to compensation referred to in the preceding paragraph, reasonable efforts shall be made to have the person who transferred the cultural object to the possessor, or any prior transferor, pay the compensation where to do so would be consistent with the law of the State in which the claim is brought.

3. Payment of compensation to the possessor by the claimant, when this is required, shall be without prejudice to the right of the claimant to recover it from any other person.
4. In determining whether the possessor exercised due diligence, regard shall be had to all the circumstances of the acquisition, including the character of the parties, the price paid, whether the possessor consulted any reasonably accessible register of stolen cultural objects, and any other relevant information and documentation which it could reasonably have obtained, and whether the possessor consulted accessible agencies or took any other step that a reasonable person would have taken in the circumstances.
5. The possessor shall not be in a more favourable position than the person from whom it acquired the cultural object by inheritance or otherwise gratuitously.

Chapter 3: Return of illegally exported cultural objects

Article 5

1. A Contracting State may request the court or other competent authority of another Contracting State to order the return of a cultural object illegally exported from the territory of the requesting State.
2. A cultural object which has been temporarily exported from the territory of the requesting State, for purposes such as exhibition, research or restoration, under a permit issued according to its law regulating its export for the purpose of protecting its cultural heritage and not returned in accordance with the terms of that permit shall be deemed to have been illegally exported.
3. The court or other competent authority of the State addressed shall order the return of an illegally exported cultural object if the requesting State establishes that the removal of the object from its territory significantly impairs one or more of the following interests:

   a. the physical Preservation of the object or of its context;
   b. the integrity of a complex object;
   c. the preservation of information of, for example, a scientific or historical character;
   d. the traditional or ritual use of the object by a tribal or indigenous community, or establishers that the object is of significant cultural importance for the requesting State.

4. Any request made under paragraph 1 of this article shall contain or be accompanied by such information of a factual or legal nature as may assist the court or other competent authority of the State addressed in determining whether the requirements of paragraphs 1–3 have been met.

5. Any request for return shall be brought within a period of 3 years from the time when the requesting State knew the location of the cultural object and the identity of its possessor, and in any case within a period of 50 years from the date of the export or from the date on which the object should have been returned under a permit referred to in paragraph 2 of this article.

Article 6

1. The possessor of a cultural object who acquired the object after it was illegally exported shall be entitled, at the time of its return, to payment by the requesting State of fair and reason compensation, provided that the possessor neither knew nor ought reasonably to have known at the time of acquisition that the object had been illegally exported.
2. In determining whether the possessor knew or ought reasonably to have known that the cultural object had been illegally exported, regard shall be had to the circumstances of the acquisition, including the absence of an export certificate required under the law of the requesting State.
3. Instead of compensation, and in agreement with the requesting State, the possessor required to return the cultural object to that State may decide:

   a. to retain ownership of the object; or
   b. to transfer ownership against payment or gratuitously to a person of its choice residing in the requesting State who provides the necessary guarantees.

4. The cost of returning the cultural object in accordance with this article shall be borne by the requesting State, without prejudice to the right of that State to recover costs from any other person.
5. The possessor shall not be in a more favourable position than the person from whom it acquired the cultural object by inheritance or otherwise gratuitously.

Article 7

1. The provisions of this Chapter shall not apply where:

   a. the export of a cultural object is no longer illegal at the time at which the return is requested; or
   b. the object was exported during the lifetime of the person who created it or within a period of 50 years following the death of that person.

2. Notwithstanding the provisions of sub-paragraph (b) of the preceding paragraph, the provisions of this Chapter shall apply where a cultural object was made by a member or members of a tribal or indigenous community for traditional or ritual use by that community and the object will be returned to that community.

Chapter IV: General Provisions

Article 8

1. A claim under Chapter II and a request under Chapter III may be brought before the courts or other competent authorities of the Contracting State where the cultural object is located, in addition to the courts or other competent authorities otherwise having jurisdiction under the rules in force in Contracting States.
2. The parties may agree to submit the dispute to any court or other competent authority or to arbitration.
3. Resort may be had to the provisional, including protective, measures available under the law of the Contracting State where the object is located even when the claim for restitution or request for return of the object is brought before the courts or other competent authorities of another Contracting State.

Article 9

1. Nothing in this Convention shall prevent a Contracting State from applying any rules more favourable to the restitution or the return of stolen or illegally exported cultural objects than provided for by this Convention.
2. This article shall not be interpreted as creating an obligation to recognise or enforce a decision of a court or other competent authority of another Contracting State that departs from the provisions of this Convention.

Article 10

1. The provisions of Chapter II shall apply only in respect of a cultural object that is stolen after this Convention enters into force in respect of the State where the claim is brought, provided that:

   a. the object was stolen from the territory of a Contracting State after the entry into force of this Convention for that State; or
   b. the object is located in a Contracting State after the entry into force of the Convention for that State.

2. The provisions of Chapter III shall apply only in respect of a cultural object that is illegally exported after this Convention enters into force for the requesting State as well as the State where the request is brought.
3. This Convention does not in any way legitimise any illegal transaction of whatever which has taken place before the entry into force of this Convention or which is excluded under paragraphs (1) or (2) of this article, nor limit any right of a State or other person to make a claim under remedies available outside the framework of this Convention for the restitution or return of a cultural object stolen or illegally exported before the entry into force of this Convention.

Chapter V: Final Provisions

Article 11

1. This Convention is open for signature at the concluding meeting of the Diplomatic Conference for the adoption of the draft Unidroit Convention on the International Return of Stolen or Illegally Exported Cultural Objects and will remain open for signature by all States at Rome until June 1996.
2. This Convention is subject to ratification, acceptance or approval by States which have signed it.
3. This Convention is open for accession by all States which are not signatory States as from the date it is open for signature.
4. Ratification, acceptance, approval or accession is subject to the deposit of a formal instrument to that effect with the depositary.

Article 12

1. This Convention shall enter into force on the 1st day of the 6th month following the date of deposit of the fifth instrument of ratification, acceptance, approval or accession.
2. For each State that ratifies, accepts, approves or accedes to this Convention after the deposit of the fifth instrument of ratification, acceptance, approval or accession, this Convention shall enter into force in respect of that State on the 1st day of the 6th month following the date of deposit of its instrument of ratification, acceptance, approval or accession.

Article 13

1. This Convention does not affect any international instrument by which any Contracting State is legally bound and which contains provisions on matters governed by this Convention, unless a contrary declaration is made by the States bound by such instrument.
2. Any Contracting State may enter into agreements with one or more Contracting States, with a view to improving the application of this Convention in their mutual relations. The States which have concluded such an agreement shall transmit a copy to the depositary.
3. In their relations with each other, Contracting States which are Members of organisations of economic integration or regional bodies may declare that they will apply. The internal rules of these organisations or bodies and will not therefore apply as between these States the provisions of this Convention the scope of application of which coincides with that of those rules.

Article 14

1. If a Contracting State has two or more territorial units, whether or not possessing different systems of law applicable in relation to the matters dealt with in this Convention, it may, at the time of signature or of the deposit of its instrument of ratification, acceptance, approval or accession, declare that this Convention is to extend to all its territorial units or only to one or more of them, and may substitute for its declaration another declaration at any time.
2. These declarations are to be notified to the depositary and are to state expressly the territorial units to which the Convention extends.
3. If, by virtue of a declaration under this article, this Convention extends to one or more but not all of the territorial units of a Contracting State the reference to:

    a. the territory of a Contracting State in Article 1 shall be construed as referring to the territory of a territorial unit of that State;
    b. a court or other competent authority of the Contracting State or of the State addressed shall be construed as referring to the court or other competent authority of a territorial unit of that State;
    c. the Contracting State where the cultural object is located in Article 8 (1) shall b construed as referring to the territorial unit of that State where the object is located;
    d. the law of the Contracting State where the object is located in Article 8 (3) shall be construed as referring to the law of the territorial unit of that State where the object is located; and
    e. a Contracting State in Article 9 shall be construed as referring to a territorial unit of that State.

4. If a Contracting State makes no declaration under paragraph 1 of this article, this Convention is to extend to all territorial units of that State.

Article 15

1. Declarations made under this Convention at the time of signature are subject to confirmation upon ratification, acceptance or approval.
2. Declarations and confirmations of declarations are to be in writing and to be formally notified to the depositary.
3. A declaration shall take effect simultaneously with the entry into force of this Convention in respect of the State concerned. However, a declaration of which the depositary receives formal notification after such entry into force shall take effect on the 1st day of the 6th month following the date of its deposit with the depositary.
4. Any State which makes a declaration. Under this Convention may withdraw it at any time by a formal notification in writing addressed to the depositary. Such withdrawal shall take effect on the 1st day of the 6th month following the date of the deposit of the notification.

Article 16

1. Each Contracting State shall at the time of signature, ratification, acceptance, approval or accession, declare that claims for the restitution, or requests for the return, of cultural objects brought by a State under Article 8 may be submitted to it under one or more of the following procedures:

   a. directly to the courts or other competent authorities of the declaring State;
   b. through an authority or authorities designated by that State to receive such claims or requests and to forward them to the courts or other competent authorities of that State;
   c. through diplomatic or consular channels.

2. Each Contracting State may also designate the courts or other authorities competent to order the restitution or return of cultural objects under the provisions of Chapters II and III.
3. Declarations made under paragraphs 1 and 2 of this article may be modified at any time by a new declaration.
4. The provisions of paragraphs 1–3 of this article do not affect bilateral or multilateral agreements on judicial assistance in respect of civil and commercial matters that may exist between Contracting States.

Article 17

Each Contracting State shall, no later than 6 months following the date of deposit of its instrument of ratification, acceptance, approval or accession, provide the depositary with written information in one of the official languages of the Convention concerning the legislation regulating the export of its cultural objects. This information shall be updated from time to time as appropriate.

Article 18

No reservations are permitted except those expressly authorised in this Convention.

Article 19

1. This Convention may be denounced by any State Party, at any time after the date on which it enters into force for that State, by the deposit of an instrument to that effect with the depositary.

2. A denunciation shall take effect on the 1st day of the 6th month following the deposit of the instrument of denunciation with the depositary. Where a longer period for the denunciation to take effect is specified in the instrument of denunciation it shall take effect upon the expiration of such longer period after its deposit with the depositary.
3. Notwithstanding such a denunciation, this Convention shall nevertheless apply to a claim for restitution or a request for return of a cultural object submitted prior to the date on which the denunciation takes effect.

Article 20

The President of the International Institute for the Unification of Private Law (Unidroit) may at regular intervals, or at any time at the request of five Contracting States, convene a special committee in order to review the practical operation of this Convention.

Article 21

1. This Convention shall be deposited with the Government of the Italian Republic.
2. The Government of the Italian Republic shall:

   a. inform all States which have signed or acceded to this Convention and the President of the International Institute for the Unification of Private Law (Unidroit) of:

      i. each new signature or deposit of an instrument of ratification, acceptance approval or accession, together with the date thereof;
      ii. each declaration made in accordance with this Convention;
      iii. the withdrawal of any declaration;
      iv. the date of entry into force of this Convention;
      v. the agreements referred to in Article 13;
      vi. the deposit of an instrument of denunciation of this Convention together with the date of its deposit and the date on which it takes effect;

   b. transmit certified true copies of this Convention to all signatory States, to all States acceding to the Convention and to the President of the International Institute for Unification of Private Law (Unidroit);
   c. perform such other functions customary for depositaries.

In witness whereof the undersigned plenipotentiaries, being duly authorised, have signed this Convention.

Done at Rome, this 24th day of June, 1995, in a single original, in the English and French languages, both texts being equally authentic.

Annex

a. Rare collections and specimens of fauna, flora, minerals and anatomy, and objects of palaeontological interest;
b. property relating to history, including the history of science and technology and military and social history, to the life of national leaders, thinkers, scientists and artists and to events of national importance;
c. products of archaeological excavations (including regular and clandestine) or of archaeological discoveries;
d. elements of artistic or historical monuments or archaeological sites which have been dismembered;
e. antiquities more than 100 years old, such as inscriptions, coins and engraved seals;
f. objects of ethnological interest;
g. property of artistic interest, such as:
    i. pictures, paintings and drawings produced entirely by hand on any support and in any material (excluding industrial designs and manufactured articles decorated by hand);
    ii. original works of statuary art and sculpture in any material;
    iii. original engravings, prints and lithographs;
    iv. original artistic assemblages and montages in any material;
h. rare manuscripts and incunabula, old books, documents and publications of special interest (historical, artistic, scientific, literary, etc.) singly or in collections;
i. postage, revenue and similar stamps, singly or in collections;
j. archives, including sound, photographic and cinematographic archives;
k. articles of furniture more than 100 years old and old musical instruments.

[http://www.unidroit.org|English language homepage|UNIDROIT Conventions – Main Page|UNIDROIT Conventions: signatures and ratifications|1995 UNIDROIT Convention on Stolen or Illegally Exported Cultural Objects – Main page]

Appendix XIII

European Convention on the Protection of the Archaeological Heritage

London, 6 June 1969

The member States of the Council of Europe, signatory hereto,

Considering that the aim of the Council of Europe is to achieve a greater unity between its members for the purpose, in particular, of safeguarding and realising the ideals and principles which are their common heritage;

Having regard to the European Cultural Convention, signed at Paris on 19 December 1954, and inter alia Article 5 of that Convention;

Affirming that the archaeological heritage is essential to a knowledge of the history of civilisations;

Recognising that while the moral responsibility for protecting the European archaeological heritage, the earliest source of European history, which is seriously threatened with destruction, rests in the first instance with the State directly concerned, it is also the concern of European States jointly;

Considering that the first step towards protecting this heritage should be to apply the most stringent scientific methods to archaeological research or discoveries, in order to preserve their full historical significance and render impossible the irremediable loss of scientific information that may result from illicit excavation;

Considering that the scientific protection thus guaranteed to archaeological objects:

a. would be in the interests, in particular, of public collections, and
b. would promote a much-needed reform of the market in archaeological finds;

Considering that it is necessary to forbid clandestine excavations and to set up a scientific control of archaeological objects as well as to seek through education to give to archaeological excavations their full scientific significance,

Have agreed as follows:

Article 1

For the purposes of this Convention, all remains and objects, or any other traces of human existence, which bear witness to epochs and civilisations for which excavations or discoveries are the main source or one of the main sources of scientific information, shall be considered as archaeological objects.

Article 2

With the object of ensuring the protection of deposits and sites where archaeological objects lie hidden, each Contracting Party undertakes to take such measures as may be possible in order:

a. to delimit and protect sites and areas of archaeological interest;
b. to create reserve zones for the preservation of material evidence to be excavated by later generations of archaeologists.

Article 3

To give full scientific significance to archaeological excavations in the sites, areas and zones designated in accordance with Article 2 of this Convention, each Contracting Party undertakes, as far as possible, to:

a. prohibit and restrain illicit excavations;
b. take the necessary measures to ensure that excavations are, by special authorisation, entrusted only to qualified persons;
c. ensure the control and conservation of the results obtained.

Article 4

1. Each Contracting Party undertakes for the purpose of the study and distribution of information on archaeological finds, to take all practicable measures necessary to ensure the most rapid and complete dissemination of information in scientific publications on excavation and discoveries.
2. Moreover, each Contracting Party shall also consider ways and means of:

   a. establishing a national inventory of publicly owned and, where possible, privately owned archaeological objects;
   b. preparing a scientific catalogue of publicly owned and, where possible, privately owned archaeological objects.

Article 5

With a view to the scientific, cultural and educational aims of this Convention, each Contracting Party undertakes to:

a. facilitate the circulation of archaeological objects for scientific, cultural and educational purposes;
b. encourage exchanges of information on:

   i. archaeological objects,
   ii. authorised and illicit excavations between scientific institutions, museums and the competent national departments;

c. do all in its power to assure that the competent authorities in the States of origin, Contracting Parties to this Convention, are informed of any offer suspected of coming either from illicit excavations or unlawfully from official excavations, together with the necessary details thereon;
d. endeavour by educational means to create and develop in public opinion a realisation of the value of archaeological finds for the knowledge of the history of civilisation, and the threat caused to this heritage by uncontrolled excavations.

Article 6

1. Each Contracting Party undertakes to cooperate in the most appropriate manner in order to ensure that the international circulation of archaeological objects shall in no way prejudice the protection of the cultural and scientific interest attaching to such objects.
2. Each Contracting Party undertakes specifically:

   a. as regards museums and other similar institutions whose acquisition policy is under State control, to take the necessary measures to avoid their acquiring archaeological objects suspected, for a specific reason, of having originated from clandestine excavations or of coming unlawfully from official excavations;
   b. as regards museums and other similar institutions, situated in the territory of a Contracting Party but enjoying freedom from State control in their acquisition policy:

      i. to transmit the text of this Convention, and
      ii. to spare no effort to obtain the support of the said museums and institutions for the principles set out in the preceding paragraph;

   c. to restrict, as far as possible, by education, information, vigilance and cooperation, the movement of archaeological objects suspected, for a specific reason, of having been obtained from illicit excavations or unlawfully from official excavations.

Article 7

In order to ensure the application of the principle of co-operation in the protection of the archaeological heritage which is the basis of this Convention, each Contracting Party undertakes, within the context of the obligations accepted under the terms of this Convention, to give consideration to any questions of identification and authentication raised by any other Contracting Party, and to co-operate actively to the extent permitted by its national legislation.

Article 8

The measures provided for in this Convention cannot restrict lawful trade in or ownership of archaeological objects, nor affect the legal rules governing the transfer of such objects.

Article 9

Each Contracting Party shall notify the Secretary General of the Council of Europe in due course of measures it may have taken in respect of the application of the provisions of this Convention.

Article 10

1. This Convention shall be open to signature by the member States of the Council of Europe. It shall be subject to ratification or acceptance. Instruments of ratification or acceptance shall be deposited with the Secretary General of the Council of Europe.
2. This Convention shall enter into force 3 months after the date of the deposit of the third instrument of ratification or acceptance.
3. In respect of a signatory State ratifying or accepting subsequently, the Convention shall come into force 3 months after the date of the deposit of its instrument of ratification or acceptance.

Article 11

1. After entry into force of this Convention:

   a. any non-member State of the Council of Europe which is a Contracting Party to the European Cultural Convention signed at Paris on 19 December 1954 may accede to this Convention;

b. the Committee of Ministers of the Council of Europe may invite any other non-member State to accede thereto.

2. Such accession shall be effected by depositing with the Secretary General of the Council of Europe an instrument of accession which shall take effect 3 months after the date of its deposit.

Article 12

1. Each signatory State, at the time of signature or when depositing its instrument of ratification or acceptance, or each acceding State, when depositing its instrument of accession, may specify the territory or territories to which this Convention shall apply.
2. Each signatory State, when depositing its instrument of ratification or acceptance or at any later date, or each acceding State, when depositing its instrument of accession or at any later date, by declaration addressed to the Secretary General of the Council of Europe, may extend this Convention to any other territory or territories specified in the declaration and for whose international relations it is responsible or on whose behalf it is authorised to give undertakings.
3. Any declaration made in pursuance of the preceding paragraph may, in respect of any territory mentioned in such declaration, be withdrawn according to the procedure laid down in Article 13 of this Convention.

Article 13

1. This Convention shall remain in force indefinitely.
2. Any Contracting Party may, in so far as it is concerned, denounce this Convention by means of a notification addressed to the Secretary General of the Council of Europe.
3. Such denunciation shall take effect 6 months after the date of receipt by the Secretary General of such notification.

Article 14

The Secretary General of the Council of Europe shall notify the member States of the Council and any State which has acceded to this Convention of:

a. any signature;
b. any deposit of an instrument of ratification, acceptance or accession;

c. any date of entry into force of this Convention in accordance with Article 10 thereof;
d. any declaration received in pursuance of the provisions of paragraphs 2 and 3 of Article 12;
e. any notification received in pursuance of the provisions of Article 13 and the date on which denunciation takes effect.

In witness whereof the undersigned, being duly authorised thereto, have signed this Convention.

Done at London, this 6th day of May 1969, in English and in French, both texts being equally authoritative, in a single copy which shall remain deposited in the archives of the Council of Europe. The Secretary General of the Council of Europe shall transmit certified copies to each of the signatory and acceding States.

Appendix XIV

European Convention on Offences Relating to Cultural Property

Delphi, 23 June 1985

The member States of the Council of Europe, signatory hereto,

Considering that the aim of the Council of Europe is to achieve a greater unity between its members;

Believing that such unity is founded to a considerable extent in the existence of a European cultural heritage;

Conscious of the social and economic value of that common heritage;

Desirous of putting an end to the offences that too often affect that heritage and urgently adopting international standards to this end;

Recognising their common responsibility and solidarity in the protection of the European cultural heritage;

Having regard to the European Conventions in the criminal and cultural fields,

Have agreed as follows:

Part I: Definitions

Article 1

For the purposes of this Convention:

a. "offence" comprises acts dealt with under the criminal law and those dealt with under the legal provisions listed in Appendix I to this Convention on condition that where an administrative authority is competent to deal with the offence it must be possible for the person concerned to have the case tried by a court;
b. "proceedings" means any procedure instituted in respect of an offence;

c. "judgment" means any final decision delivered by a criminal court or by an administrative body as a result of a procedure instituted in pursuance of one of the legal provisions listed in Appendix I;
d. "sanction" means any punishment or measure incurred or pronounced in respect of an offence.

Part II: Scope

Article 2

1. This Convention shall apply to the cultural property listed in Appendix II, paragraph 1.
2. Any Contracting State may, at any time, declare that for the purposes of this Convention it also considers any one or more of the categories of property listed in Appendix II, paragraph 2, as cultural property.
3. Any Contracting State may, at any time, declare that for the purposes of this Convention it also considers as cultural property any category of movable or immovable property, presenting an artistic, historical, archaeological, scientific or other cultural interest, that is not included in Appendix II.

Article 3

1. For the purposes of this Convention, the acts and omissions listed in Appendix III, paragraph 1, are offences relating to cultural property.
2. Any Contracting State may, at any time, declare that, for the purposes of this Convention, it also deems to be offences relating to cultural property the acts and omissions listed in any one or more sub-paragraphs of Appendix III, paragraph 2.
3. Any Contracting State may, at any time, declare that, for the purposes of this Convention, it also deems to be offences relating to cultural property any one or more acts and omissions that affect cultural property and are not listed in Appendix III.

Part III: Protection of cultural property

Article 4

Each Party shall take appropriate measures to enhance public awareness of the need to protect cultural property.

Article 5

The Parties shall take appropriate measures with a view to co-operating in the prevention of offences relating to cultural property and the discovery of cultural property removed subsequent to such offences.

Part IV: Restitution of cultural property

Article 6

The Parties undertake to co-operate with a view to the restitution of cultural property found on their territory, which has been removed from the territory of another Party subsequent to an offence relating to cultural property committed in the territory of a Party, notably in conformity with the provisions that follow.

Article 7

1. Any Party that is competent under Article 13 shall, if it thinks fit, notify as soon as possible the Party or Parties to whose territory cultural property has been removed, or is believed to have been removed, subsequent to an offence relating to cultural property.
2. Any Party from whose territory cultural property has been removed, or is believed to have been removed, subsequent to an offence relating to cultural property, shall notify as soon as possible the Party that is competent in accordance with Article 13, paragraph 1, sub-paragraph e.
3. If such cultural property is found on the territory of a Party which has been duly notified, that Party shall immediately inform the Party or Parties concerned.
4. If cultural property is found on the territory of a Party and if that Party has reasonable grounds to believe that the property in question has been removed from the territory of another Party subsequent to an offence relating to cultural property, it shall immediately inform the other Party or Parties presumed to be concerned.
5. The communications referred to in the preceding paragraphs shall contain all information concerning the identification of the property in question, the offence subsequent to which it was removed and the circumstances concerning the discovery.
6. The Parties shall ensure the fullest possible distribution of the notifications which they receive pursuant to the provisions of paragraph 1.

Article 8

1. Each Party shall execute in the manner provided for by its law any letters rogatory relating to proceedings addressed to it by the competent authorities of a Party that is competent in accordance with Article 13 for the purpose of procuring evidence or transmitting articles to be produced in evidence, records or documents.
2. Each Party shall execute in the manner provided for by its law any letters rogatory relating to proceedings addressed to it by the competent authorities of a Party that is competent in accordance with Article 13 for the purpose of seizure and restitution of cultural property which has been removed to the territory of the requested Party subsequent to an offence relating to cultural property. Restitution of the property in question is, however, subject to the conditions laid down in the law of the requested Party.
3. Each Party shall likewise execute any letters rogatory relating to the enforcement of judgments delivered by the competent authorities of the requesting Party in respect of an offence relating to cultural property for the purpose of seizure and restitution of cultural property found on the territory of the requested Party to the person designated by the judgment or that person's successors in title. To this end the Parties shall take such legislative measures as they may consider necessary and shall determine the conditions under which such letters rogatory are executed.
4. Where there is a request for extradition, the return of the cultural property mentioned in paragraphs 2 and 3 shall take place even if extradition, having been agreed to, cannot be carried out owing to the death or escape of the person claimed or to other reasons of fact.
5. The requested Party may not refuse to return the cultural property on the grounds that it has seized, confiscated or otherwise acquired rights to the property in question as the result of a fiscal or customs offence committed in respect of that property.

Article 9

1. Unless the Parties otherwise agree, letters rogatory shall be in the language of the requested Party, or in the official language of the Council of Europe that is indicated by the requested Party in a declaration addressed to the Secretary General of the Council of Europe, or where no such declaration has been made in either of the official languages of the Council of Europe.
2. They shall indicate:

   a. the authority making the request,
   b. the object of and the reason for the request,
   c. the identity of the person concerned,
   d. the detailed identification of the cultural property in question,
   e. a summary of the facts as well as the offence they constitute and shall be accompanied by an authenticated or certified copy of the judgment whose enforcement is requested, in the cases covered by Article 8, paragraph 3.

Article 10

Evidence or documents transmitted pursuant to this Convention shall not require any form of authentication.

Article 11

Execution of requests under this Convention shall not entail refunding of expenses except those incurred by the attendance of experts and the return of cultural property.

Part V: Proceedings

Section I: Sanctioning

Article 12

The Parties acknowledge the gravity of any act or omission that affects cultural property; they shall accordingly take the necessary measures for adequate sanctioning.

Section II: Jurisdiction

Article 13

1. Each Party shall take the necessary measures in order to establish its competence to prosecute any offence relating to cultural property:
   a. committed on its territory, including its internal and territorial waters, or in its airspace;
   b. committed on board a ship or an aircraft registered in it;
   c. committed outside its territory by one of its nationals;
   d. committed outside its territory by a person having his/her habitual residence on its territory;
   e. committed outside its territory when the cultural property against which that offence was directed belongs to the said Party or one of its nationals;
   f. committed outside its territory when it was directed against cultural property originally found within its territory.
2. In the cases referred to in paragraph 1, sub-paragraphs d and f, a Party shall not be competent to institute proceedings in respect of an offence relating to cultural property committed outside its territory unless the suspected person is on its territory.

Section III: Plurality of proceedings

Article 14

1. Any Party which, before the institution or in the course of proceedings for an offence relating to cultural property, is aware of proceedings pending in another Party against the same person in respect of the same offence shall consider whether it can either waive or suspend its own proceedings.
2. If such Party considers it opportune in the circumstances not to waive or suspend its own proceedings it shall so notify the other Party in good time and in any event before judgment is given on the substance of the case.

Article 15

1. In the eventuality referred to in Article 14, paragraph 2, the Parties concerned shall through consultation endeavour as far as possible to determine, after evaluation of the circumstances of each case notably with a view to facilitating the restitution of the cultural property, which of them alone shall continue to conduct proceedings. During this consultation the Parties concerned shall stay judgment on the substance without, however, being obliged to extend that stay beyond a period of 30 days as from the despatch of the notification provided for in Article 14, paragraph 2.
2. The provisions of paragraph 1 shall not be binding:
   a. on a Party which despatches the notification provided for in Article 14, paragraph 2, if the main trial has been declared open there in the presence of the accused before despatch of the notification;
   b. on a Party to which the notification is addressed, if the main trial has been declared open there in the presence of the accused before receipt of the notification.

Article 16

In the interests of arriving at the truth, the restitution of the cultural property and the application of an adequate sanction, the Parties concerned shall examine whether it is expedient that one of them alone shall conduct proceedings and, if so, endeavour to determine which one, when:

a. several offences relating to cultural property which are materially distinct are ascribed either to a single person or to several persons having acted in unison;
b. a single offence relating to cultural property is ascribed to several persons having acted in unison.

Section IV: Ne bis in idem

Article 17

1. A person in respect of whom a final and enforceable judgment has been rendered may for the same act neither be prosecuted nor sentenced nor subjected to enforcement of a sanction in another Party:

   a. if he was acquitted;
   b. if the sanction imposed:

      i. has been completely enforced or is being enforced, or
      ii. has been wholly, or with respect to the part not enforced, the subject of a pardon or an amnesty, or
      iii. can no longer be enforced owing to the expiry of a limitation period;

   c. if the court found the offender guilty without imposing a sanction.

2. Nevertheless, a Party shall not, unless it has itself requested the proceedings, be obliged to recognise the *ne bis in idem* rule if the act which gave rise to judgment as directed against either a person or an institution or any thing having public status in that Party, or if the subject of the judgment had itself a public status in that Party.
3. Furthermore, a Party in whose territory the act was committed or considered to have been committed under the law of that Party shall not be obliged to recognise the *ne bis in idem* rule unless that Party has itself requested the proceedings.

Article 18

If new proceedings are instituted against a person who has been sentenced in another Party for the same act, then any period of deprivation of liberty imposed in the execution of that sentence shall be deducted from any sanction which may be imposed.

Article 19

This section shall not prevent the application of wider domestic provisions relating to the *ne bis in idem* rule attached to judicial decisions.

Part VI: Final clauses

Article 20

This Convention shall be open for signature by the member States of the Council of Europe. It is subject to ratification, acceptance or approval. Instruments of ratification, acceptance or approval shall be deposited with the Secretary General of the Council of Europe.

Article 21

1. This Convention shall enter into force on the first day of the month following the expiration of a period of 1 month after the date on which three member States of the Council of Europe have expressed their consent to be bound by the Convention in accordance with the provisions of Article 20.
2. In respect of any member State which subsequently expresses its consent to be bound by it the Convention shall enter into force on the first day of the month following the expiration of a period of 1 month after the date of deposit of the instrument of ratification, acceptance or approval.

Article 22

1. After the entry into force of this Convention, the Committee of Ministers of the Council of Europe may invite any State not a member of the Council to accede to this Convention, by a decision taken by the majority provided for in Article 20.d of the Statute of the Council of Europe and by the unanimous vote of the representatives of the Contracting States entitled to sit on the Committee.
2. In respect of any acceding State, the Convention shall enter into force on the first day of the month following the expiration of a period of 1 month after the date of deposit of the instrument of accession with the Secretary General of the Council of Europe.

Article 23

No Party is bound to apply this Convention to the offences relating to cultural property committed before the date of entry into force of the Convention in respect of that Party.

Article 24

1. Any State may at the time of signature or when depositing its instrument of ratification, acceptance, approval or accession, specify the territory or territories to which this Convention shall apply.
2. Any State may at any later date, by a declaration addressed to the Secretary General of the Council of Europe, extend the application of this Convention to

any other territory specified in the declaration. In respect of such territory the Convention shall enter into force on the first day of the month following the expiration of a period of 1 month after the date of receipt of such declaration by the Secretary General.

3. Any declaration made under the two preceding paragraphs may, in respect of any territory specified in such declaration, be withdrawn by a notification addressed to the Secretary General. The withdrawal shall become effective on the first day of the month following the expiration of a period of 6 months after the date of receipt of such notification by the Secretary General.

Article 25

The following provisions shall apply to those States Parties to this Convention which have a federal or non-unitary constitutional system:

a. with regard to the provisions of this Convention, the implementation of which comes under the legal jurisdiction of the federal or central legislative power, the obligations of the federal or central government shall be the same as for those States Parties which are not federal or non-unitary States;
b. with regard to the provisions of this Convention, the implementation of which comes under the legal jurisdiction of individual constituent States, countries, provinces or cantons that are not obliged by the constitutional system of the federation to take legislative measures, the federal government shall inform the competent authorities of such States, countries, provinces or cantons of the said provisions with its favourable opinion.

Article 26

In no case may a Party claim application of this Convention by another Party save in so far as it would itself apply this Convention in similar cases.

Article 27

Any Party may decide not to apply the provisions of Articles 7 and 8 either where the request is in respect of offences that it regards as political or where it considers that the application is likely to prejudice its sovereignty, security or "*ordre public.*"

Article 28

1. Any State may, at the time of signature or when depositing its instrument of ratification, acceptance, approval or accession, declare that it avails itself of the right not to apply any one or more provisions of Articles 8, paragraph 3, 10, 13 and 18. No other reservation may be made.
2. Any State which has made a reservation shall withdraw it as soon as circumstances permit. Such withdrawal shall be made by notification to the Secretary General of the Council of Europe.

Article 29

1. Any Contracting State may, at any time, by declaration addressed to the Secretary General of the Council of Europe, set out the legal provisions to be included in Appendix I to this Convention.
2. Any change of the national provisions listed in Appendix I shall be notified to the Secretary General of the Council of Europe if such a change renders the information in this appendix incorrect.
3. Any changes made in Appendix I in application of the preceding paragraphs shall take effect in each Party on the first day of the month following the expiration of a period of 1 month after the date of their notification by the Secretary General of the Council of Europe.

Article 30

The declarations provided for in Articles 2 and 3 shall be addressed to the Secretary General of the Council of Europe. They shall become effective in respect of each Party on the first day of the month following the expiration of a period of 1 month after the date of their notification by the Secretary General of the Council of Europe.

Article 31

The European Committee on Crime Problems of the Council of Europe shall follow the application of this Convention and shall do whatever is needed to facilitate a friendly settlement of any difficulty which may arise out of its execution.

Article 32

1. The European Committee on Crime Problems may formulate and submit to the Committee of Ministers of the Council of Europe proposals designed to alter the contents of Appendices II and III or their paragraphs.
2. Any proposal submitted in accordance with the provisions of the preceding paragraph shall be examined by the Committee of Ministers which, by a decision taken by the majority provided for in Article 20.d of the Statute of the Council of Europe and by the unanimous vote of the representatives of the Contracting States entitled to sit on the Committee, may approve it and instruct the Secretary General of the Council of Europe to notify the Contracting States thereof.
3. Any alteration approved in accordance with the provisions of the preceding paragraph shall enter into force on the first day of the month following the expiration of a period of 6 months after the date of despatch of the notification provided for in that paragraph unless a Contracting State notifies an objection to the entry into force. In the event of such an objection being made, the alteration will only enter force if the objection is subsequently lifted.

Article 33

1. The notifications and information provided for in Article 7 shall be exchanged between the competent authorities of the Parties. However, they may be sent through the International Criminal Police Organisation – Interpol.
2. The requests provided for in this Convention and any communication made under the provisions of Part V, Section III, shall be addressed by the competent authority of a Party to the competent authority of another Party.
3. Any Contracting State may, by a declaration addressed to the Secretary General of the Council of Europe, designate which authorities will be its competent authorities within the meaning of this article. Where such declaration is not made the Ministry of Justice of the State in question will be deemed to be its competent authority.

Article 34

1. Nothing in this Convention shall prejudice the application of the provisions of any other international treaties or conventions in force between two or more Parties on the matters dealt with in this Convention provided that the said provisions are more compelling with respect to the duty to restitute cultural property affected by an offence.

2. The Parties may not conclude bilateral or multilateral agreements with one another on the matters dealt with in this Convention, except in order to supplement its provisions or facilitate the application of the principles embodied in it.
3. However, if two or more Parties have already established their relations in this matter on the basis of uniform legislation, or instituted a special system of their own, or should they in the future do so, they shall be entitled to regulate those relations accordingly, notwithstanding the terms of this Convention.
4. Parties ceasing to apply the terms of this Convention to their mutual relations in accordance with the provisions of the preceding paragraph shall notify the Secretary General of the Council of Europe to that effect.

Article 35

1. Any Party may at any time denounce this Convention by means of a notification addressed to the Secretary General of the Council of Europe.
2. Such denunciation shall become effective on the first day of the month following the expiration of a period of 6 months after the date of receipt of the notification by the Secretary General.

Article 36

The Secretary General of the Council of Europe shall notify the member States of the Council and any State which has acceded to this Convention of:

a. any signature;
b. the deposit of any instrument of ratification, acceptance, approval or accession;
c. any date of entry into force of this Convention in accordance with Articles 21 and 22;
d. any other act, notification or communication relating to this Convention.

In witness whereof the undersigned, being duly authorised thereto, have signed this Convention.

Done at Delphi, this 23rd day of June 1985, in English and French, both texts being equally authentic, in a single copy which shall be deposited in the archives of the Council of Europe. The Secretary General of the Council of Europe shall transmit certified copies to each member State of the Council of Europe.

Appendix I

List of legal provisions that provide for offences other than offences dealt with under criminal law

Appendix II

1.

a. products of archaeological exploration and excavations (including regular and clandestine) conducted on land and underwater;
b. elements of artistic or historical monuments or archaeological sites which have been dismembered;
c. pictures, paintings and drawings produced entirely by hand on any support and in any material which are of great importance from an artistic, historical, archaeological, scientific or otherwise cultural point of view;
d. original works of statuary art and sculpture in any material which are of great importance from an artistic, historical, archaeological, scientific or otherwise cultural point of view and items resulting from the dismemberment of such works;
e. original engravings, prints, lithographs and photographs which are of great importance from an artistic, historical, archaeological, scientific or otherwise cultural point of view;
f. tools, pottery, inscriptions, coins, seals, jewellery, weapons and funerary remains, including mummies, more than 100 years old;
g. articles of furniture, tapestries, carpets and dress more than 100 years old;
h. musical instruments more than 100 years old;
i. rare manuscripts and incunabula, singly or in collections.

2.

a. original artistic assemblages and montages in any material which are of great importance from an artistic, historical, archaeological, scientific or otherwise cultural point of view;
b. works of applied art in such materials as glass, ceramics, metal, wood, etc. which are of great importance from an artistic, historical, archaeological, scientific or otherwise cultural point of view;
c. old books, documents and publications of special interest (historical, artistic, scientific, literary, etc.) singly or in collections;
d. archives, including textual records, maps and other cartographic materials, photographs, cinematographic films, sound recordings and machine-readable records which are of great importance from an artistic, historical, archaeological, scientific or otherwise cultural point of view;

e. property relating to history, including the history of science and technology and military and social history;
f. property relating to life of national leaders, thinkers, scientists and artists;
g. property relating to events of national importance;
h. rare collections and specimens of fauna;
i. rare collections and specimens of flora;
j. rare collections and specimens of minerals;
k. rare collections and specimens of anatomy;
l. property of paleontological interest;
m. material of anthropological interest;
n. property of ethnological interest;
o. property of philatelic interest;
p. rare property of numismatic interest (medals and coins);
q. all remains and objects, or any other traces of human existence, which bear witness to epochs and civilisations for which excavations or discoveries are the main source or one of the main sources of scientific information;
r. monuments of architecture, art or history;
s. archaeological and historic or scientific sites of importance, structures or other features of important historic, scientific, artistic or architectural value, whether religious or secular, including groups of traditional structures, historic quarters in urban or rural built-up areas and the ethnological structures of previous cultures still existent in valid form.

Appendix III

1.

   a. Thefts of cultural property.
   b. Appropriating cultural property with violence or menace.
   c. Receiving of cultural property where the original offence is listed in this paragraph and regardless of the place where the latter was committed.

2.

   a. Acts which consist of illegally appropriating the cultural property of another person, whether such acts be classed by national law as misappropriation, fraud, breach of trust or otherwise.
   b. Handling cultural property obtained as the result of an offence against property other than theft.
   c. The acquisition in a grossly negligent manner of cultural property obtained as the result of theft or of an offence against property other than theft.
   d. Destruction or damaging of cultural property of another person.
   e. Any understanding followed by overt acts, between two or more persons, with a view to committing any of the offences referred to in paragraph 1 of this appendix.

f.

i. alienation of cultural property which is inalienable according to the law of a Party;
ii. acquisition of such property as referred to under i, if the person who acquires it acts knowing that the property is inalienable;
iii. alienation of cultural property in violation of the legal provisions of a Party which make alienation of such property conditional on prior authorisation by the competent authorities;
iv. acquisition of such property as referred to under iii, if the person who acquires it acts knowing that the property is alienated in violation of the legal provisions referred to under iii;
v. violation of the legal provisions of a Party according to which the person who alienates or acquires cultural property is held to notify the competent authorities of such alienation or acquisition.

g.

i. violation of the legal provisions of a Party according to which the person who fortuitously discovers archaeological property is held to declare such property to the competent authorities;
ii. concealment or alienation of such property as referred to under i;
iii. acquisition of such property as referred to under i, if the person who acquires it acts knowing that the property was obtained in violation of the legal provisions referred to under i;
iv. violation of the legal provisions of a Party according to which archaeological excavations may only be carried out with the authorisation of the competent authorities;
v. concealment or alienation of archaeological property discovered as a result of excavations carried out in violation of the legal provisions referred to under iv;
vi. acquisition of archaeological property discovered as a result of excavations carried out in violation of the legal provisions referred to under iv, if the person who acquires it acts knowing that the property was obtained as a result of such excavations;
vii. violation of the legal provisions of a Party, or of an excavation licence issued by the competent authorities, according to which the person who discovers archaeological property as a result of duly authorised excavations is held to declare such property to the competent authorities;
viii. concealment or alienation of such property as referred to under vii;
ix. acquisition of such property as referred to under vii, if the person who acquires it acts knowing that the property was obtained in violation of the legal provisions referred to under vii;
x. violation of the legal provisions of a Party according to which the use of metal detectors in archaeological contexts is either prohibited or subject to conditions.

h.

i. actual or attempted exportation of cultural property the exportation of which is prohibited by the law of a Party;
ii. exportation or attempted exportation, without authorisation of the competent authorities, of cultural property the exportation of which is made conditional on such an authorisation by the law of a Party.

i. Violation of the legal provisions of a Party:

i. which make modifications to a protected monument of architecture, a protected movable monument, a protected monumental ensemble or a protected site, conditional on prior authorisation by the competent authorities, or
ii. according to which the owner or the possessor of a protected monument of architecture, a protected movable monument, a protected monumental ensemble or a protected site, is held to preserve it in adequate condition or to give notice of defects which endanger its preservation.

j. Receiving of cultural property where the original offence is listed in this paragraph and regardless of the place where the latter was committed.

Appendix XV

European Convention on the Protection of the Archaeological Heritage (Revised)

Valletta, 16 January 1992

Preamble

The member States of the Council of Europe and the other States party to the European Cultural Convention signatory hereto,

Considering that the aim of the Council of Europe is to achieve a greater unity between its members for the purpose, in particular, of safeguarding and realising the ideals and principles which are their common heritage;

Having regard to the European Cultural Convention signed in Paris on 19 December 1954, in particular Articles 1 and 5 thereof;

Having regard to the Convention for the Protection of the Architectural Heritage of Europe signed in Granada on 3 October 1985;

Having regard to the European Convention on Offences relating to Cultural Property signed in Delphi on 23 June 1985;

Having regard to the recommendations of the Parliamentary Assembly relating to archaeology and in particular Recommendations 848 (1978), 921 (1981) and 1072 (1988);

Having regard to Recommendation No. R (89) 5 concerning the protection and enhancement of the archaeological heritage in the context of town and country planning operations;

Recalling that the archaeological heritage is essential to a knowledge of the history of mankind;

Acknowledging that the European archaeological heritage, which provides evidence of ancient history, is seriously threatened with deterioration because of the increasing number of major planning schemes, natural risks, clandestine or unscientific excavations and insufficient public awareness;

Affirming that it is important to institute, where they do not yet exist, appropriate administrative and scientific supervision procedures, and that the need to protect the archaeological heritage should be reflected in town and country planning and cultural development policies;

Stressing that responsibility for the protection of the archaeological heritage should rest not only with the State directly concerned but with all European countries, the aim being to reduce the risk of deterioration and promote conservation by encouraging exchanges of experts and the comparison of experiences;

Noting the necessity to complete the principles set forth in the European Convention for the Protection of the Archaeological Heritage signed in London on 6 May 1969, as a result of evolution of planning policies in European countries,

Have agreed as follows:

Definition of the archaeological heritage

Article 1

1. The aim of this (revised) Convention is to protect the archaeological heritage as a source of the European collective memory and as an instrument for historical and scientific study.
2. To this end shall be considered to be elements of the archaeological heritage all remains and objects and any other traces of mankind from past epochs:
   a. the preservation and study of which help to retrace the history of mankind and its relation with the natural environment;
   b. for which excavations or discoveries and other methods of research into mankind and the related environment are the main sources of information; and
   c. which are located in any area within the jurisdiction of the Parties.
3. The archaeological heritage shall include structures, constructions, groups of buildings, developed sites, moveable objects, monuments of other kinds as well as their context, whether situated on land or under water.

Identification of the heritage and measures for protection

Article 2

Each Party undertakes to institute, by means appropriate to the State in question, a legal system for the protection of the archaeological heritage, making provision for:

i. the maintenance of an inventory of its archaeological heritage and the designation of protected monuments and areas;

ii. the creation of archaeological reserves, even where there are no visible remains on the ground or under water, for the preservation of material evidence to be studied by later generations;
iii. the mandatory reporting to the competent authorities by a finder of the chance discovery of elements of the archaeological heritage and making them available for examination.

Article 3

To preserve the archaeological heritage and guarantee the scientific significance of archaeological research work, each Party undertakes:

i. to apply procedures for the authorisation and supervision of excavation and other archaeological activities in such a way as:
   a. to prevent any illicit excavation or removal of elements of the archaeological heritage;
   b. to ensure that archaeological excavations and prospecting are undertaken in a scientific manner and provided that:
      – non-destructive methods of investigation are applied wherever possible;
      – the elements of the archaeological heritage are not uncovered or left exposed during or after excavation without provision being made for their proper preservation, conservation and management;
ii. to ensure that excavations and other potentially destructive techniques are carried out only by qualified, specially authorised persons;
iii. to subject to specific prior authorisation, whenever foreseen by the domestic law of the State, the use of metal detectors and any other detection equipment or process for archaeological investigation.

Article 4

Each Party undertakes to implement measures for the physical protection of the archaeological heritage, making provision, as circumstances demand:

i. for the acquisition or protection by other appropriate means by the authorities of areas intended to constitute archaeological reserves;
ii. for the conservation and maintenance of the archaeological heritage, preferably in situ;
iii. for appropriate storage places for archaeological remains which have been removed from their original location.

Integrated conservation of the archaeological heritage

Article 5

Each Party undertakes:

i. to seek to reconcile and combine the respective requirements of archaeology and development plans by ensuring that archaeologists participate:

  a. in planning policies designed to ensure well-balanced strategies for the protection, conservation and enhancement of sites of archaeological interest;
  b. in the various stages of development schemes;

ii. to ensure that archaeologists, town and regional planners systematically consult one another in order to permit:

  a. the modification of development plans likely to have adverse effects on the archaeological heritage;
  b. the allocation of sufficient time and resources for an appropriate scientific study to be made of the site and for its findings to be published;

iii. to ensure that environmental impact assessments and the resulting decisions involve full consideration of archaeological sites and their settings;
iv. to make provision, when elements of the archaeological heritage have been found during development work, for their conservation in situ when feasible;
v. to ensure that the opening of archaeological sites to the public, especially any structural arrangements necessary for the reception of large numbers of visitors, does not adversely affect the archaeological and scientific character of such sites and their surroundings.

Financing of archaeological research and conservation

Article 6

Each Party undertakes:

i. to arrange for public financial support for archaeological research from national, regional and local authorities in accordance with their respective competence;
ii. to increase the material resources for rescue archaeology:

  a. by taking suitable measures to ensure that provision is made in major public or private development schemes for covering, from public sector or private sector resources, as appropriate, the total costs of any necessary related archaeological operations;

b. by making provision in the budget relating to these schemes in the same way as for the impact studies necessitated by environmental and regional planning precautions, for preliminary archaeological study and prospection, for a scientific summary record as well as for the full publication and recording of the findings.

Collection and dissemination of scientific information

Article 7

For the purpose of facilitating the study of, and dissemination of knowledge about, archaeological discoveries, each Party undertakes:

i. to make or bring up to date surveys, inventories and maps of archaeological sites in the areas within its jurisdiction;
ii. to take all practical measures to ensure the drafting, following archaeological operations, of a publishable scientific summary record before the necessary comprehensive publication of specialised studies.

Article 8

Each Party undertakes:

i. to facilitate the national and international exchange of elements of the archaeological heritage for professional scientific purposes while taking appropriate steps to ensure that such circulation in no way prejudices the cultural and scientific value of those elements;
ii. to promote the pooling of information on archaeological research and excavations in progress and to contribute to the organisation of international research programmes.

Promotion of public awareness

Article 9

Each Party undertakes:

i. to conduct educational actions with a view to rousing and developing an awareness in public opinion of the value of the archaeological heritage for understanding the past and of the threats to this heritage;
ii. to promote public access to important elements of its archaeological heritage, especially sites, and encourage the display to the public of suitable selections of archaeological objects.

Prevention of the illicit circulation of elements of the archaeological heritage

Article 10

Each Party undertakes:

i. to arrange for the relevant public authorities and for scientific institutions to pool information on any illicit excavations identified;
ii. to inform the competent authorities in the State of origin which is a Party to this Convention of any offer suspected of coming either from illicit excavations or unlawfully from official excavations, and to provide the necessary details thereof;
iii. to take such steps as are necessary to ensure that museums and similar institutions whose acquisition policy is under State control do not acquire elements of the archaeological heritage suspected of coming from uncontrolled finds or illicit excavations or unlawfully from official excavations;
iv. as regards museums and similar institutions located in the territory of a Party but the acquisition policy of which is not under State control:

    i. to convey to them the text of this (revised) Convention;
    ii. to spare no effort to ensure respect by the said museums and institutions for the principles set out in paragraph 3 above;

v. to restrict, as far as possible, by education, information, vigilance and co-operation, the transfer of elements of the archaeological heritage obtained from uncontrolled finds or illicit excavations or unlawfully from official excavations.

Article 11

Nothing in this (revised) Convention shall affect existing or future bilateral or multilateral treaties between Parties, concerning the illicit circulation of elements of the archaeological heritage or their restitution to the rightful owner.

Mutual technical and scientific assistance

Article 12

The Parties undertake:

i. to afford mutual technical and scientific assistance through the pooling of experience and exchanges of experts in matters concerning the archaeological heritage;

ii. to encourage, under the relevant national legislation or international agreements binding them, exchanges of specialists in the preservation of the archaeological heritage, including those responsible for further training.

Control of the application of the (revised) Convention

Article 13

For the purposes of this (revised) Convention, a committee of experts, set up by the Committee of Ministers of the Council of Europe pursuant to Article 17 of the Statute of the Council of Europe, shall monitor the application of the (revised) Convention and in particular:

i. report periodically to the Committee of Ministers of the Council of Europe on the situation of archaeological heritage protection policies in the States Parties to the (revised) Convention and on the implementation of the principles embodied in the (revised) Convention;
ii. propose measures to the Committee of Ministers of the Council of Europe for the implementation of the (revised) Convention's provisions, including multilateral activities, revision or amendment of the (revised) Convention and informing public opinion about the purpose of the (revised) Convention;
iii. make recommendations to the Committee of Ministers of the Council of Europe regarding invitations to States which are not members of the Council of Europe to accede to this (revised) Convention.

Final clauses

Article 14

1. This (revised) Convention shall be open for signature by the member States of the Council of Europe and the other States party to the European Cultural Convention. It is subject to ratification, acceptance or approval. Instruments of ratification, acceptance or approval shall be deposited with the Secretary General of the Council of Europe.
2. No State party to the European Convention on the Protection of the Archaeological Heritage, signed in London on 6 May 1969, may deposit its instrument of ratification, acceptance or approval unless it has already denounced the said Convention or denounces it simultaneously.
3. This (revised) Convention shall enter into force 6 months after the date on which four States, including at least three member States of the Council of Europe, have expressed their consent to be bound by the (revised) Convention in accordance with the provisions of the preceding paragraphs.

4. Whenever, in application of the preceding two paragraphs, the denunciation of the Convention of 6 May 1969 would not become effective simultaneously with the entry into force of this (revised) Convention, a Contracting State may, when depositing its instrument of ratification, acceptance or approval, declare that it will continue to apply the Convention of 6 May 1969 until the entry into force of this (revised) Convention.
5. In respect of any signatory State which subsequently expresses its consent to be bound by it, the (revised) Convention shall enter into force 6 months after the date of the deposit of the instrument of ratification, acceptance or approval.

Article 15

1. After the entry into force of this (revised) Convention, the Committee of Ministers of the Council of Europe may invite any other State not a member of the Council and the European Economic Community, to accede to this (revised) Convention by a decision taken by the majority provided for in Article 20.d of the Statute of the Council of Europe and by the unanimous vote of the representatives of the Contracting States entitled to sit on the Committee.
2. In respect of any acceding State or, should it accede, the European Economic Community, the (revised) Convention shall enter into force 6 months after the date of deposit of the instrument of accession with the Secretary General of the Council of Europe.

Article 16

1. Any State may, at the time of signature or when depositing its instrument of ratification, acceptance, approval or accession, specify the territory or territories to which this (revised) Convention shall apply.
2. Any State may at any later date, by a declaration addressed to the Secretary General of the Council of Europe, extend the application of this (revised) Convention to any other territory specified in the declaration. In respect of such territory the (revised) Convention shall enter into force 6 months after the date of receipt of such declaration by the Secretary General.
3. Any declaration made under the two preceding paragraphs may, in respect of any territory specified in such declaration, be withdrawn by a notification addressed to the Secretary General. The withdrawal shall become effective 6 months after the date of receipt of such notification by the Secretary General.

Article 17

1. Any Party may at any time denounce this (revised) Convention by means of a notification addressed to the Secretary General of the Council of Europe.

2. Such denunciation shall become effective 6 months following the date of receipt of such notification by the Secretary General.

Article 18

The Secretary General of the Council of Europe shall notify the member States of the Council of Europe, the other States party to the European Cultural Convention and any State or the European Economic Community which has acceded or has been invited to accede to this (revised) Convention of:

i. any signature;
ii. the deposit of any instrument of ratification, acceptance, approval or accession;
iii. any date of entry into force of this (revised) Convention in accordance with Articles 14, 15 and 16;
iv. any other act, notification or communication relating to this (revised) Convention.

In witness whereof the undersigned, being duly authorised thereto, have signed this revised Convention.

Done at Valletta, this 16th day of January 1992, in English and French, both texts being equally authentic, in a single copy which shall be deposited in the archives of the Council of Europe. The Secretary General of the Council of Europe shall transmit certified copies to each member State of the Council of Europe, to the other States party to the European Cultural Convention, and to any non-member State or the European Economic Community invited to accede to this (revised) Convention.

Appendix XVI

Council of Europe Framework Convention on the Value of Cultural Heritage for Society

Preamble

The member States of the Council of Europe, Signatories hereto,

Considering that one of the aims of the Council of Europe is to achieve greater unity between its members for the purpose of safeguarding and fostering the ideals and principles, founded upon respect for human rights, democracy and the rule of law, which are their common heritage;

Recognising the need to put people and human values at the centre of an enlarged and cross-disciplinary concept of cultural heritage;

Emphasising the value and potential of cultural heritage wisely used as a resource for sustainable development and quality of life in a constantly evolving society;

Recognising that every person has a right to engage with the cultural heritage of their choice, while respecting the rights and freedoms of others, as an aspect of the right to freely participate in cultural life enshrined in the United Nations Universal Declaration of Human Rights (1948) and guaranteed by the International Covenant on Economic, Social and Cultural Rights (1966);

Convinced of the need to involve everyone in society in the ongoing process of defining and managing cultural heritage;

Convinced of the soundness of the principle of heritage policies and educational initiatives which treat all cultural heritages equitably and so promote dialogue among cultures and religions;

Referring to the various instruments of the Council of Europe, in particular the European Cultural Convention (1954), the Convention for the Protection of the Architectural Heritage of Europe (1985), the European Convention on the Protection of the Archaeological Heritage (1992, revised) and the European Landscape Convention (2000);

Convinced of the importance of creating a pan-European framework for co-operation in the dynamic process of putting these principles into effect;

Have agreed as follows:

Section I: Aims, definitions and principles

Article 1: Aims of the Convention

The Parties to this Convention agree to:

a. recognise that rights relating to cultural heritage are inherent in the right to participate in cultural life, as defined in the Universal Declaration of Human Rights;
b. recognise individual and collective responsibility towards cultural heritage;
c. emphasise that the conservation of cultural heritage and its sustainable use have human development and quality of life as their goal;
d. take the necessary steps to apply the provisions of this Convention concerning:
   - the role of cultural heritage in the construction of a peaceful and democratic society, and in the processes of sustainable development and the promotion of cultural diversity;
   - greater synergy of competencies among all the public, institutional and private actors concerned.

Article 2: Definitions

For the purposes of this Convention,

a. cultural heritage is a group of resources inherited from the past which people identify, independently of ownership, as a reflection and expression of their constantly evolving values, beliefs, knowledge and traditions. It includes all aspects of the environment resulting from the interaction between people and places through time;
b. a heritage community consists of people who value specific aspects of cultural heritage which they wish, within the framework of public action, to sustain and transmit to future generations.

Article 3: The common heritage of Europe

The Parties agree to promote an understanding of the common heritage of Europe, which consists of:

a. all forms of cultural heritage in Europe which together constitute a shared source of remembrance, understanding, identity, cohesion and creativity, and

b. the ideals, principles and values, derived from the experience gained through progress and past conflicts, which foster the development of a peaceful and stable society, founded on respect for human rights, democracy and the rule of law.

Article 4: Rights and responsibilities relating to cultural heritage

The Parties recognise that:

a. everyone, alone or collectively, has the right to benefit from the cultural heritage and to contribute towards its enrichment;
b. everyone, alone or collectively, has the responsibility to respect the cultural heritage of others as much as their own heritage, and consequently the common heritage of Europe;
c. exercise of the right to cultural heritage may be subject only to those restrictions which are necessary in a democratic society for the protection of the public interest and the rights and freedoms of others.

Article 5: Cultural heritage law and policies

The Parties undertake to:

a. recognise the public interest associated with elements of the cultural heritage in accordance with their importance to society;
b. enhance the value of the cultural heritage through its identification, study, interpretation, protection, conservation and presentation;
c. ensure, in the specific context of each Party, that legislative provisions exist for exercising the right to cultural heritage as defined in Article 4;
d. foster an economic and social climate which supports participation in cultural heritage activities;
e. promote cultural heritage protection as a central factor in the mutually supporting objectives of sustainable development, cultural diversity and contemporary creativity;
f. recognise the value of cultural heritage situated on territories under their jurisdiction, regardless of its origin;
g. formulate integrated strategies to facilitate the implementation of the provisions of this Convention.

Article 6: Effects of the Convention

No provision of this Convention shall be interpreted so as to:

a. limit or undermine the human rights and fundamental freedoms which may be safeguarded by international instruments, in particular, the Universal Declaration of Human Rights and the Convention for the Protection of Human Rights and Fundamental Freedoms;

b. affect more favourable provisions concerning cultural heritage and environment contained in other national or international legal instruments;
c. create enforceable rights.

Section II: Contribution of cultural heritage to society and human development

Article 7: Cultural heritage and dialogue

The Parties undertake, through the public authorities and other competent bodies, to:

a. encourage reflection on the ethics and methods of presentation of the cultural heritage, as well as respect for diversity of interpretations;
b. establish processes for conciliation to deal equitably with situations where contradictory values are placed on the same cultural heritage by different communities;
c. develop knowledge of cultural heritage as a resource to facilitate peaceful coexistence by promoting trust and mutual understanding with a view to resolution and prevention of conflicts;
d. integrate these approaches into all aspects of lifelong education and training.

Article 8: Environment, heritage and quality of life

The Parties undertake to utilise all heritage aspects of the cultural environment to:

a. enrich the processes of economic, political, social and cultural development and land-use planning, resorting to cultural heritage impact assessments and adopting mitigation strategies where necessary;
b. promote an integrated approach to policies concerning cultural, biological, geological and landscape diversity to achieve a balance between these elements;
c. reinforce social cohesion by fostering a sense of shared responsibility towards the places in which people live;
d. promote the objective of quality in contemporary additions to the environment without endangering its cultural values.

Article 9: Sustainable use of the cultural heritage

To sustain the cultural heritage, the Parties undertake to:

a. promote respect for the integrity of the cultural heritage by ensuring that decisions about change include an understanding of the cultural values involved;
b. define and promote principles for sustainable management, and to encourage maintenance;
c. ensure that all general technical regulations take account of the specific conservation requirements of cultural heritage;

d. promote the use of materials, techniques and skills based on tradition, and explore their potential for contemporary applications;
e. promote high-quality work through systems of professional qualifications and accreditation for individuals, businesses and institutions.

Article 10: Cultural heritage and economic activity

In order to make full use of the potential of the cultural heritage as a factor in sustainable economic development, the Parties undertake to:

a. raise awareness and utilise the economic potential of the cultural heritage;
b. take into account the specific character and interests of the cultural heritage when devising economic policies; and
c. ensure that these policies respect the integrity of the cultural heritage without compromising its inherent values.

Section III: Shared responsibility for cultural heritage and public participation

Article 11: The organisation of public responsibilities for cultural heritage

In the management of the cultural heritage, the Parties undertake to:

a. promote an integrated and well-informed approach by public authorities in all sectors and at all levels;
b. develop the legal, financial and professional frameworks which make possible joint action by public authorities, experts, owners, investors, businesses, non-governmental organisations and civil society;
c. develop innovative ways for public authorities to co-operate with other actors;
d. respect and encourage voluntary initiatives which complement the roles of public authorities;
e. encourage non-governmental organisations concerned with heritage conservation to act in the public interest.

Article 12: Access to cultural heritage and democratic participation

The Parties undertake to:

a. encourage everyone to participate in:

  - the process of identification, study, interpretation, protection, conservation and presentation of the cultural heritage;
  - public reflection and debate on the opportunities and challenges which the cultural heritage represents;

b. take into consideration the value attached by each heritage community to the cultural heritage with which it identifies;
c. recognise the role of voluntary organisations both as partners in activities and as constructive critics of cultural heritage policies;
d. take steps to improve access to the heritage, especially among young people and the disadvantaged, in order to raise awareness about its value, the need to maintain and preserve it, and the benefits which may be derived from it.

Article 13: Cultural heritage and knowledge

The Parties undertake to:

a. facilitate the inclusion of the cultural heritage dimension at all levels of education, not necessarily as a subject of study in its own right, but as a fertile source for studies in other subjects;
b. strengthen the link between cultural heritage education and vocational training;
c. encourage interdisciplinary research on cultural heritage, heritage communities, the environment and their inter-relationship;
d. encourage continuous professional training and the exchange of knowledge and skills, both within and outside the educational system.

Article 14: Cultural heritage and the information society

The Parties undertake to develop the use of digital technology to enhance access to cultural heritage and the benefits which derive from it, by:

a. encouraging initiatives which promote the quality of contents and endeavour to secure diversity of languages and cultures in the information society;
b. supporting internationally compatible standards for the study, conservation, enhancement and security of cultural heritage, whilst combating illicit trafficking in cultural property;
c. seeking to resolve obstacles to access to information relating to cultural heritage, particularly for educational purposes, whilst protecting intellectual property rights;
d. recognising that the creation of digital contents related to the heritage should not prejudice the conservation of the existing heritage.

Section IV: Monitoring and co-operation

Article 15: Undertakings of the Parties

The Parties undertake to:

a. develop, through the Council of Europe, a monitoring function covering legislations, policies and practices concerning cultural heritage, consistent with the principles established by this Convention;

b. maintain, develop and contribute data to a shared information system, accessible to the public, which facilitates assessment of how each Party fulfils its commitments under this Convention.

Article 16: Monitoring mechanism

a. The Committee of Ministers, pursuant to Article 17 of the Statute of the Council of Europe, shall nominate an appropriate committee or specify an existing committee to monitor the application of the Convention, which will be authorised to make rules for the conduct of its business;
b. The nominated committee shall:

   - establish rules of procedure as necessary;
   - manage the shared information system referred to in Article 15, maintaining an overview of the means by which each commitment under this Convention is met;
   - at the request of one or more Parties, give an advisory opinion on any question relating to the interpretation of the Convention, taking into consideration all Council of Europe legal instruments;
   - on the initiative of one or more Parties, undertake an evaluation of any aspect of their implementation of the Convention;
   - foster the trans-sectoral application of this Convention by collaborating with other committees and participating in other initiatives of the Council of Europe;
   - report to the Committee of Ministers on its activities.

The committee may involve experts and observers in its work.

Article 17: Co-operation in follow-up activities

The Parties undertake to co-operate with each other and through the Council of Europe in pursuing the aims and principles of this Convention, and especially in promoting recognition of the common heritage of Europe, by:

a. putting in place collaborative strategies to address priorities identified through the monitoring process;
b. fostering multilateral and transfrontier activities, and developing networks for regional co-operation in order to implement these strategies;
c. exchanging, developing, codifying and assuring the dissemination of good practices;
d. informing the public about the aims and implementation of this Convention.

Any Parties may, by mutual agreement, make financial arrangements to facilitate international co-operation.

Section V: Final clauses

Article 18: Signature and entry into force

a. This Convention shall be open for signature by the member States of the Council of Europe.
b. It shall be subject to ratification, acceptance or approval. Instruments of ratification, acceptance or approval shall be deposited with the Secretary General of the Council of Europe.
c. This Convention shall enter into force on the first day of the month following the expiration of a period of 3 months after the date on which ten member States of the Council of Europe have expressed their consent to be bound by the Convention in accordance with the provisions of the preceding paragraph.
d. In respect of any signatory State which subsequently expresses its consent to be bound by it, this Convention shall enter into force on the first day of the month following the expiration of a period of 3 months after the date of deposit of the instrument of ratification, acceptance or approval.

Article 19: Accession

a. After the entry into force of this Convention, the Committee of Ministers of the Council of Europe may invite any State not a member of the Council of Europe, and the European Community, to accede to the Convention by a decision taken by the majority provided for in Article 20.d of the Statute of the Council of Europe and by the unanimous vote of the representatives of the Contracting States entitled to sit on the Committee of Ministers.
b. In respect of any acceding State, or the European Community in the event of its accession, this Convention shall enter into force on the first day of the month following the expiration of a period of 3 months after the date of deposit of the instrument of accession with the Secretary General of the Council of Europe.

Article 20: Territorial application

a. Any State may, at the time of signature or when depositing its instrument of ratification, acceptance, approval or accession, specify the territory or territories to which this Convention shall apply.
b. Any State may, at any later date, by a declaration addressed to the Secretary General of the Council of Europe, extend the application of this Convention to any other territory specified in the declaration. In respect of such territory, the Convention shall enter into force on the first day of the month following the

expiration of a period of 3 months after the date of receipt of such declaration by the Secretary General.

c. Any declaration made under the two preceding paragraphs may, in respect of any territory specified in such declaration, be withdrawn by a notification addressed to the Secretary General. The withdrawal shall become effective on the first day of the month following the expiration of a period of 6 months after the date of receipt of such notification by the Secretary General.

Article 21: Denunciation

a. Any Party may, at any time, denounce this Convention by means of a notification addressed to the Secretary General of the Council of Europe.
b. Such denunciation shall become effective on the first day of the month following the expiration of a period of 6 months after the date of receipt of the notification by the Secretary General.

Article 22: Amendments

a. Any Party, and the committee mentioned in Article 16, may propose amendments to this Convention.
b. Any proposal for amendment shall be notified to the Secretary General of the Council of Europe, who shall communicate it to the member States of the Council of Europe, to the other Parties, and to any non-member State and the European Community invited to accede to this Convention in accordance with the provisions of Article 19.
c. The committee shall examine any amendment proposed and submit the text adopted by a majority of three-quarters of the Parties' representatives to the Committee of Ministers for adoption. Following its adoption by the Committee of Ministers by the majority provided for in Article 20.d of the Statute of the Council of Europe, and by the unanimous vote of the States Parties entitled to hold seats in the Committee of Ministers, the text shall be forwarded to the Parties for acceptance.
d. Any amendment shall enter into force in respect of the Parties which have accepted it, on the first day of the month following the expiry of a period of 3 months after the date on which ten member States of the Council of Europe have informed the Secretary General of their acceptance. In respect of any Party which subsequently accepts it, such amendment shall enter into force on the first day of the month following the expiry of a period of 3 months after the date on which the said Party has informed the Secretary General of its acceptance.

Article 23: Notifications

The Secretary General of the Council of Europe shall notify the member States of the Council of Europe, any State which has acceded or been invited to accede to this Convention, and the European Community having acceded or been invited to accede, of:

a. any signature;
b. the deposit of any instrument of ratification, acceptance, approval or accession;
c. any date of entry into force of this Convention in accordance with the provisions of Articles 18, 19 and 20;
d. any amendment proposed to this Convention in accordance with the provisions of Article 22, as well as its date of entry into force;
e. any other act, declaration, notification or communication relating to this Convention.

In witness whereof the undersigned, being duly authorized thereto, have signed this Convention.

Done at Faro, this 27th day of October 2005, in English and in French, both texts being equally authentic, in a single copy which shall be deposited in the archives of the Council of Europe. The Secretary General of the Council of Europe shall transmit certified copies to each member State of the Council of Europe and to any State or the European Community invited to accede to it.

Appendix XVII

Council Directive 93/7/EEC of 15 March 1993 on the Return of Cultural Objects Unlawfully Removed from the Territory of a Member State

The Council of the European Communities,

Having regard to the Treaty establishing the European Economic Community, and in particular Article 100a thereof,

Having regard to the proposal from the Commission,[47]

In cooperation with the European Parliament,[48]

Having regard to the opinion of the Economic and Social Committee,[49]

Whereas Article 8a of the Treaty provides for the establishment, not later than 1 January 1993, of the internal market, which is to comprise an area without internal frontiers in which the free movement of goods, persons, services and capital is ensured in accordance with the provisions of the Treaty;

Whereas, under the terms and within the limits of Article 36 of the Treaty, Member States will, after 1992, retain the right to define their national treasures and to take the necessary measures to protect them in this area without internal frontiers;

Whereas arrangements should therefore be introduced enabling Member States to secure the return to their territory of cultural objects which are classified as national treasures within the meaning of the said Article 36 and have been removed from their territory in breach of the abovementioned national measures or of Council Regulation (EEC) No 3911/92 of 9 December 1992 on the export of cultural goods;[50] whereas the implementation of these arrangements should be as simple and efficient as possible; whereas, to facilitate cooperation with regard to return, the scope of the arrangements should be confined to items belonging to

[47] OJ No. C 53, 28. 2. 1992, p. 11, and OJ No. C 172, 8. 7. 1992, p. 7.

[48] OJ No. C 176, 13. 7. 1992, p. 129 and OJ No. C 72, 15. 3. 1993.

[49] OJ No. C 223, 31. 8. 1992, p. 10.

[50] OJ No. L 395, 31. 12. 1992, p. 1.

common categories of cultural object; whereas the Annex to this Directive is consequently not intended to define objects which rank as "national treasures" within the meaning of the said Article 36, but merely categories of object which may be classified as such and may accordingly be covered by the return procedure introduced by this Directive;

Whereas cultural objects classified as national treasures and forming an integral part of public collections or inventories of ecclesiastical institutions but which do not fall within these common categories should also be covered by this Directive;

Whereas administrative cooperation should be established between Member States as regards their national treasures, in close liaison with their cooperation in the field of stolen works of art and involving in particular the recording, with Interpol and other qualified bodies issuing similar lists, of lost, stolen or illegally removed cultural objects forming part of their national treasures and their public collections;

Whereas the procedure introduced by this Directive is a first step in establishing cooperation between Member States in this field in the context of the internal market; whereas the aim is mutual recognition of the relevant national laws; whereas provision should therefore be made, in particular, for the Commission to be assisted by an advisory committee;

Whereas Regulation (EEC) No 3911/92 introduces, together with this Directive, a Community system to protect Member States' cultural goods; whereas the date by which Member States have to comply with this Directive has to be as close as possible to the date of entry into force of that Regulation; whereas, having regard to the nature of their legal systems and the scope of the changes to their legislation necessary to implement this Directive, some Member States will need a longer period,

Has adopted this directive:

Article 1

For the purposes of this Directive:

1. "Cultural object" shall mean an object which:
   a. is classified, before or after its unlawful removal from the territory of a Member State, among the "national treasures possessing artistic, historic or archaeological value" under national legislation or administrative procedures within the meaning of Article 36 of the Treaty, and
   b. belongs to one of the categories listed in the Annex or does not belong to one of these categories but forms an integral part of:
   c. public collections listed in the inventories of museums, archives or libraries' conservation collection.

   For the purposes of this Directive, "public collections" shall mean collections which are the property of a Member State, local or regional authority within a Member States or an institution situated in the territory of a Member State and defined as public in accordance with the legislation of that Member State, such institution being the property of, or significantly financed by, that Member State or a local or regional authority;

- the inventories of ecclesiastical institutions.

2. "Unlawfully removed from the territory of a Member State" shall mean:

   a. removed from the territory of a Member State in breach of its rules on the protection of national treasures or in breach of Regulation (EEC) No 3911/92, or
   b. not returned at the end of a period of lawful temporary removal or any breach of another condition governing such temporary removal.

3. "Requesting Member State" shall mean the Member State from whose territory the cultural object has been unlawfully removed.
4. "Requested Member State" shall mean the Member State in whose territory a cultural object unlawfully removed from the territory of another Member State is located.
5. "Return" shall mean the physical return of the cultural object to the territory of the requesting Member State.
6. "Possessor" shall mean the person physically holding the cultural object on his own account.
7. "Holder" shall mean the person physically holding the cultural object for third parties.

Article 2

Cultural objects which have been unlawfully removed from the territory of a Member State shall be returned in accordance with the procedure and in the circumstances provided for in this Directive.

Article 3

Each Member State shall appoint one or more central authorities to carry out the tasks provided for in this Directive.

Member States shall inform the Commission of all the central authorities they appoint pursuant to this Article.

The Commission shall publish a first of these central authorities and any changes concerning them in the C series of the Official Journal of the European Communities.

Article 4

Member States' central authorities shall cooperate and promote consultation between the Member States' competent national authorities. The latter shall in particular:

1. upon application by the requesting Member State, seek a specified cultural object which as been unlawfully removed from its territory, identifying the possessor and/or holder. The application must include all information needed to facilitate this search, with particular reference to the actual or presumed location of the object;
2. notify the Member States concerned, where a cultural object is found in their own territory and there are reasonable grounds for believing that it has been unlawfully removed from the territory of another Member State;
3. enable the competent authorities of the requesting Member State to check that the object in question is a cultural object, provided that the check is made within 2 months of the notification provided for in paragraph 2. If it is not made within the stipulated period, paragraphs 4 and 5 shall cease to apply;
4. take any necessary measures, in cooperation with the Member State concerned, for the physical preservation of the cultural object;
5. prevent, by the necessary interim measures, any action to evade the return procedure;
6. act as intermediary between the possessor and/or holder and the requesting Member State with regard to return. To this end, the competent authorities of the requested Member States may, without prejudice to Article 5, first facilitate the implementation of an arbitration procedure, in accordance with the national legislation of the requested State and provided that the requesting State and the possessor or holder give their formal approval.

Article 5

The requesting Member State may initiate, before the competent court in the requested Member State, proceedings against the possessor or, failing him, the holder, with the aim of securing the return of a cultural object which has been unlawfully removed from its territory.

Proceedings may be brought only where the document initiating them is accompanied by:

- a document describing the object covered by the request and stating that it is a cultural object,
- a declaration by the competent authorities of the requesting Member State that the cultural object has been unlawfully removed from its territory.

Article 6

The central authority of the requesting Member State shall forthwith inform the central authority of the requested Member State that proceedings have been initiated with the aim of securing the return of the object in question.

The central authority of the requested Member State shall forthwith inform the central authorities of the other Member States.

Article 7

1. Member States shall lay down in their legislation that the return proceedings provided for in this Directive may not be brought more than 1 year after the requesting Member State became aware of the location of the cultural object and of the identity of its possessor or holder.

   Such proceedings may, at all events, not be brought more than 30 years after the object was unlawfully removed from the territory of the requesting Member State. However, in the case of objects forming part of public collections, referred to in Article 1 (1), and ecclesiastical goods in the Member States where they are subject to special protection arrangements under national law, return proceedings shall be subject to a time-limit of 75 years, except in Member States where proceedings are not subject to a time-limit or in the case of bilateral agreements between Member States laying down a period exceeding 75 years.
2. Return proceedings may not be brought if removal from the national territory of the requesting Member State is no longer unlawful at the time when they are to be initiated.

Article 8

Save as otherwise provided in Articles 7 and 13, the competent court shall order the return of the cultural object in question where it is found to be a cultural object within the meaning of Article 1 (1) and to have been removed unlawfully from national territory.

Article 9

Where return of the object is ordered, the competent court in the requested States shall award the possessor such compensation as it deems fair according to the circumstances of the case, provided that it is satisfied that the possessor exercised due care and attention in acquiring the object.

The burden of proof shall be governed by the legislation of the requested Member State.

In the case of a donation or succession, the possessor shall not be in a more favourable position than the person from whom he acquired the object by that means.

The requesting Member State shall pay such compensation upon return of the object.

Article 10

Expenses incurred in implementing a decision ordering the return of a cultural object shall be borne by the requesting Member State. The same applies to the costs of the measures referred to in Article 4 (4).

Article 11

Payment of the fair compensation and of the expenses referred to in Articles 9 and 10, respectively, shall be without prejudice to the requesting Member State's right to take action with a view to recovering those amounts from the persons responsible for the unlawful removal of the cultural object from its territory.

Article 12

Ownership of the cultural object after return shall be governed by that law of the requesting Member State.

Article 13

This Directive shall apply only to cultural objects unlawfully removed from the territory of a Member State on or after 1 January 1993.

Article 14

1. Each Member State may extend its obligation to return cultural objects to cover categories of objects other than those listed in the Annex.

2. Each Member State may apply the arrangements provided for by this Directive to requests for the return of cultural objects unlawfully removed from the territory of other Member States prior to 1 January 1993.

Article 15

This Directive shall be without prejudice to any civil or criminal proceedings that may be brought, under the national laws of the Member States, by the requesting Member State and/or the owner of a cultural object that has been stolen.

Article 16

1. Member States shall send the Commission every 3 years, and for the first time in February 1996, a report on the application of this Directive.
2. The Commission shall send the European Parliament, the Council and the Economic and Social Committee, every 3 years, a report reviewing the application of this Directive.
3. The Council shall review the effectiveness of this Directive after a period of application of 3 years and, acting on a proposal from the Commission, make any necessary adaptations.
4. In any event, the Council acting on a proposal from the Commission, shall examine every 3 years and, where appropriate, update the amounts indicated in the Annex, on the basis of economic and monetary indicators in the Community.

Article 17

The Commission shall be assisted by the Committee set up by Article 8 of Regulation (EEC) No 3911/92.

The Committee shall examine any question arising from the application of the Annex to this Directive which may be tabled by the chairman either on his own initiative or at the request of the representative of a Member State.

Article 18

Member States shall bring into force the laws, regulations and administrative provisions necessary to comply with this Directive within 9 months of its adoption, except as far as the Kingdom of Belgium, the Federal Republic of Germany and the

Kingdom of the Netherlands are concerned, which must conform to this Directive at the latest 12 months from the date of its adoption. They shall forthwith inform the Commission thereof.

When Member States adopt these measures, they shall contain a reference to this Directive or shall be accompanied by such reference on the occasion of their official publication. The methods of making such a reference shall be laid down by the Member States.

Article 19

This Directive is addressed to the Member States.

Done at Brussels, 15 March 1993.

For the Council

The President

M. JELVED

Annex

Categories referred to in the second indent of Article 1[51] to which objects classified as "national treasures" within the meaning of Article 36 of the Treaty must belong in order to qualify for return under this Directive.

A. 1. Archaeological objects more than 100 years old which are the products of:

a. and or underwater excavations and finds,
b. archaeological sites,
c. archaeological collections.

2. Elements forming an integral part of artistic, historical or religious monuments which have been dismembered, more than 100 years old.
3. Pictures and paintings, other than those included in category 3A or 4, executed entirely by hand on any material and in any medium.[5]
4. Water-colours, gouaches and pastels executed entirely by hand on any material.[5]
5. Mosaics other than those in category 1 or category 2 and drawings executed entirely by hand, on any medium and in any material.[5]
6. Original engravings, prints, serigraphs and lithographs with their respective plates and original posters.[5]
7. Original sculptures or statuary and copies produced by the same process as the original[5] other than those in category 1.
8. Photographs, films and negatives thereof.[5]
9. Incunabula and manuscripts, including maps and musical scores, singly or in collections.[5]

[51] Which are more than 50 years old and do not belong to their originators.

10. Books more than 100 years old, singly or in collections.
11. Printed maps more than 200 years old.
12. Archives and any elements thereof, of any kind, on any medium, comprising elements more than 50 years old.
13.
    a. Collections[52] and specimens from zoological, botanical, mineralogical or anatomical collections;
    b. Collections[6] of historical, palaeontological, ethnographic or numismatic interest.
14. Means of transport more than 75 years old. Any other antique item not included in categories A 1 to A 13, more than 50 years old.

B. Financial thresholds applicable to certain categories under A (in ecus) Value:

- 0
  - 1 (Archaeological objects)
  - 2 (Dismembered monuments)
  - 8 (Incunabula and manuscripts)
  - 11 (Archives)
- 15,000
  - 4 (Mosaics and drawings)
  - 5 (Engravings)
  - 7 (Photographs)
  - 10 (Printed maps)
- 30,000
  - 3A (Water colours, gouches and pastels)
- 50,000
  - 6 (Statuary)
  - 9 (Books)
  - 12 (Collections)
  - 13 (Means of transport)
  - 14 (Any other object)
- 150,000
  - 3 (Pictures)

[52] As defined by the Court of Justice in its Judgment in Case 252/84, as follows: "Collectors" pieces within the meaning of Heading No. 99.05 of the Common Customs Tariff are articles which possess the requisite characteristics for inclusion in a collection, that is to say, articles which are relatively rare, are not normally used for their original purpose, are the subject of special transactions outside the normal trade in similar utility articles and are of high value.

The cultural objects in categories A 1 to A 14 are covered by this Directive only if their value corresponds to, or exceeds, the financial thresholds under B.

The assessment of whether or not the conditions relating to financial value are fulfilled must be made when return is requested. The financial value is that of the object in the requested Member State.

For the Member States which do not have the euro as their currency, the values expressed in euro in the Annex shall be converted and expressed in national currencies at the rate of echange on 31 December 2001 published in the *Official Journal of the European Communities*. This countervalue in national currencies shall be reviewed every two years with effect from 31 December 2001. Calculation of this countervalue shall be based on the average daily value of those currencies, expressed in euro, during the 24 months ending on the last day of August preceeding the revision which takes effect on 31 December. The Advisory Committee on Cultural Goods shall review this method of calculation, on a proposal from the Commission, in principle two years after the first application. For each revision, the values expressed in euro and their countervalues in natinal currency shall be published periodically in the *Official Journal of the European Communities* in the first days of the month of November preceeding the date on which the revision takes effect.

Appendix XVIII

Council Regulation (EEC) No. 3911/92 of 9 December 1992 on the Export of Cultural Goods

The Council of the European Communities,

Having regard to the Treaty establishing the European Economic Community, and in particular Article 113 thereof,

Having regard to the proposal from the Commission,[53]

Having regard to the opinion of the European Parliament,[54]

Having regard to the opinion of the Economic and Social Committee,[55]

Whereas, in view of the completion of the internal market, rules on trade with third countries are needed for the protection of cultural goods;

Whereas, in the light of the conclusions of the Council meeting on 19 November 1990, it seems necessary to take measures in particular to ensure that exports of cultural goods are subject to uniform controls at the Community's external borders;

Whereas such a system should require the presentation of a licence issued by the competent Member State prior to the export of cultural goods covered by this Regulation; whereas this necessitates a clear definition of the scope of such measures and the procedures for their implementation; whereas the implementation of the system should be as simple and efficient as possible; whereas a Committee should be set up to assist the Commission in carrying out the responsibilities conferred on it by this Regulation;

Whereas, in view of the considerable experience of the Member States' authorities in the application of Council Regulation (EEC) No. 1468/81 of 19 May 1981 on mutual assistance between the administrative authorities of the Member States and cooperation between the latter and the Commission to ensure the correct application of the law on customs or agricultural matters,[56] the said Regulation should be applied to this matter;

---

[53] OJ No. C 53, 28. 2. 1992, p. 8.

[54] OJ No. C 176, 13. 7. 1992, p. 31.

[55] OJ No. C 223, 31. 8. 1992, p. 10.

[56] OJ No. L 144, 2. 6. 1981, p. 1. Regulation as amended by Regulation (EEC) No. 945/87 (OJ No. L 90, 2. 4. 1987, p. 3).

Whereas the Annex to this Regulation is aimed at making clear the categories of cultural goods which should be given particular protection in trade with third countries, but is not intended to prejudice the definition, by Member States, of national treasures within the meaning of Article 36 of the Treaty,

Has adopted this regulation:

Article 1

Without prejudice to Member States' powers under Article 36 of the Treaty, the term "cultural goods" shall refer, for the purposes of this Regulation, to the items listed in the Annex.

Export licence

Article 2

1. The export of cultural goods outside the customs territory of the Community shall be subject to the presentation of an export licence.
2. The export licence shall be issued at the request of the person concerned:
    a. by a competent authority of the Member State in whose territory the cultural object in question was lawfully and definitively located on 1 January 1993,
    b. or, thereafter, by a competent authority of the Member State in whose territory it is located following either lawful and definitive dispatch from another Member State, or importation from a third country, or reimportation from a third country after lawful dispatch from a Member State to that country.

    However, without prejudice to paragraph 4, the Member State which is competent in accordance with the two indents in the first subparagraph may not require export licences for the cultural goods specified in the first and second indents of category A1 of the Annex where they are of limited archaeological or scientific interest, and provided that they are not the direct product of excavations, finds and archaeological sites within a Member State, and that their presence on the market is lawful.

    The export licence may be refused, for the purposes of this Regulation, where the cultural goods in question are covered by legislation protecting national treasures of artistic, historical or archaeological value in the Member State concerned.

    Where necessary, the authority referred to in the second indent of the first subparagraph shall enter into contact with the competent authorities of the

Member State from which the cultural object in question came, and in particular the competent authorities within the meaning of Council Directive 93.../EEC of... on the return of cultural objects unlawfully removed from the territory of a Member State.[57]

3. The export licence shall be valid throughout the Community.
4. Without prejudice to the provisions of this Article, direct export from the customs territory of the Community of national treasures having artistic, historic or archaeological value which are not cultural goods within the meaning of this Regulation is subject to the national law of the Member State of export.

Article 3

1. Member States shall furnish the Commission with a list of the authorities empowered to issue export licences for cultural goods.
2. The Commission shall publish a list of these authorities and any amendment to that list in the "C" series of the Official Journal of the European Communities.

Article 4

The export licence shall be presented, in support of the export declaration, when the customs export formalities are carried out, at the customs office which is competent to accept that declaration.

Article 5

1. Member States may restrict the number of customs offices empowered to handle formalities for the export of cultural goods.
2. Member States availing themselves of the option afforded by paragraph 1 shall inform the Commission of the customs offices duly empowered.

The Commission shall publish this information in the "C" series of the Official Journal of the European Communities. The commission shall publish this information in the 'C' series of the *Official Journal of the European Communities.*

---

[57] Not yet adopted at the time of this publication; in accordance with Article 11 below, the present Regulation will enter into force on the 3rd day following that of publication of the Directive in the Official Journal of the European Communities.

Administrative cooperation

Article 6

For the purposes of implementing this Regulation, the provisions of Regulation (EEC) No. 1468/81, and in particular the provisions on the confidentiality of information, shall apply mutatis mutandis.

In addition to the cooperation provided for under the first subparagraph, Member States shall take all necessary steps to establish, in the context of their mutual relations, cooperation between the customs authorities and the competent authorities referred to in Article 4 of Directive 93/.../EEC.[58]

General and final provisions

Article 7

The provisions necessary for the implementation of this Regulation, in particular those concerning the form to be used (for example, the model and technical properties) shall be adopted in accordance with the procedure laid down in Article 8(2).

Article 8

1. The Commission shall be assisted by a committee.
2. Where reference is made to this paragraph, Articles 3 and 7 of Decision 1999/468/EC shall apply.
3. The Committee shall adopt its Rules of Procedure.

[58] See footnote No. 5.

Article 9

Each Member State shall determine the penalties to be applied for infringement of the provisions of this Regulation. The penalties shall be sufficient to promote compliance with those provisions.

Article 10

Each Member State shall inform the Commission of the measures taken pursuant to this Regulation.

The Commission shall pass on this information to the other Member States.

Every 3 years the Commission shall present a report to the European Parliament, the Council and the Economic and Social Committee on the implementation of this Regulation.

The Council shall review the effectiveness of the Regulation after a period of application of 3 years and, acting on a proposal from the Commission, make any necessary adaptations.

In any event, the Council, acting on a proposal from the Commission, shall examine every 3 years and, where appropriate, update the amounts indicated in the Annex, on the basis of economic and monetary indicators in the Community.

Article 11

This Regulation shall enter into force on the third day following that of publication in the Official Journal of the European Communities of Directive 93/.../EEC.[59]

This Regulation shall be binding in its entirety and directly applicable in all Member States.

Done at Brussels, 9 December 1992.

For the Council

The President

W. Waldegrave

---

[59] The Directive on the return of cultural objects unlawfully removed from the territory of a Member State, already referred to in Articles 2(2) and 6, has not yet been adopted at the time of this publication.

Annex

Categories of Cultural Objects Covered by Article 1

A. 1. Archaeological objects more than 100 years old which are the products of:

- excavations and finds on land or under water
  9705 00 00
- archaeological sites
  9706 00 00
- archaelogical collections

2. Elements forming an integral part of artistic, historical or religious monuments which have been dismembered, of an age exceeding 100 years
   9705 00 00
   9706 00 00

3. Pictures and paintings executed entirely by hand, on any medium and in any material[60]
   9701

3A. Water-colours, gouaches and pastels executed entirely by hand on any material[8]

4. Mosaics other than those in categories 1 or 2 and drawings executed entirely by hand, on any medium and in any material[8]
   6914
   9701

5. Original engravings, prints, serigraphs and lithographs with their respective plates and original posters[8]
   Chapter 49
   9702 00 00
   8442 50 99

6. Original sculptures or statuary and copies produced by the same process as the original,[8] other than those in category 1
   9703 00 00

7. Photographs, films and negatives thereof[8]
   3704
   3705
   3706
   4911 91 80

[60] Which are more than 50 years old and do not belong to their originators.

8. Incunabula and manuscripts, including maps and musical scores, singly or in collections[8]
   9702 00 00
   9706 00 00
   4901 10 00
   4901 99 00
   4904 00 00
   4905 91 00
   4905 99 00
   4906 00 00

9. Books more than 100 years old, singly or in collections
   9705 00 00
   9706 00 00

10. Printed maps more than 200 years old
    9706 00 00

11. Archives, and any elements thereof, of any kind or any medium which are more than 50 years old
    3704
    3705
    3706
    4901
    4906
    9705 00 00
    9706 00 00

12.
    a. Collections[61] and specimens from zoological, botanical, mineralogical or anatomical collections;
       9705 00 00
    b. Collections[9] of historical, palaeontological, ethnographic or numismatic interest
       9705 00 00

13. Means of transport more than 75 years old
    9705 00 00
    Chapters
    86–89

[61] As defined by the Court of Justice in its judgment in Case 252/84, as follows: "Collectors" pieces within the meaning of heading No. 97.05 of the Common Customs Tariff are articles which possess the requisite characteristics for inclusion in a collection, that is to say, articles which are relatively rare, are not normally used for their original purpose, are the subject of special transactions outside the normal trade in similar utility articles and are of high value.

14. Any other antique items not included in categories A.1 to A.13

   a. between 50 and 100 years old:

   - toys, games
     Chapter 95
   - glassware
     7013
   - articles of goldsmiths' or silversmiths' wares
     7114
   - furniture
     Chapter 94
   - optical, photographic or cinematographic apparatus
     Chapter 90
   - musical instruments
     Chapter 92
   - clocks and watches and parts thereof
     Chapter 91
   - articles of wood
     Chapter 44
   - pottery
     Chapter 69
   - tapestries
     5805 00 00
   - carpets
     Chapter 57
   - wallpaper
     4814
   - arms
     Chapter 93

   b. more than 100 years old
     9706 00 00

The cultural objects in categories A.1 to A.14 are covered by this Regulation only if their value corresponds to, or exceeds, the financial thresholds under B.

B. Financial thresholds applicable to certain categories under A (in ecus)

- Value: Whatever the value
  - 1 (Archaeological objects)
  - 2 (Dismembered monuments)
  - 8 (Incunabula and manuscripts)
  - 11 (Archives)
- 15,000
  - 4 (Mosaics and drawings)
  - 5 (Engravings)

  - 7 (Photographs)
  - 10 (Printed maps)

- 30,000

  - 3A. (Water colours, gouaches and pastels)

- 50,3000

  - 6 (Statuary)
  - 9 (Books)
  - 12 (Collections)
  - 13 (Means of transport)
  - 14 (Any other object)

- 150,000

  - 3 (Pictures)

The assessment of whether or not the conditions relating to financial value are fulfilled must be made when an application for an export licence is submitted. The financial value is that of the cultural object in the Member State referred to in Article 2 (2) of the Regulation.

For the Member States which do not have the euro as their currency, the values expressed in euro in the Annex shall be converted and expressed in national currencies at the rate of exchange on 31 December 2001 published in the *Official Journal of the European Communities*. This countervalue in national currencies shall be reviewed every two years with effect from 31 December 2001. Calculation of this countervalue shall be based on the average daily value of those currencies, expressed in euro, during the 24 months ending on the last day of August preceeding the revision which takes effect on 31 December. This method of calculation shall be reviewed, on a proposal from the Commission, by the Advisory Committee on Cultural Goods, in principle two years after the first application. For each revision, the values expressed in euro and their countervalues in national currency shall be published periodically in the *Official Journal of the European Communities* in the first days of the month of November preceeding the date on which the revision takes effect.

Appendix XIX

Council Regulation (EC) 116/2009 of 18 December 2008 on the export of cultural goods (Codified version), Official Journal L 039, 10/02/2009, p. 1–7.

The Council of the European Union,

Having regard to the Treaty establishing the European Community, and in particular Article 133 thereof,

Having regard to the proposal from the Commission,

Whereas:

1. Council Regulation (EEC) No. 3911/92 of 9 December 1992 on the export of cultural goods[62] has been substantially amended several times.[63] In the interests of clarity and rationality the said Regulation should be codified.
2. In order to maintain the internal market, rules on trade with third countries are needed for the protection of cultural goods.
3. It seems necessary to take measures in particular to ensure that exports of cultural goods are subject to uniform controls at the Community's external borders.
4. Such a system should require the presentation of a licence issued by the competent Member State prior to the export of cultural goods covered by this Regulation. This necessitates a clear definition of the scope of such measures and the procedures for their implementation. The implementation of the system should be as simple and efficient as possible.
5. The measures necessary for the implementation of this Regulation should be adopted in accordance with Council Decision 1999/468/EC of 28 June 1999 laying down the procedures for the exercise of implementing powers conferred on the Commission.[64]

---

[62] OJ L 395, 31.12.1992, p. 1.

[63] See Annex II.

[64] OJ L 184, 17.7.1999, p. 23.

6. In view of the considerable experience of the Member States' authorities in the application of Council Regulation (EC) No. 515/97 of 13 March 1997 on mutual assistance between the administrative authorities of the Member States and cooperation between the latter and the Commission to ensure the correct application of the law on customs and agricultural matters,[65] the said Regulation should be applied to this matter.
7. Annex I to this Regulation is aimed at making clear the categories of cultural goods which should be given particular protection in trade with third countries but is not intended to prejudice the definition, by Member States, of national treasures within the meaning of Article 30 of the Treaty,

Has adopted this regulation:

Article 1

Definition

Without prejudice to Member States' powers under Article 30 of the Treaty, the term "cultural goods" shall refer, for the purposes of this Regulation, to the items listed in Annex I.

Article 2

Export licence

1. The export of cultural goods outside the customs territory of the Community shall be subject to the presentation of an export licence.
2. The export licence shall be issued at the request of the person concerned:

   a. by a competent authority of the Member State in whose territory the cultural object in question was lawfully and definitively located on 1 January 1993;
   b. or, thereafter, by a competent authority of the Member State in whose territory it is located following either lawful and definitive dispatch from another Member State, or importation from a third country, or re-importation from a third country after lawful dispatch from a Member State to that country.
   However, without prejudice to paragraph 4, the Member State which is competent in accordance with points (a) or (b) of the first subparagraph is authorised not to require export licences for the cultural goods specified in the first and second indents of category A.1 of Annex I where they are of limited archaeological or scientific interest, and provided that they are not the direct product of excavations, finds or archaeological sites within a Member State, and that their presence on the market is lawful.

[65] OJ L 82, 22.3.1997, p. 1.

The export licence may be refused, for the purposes of this Regulation, where the cultural goods in question are covered by legislation protecting national treasures of artistic, historical or archaeological value in the Member State concerned.

Where necessary, the authority referred to in point (b) of the first subparagraph shall enter into contact with the competent authorities of the Member State from which the cultural object in question came, and in particular the competent authorities within the meaning of Council Directive 93/7/EEC of 15 March 1993 on the return of cultural objects unlawfully removed from the territory of a Member State.[66]

3. The export licence shall be valid throughout the Community.
4. Without prejudice to the provisions of paragraphs 1, 2 and 3, direct export from the customs territory of the Community of national treasures having artistic, historic or archaeological value which are not cultural goods within the meaning of this Regulation is subject to the national law of the Member State of export.

Article 3

Competent authorities

1. Member States shall furnish the Commission with a list of the authorities empowered to issue export licences for cultural goods.
2. The Commission shall publish a list of the authorities and any amendment to that list in the "C" series of the Official Journal of the European Union.

Article 4

Presentation of licence

The export licence shall be presented, in support of the export declaration, when the customs export formalities are carried out, at the customs office which is competent to accept that declaration.

Article 5

Limitation of competent customs offices

1. Member States may restrict the number of customs offices empowered to handle formalities for the export of cultural goods.

[66] OJ L 74, 27.3.1993, p. 74.

2. Member States availing themselves of the option afforded by paragraph 1 shall inform the Commission of the customs offices duly empowered.

The Commission shall publish this information in the "C" series of the Official Journal of the European Union.

Article 6

Administrative cooperation

For the purposes of implementing this Regulation, the provisions of Regulation (EC) No. 515/97, and in particular the provisions on the confidentiality of information, shall apply mutatis mutandis.

In addition to the cooperation provided for under the first paragraph, Member States shall take all necessary steps to establish, in the context of their mutual relations, cooperation between the customs authorities and the competent authorities referred to in Article 4 of Directive 93/7/EEC.

Article 7

Implementing measures

The measures necessary for the implementation of this Regulation, in particular those concerning the form to be used (for example, the model and technical properties) shall be adopted in accordance with the procedure referred to in Article 8(2).

Article 8

Committee

1. The Commission shall be assisted by a committee.
2. Where reference is made to this paragraph, Articles 3 and 7 of Decision 1999/468/EC shall apply.

Article 9

Penalties

The Member States shall lay down the rules on penalties applicable to infringements of the provisions of this Regulation and shall take all measures necessary to ensure that they are implemented. The penalties provided for must be effective, proportionate and dissuasive.

Article 10

Reporting

1. Each Member State shall inform the Commission of the measures taken pursuant to this Regulation.
2. The Commission shall pass on this information to the other Member States.
3. Every 3 years the Commission shall present a report to the European Parliament, the Council and the European Economic and Social Committee on the implementation of this Regulation.

The Council, acting on a proposal from the Commission, shall examine every 3 years and, where appropriate, update the amounts indicated in Annex I, on the basis of economic and monetary indicators in the Community.

Article 11

Repeal

Regulation (EEC) No. 3911/92, as amended by the Regulations listed in Annex II, is repealed.

References to the repealed Regulation shall be construed as references to this Regulation and shall be read in accordance with the correlation table in Annex III.

Article 12

Entry into force

This Regulation shall enter into force on the 20th day following its publication in the Official Journal of the European Union.

This Regulation shall be binding in its entirety and directly applicable in all Member States.

Done at Brussels, 18 December 2008.

For the Council

The President

M. Barnier

Annex I

Categories of cultural objects covered by Article 1

1. Archaeological objects more than 100 years old which are the products of:
   - excavations and finds on land or under water, 9705 00 00;

- archaeological sites, 9706 00 00;
- archaeological collections.

2. Elements forming an integral part of artistic, historical or religious monuments which have been dismembered, of an age exceeding 100 years, 9705 00 00 9706 00 00.
3. Pictures and paintings, other than those included in category 3A or 4, executed entirely by hand on any material and in any medium,[67] 9701.

3A. Water-colours, gouaches and pastels executed entirely by hand on any material,[67] 9701.

4. Mosaics in any material executed entirely by hand, other than those falling in categories 1 or 2, and drawings in any medium executed entirely by hand on any material,[6] 6914 9701.
5. Original engravings, prints, serigraphs and lithographs with their respective plates and original posters,[6] Chapter 49, 9702 00 00 8442 50 99.
6. Original sculptures or statuary and copies produced by the same process as the original,[6] other than those in category 1, 9703 00 00.
7. Photographs, films and negatives thereof,[1] 3704 3705 3706 4911 91 80.
8. Incunabula and manuscripts, including maps and musical scores, singly or in collections,[6] 9702 00 00 9706 00 00 4901 10 00 4901 99 00 4904 00 00 4905 91 00 4905 99 00 4906 00 00.
9. Books more than 100 years old, singly or in collections, 9705 00 00 9706 00 00.
10. Printed maps more than 200 years old 9706 00 00.
11. Archives, and any elements thereof, of any kind or any medium which are more than 50 years old 3704 3705 3706 4901 4906 9705 00 00 9706 00 00.
12.
    a. Collections[68] and specimens from zoological, botanical, mineralogical or anatomical collections; 9705 00 00.
    b. Collections[7] of historical, palaeontological, ethnographic or numismatic interest 9705 00 00.
13. Means of transport more than 75 years old 9705 00 00 Chapters 86–89.
14. Any other antique items not included in categories A.1 to A.14:
    a.

       between 50 and 100 years old;
       toys, games, Chapter 95;

---

[67] Which are more than 50 years old and do not belong to their originators.

[68] As defined by the Court of Justice in its judgment in Case 252/84, as follows: "Collectors' pieces within the meaning of heading No. 97.05 of the Common Customs Tariff are articles which possess the requisite characteristics for inclusion in a collection, that is to say, articles which are relatively rare, are not normally used for their original purpose, are the subject of special transactions outside the normal trade in similar utility articles and are of high value."

glassware, 7013;
articles of goldsmiths' or silversmiths' wares, 7114;
furniture, Chapter 94
optical, photographic or cinematographic apparatus, Chapter 90;
musical instruments, Chapter 92;
clocks and watches and parts thereof, Chapter 91;
articles of wood, Chapter 44;
pottery, Chapter 69;
tapestries, 5805 00 00;
carpets, Chapter 57;
wallpaper, 4814;
arms, Chapter 93;

b. more than 100 years old, 9706 00 00.

A. The cultural objects in categories A.1 to A.15 are covered by this Regulation only if their value corresponds to, or exceeds, the financial thresholds under B.
B. Financial thresholds applicable to certain categories under A (in euro)

Value:

- Whatever the value
  - 1 (Archaeological objects).
  - 2 (Dismembered monuments).
  - 9 (Incunabula and manuscripts).
  - 12 (Archives).
- 15,000
  - 5 (Mosaics and drawings).
  - 6 (Engravings).
  - 8 (Photographs).
  - 11 (Printed maps).
- 30,000
  - 4 (Watercolours, gouaches and pastels).
- 50,000
  - 7 (Statuary).
  - 10 (Books).
  - 13 (Collections).
  - 14 (Means of transport).
  - 15 (Any other object).
- 150,000
  - 3 (Pictures).

The assessment of whether or not the conditions relating to financial value are fulfilled must be made when an application for an export licence is submitted. The financial value is that of the cultural object in the Member State referred to in Article 2(2).

For the Member States which do not have the euro as their currency, the values expressed in euro in Annex I shall be converted and expressed in national currencies at the rate of exchange on 31 December 2001 published in the Official Journal of the European Communities. This countervalue in national currencies shall be reviewed every 2 years with effect from 31 December 2001. Calculation of this countervalue shall be based on the average daily value of those currencies, expressed in euro, during the 24 months ending on the last day of August preceding the revision which takes effect on 31 December. This method of calculation shall be reviewed, on a proposal from the Commission, by the Advisory Committee on Cultural Goods, in principle 2 years after the first application. For each revision, the values expressed in euro and their countervalues in national currency shall be published periodically in the Official Journal of the European Union in the first days of the month of November preceding the date on which the revision takes effect.

Annex II

Repealed Regulation with its successive amendments

Council Regulation (EEC) No. 3911/92 (OJ L 395, 31.12.1992, p. 1).

Council Regulation (EC) No. 2469/96 (OJ L 335, 24.12.1996, p. 9).

Council Regulation (EC) No. 974/2001 (OJ L 137, 19.5.2001, p. 10).

Council Regulation (EC) No. 806/2003 (OJ L 122, 16.5.2003, p. 1), Annex I, point 2 only.

Annex III

Correlation Table

Regulation (EEC) No. 3911/92, This Regulation;

Article 1, Article 1;

Article 2(1), Article 2(1);

Article 2(2), first subparagraph, introductory wording, Article 2(2), first subparagraph, introductory wording;

Article 2(2), first subparagraph, first indent, Article 2(2), first subparagraph, point (a);

Article 2(2), first subparagraph, second indent, Article 2(2), first subparagraph, point (b);

Article 2(2), second subparagraph, Article 2(2), second subparagraph;

Article 2(2), third subparagraph, Article 2(2), third subparagraph;

Article 2(2), fourth subparagraph, Article 2(2), fourth subparagraph;
Article 2(3), Article 2(3);
Article 2(4), Article 2(4);
Articles 3 to 9, Articles 3 to 9;
Article 10, first paragraph, Article 10(1), first subparagraph;
Article 10, second paragraph, Article 10(1), second subparagraph;
Article 10, third paragraph, Article 10(2), first subparagraph;
Article 10, fourth paragraph;
Article 10, fifth paragraph, Article 10(2), second subparagraph;
Article 11, Article 11;
Article 12;
Annex, points A.1, A.2 and A.3, Annex I, points A.1, A.2 and A.3;
Annex, point A.3A, Annex I, point A.4;
Annex, point A.4, Annex I, point A.5;
Annex, point A.5, Annex I, point A.6;
Annex, point A.6, Annex I, point A.7;
Annex, point A.7, Annex I, point A.8;
Annex, point A.8, Annex I, point A.9;
Annex, point A.9, Annex I, point A.10;
Annex, point A.10, Annex I, point A.11;
Annex, point A.11, Annex I, point A.12;
Annex, point A.12, Annex I, point A.13;
Annex, point A.13, Annex I, point A.14;
Annex, point A.14, Annex I, point A.15;
Annex, point B, Annex I, point B;
Annex II;
Annex III.

Appendix XX

Directive 96/100/EC of the European Parliament and of the Council of 17 February 1997 amending the Annex to Directive 93/7/EEC on the return of cultural objects unlawfully removed from the territory of a Member State, Official Journal L 060, 01/03/1997, p. 59–60

The European Parliament and the Council of the European Union,

Having regard to the Treaty establishing the European Community, and in particular Article 100a thereof,

Having regard to the proposal from the Commission,[69]

Having regard to the opinion of the Economic and Social Committee,[70]

Acting in accordance with the procedure laid down in Article 189b of the Treaty,[71]

Whereas according to different artistic traditions within the Community water-colour, gouache and pastel pictures are variously regarded as being either paintings or drawings; whereas Category 4 of the Annex to Directive No. 93/7/EEC[72] includes drawings executed entirely by hand on any medium in any material, and Category 3 includes pictures and paintings executed entirely by hand on any medium in any material; whereas the financial thresholds which apply to these two categories are different; whereas in the internal market this could lead to serious differences of treatment for water-colour, gouache and pastel pictures depending upon the Member

---

[69] OJ No. C 6, 11. 1. 1996, p. 15.

[70] OJ No. C 97, 1. 4. 1996, p. 28.

[71] Opinion of the European Parliament of 21 May 1996 (OJ No. C 166, 10. 6. 1996, p. 38), Council Common Position of 8 July 1996 (OJ No. C 264, 11. 9. 1996, p. 66) and Decision of the European Parliament of 13 November 1996 (OJ No. C 362, 2. 12. 1996). Council Decision of 20 December 1996.

[72] OJ No. L 74, 27. 3. 1993, p. 74.

State in which they are situated; whereas it is necessary to decide for the purposes of the application of the Directive into which category they shall fall to ensure that the financial thresholds applied shall be the same throughout the Community;

Whereas experience shows that the prices realized by water-colour, gouache and pastel pictures tend to be rather higher than those realized by drawings and much lower than those fetched by paintings in oil or tempora; whereas accordingly it is expedient to place water-colour, gouache and pastel pictures into a new separate category with a threshold of ECU 30 000 which would ensure that works of major significance unlawfully removed from the territory of a Member State can be returned,

Have adopted this directive:

Article 1

The Annex to Directive No. 93/7/EEC shall be amended as follows:

1. in heading A:
   a. point 3 shall be replaced by: "3. Pictures and paintings, other than those included in Category 3A or 4, executed entirely by hand on any material and in any medium[1]";
   b. the following point shall be inserted: "3A. Water-colours, gouaches and pastels executed entirely by hand on any material[1]";
   c. point 4 shall be replaced by the following: "4. Mosaics in any material executed entirely by hand, other than those falling in Categories 1 or 2, and drawings in any medium executed entirely by hand on any material[1]";
2. in heading B:
   The following Category shall be inserted: "30 000-3A. (Water colours, gouaches and pastels)".

Article 2

Member States shall bring into force the laws, regulations and administrative provisions necessary to comply with this Directive within 6 months of the date of its publication in the Official Journal of the European Communities. They shall forthwith inform the Commission thereof.

When Member States adopt these measures, they shall contain a reference to this Directive or shall be accompanied by such reference on the occasion of their official publication. The methods of making such a reference shall be laid down by the Member States.

Article 3

This Directive is addressed to the Member States.

Done at Brussels, 17 February 1997.

For the European Parliament

The President

J. M. GIL-ROBLES

For the Council

The President

G. ZALM

Appendix XXI

Directive 2001/38/EC of the European Parliament and of the Council of 5 June 2001 amending Council Directive 93/7/EEC on the return of cultural objects unlawfully removed from the territory of a Member State, Official Journal L 187, 10/07/2001, p. 43–44

The European Parliament and the Council of the European Union,

Having regard to the Treaty establishing the European Community, and in particular Article 95 thereof,

Having regard to the proposal from the Commission,[73]

Having regard to the opinion of the Economic and Social Committee,

Having regard to the opinion of the Committee of the Regions,

Acting in accordance with the procedure referred to in Article 251 of the Treaty,[74]

Whereas:

1. The establishment of Economic and Monetary Union and the changeover to the euro have an effect on the last subparagraph under heading B of the Annex to Council Directive 93/7/EEC[75] laying down the values, expressed in ecu, of the cultural goods subject to the application of the Directive. That subparagraph lays down that the date for the conversion of such values into national currencies is to be 1 January 1993.
2. Pursuant to Council Regulation (EC) No. 1103/97 of 17 June 1997 on certain provisions relating to the introduction of the euro,[76] any reference to the ecu in legal instruments became, as from 1 January 1999, a reference to the euro, after

[73] OJ C 120 E, 24.4.2001, p. 182.

[74] Opinion of the European Parliament of 14 February 2001 and Council Decision of 14 May 2001.

[75] OJ L 74, 27.3.1993, p. 74. Directive as amended by Directive 96/100/EC of the European Parliament and of the Council (OJ L 60, 1.3.1997, p. 59).

[76] OJ L 162, 19.6.1997, p. 1.

conversion at the rate of one to one. Without an amendment to Directive 93/7/EEC, and hence to the fixed exchange rate corresponding to the rate in force on 1 January 1993, the Member States having the euro as their currency would continue to apply different amounts converted on the basis of the exchange rates of 1993, and not the conversion rates irrevocably fixed on 1 January 1999, and this situation would persist as long as the conversion rule remained an integral part of the Directive.

3. The last subparagrah under heading B of the Annex to Directive 93/7/EEC should therefore be amended in such a way that, as from 1 January 2002, the Member States having the euro as their currency directly apply the values in euro laid down in Community legislation. For the other Member States, which will continue to convert these thresholds into national currencies, an exchange rate should be adopted on an appropriate date before 1 January 2002, and provision should be made for those Member States to adapt that rate automatically and periodically in order to compensate for variations in the exchange rate between the national currency and the euro.
4. It would appear that the value 0 (zero) under heading B of the Annex to Directive 93/7/EEC, applicable as the financial threshold for certain categories of cultural objects, could be interpreted in such a way as to jeopardise the effective application of the Directive. Whereas this value 0 (zero) means that goods belonging to the categories in question, whatever their value – even if it is negligible or zero – are to be considered "cultural objects" within the meaning of the Directive, certain authorities have interpreted it in such a way that the cultural object in question has no value at all, thereby depriving those categories of goods of the protection afforded by the Directive.
5. To avoid any confusion in this respect, therefore, the figure 0 should be replaced by a clearer expression which leaves no doubt as to the need to protect the goods in question,

Have adopted this directive:

Article 1

In the Annex to Directive 93/7/EEC, the text under heading B is hereby amended as follows:

1. The title "VALUE: 0 (zero)" shall be replaced by: "VALUE: Whatever the value."
2. The last subparagraph, relating to the conversion into national currencies of the values expressed in ecus, shall be replaced by the following: "For the Member States which do not have the euro as their currency, the values expressed in euro in the Annex shall be converted and expressed in national currencies at the rate of exchange on 31 December 2001 published in the Official Journal of the European Communities. This countervalue in national currencies shall be reviewed every 2

years with effect from 31 December 2001. Calculation of this countervalue shall be based on the average daily value of those currencies, expressed in euro, during the 24 months ending on the last day of August preceding the revision which takes effect on 31 December. The Advisory Committee on Cultural Goods shall review this method of calculation, on a proposal from the Commission, in principle 2 years after the first application. For each revision, the values expressed in euro and their countervalues in national currency shall be published periodically in the Official Journal of the European Communities in the first days of the month of November preceding the date on which the revision takes effect".

Article 2

Member States shall bring into force the laws, regulations and administrative provisions necessary to comply with this Directive by 31 December 2001. They shall immediately inform the Commission thereof.

When Member States adopt these measures, they shall contain a reference to this Directive or shall be accompanied by such reference on the occasion of their official publication. The methods of making such reference shall be laid down by Member States.

Article 3

This Directive shall enter into force on the 20th day following that of its publication in the Official Journal of the European Communities.

Article 4

This Directive is addressed to the Member States.

Done at Luxembourg, 5 June 2001.

For the European Parliament
The President
N. Fontaine
For the Council
The President
L. Engqvist

Appendix XXII

Unesco International Code of Ethics for Dealers in Cultural Property[77]

Members of the trade in cultural property recognize the key role that trade has traditionally played in the dissemination of culture and in the distribution to museums and private collectors of foreign cultural property for the education and inspiration of all peoples.

They acknowledge the world wide concern over the traffic in stolen, illegally alienated, clandestinely excavated and illegally exported cultural property and accept as binding the following principles of professional practice intended to distinguish cultural property being illicitly traded from that in licit trade and they will seek to eliminate the former from their professional activities.

Article 1 Professional traders in cultural property will not import, export or transfer the ownership of this property when they have reasonable cause to believe it has been stolen, illegally alienated, clandestinely excavated or illegally exported.

Article 2 A trader who is acting as agent for the seller is not deemed to guarantee title to the property, provided that he makes known to the buyer the full name and address of the seller. A trader who is himself the seller is deemed to guarantee to the buyer the title to the goods.

Article 3 A trader who has reasonable cause to believe that an object has been the product of a clandestine excavation, or has been acquired illegally or dishonestly from an official excavation site or monument will not assist in any further transaction with that object, except with the agreement of the country where the site or monument exists. A trader who is in possession of the object, where that country seeks its return within a reasonable period of time, will take all legally permissible steps to co-operate in the return of that object to the country of origin.

[77] Adopted by the UNESCO intergovernmental Committee for Promoting the Return of Cultural Property to its Countries of Origin or its Restitution in Case of Illicit Appropriation at its Tenth Session, January 1999 and endorsed by the 30th General Conference of UNESCO, November 1999.

Article 4 A trader who has reasonable cause to believe that an item of cultural property has been illegally exported will not assist in any further transaction with that item, except with the agreement of the country of export. A trader who is in possession of the item, where the country of export seeks its return within a reasonable period of time, will take all legally permissible steps to co-operate in the return of that object to the country of export.

Article 5 Traders in cultural property will not exhibit, describe, attribute, appraise or retain any item of cultural property with the intention of promoting or failing to prevent its illicit transfer or export. Traders will not refer the seller or other person offering the item to those who may perform such services.

Article 6 Traders in cultural property will not dismember or sell separately parts of one complete item of cultural property.

Article 7 Traders in cultural property undertake to the best of their ability to keep together items of cultural heritage that were originally meant to be kept together.

Article 8 Violations of this Code of Ethics will be rigorously investigated by (*a body to be nominated by participating dealers*). A person aggrieved by the failure of a trader to adhere to the principles of this Code of Ethics may lay a complaint before that body, which shall investigate that complaint before that body, which shall investigate that complaint. Results of the complaint and the principles applied will be made public.

Why a Code?

Countless transactions take place every day all over the world concerning cultural property. They are part of the vibrant dialogue between cultures which UNESCO supports.

But unfortunately every day there are also ancient tombs broken into, libraries stolen from, monuments dismembered and collections robbed. Not only is the context and history of the purloined items lost, but very often the objects themselves are damaged and their place of origin destroyed for serious scholarship. A trail of desecrated religious places, damaged monuments and broken fragments witness the activities of the looters.

Much of the spoils find its way into the legal trade in art, antiquities and antiquarian books. Many collectors are today conscious of the damage done to cultures which they love and would like to help protect them. But how is one to know whether the object one wants to buy was properly transferred and legally dealt with?

One way is to be sure to buy from a dealer who espouses the highest principles of ethics devised by professionals in the care of cultural property and who is scrupulous to check the provenance of the works he deals in. Anyone can call himself a dealer. Thus objects sold from the back of a truck at 3 a.m. in the morning may gradually work their way up the chain from the thief to the local flea market, to, an antiques fair, to a small dealer and eventually find themselves in the international market at a dealers' or auction house where a collector may assume that he is dealing with a responsible handler of the cultural heritage.

The best dealers have the ethical dimensions of their work in mind when working with the cultures whose values they handle. But how is the collector to separate them from the less scrupulous?

The UNIDROIT Convention on Stolen or Illegally Exported Cultural Objects 1995 provides that a stolen cultural object must be returned. A purchaser in those systems which protect the *bona fide* purchaser will, however, receive compensation where it is otherwise entitled to retain the object if it has used the required diligence in acquiring the object. Indications of such diligence include the circumstances of the acquisition, including:

- the character of the parties,
- the price paid,
- whether the possessor consulted any reasonably accessible register of stolen cultural objects,
- any other relevant information and documentation which it could reasonably have obtained,
- whether the possessor consulted accessible agencies or,
- whether the possessor took any other step that a reasonable person would have taken in the circumstances.

The character of the parties and the reasonable steps which could be taken would include purchase from a reputable dealer.

UNESCO has therefore decided to assist in the process of establishing who are dealers who have acceptable standards by establishing an international code of conduct for dealers. Dealers who adopt it will be recognizable and the public will be entitled to expect that those dealers have been diligent in ascertaining the origin of the objects concerned and will be able to give assurances of their good provenance. Such dealers will be under the particular scrutiny of their fellow dealers and of the media to ensure that these high standards are kept. UNESCO will follow closely the practice of the dealers who use the Code.

History of the Code

The adoption of a Code was requested by the fifth session of the UNESCO Intergovernmental Committee for Promoting the Return of Cultural Property to its Countries of Origin or its Restitution in case of Illicit Appropriation in 1987 and was considered by that Committee in its subsequent sessions. Approved for adoption in 1999 by the Committee, it was endorsed by the 30th General Conference of UNESCO in November 1999.

While the work was in progress contributions and comments on the work were invited from dealers and dealer groups.

The Code builds on the principles developed in the UNESCO Convention on the Means of Prohibiting and Preventing the Illicit Import, Export and Transfer of Ownership of Cultural Property 1970 and subsequently in the UNIDROIT Convention on Stolen or Illegally Exported Cultural Objects 1995.

It also relies on the experience of various national Dealers' Codes including those of France, the Netherlands, Switzerland and the United Kingdom, as well as the code of the *Confédération internationale des Négociants d'Oeuvres d'Art* (CINOA). There were some differences between these Codes which have been harmonized in the UNESCO text. Experience had also shown that there were some loopholes which allowed cultural material to be handled even though it had been abstracted from its country of origin with some illegality. These areas have been tightened up.

The new *International Code of Ethics for Dealers in Cultural Property* is also close to the model rule on the Acquisitions Policies of Museums found in the Code of Professional Ethics of the International Council of Museums (ICOM).

If you would like more information as to how the Code was developed you may wish to consult the UNESCO Document "Feasibility of an International Code of Ethics for Dealers in Cultural Property for the Purpose of More Effective Control of Illicit Traffic in Cultural Property", Document CLT/94/WS/11.

Contents of the Code

The key clause is Article 1 which reads:

Professional traders in cultural property will not import, export or transfer the ownership of this property when they have reasonable cause to believe it has been stolen, illegally alienated, clandestinely excavated or illegally exported.

The effect of the phrase "reasonable cause to believe" is set out in later clauses. However, it is to be read as requiring traders to investigate the provenance of the material they handle. It is not sufficient to trade in material without questions and consider that the clause only comes into effect when somehow evidence of the illegality is fortuitously acquired. To satisfy this requirement, traders must actively examine the background of the objects they are offered and question the person concerned. They must pay attention to any circumstances likely to arouse suspicions, such as a demand for a large payment in cash or too low a price asked for a valuable object. That having been said, if there are no suspicious circumstances and questions are answered satisfactorily, traders can proceed with the transaction having no reasonable cause to believe there is any illegality.

Advantages of the Code

For Collectors

The issue of the Code gives collectors who have a serious concern for the fate of the cultures which they are attracted to the possibility of showing their preference for the legal over the illegal trade by bestowing their custom on ethical dealers.

They are also giving themselves some insurance that, if the status of an object in their collection is challenged, they will have evidence that they did their best to ensure that provenance of the object was legal and that they only dealt with a dealer who follows appropriate standards designed to avoid the transfer of illicitly acquired cultural property into the legal market.

For Dealers

Adopting the Code gives dealers a way of distancing themselves from disreputable people who claim to be dealers and in fact make no inquiry into provenance or even themselves knowingly instigate illegal acquisitions.

It therefore attracts to them the business of ethical collectors and raises the reputation of the ethical dealer community in the minds of the public and the media.

In cases where dealers themselves are selling as owners and not only as agents, it also gives them the right arguments to insist on proper evidence of legal acquisition from their suppliers.

For the Public

Adoption of the Code by dealers indicates that there is an ethical body of dealers who are not to be confused with those exposed by the media as instigating and commissioning thefts, clandestine excavations and illegal exports of cultural property.

It will show that there is a real and serious effort to prevent damage and destruction of the cultural heritage by a coalition of international organizations, museum and other cultural professionals, dealers, governments and local peoples in source countries in order to fight against the illegal trade.

International law on the illicit trade

Codes of Ethics do not replace the law – they complement it. The chief international instruments on the illicit trade are:

- *Protocol to the Hague Convention for the Protection of Cultural Property in the Event of Armed Conflict 1954* which provides for the return of cultural property illegally exported from occupied territory. Eighty-two States are Party to this Protocol.
- *UNESCO Convention on the Means of Prohibiting and Preventing the Illicit Import, Export and Transfer of Ownership of Cultural Property 1970* which creates co-operation strategies between States to prevent illicit traffic and co-operate on the return of cultural property. Ninety-one States are party to this Convention and a number of others are currently considering accession. It also

includes a provision on illegal export from occupied territories and, as some of the States party to this Convention are not party to the Hague Protocol, it widens the circle of States which are committed to return cultural property displaced as a result of conflict. It operates on a State to State basis.

- *UNIDROIT Convention on Stolen or Illegally Exported Cultural Objects 1995* which ensures that private owners have direct access to the courts of another country where cultural property stolen from their owners is found. It also allows States to sue in the courts of such a country for important cultural property belonging to certain categories which has been illegally exported. Twelve countries are already party to this Convention which is in force. Fourteen States have signed but not yet ratified and others are currently considering accession.

Other action on illicit trade

Codes of Ethics and international treaties are two important elements of the current major international effort to prevent the damage caused by the illegal trade.

Other efforts include action by UNESCO to

- Heighten awareness in source countries among local populations to the importance of protecting their cultural heritage.
- Help source countries update their legislation.
- Hold regional workshops so that experts can compare their laws and strategies and improve implementation of the Convention.
- Publicize simple but effective inventory systems which will help in the tracing of cultural property such as "Object-ID."
- Publicize the laws of source countries so that they are known and understood by local and international dealers.
- Publish handbooks and other information on preventing the illicit trade.
- Co-operate with INTERPOL, The World Customs Organization (WCO) and ICOM.

Appendix XXIII

ICOM Code of Ethics for Museums, 2006

Introduction

This edition of the *ICOM Code of Ethics for Museums* is the culmination of 6 years' revision. Following a thorough review of the ICOM's *Code* in the light of contemporary museum practice, a revised version, structured on the earlier edition, was issued in 2001. As envisaged at that time, this has now been completely reformatted to give it the look and feel of the museum profession and is based on key principles of professional practice, elaborated to provide general ethical guidance. The *Code* has been the subject of three periods of consultation with the membership. It was approved at the 21st General Assembly of ICOM, Seoul in 2004 with acclamation.

The whole ethos of the document continues to be that of service to society, the community, the public and its various constituencies, and the professionalism of museum practitioners. While there is a changed emphasis throughout the document resulting from the new structure, the accentuation of key points and the use of shorter paragraphs, very little is totally new. The new features will be found in paragraph 2.11 and the principles outlined in Sects. 3, 5 and 6.

The *Code of Ethics for Museums* provides a means of professional self-regulation in a key area of public provision where legislation at a national level is variable and far from consistent. It sets minimum standards of conduct and performance to which museum professional staff throughout the world may reasonably aspire as well as a providing a statement of reasonable public expectation from the museum profession.

ICOM issued its Ethics of Acquisition in 1970 and a full *Code of Professional Ethics* in 1986. The present edition – and its interim document of 2001 – owe much to that early work. The major work of revision and restructuring, however, fell on the members of the Ethics Committee. Their contribution in meetings – both actual and electronic – and their determination to meet both target and schedule is gratefully acknowledged. Their names are listed for reference.

Having completed our mandate, we pass responsibility for the Code to a largely new committee membership, headed by Bernice Murphy, who brings to the work all the knowledge and experience of a past Vice-President of ICOM and a previous member of the Ethics Committee.

Like its precursors, the present *Code* provides a global minimum standard on which national and specialist groups can build to meet their particular requirements. ICOM encourages the development of national and specialist codes of ethics to meet particular needs and will be pleased to receive copies of these. They should be sent to the Secretary-General of ICOM, Maison de l'UNESCO, 1 rue Miollis, 75732 Paris Cedex 15, France. E-mail: secretariat@icom.museum

Geoffrey Lewis Chair, ICOM Ethics Committee (1997–2004), President of ICOM (1983–1989)

ICOM Ethics Committee for the period 2001–2004

Chair: Geoffrey Lewis (UK)

Members: Gary Edson (USA); Per Kåks (Sweden); Byung-mo Kim (Rep. of Korea); Pascal Makambila (Congo) – from 2002; Jean-Yves Marin (France); Bernice Murphy (Australia) to 2002; Tereza Scheiner (Brazil); Shaje'a Tshiluila (Democratic Rep. of Congo); Michel Van-Praët (France).

Ethical issues that require the attention and/or consideration of the ICOM Ethics Committee may be addressed to its Chair by e-mail: ethics@icom.museum.

Preamble

Status of the ICOM *Code of Ethics for Museums*

The *ICOM Code of Ethics for Museums* has been prepared by the International Council of Museums. It is the statement of ethics for museums referred to in the *ICOM Statutes*. The Code reflects principles generally accepted by the international museum community. Membership in ICOM and the payment of the annual subscription to ICOM are an affirmation of the *ICOM Code of Ethics for Museums*.

A Minimum Standard for Museums

The ICOM Code represents a minimum standard for museums. It is presented as a series of principles supported by guidelines for desirable professional practice. In some countries, certain minimum standards are defined by law or government regulation. In others, guidance on and assessment of minimum professional standards may be available in the form of "Accreditation," "Registration," or similar evaluative schemes. Where such standards are not defined, guidance can be obtained through the ICOM Secretariat, a relevant National Committee of ICOM, or the appropriate International Committee of ICOM. It is also intended that individual nations and the specialized subject organizations connected with museums should use this Code as a basis for developing additional standards.

Translations of the *ICOM Code of Ethics for Museums*

The *ICOM Code of Ethics for Museums* is published in the three official languages of the organization: English, French and Spanish. ICOM welcomes the translation of the Code into other languages. However, a translation will be regarded as "official" only if it is endorsed by at least one National Committee of a country in which the language is spoken, normally as the first language. Where the language is spoken in more than one country, it is preferable that the National Committees of these countries also be consulted. Attention is drawn to the need for linguistic as well as professional museum expertise in providing official translations. The language version used for a translation and the names of the National Committees involved should be indicated. These conditions do not restrict translations of the Code, or parts of it, for use in educational work or for study purposes.

Museums preserve, interpret and promote the natural and cultural inheritance of humanity

Principle: *Museums are responsible for the tangible and intangible natural and cultural heritage. Governing bodies and those concerned with the strategic direction and oversight of museums have a primary responsibility to protect and promote this heritage as well as the human, physical and financial resources made available for that purpose.*

Institutional Standing

Enabling documentation – The governing body should ensure that the museum has a written and published constitution, statute or other public document, in accordance with national laws which clearly states the museum's legal status, mission, permanence, and non-profit nature.
Statement of the Mission, Objectives, and Policies – The governing body should prepare, publicize and be guided by a statement of the mission, objectives, and policies of the museum and of the role and composition of the governing body.

Physical Resources

Premises – The governing body should ensure adequate premises with a suitable environment for the museum to fulfil the basic functions defined in its mission.

Access – The governing body should ensure that the museum and its collections are available to all during reasonable hours and for regular periods. Particular regard should be given to those persons with special needs.
Health and Safety – The governing body should ensure that institutional standards of health, safety, and accessibility apply to its personnel and visitors.
Protection Against Disasters – The governing body should develop and maintain policies to protect the public and personnel, the collections and other resources, against natural and human-made disasters.
Security Requirements – The governing body should ensure appropriate security to protect collections against theft or damage in displays, exhibitions, working or storage areas, and while in transit.
Insurance and Indemnity – Where commercial insurance is used for collections, the governing body should ensure that such cover is adequate and includes objects in transit or on loan and other items that are the responsibility of the museum. When an indemnity scheme is in use, it is necessary that material not in the ownership of the museum is adequately covered.

Financial Resources

Funding – The governing body should ensure that there are sufficient funds to carry out and develop the activities of the museum. All funds must be accounted for in a professional manner.
Income-Generating Policy – The governing body should have a written policy regarding sources of income that it may generate through its activities or accept from outside sources. Regardless of funding source, museums should maintain control of the content and integrity of their programmes, exhibitions and activities. Income-generating activities should not compromise the standards of the institution or its public (See 6.6).

Personnel

Employment Policy– The governing body should ensure that all action concerning personnel is taken in accordance with the policies of the museum as well as the proper and legal procedures.
Appointment of the Director or Head – The director or head of the museum is a key post and when making an appointment, governing bodies should have regard for the knowledge and skills required to fill the post effectively. These qualities should include adequate intellectual ability and professional knowledge, complemented by a high standard of ethical conduct.
Access to Governing Bodies – The director or head of a museum should be directly responsible, and have direct access, to the relevant governing bodies.

Competence of Museum Personnel – The employment of qualified personnel with the expertise required to meet all responsibilities is necessary (See also 2.18, 2.24 and 8.12).
Training of Personnel – Adequate opportunities for the continuing education and professional development of all museum personnel should be arranged to maintain an effective workforce.
Ethical Conflict – The governing body should never require museum personnel to act in a way that could be considered to conflict with the provisions of this *Code of Ethics*, or any national law or specialist code of ethics.
Museum Personnel and Volunteers – The governing body should have a written policy on volunteer work which promotes a positive relationship between volunteers and members of the museum profession.
Volunteers and Ethics – The governing body should ensure that volunteers, when conducting museum and personal activities, are fully conversant with the *ICOM Code of Ethics for Museums* and other applicable codes and laws.

Museums that maintain collections hold them in trust for the benefit of society and its development

Principle: *Museums have the duty to acquire, preserve and promote their collections as a contribution to safeguarding the natural, cultural and scientific heritage. Their collections are a significant public inheritance, have a special position in law and are protected by international legislation. Inherent in this public trust is the notion of stewardship that includes rightful ownership, permanence, documentation, accessibility and responsible disposal.*

Acquiring Collections

Collections Policy – The governing body for each museum should adopt and publish a written collections policy that addresses the acquisition, care and use of collections. The policy should clarify the position of any material that will not be catalogued, conserved, or exhibited (See 2.7 and 2.8).
Valid Title – No object or specimen should be acquired by purchase, gift, loan, bequest, or exchange unless the acquiring museum is satisfied that a valid title is held. Evidence of lawful ownership in a country is not necessarily valid title.
Provenance and Due Diligence – Every effort must be made before acquisition to ensure that any object or specimen offered for purchase, gift, loan, bequest, or exchange has not been illegally obtained in or exported from, its country of origin or any intermediate country in which it might have been owned legally (including the museum's own country). Due diligence in this regard should establish the full history of the item from discovery or production.

Objects and Specimens from Unauthorized or Unscientific Fieldwork – Museums should not acquire objects where there is reasonable cause to believe their recovery involved the unauthorised, unscientific, or intentional destruction or damage of monuments, archaeological or geological sites, or species and natural habitats. In the same way, acquisition should not occur if there has been a failure to disclose the finds to the owner or occupier of the land, or to the proper legal or governmental authorities.

Culturally Sensitive Material – Collections of human remains and material of sacred significance should be acquired only if they can be housed securely and cared for respectfully. This must be accomplished in a manner consistent with professional standards and the interests and beliefs of members of the community, ethnic or religious groups from which the objects originated, where these are known (See also 3.7 and 4.3).

Protected Biological or Geological Specimens – Museums should not acquire biological or geological specimens that have been collected, sold, or otherwise transferred in contravention of local, national, regional or international law or treaty relating to wildlife protection or natural history conservation.

Living Collections – When the collections include live botanical and zoological specimens, special considerations should be made for the natural and social environment from which they are derived as well as any local, national, regional or international law, or treaty relating to wildlife protection or natural history conservation.

Working Collections – The collections policy may include special considerations for certain types of working collection where the emphasis is on preserving cultural, scientific or technical process rather than the object, or where objects or specimens are assembled for regular handling and teaching purposes (See also 2.1).

Acquisition Outside Collections Policy – The acquisition of objects or specimens outside the museum's stated policy should only be made in exceptional circumstances. The governing body should consider the professional opinions available to them, and the views of all interested parties. Consideration will include the significance of the object or specimen including its context in the cultural or natural heritage, and the special interests of other museums collecting such material. However, even in these circumstances, objects without a valid title should not be acquired (See also 3.4).

Acquisition by Members of the Governing Body and Museum Personnel – Special care is required in considering any item, either for sale, as a donation or as a tax-benefit gift, from members of governing bodies, museum personnel, or the families and close associates of these persons.

Repositories of Last Resort – Nothing in this *Code of Ethics* should prevent a museum from acting as an authorized repository for unprovenanced, illicitly collected or recovered specimens and objects from the territory over which it has lawful responsibility.

Removing Collections

Legal or Other Powers of Disposal – Where the museum has legal powers permitting disposals, or has acquired objects subject to conditions of disposal, the legal or other requirements and procedures must be complied with fully. Where the original acquisition was subject to mandatory or other restrictions these conditions must be observed, unless it can be shown clearly that adherence to such restrictions is impossible or substantially detrimental to the institution and, if appropriate, relief may be sought through legal procedures.
Deaccessioning from Museum Collections – The removal of an object or specimen from a museum collection must only be undertaken with a full understanding of the significance of the item, its character (whether renewable or non-renewable), legal standing, and any loss of public trust that might result from such action.
Responsibility for Deaccessioning – The decision to deaccession should be the responsibility of the governing body acting in conjunction with the director of the museum and the curator of the collection concerned. Special arrangements may apply to working collections (See 2.7 and 2.8).
Disposal of Objects Removed from the Collections – Each museum should have a policy defining authorized methods for permanently removing an object from the collections through donation, transfer, exchange, sale, repatriation, or destruction, and that allows the transfer of unrestricted title to the receiving agency. Complete records must be kept of all deaccessioning decisions, the objects involved, and the disposition of the object. There will be a strong presumption that a deaccessioned item should first be offered to another museum.
Income from Disposal of Collections – Museum collections are held in public trust and may not be treated as a realizable asset. Money or compensation received from the deaccessioning and disposal of objects and specimens from a museum collection should be used solely for the benefit of the collection and usually for acquisitions to that same collection.
Purchase of Deaccessioned Collections – Museum personnel, the governing body, or their families or close associates, should not be permitted to purchase objects that have been deaccessioned from a collection for which they are responsible.

Care of Collections

2.18 Collection Continuity – The museum should establish and apply policies to ensure that its collections (both permanent and temporary) and associated information, properly recorded, are available for current use and will be passed on to future generations in as good and safe a condition as practicable, having regard to current knowledge and resources.

Delegation of Collection Responsibility – Professional responsibilities involving the care of the collections should be assigned to persons with appropriate knowledge and skill or who are adequately supervised (See also 8.11).

Documentation of Collections – Museum collections should be documented according to accepted professional standards. Such documentation should include a full identification and description of each item, its associations, provenance, condition, treatment and present location. Such data should be kept in a secure environment and be supported by retrieval systems providing access to the information by the museum personnel and other legitimate users.

Protection Against Disasters – Careful attention should be given to the development of policies to protect the collections during armed conflict and other human-made or natural disasters.

Security of Collection and Associated Data – The museum should exercise control to avoid disclosing sensitive personal or related information and other confidential matters when collection data is made available to the public.

Preventive Conservation – Preventive conservation is an important element of museum policy and collections care. It is an essential responsibility of members of the museum profession to create and maintain a protective environment for the collections in their care, whether in store, on display, or in transit.

Collection Conservation and Restoration – The museum should carefully monitor the condition of collections to determine when an object or specimen may require conservation-restoration work and the services of a qualified conservator-restorer. The principal goal should be the stabilization of the object or specimen. All conservation procedures should be documented and as reversible as possible, and all alterations should be clearly distinguishable from the original object or specimen.

Welfare of Live Animals – A museum that maintains living animals should assume full responsibility for their health and well-being. It should prepare and implement a safety code for the protection of its personnel and visitors, as well as of the animals, that has been approved by an expert in the veterinary field. Genetic modification should be clearly identifiable.

Personal Use of Museum Collections – Museum personnel, the governing body, their families, close associates, or others should not be permitted to expropriate items from the museum collections, even temporarily, for any personal use.

Museums hold primary evidence for establishing and furthering knowledge

Principle: *Museums have particular responsibilities to all for the care, accessibility and interpretation of primary evidence collected and held in their collections.*

Primary Evidence

Collections as Primary Evidence. – The museum collections policy should indicate clearly the significance of collections as primary evidence. The policy should not be governed only by current intellectual trends or present museum usage.
Availability of Collections – Museums have a particular responsibility for making collections and all relevant information available as freely as possible, having regard to restraints arising for reasons of confidentiality and security.

Museum Collecting and Research

Field Collecting – Museums undertaking field collecting should develop policies consistent with academic standards and applicable national and international laws and treaty obligations. Fieldwork should only be undertaken with respect and consideration for the views of local communities, their environmental resources and cultural practices as well as efforts to enhance the cultural and natural heritage.
Exceptional Collecting of Primary Evidence – In exceptional cases an item without provenance may have such an inherently outstanding contribution to knowledge that it would be in the public interest to preserve it. The acceptance of such an item into a museum collection should be the subject of a decision by specialists in the discipline concerned and without national or international prejudice (See also 2.11).
Research – Research by museum personnel should relate to the museum's mission and objectives and conform to established legal, ethical and academic practices.
Destructive Analysis – When destructive analytical techniques are undertaken, a complete record of the material analyzed, the outcome of the analysis and the resulting research, including publications, should become a part of the permanent record of the object.
Human Remains and Material of Sacred Significance – Research on human remains and materials of sacred significance must be accomplished in a manner consistent with professional standards and take into account the interests and beliefs of the community, ethnic or religious groups from whom the objects originated, where these are known (See also 2.5 and 4.3).
Retention of Rights to Research Materials – When museum personnel prepare material for presentation or to document field investigation, there must be clear agreement with the sponsoring museum regarding all rights to such work.
Shared Expertise – Members of the museum profession have an obligation to share their knowledge and experience with colleagues, scholars and students in relevant fields. They should respect and acknowledge those from whom they have learned and should pass on such advancements in techniques and experience that may be of benefit to others.

Co-operation Between Museums & Other Institutions – Museum personnel should acknowledge and endorse the need for co-operation and consultation between institutions with similar interests and collecting practices. This is particularly so with institutes of higher education and certain public utilities where research may generate important collections for which there is no long-term security.

Museums provide opportunities for the appreciation, understanding and promotion of the natural and cultural heritage

Principle: *Museums have an important duty to develop their educational role and attract wider audiences from the community, locality, or group they serve. Interaction with the constituent community and promotion of their heritage is an integral part of the educational role of the museum.*

Display and Exhibition

Displays, Exhibitions and Special Activities – Displays and temporary exhibitions, physical or electronic, should be in accordance with the stated mission, policy and purpose of the museum. They should not compromise either the quality or the proper care and conservation of the collections.
Interpretation of Exhibits – Museums should ensure that the information they present in displays and exhibitions is well-founded, accurate and gives appropriate consideration to represented groups or beliefs.
Exhibition of Sensitive Materials – Human remains and materials of sacred significance must be displayed in a manner consistent with professional standards and, where known, taking into account the interests and beliefs of members of the community, ethnic or religious groups from whom the objects originated. They must be presented with great tact and respect for the feelings of human dignity held by all peoples.
Removal from Public Display – Requests for removal from public display of human remains or material of sacred significance from the originating communities must be addressed expeditiously with respect and sensitivity. Requests for the return of such material should be addressed similarly. Museum policies should clearly define the process for responding to such requests.
Display of Unprovenanced Material – Museums should avoid displaying or otherwise using material of questionable origin or lacking provenance. They should be aware that such displays or usage can be seen to condone and contribute to the illicit trade in cultural property.

Other Resources

Publication – Information published by museums, by whatever means, should be well-founded, accurate and give responsible consideration to the academic disciplines, societies, or beliefs presented. Museum publications should not compromise the standards of the institution.
Reproductions – Museums should respect the integrity of the original when replicas, reproductions, or copies of items in the collection are made. All such copies should be permanently marked as facsimiles.

Museums hold resources that provide opportunities for other public services and benefits.

Principle: *Principle Museums utilize a wide variety of specialisms, skills and physical resources that have a far broader application than in the museum. This may lead to shared resources or the provision of services as an extension of the museum's activities. These should be organized in such a way that they do not compromise the museum's stated mission.*

Identification Services

Identification of Illegally or Illicitly Acquired Objects – Where museums provide an identification service, they should not act in any way that could be regarded as benefiting from such activity, directly or indirectly. The identification and authentication of objects that are believed or suspected to have been illegally or illicitly acquired, transferred, imported or exported, should not be made public until the appropriate authorities have been notified.
Authentication and Valuation (Appraisal) – Valuations may be made for the purposes of insurance of museum collections. Opinions on the monetary value of other objects should only be given on official request from other museums or competent legal, governmental or other responsible public authorities. However, when the museum itself may be the beneficiary, appraisal of an object or specimen must be undertaken independently.

Museums work in close collaboration with the communities from which their collections originate as well as those they serve

Principle: *Museum collections reflect the cultural and natural heritage of the communities from which they have been derived. As such they have a character beyond that of ordinary property which may include strong affinities with national, regional, local, ethnic, religious or political identity. It is important therefore that museum policy is responsive to this possibility.*

Origin of Collections

Co-operation – Museums should promote the sharing of knowledge, documentation and collections with museums and cultural organizations in the countries and communities of origin. The possibility of developing partnerships with museums in countries or areas that have lost a significant part of their heritage should be explored.

Return of Cultural Property – Museums should be prepared to initiate dialogues for the return of cultural property to a country or people of origin. This should be undertaken in an impartial manner, based on scientific, professional and humanitarian principles as well as applicable local, national and international legislation, in preference to action at a governmental or political level.

Restitution of Cultural Property – When a country or people of origin seeks the restitution of an object or specimen that can be demonstrated to have been exported or otherwise transferred in violation of the principles of international and national conventions, and shown to be part of that country's or people's cultural or natural heritage, the museum concerned should, if legally free to do so, take prompt and responsible steps to co-operate in its return.

Cultural Objects From an Occupied Country – Museums should abstain from purchasing or acquiring cultural objects from an occupied territory and respect fully all laws and conventions that regulate the import, export and transfer of cultural or natural materials.

Respect for Communities Served

Contemporary Communities – Where museum activities involve a contemporary community or its heritage, acquisitions should only be made based on informed and mutual consent without exploitation of the owner or informants. Respect for the wishes of the community involved should be paramount.

Funding of Community Facilities – When seeking funds for activities involving contemporary communities, their interests should not be compromised (See 1.10).

Use of Collections from Contemporary Communities – Museum usage of collections from contemporary communities requires respect for human dignity and the traditions and cultures that use such material. Such collections should be used to promote human well-being, social development, tolerance, and respect by advocating multisocial, multicultural and multilingual expression (See 4.3).

Supporting Organizations in the Community – Museums should create a favourable environment for community support (e.g., Friends of Museums and other supporting organisations), recognize their contribution and promote a harmonious relationship between the community and museum personnel.

Museums operate in a legal manner

Principle: *Museums must conform fully to international, regional, national, or local legislation and treaty obligations. In addition, the governing body should comply with any legally binding trusts or conditions relating to any aspect of the museum, its collections and operations.*

Legal Framework

National and Local Legislation – Museums should conform to all national and local laws and respect the legislation of other states as they affect their operation.
International Legislation – Museum policy should acknowledge the following international legislation which is taken as a standard in interpreting the *ICOM Code of Ethics*:

UNESCO Convention for the Protection of Cultural Property in the Event of Armed Conflict (The Hague Convention, First Protocol, 1954 and Second Protocol, 1999);
UNESCO Convention on the Means of Prohibiting and Preventing the Illicit Import, Export and Transfer of Ownership of Cultural Property (1970);
Convention on International Trade in Endangered Species of Wild Fauna and Flora (1973);
UN Convention on Biological Diversity (1992);
Unidroit Convention on Stolen and Illegally Exported Cultural Objects (1995);
UNESCO Convention on the protection of the Underwater Cultural Heritage (2001);
UNESCO Convention for the Safeguarding of the Intangible Cultural Heritage (2003).

Museums operate in a professional manner

Principle: *Members of the museum profession should observe accepted standards and laws and uphold the dignity and honour of their profession. They should safeguard the public against illegal or unethical professional conduct. Every opportunity should be used to inform and educate the public about the aims, purposes, and aspirations of the profession to develop a better public understanding of the contributions of museums to society.*

Professional Conduct

Familiarity with Relevant Legislation – Every member of the museum profession should be conversant with relevant international, national and local legislation and the conditions of their employment. They should avoid situations that could be construed as improper conduct.
Professional Responsibility – Members of the museum profession have an obligation to follow the policies and procedures of their employing institution. However, they may properly object to practices that are perceived to be damaging to a museum or the profession and matters of professional ethics.
Professional Conduct – Loyalty to colleagues and to the employing museum is an important professional responsibility and must be based on allegiance to fundamental ethical principles applicable to the profession as a whole. They should comply with the terms of the *ICOM Code of Ethics* and be aware of any other codes or policies relevant to museum work.
Academic and Scientific Responsibilities – Members of the museum profession should promote the investigation, preservation, and use of information inherent in the collections. They should, therefore, refrain from any activity or circumstance that might result in the loss of such academic and scientific data.
The Illicit Market – Members of the museum profession should not support the illicit traffic or market in natural and cultural property, directly or indirectly.
Confidentiality – Members of the museum profession must protect confidential information obtained during their work. In addition, information about items brought to the museum for identification is confidential and should not be published or passed to any other institution or person without specific authorization from the owner.
Museum and Collection Security – Information about the security of the museum or of private collections and locations visited during official duties must be held in strict confidence by museum personnel.
Exception to the Obligation for Confidentiality – Confidentiality is subject to a legal obligation to assist the police or other proper authorities in investigating possible stolen, illicitly acquired, or illegally transferred property.
Personal Independence – While members of a profession are entitled to a measure of personal independence, they must realize that no private business or professional interest can be wholly separated from their employing institution.
Professional Relationships – Members of the museums profession form working relationships with numerous other persons within and outside the museum in which they are employed. They are expected to render their professional services to others efficiently and to a high standard.

Professional Consultation – It is a professional responsibility to consult other colleagues within or outside the museum when the expertise available is insufficient in the museum to ensure good decision-making.

Conflicts of Interest

Gifts, Favours, Loans, or Other Personal Benefits – Museum employees must not accept gifts, favours, loans, or other personal benefits that may be offered to them in connection with their duties for the museum. Occasionally, professional courtesy may include the giving and receiving of gifts, but this should always take place in the name of the institution concerned.
Outside Employment or Business Interests – Members of the museum profession, although entitled to a measure of personal independence, must realize that no private business or professional interest can be wholly separated from their employing institution. They should not undertake other paid employment or accept outside commissions that are in conflict with, or may be viewed as being in conflict with the interests of the museum.
Dealing in Natural or Cultural Heritage – Members of the museum profession should not participate directly or indirectly in dealing (buying or selling for profit), in the natural or cultural heritage.
Interaction with Dealers – Museum professionals should not accept any gift, hospitality, or any form of reward from a dealer, auctioneer, or other person as an inducement to purchase or dispose of museum items, or to take or refrain from taking official action. Furthermore, a museum professional should not recommend a particular dealer, auctioneer, or appraiser to a member of the public.
Private Collecting – Members of the museum profession should not compete with their institution either in the acquisition of objects or in any personal collecting activity. An agreement between the museum professional and the governing body concerning any private collecting must be formulated and scrupulously followed.
Use of the Name and Logo of ICOM – The name of the organization, its acronym or its logo may not be used to promote or endorse any for-profit operation or product.
Other Conflicts of Interest – Should any other conflict of interest develop between an individual and the museum, the interests of the museum should prevail.

Glossary

Appraisal The authentication and valuation of an object or specimen. In certain countries the term is used for an independent assessment of a proposed gift for tax benefit purposes.

Conflict of Interest The existence of a personal or private interest that gives rise to a clash of principle in a work situation, thus restricting, or having the appearance of restricting, the objectivity of decision making.

Conservator-Restorer Museum or independent personnel competent to undertake the technical examination, preservation, conservation and restoration of cultural property. (For further information, see *ICOM News* (1986), vol. 39, No.1, 5 6.)

Cultural Heritage Any thing or concept considered of aesthetic, historical, scientific or spiritual significance.

Dealing Buying and selling items for personal or institutional gain.

Due Diligence The requirement that every endeavour is made to establish the facts of a case before deciding a course of action, particularly in identifying the source and history of an item offered for acquisition or use before acquiring it.

Governing Body The persons or organizations defined in the enabling legislation of the museum as responsible for its continuance, strategic development and funding.

Income-Generating Activities Activities intended to bring financial gain or profit for the benefit of the institution.

Legal Title Legal right to ownership of property in the country concerned. In certain countries this may be a conferred right and insufficient to meet the requirements of a due diligence search.

Minimum Standard A standard to which it is reasonable to expect all museums and museum personnel to aspire. Certain countries have their own statements of minimum standards.

Museum[1] A museum is a non-profit making permanent institution in the service of society and of its development, open to the public, which acquires, conserves, researches, communicates and exhibits, for purposes of study, education and enjoyment, the tangible and intangible evidence of people and their environment.

Museum Professional[1] Museum professionals consist the personnel (whether paid or unpaid) of museums or institutions as defined in Article 2, paragraphs 1 and 2, of the Statutes, who have received specialized training, or possess an equivalent

[1] It should be noted that the terms "museum" and "museum professional" are interim definitions for use in interpreting the *ICOM Code of Ethics for Museums*. The definitions of "museum" and "professional museum workers" used in the ICOM Statutes remain in force until the revision of that document has been completed.

practical experience in any field relevant to the management and operations of a museum, and independent persons respecting the *ICOM Code of Ethics for Museums* and working for museums or institutions as defined in the Statute quoted above, but not persons promoting or dealing with commercial products and equipment required for museums and museum services.

Natural Heritage Any natural thing, phenomenon or concept, considered to be of scientific significance or to be a spiritual manifestation.

Non-profit Organization A legally established body – corporate or unincorporated – whose income (including any surplus or profit) is used solely for the benefit of that body and its operation. The term "not-for-profit" has the same meaning.

Provenance The full history and ownership of an item from the time of its discovery or creation to the present day, from which authenticity and ownership is determined.

Valid Title Indisputable right to ownership of property, supported by full provenance of the item from discovery or production.

Appendix XXIV

7th Meeting of the Interpol Expert Group (IEG) on Stolen Cultural Property

Lyon (France), 23–24 February 2010

The participants of the 7th Meeting of the INTERPOL Expert Group (IEG) on Stolen Cultural Property, held in Lyon on 23–24 February 2010:

Aware of the serious damages to the Haitian cultural heritage as one of the consequences of the earthquake and the high risk of illicit trafficking in unlawfully removed cultural property welcomes ICOM's initiative of publishing a Red List of Haitian cultural property at risk,

Aware of the urgent need to enable all countries to effectively combat illegal importation of Haitian cultural property, encourage UNESCO and ICOM to rapidly collect information on categories of objects particularly at risk of illicit trafficking including visual material, a list of renowned Haitian artists and a list of experts of Haitian art and make this information publicly available in co-operation with relevant bodies,

Noting the important role of INTERPOL's database of stolen cultural property and the extended online access, encourage member countries to systematically provide appropriate stolen art information to the INTERPOL General Secretariat,

Recognizing the crucial lack of appropriate documentation and inventories of cultural property in many countries and the resulting need for continuous training, ask UNESCO, ICOM and INTERPOL to develop online availability of the Object ID form and a training course using an e-learning module, and invite member countries to promote the use of Object ID on a national level,

Acknowledging the importance of UNESCO's Cultural Heritage Laws Database, ask member countries to provide systematically their cultural heritage legislation to UNESCO, ensure regular updates and invite INTERPOL, international Organizations and national authorities to create a direct link from their Web sites to this database,

Taking note of the United Nations Transnational Organized Crime Convention (UNTOC) and its potential usefulness to address crime prevention and criminal justice aspects of illicit trafficking in cultural property, invite the UNODC to join the existing network between the relevant international organizations and to participate in appropriate events on the subject matter,

Acknowledging the success of individual projects in co-operation with Internet platforms on the fight against the illicit sale of endangered cultural property, encourage member countries to develop similar actions and international organizations to continue raising public awareness on illicit e-commerce.

Noting the necessity of raising public awareness of categories of particularly endangered cultural property, encourage ICOM to continue its efforts with the Red Lists and invite INTERPOL and its member countries to support their production and diffusion,

Taking note of the importance of organizing training on the fight against illicit trafficking in cultural property for the law enforcement, judicial and other authorities, invite INTERPOL and its member countries to provide appropriate training opportunities.

Appendix XXV

7th International Symposium on the Theft of and Illicit Traffic in Works of Art, cultural Property and Antiques

Lyon (France), 17–19 June 2008

The participants at the 7th International Symposium on the Theft of and Illicit Traffic in Works of Art, Cultural Property and Antiques, Lyon, France, 17–19 June 2008,

Acknowledging the relevance of INTERPOL's Stolen Works of Art Database as a global investigation tool,

Aware of the need for access to information in this database to be extended beyond law-enforcement services, to museums, art market professionals and the general public,

Considering the need to identify international networks of traffickers in order to transmit the information to operational law-enforcement services,

Alarmed by the increase in the use of the Internet for the illegal trade in cultural objects,

Noting the growth in the use of express-delivery companies for dispatching of cultural objects, which is mainly due to the trade in cultural objects over the Internet,

Aware of the constant looting of archaeological sites, both on land and under water,

Noting the need for national law enforcement services to consult recognized experts with a view to determining the origin and the authenticity of cultural objects which may have come from Iraq,

Also noting the large number of thefts committed in places of worship and the lack of inventories and security measures for religious property in such places,

Noting that there is a lack of awareness among the general public of the importance of cultural heritage and the need for it to be protected,

Recommend that member countries:

1. Regularly add updated information to the General Secretariat's Works of Art Database;
2. Send to the General Secretariat all information necessary to carry out crime analyses on international cultural property traffickers;
3. Circulate as widely as possible the INTERPOL-UNESCO-ICOM joint letter on Basic Actions concerning cultural objects being offered for sale over the Internet so that these actions can be implemented, and conclude agreements with auction platforms in order to reduce illegal sales and to monitor this type of trade as effectively as possible;
4. Monitor land and underwater archaeological sites and tackle the illegal traffic which follows looting by adopting appropriate legislation in compliance with existing international instruments;
5. In the event of a seizure of Iraqi cultural property, contact the experts on the list drawn up by UNESCO, available on the General Secretariat's secure Web site;
6. Make the owners of cultural property aware of the need to draw up inventories of the property and make arrangements for its protection;

Recommend that the General Secretariat:

Pursue the initiative of granting the widest possible access to INTERPOL's Stolen Works of Art Database via the Web site;

Recommend that INTERPOL, UNESCO and ICOM:

Jointly seek ways of raising awareness among law-enforcement services, those responsible for safeguarding religious heritage, the major players in the art market and the conservation world, and the general public, with regard to protecting cultural property and combating illegal trafficking.

Appendix XXVI

"Carta di Courmayeur" sul patrimonio artistico e culturale (ONU – UNESCO)

"Charte de Courmayeur" sur le patrimoine artistique et culturel

Workshop internazionale promosso dal Consiglio internazionale consultivo scientifico e tecnico delle Nazioni Unite – ISPAC

in collaborazione con:

Nazioni Unite

Division of Cultural Patrimony of the United Nations Educational Scientific and Cultural Organization – UNESCO

Courmayeur Mont Blanc, 25–27 giugno 1992

- Aide-Mémoire
- Charter of Courmayeur/Report
- Charte de Courmayeur/Rapport
- Elenco dei partecipanti

Aide-Mémoire

Background

1. The Eighth United Nations Congress on the Prevention of Crime and the Treatment of Offenders, alarmed by the growing illicit trade on movable cultural property, a development that, in the opinion of experts, threatens to gravely damage the cultural heritage of many countries and, through that, the identity of their peoples, adopted two resolutions aimed at assisting the international community in combating this trend. The first of these contained, as an annex, the model treaty for the prevention of crimes that infringe on the cultural heritage of peoples in the form of movable property, recommended to Member States to consider the model treaty as a framework that could be of assistance to interested

States in negotiating and drawing up bilateral agreements designed to improve co-operation in this area, inviting those that had not yet established relevant treaty resolutions to take the model into consideration when so doing, and urging them to continue strengthening co-operation and mutual assistance in their prevention efforts.

2. The second resolution requested the Secretary-General, *inter alia*, to make arrangements, in co-operation with Member States, intergovernmental and non-governmental organizations, aimed at the establishment of national and international computer databases containing information, to be used by the competent authorities, on stolen or illegally exported cultural property, national legislation and international instruments related to the protection of cultural heritage. Further, this resolution urged Member States to co-operate in this endeavour by providing the corresponding information and using the databases for the prevention and control of crimes against the cultural patrimony.

Scope

3. In view of the above, the Fondazione Centro Internazionale su Diritto, Società e Economia is convening, on behalf of the International Scientific Professional Advisory Council (ISPAC), a 3-day workshop in which representatives of Governments, of intergovernmental and non-governmental organizations, and of interested private institutions, would discuss means and modalities to implement those instruments and formulate relevant recommendations for action by the international community. The project is being realized with the co-operation of the United Nations Educational, Scientific and Cultural Organization's (UNESCO) Division of Cultural Patrimony and the United Nations Crime Prevention and Criminal Justice Programme of the United Nations Office at Vienna.
4. The invited Governments are, taking into consideration a fair and representative geographical distribution, the following: Albania, Benin, Canada, China, Czech and Slovak Federal Republic, Egypt, France, Germany, Greece, Guatemala, India, Italy, Japan, Mexico, Nigeria, Peru, the Russian Federation, Senegal, Spain, Thailand, the United Kingdom and the United States of America.
5. Each country is requested to appoint two participants, one having a professional involvement with ministries of culture, museum administration, or some other official function in the area of cultural property, while the second should have duties in the area of law enforcement with respect to the protection of such property.
6. In addition, invitations have been extended to Lloyd's of London, ICPO/INTERPOL, and the International Museum Association (ICOM).
7. Further, Italian computer companies will provide experts in electronic information processing, who would be in the position to provide valuable technical assistance to the workshop.

Major themes of the workshop

8. The workshop will explore ways and means to promote action on the part of Governments aimed at initiating bilateral negotiations for the purpose of formalizing their co-operation in the area in question, and their utilization thereto, as a useful framework, of the model treaty annexed to resolution B1 of the Eighth Congress. In this connection, the need for technical assistance to requesting countries will need the attention of the participants, who will be expected to provide suggestions concerning the form, extension and financing of such assistance.
9. With respect to the establishment of databanks, the workshop will, first and foremost, examine its technical feasibility, taking into account existing initiatives at the national and international levels, e.g. Canada and INTERPOL.
10. Further, the workshop is expected to consider the possible centralization of the data in one institution or organization, without precluding the existence of national databases which, on the contrary, should be promoted and supported. For the accomplishment of the latter endeavour, the modalities of technical assistance would have to be examined. The end product to be kept in focus is the graded emergence of an international network connected through a central module.
11. In connection with the above, a crucial issue is the accessibility by the competent authorities, both to insert relevant data and to retrieve them, as needed. In this respect, the workshop should carefully examine the implications of such a system for the right to privacy, the protection of which must be fully ensured.
12. The workshop will further examine the possible costs of the project, both at the local and the international levels, and the most effective means to finance such costs.
13. Finally, the participants will examine the issue of juridical compatibility of the project with the existing legislation in the participating countries, formulating recommendations as to how solve problems in this area, if any.

Charter of Courmayeur

The International Workshop on the Protection of Artistic and Cultural Patrimony held at Courmayeur, Aosta Valley, Italy, 25–27 June 1992, adopted the following recommendations:

National and international action against the illicit trade with objects belonging to the cultural patrimony of nations

Aware of the sharp increase registered in the illicit trade with art objects and archeological items belonging to the cultural patrimony of nations,

Convinced that such criminal activities are causing grave damage to the cultural patrimony of many countries,

Convinced also that its cultural patrimony is a crucial component of the identity and self-understanding of a people,

Mindful of the imperative need to protect the cultural patrimony, preserving thereby the social, historical and artistic components of this identity and self-understanding,

Desirous to assist Governments and international organizations in their efforts to curtail the illicit trade with art objects and items belonging to the cultural patrimony,

Recalling the principles contained in the International Covenant on Economic, Social and Cultural Rights,

Recalling also the principles contained in the 1970 UNESCO Convention on the Means of Prohibiting and Preventing the Illicit Import, Export and Transfer of ownership of Cultural Property,

Recalling further the principles on protection of moveable cultural property contained in the Protocol to the 1954 UNESCO Convention on the Protection of Cultural Property in the Event of Armed Conflict,

Recognizing the usefulness of the model treaty for the prevention of crimes against the cultural heritage of peoples, as annexed to resolution B-1 of the Eighth United Nations Congress on the Prevention of Crime and the Treatment of Offenders,

Aware of the draft convention of stolen and illegally exported cultural property which is under preparation in the framework of the International Institute for the Unification of Private Law (UNIDROIT),

Adopts the following recommendations for national and international action aimed at bringing under control the illicit trade with objects belonging to the cultural patrimony of nations:

i. Concerned Governments should make a concerted effort, on the occasion of the 47th session of the General Assembly of the United Nations and of the next General Conference of UNESCO, to obtain the adoption of resolutions strongly urging Member States to initiate multilateral and bilateral negotiations aimed at concluding treaties for the protection of the cultural patrimony of nations. The same resolutions should also urge Governments to upgrade, in their crime prevention programmes, the importance of protecting the cultural property of nations, granting top priority to these activities,
ii. In view of the need for international co-operation to cope with the illicit trade with cultural objects, Governments should establish focal points that would handle, in close collaboration with ICPO/INTERPOL, all matters related with the transnational traffic with art objects and items belonging to the cultural patrimony, including requests for international co-operation,
iii. Detailed and extensive information concerning the cultural patrimony of every nation is of the foremost importance. Consequently, Governments should consider establishing inventories of their cultural patrimony, containing, when possible, a description of each item adequate for its identification and a photographic reproduction of it. In addition, Governments should examine the possibility of establishing public registers of works of art, identified by categories, as goods linked to possession. Further, national inventories should remain open to new items, as these come to light.

iv. In view of the scarcity of resources prevailing in many countries, Member States should be disposed to provide technical and, eventually, material assistance to requesting Governments interested in establishing the above-mentioned national inventories. Such technical assistance could take the form of provision of expert advice, training and/or hardware, as needed, and may be provided bilaterally or through international organizations.

v. For the purpose of enhancing awareness on the part of government officials of the seriousness and gravity of the problem in question, the United Nations and UNESCO, in co-operation with ICPO/INTERPOL and interested intergovernmental and non-governmental organizations, are requested to prepare a document, to be submitted to national authorities, explaining in detail the dimensions of the problem, including available relevant statistical data. The document should also cover the links between the illicit traffic with objects belonging to the cultural patrimony of nations, and other manifestations of transnational criminality, such as the illicit traffic with narcotic drugs.

vi. Governments are urged to consider the introduction of new legislation, as needed, that would criminalize the illicit export and import of cultural objects.

vii. Governments should consider establishing regulations whereby any imported cultural object should be accompanied by an export permission issued by the relevant authorities of the country of origin. Governments should also determine the adequate sanctions in case of violations of any regulations so established.

viii. With respect to the return of illicitly exported objects, it has been noted that excessive demands for information posed by the requested Governments may in practice render ineffective the dispositions of a bilateral agreement. For instance, the request for the exact date of the theft, or the illicit exportation, may be impossible to fulfil. This is particularly true in the case of clandestine archeological digs. Consequently, Governments are urged to show greater flexibility and understanding for the difficulties facing the authorities of the requesting countries.

ix. In the same vein, it has been observed that high judicial costs in the requested country may deter requesting countries from initiating action for the return of illicitly exported objects. In fact, in some cases, such costs may exceed the price of the item in question. Consequently, Governments are reminded that they are free to explore the possibility of friendly settlement, or, where the parties agree, of binding arbitration procedures in order to secure the return of such illicitly exported objects to their countries of origin.

x. The United Nations and UNESCO, in consultation with Governments and in co-operation with relevant organizations, should explore the possibility of creating an internationally recognized licensing system for art dealers, which would serve to weed out the criminal elements of an otherwise respectable professional group.

xi. The co-operation between the United Nations, UNESCO and INTERPOL in the area of the illicit trade with cultural objects should be intensified and streamlined, so as to obtain higher effectiveness and better possibilities of providing advice and assistance to requesting Governments.

xii. Regional and interregional crime prevention institutes should add to their programmes of work elements concerning the prevention of crimes against the cultural patrimony of nations, so as to be able to assist requesting Governments and to support the corresponding activities of the United Nations.

xiii. It is indispensable that the international community gain full awareness of the crucial moral dimensions of the illicit transnational trade with the cultural patrimony. It is a fact that a considerable share of this trade flows from developing to developed countries. Consequently, developed countries should be respectful of the cultural heritage of developing countries, and should provide full co-operation to the victims of illicit trade with cultural objects, thereby dispelling any misunderstanding and placing themselves above any suspicion of possible complicity or complacency.

Improvement of information exchanges and establishment of databanks

Recognizing that recording and dissemination of information about the legal status of cultural items and about crimes against the cultural patrimony are important means of combating international illicit traffic in movable cultural property,

Noting with satisfaction the existence of databases already established, *inter alia*, by the Italian Republic, Arma dei Carabinieri, since 1980, and by Canada, since 1983, as well as those established by ICPO/INTERPOL and the Art Loss Register,

Acknowledging the action of UNESCO and the International Council of Museums (ICOM) in assisting countries in the preparation of inventories and appropriate legislation, in providing training for specialized personnel and in co-ordinating the concerns of museums with respect to crimes against cultural property,

Recognizing also the cultural importance of assisting developing countries to protect their cultural patrimonies from the criminal depredations to which they are increasingly subjected,

Acknowledging with appreciation the willingness of the Governments of Canada and Italy to provide assistance to international efforts to achieve an optimal diffusion of information concerning stolen and illegally exported movable cultural property as well as national laws related to its protection,

Aware of the fruitful co-operation established between the United Nations and UNESCO in relation to the prevention of crimes against the cultural patrimony,

Recalling the 1970 UNESCO Convention on the Means of Prohibiting and Preventing the Illicit Import, Export and Transfer of Ownership of Cultural Property, in particular article 5 thereof concerning the need to give appropriate publicity by States parties to the Convention to the disappearance of any items of cultural property,

Noting the 1989 ICOM General Conference resolution on the importance of national inventories,

Strongly underlining the importance of the resolution on the use of automated information exchange to combat crimes against movable cultural property adopted by the Eighth United Nations Congress on the Prevention of Crime and the Treatment of Offenders,

Adopts the following recommendations for national and international action aimed at the improvement of information exchanges related to the prevention of crimes against the cultural patrimony of nations:

i. The United Nations, in co-operation with UNESCO, should play a central role in the co-ordination of information exchanges between Governments, relevant intergovernmental and non-governmental organizations and private institutions, so as to ensure an optimal diffusion of data concerning movable cultural patrimonies and crimes committed against them;
ii. The United Nations, in close collaboration with UNESCO, should organize, subject to the availability of extrabudgetary resources, yearly export meetings for the purpose of carrying out a continuous technical evaluation of the difficulties encountered in establishing the co-ordination mentioned in recommendation (i), above;
iii. The United Nations, in collaboration with UNESCO and in co-operation with relevant international agencies and organizations, should formulate specific country projects, intended to assist Member States in improving their capability to cope with the challenge of crimes against cultural property. These projects, which should address, *inter alia*, such areas as legal reforms, establishment of databases, museum security and training of law enforcement officials and customs personnel in the identification of cultural objects, would be submitted to potential donor countries for the purpose of funding. The United Nations and UNESCO should act as executing agencies for funded projects;
iv. Member States should examine the possibility of supporting the United Nations Criminal Justice Information Network (UNCJIN), thus contributing to improve its capability;
v. The United Nations and UNESCO, in close collaboration with ICOM and other interested non-governmental organizations, should encourage close co-operation between emerging initiatives in the private and public sector that are developing databases about stolen cultural property. The feasibility of establishing a network of these databases should be carefully explored;
vi. The United Nations and UNESCO, in co-operation with ICOM and other relevant non-government organizations, should promote the development of national inventories of cultural properties, and should provide expert advice to requesting countries on standards and technical methods for establishing such inventories;

vii. The intended direct accessibility of the IGPO/INTERPOL Central Database on Stolen or Unidentified Works of Art to national law enforcement agencies should be strongly encouraged;
viii. The diffusion of information concerning national and international legislation concerning cultural patrimonies should be strongly encouraged. UNESCO should promote the development of a database about such legislation, making them accessible to Governments, intergovernmental and non-governmental organizations and to relevant private institutions;
ix. The United Nations and UNESCO, in co-operation with concerned Governments, with ICPO/INTERPOL and with relevant private sector organizations, should provide museums and other public sector organizations with information concerning stolen cultural property, if possible through access to the corresponding databases;
x. Since the bulk of information concerning stolen or unidentified works of art it still kept in national registers or databases, it appears desirable that the INTERPOL Computer Network be granted easy access to this information, particularly in those cases in which the possibility of international illicit traffic cannot be excluded, thereby facilitating an increase of seizures and recovery at the international level.

Report

1. The Eighth United Nations Congress on the Prevention of Crime and the Treatment of Offenders, held at Havana, Cuba, from 27 August to 7 September 1990, adopted the Model Treaty for the Prevention of Crimes that Infringe on the Cultural Heritage of Peoples in the Form of Movable Property, recommending it as a framework that could be of assistance to Member States interested in negotiating and drawing bilateral agreements in this area (Congress resolution B1).
2. The Eighth Congress also adopted a resolution on the use of automated information exchange to combat crimes against movable cultural property (Congress resolution C6), in which it requested the Secretary-General of the United Nations, *inter alia*, to make arrangements, in co-operation with Member States, intergovernmental and non-governmental organizations and other organizations, for the establishment of national and international computer databases that would be used by competent authorities for the purpose of preventing and combating crimes against the cultural heritage, which would be available to Member States and to specialized sectors through appropriate information networks. Further, the resolution urged Member States to.
3. In pursuance of the above, and for the purpose of assisting the United Nations in the fulfilment of its mandates, an International Workshop on the Protection of Artistic and Cultural Patrimony has taken place, organized by the Fondazione Centro internazionale su diritto società e economia. The Meeting was prepared by the International Scientific and Professional Advisory Council of the United Nations for Crime Prevention and Criminal Justice (ISPAC), in cooperation

with the Crime Prevention and Criminal Justice Branch of the United Nations Office at Vienna and the Division of Physical Heritage of UNESCO. For the programme outline of the Workshop, see Annex I.

4. The Workshop was held at Courmayeur, Aosta Valley, Italy, from 25 to 27, June 1992, and was attended by representatives of 15 countries and of ICPO/INTERPOL and of the International Council of Museums (ICOM). For the list of participants, see Annex II.
5. The Chairman of the Executive Board of ISPAC opened the meeting, welcoming the participants and thanking them for their willingness to participate in the event.
6. The President of the Autonomous Region of the Aosta Valley also addressed the Workshop, welcoming the participants and emphasizing the importance for his region of the items to be discussed, in view of the numerous works of art to be found in it, which could quite conceivably arouse the interest of art thieves. Courmayeur had already hosted other meetings aimed at assisting the international community to cope with the problems generated by transnational criminality. He certainly hoped that other similar events would take place in the region in the near future.
7. The representative of the Italian Ministry of Foreign Affairs greeted the Workshop on behalf of the Director-General of Cultural Relations of that Ministry, who took a personal interest in the protection of the artistic and cultural patrimony. Further, she addressed herself to the new circumstances emerging from the establishment of the European Common Market in which national boundaries will disappear, and informed the workshop of the initiatives undertaken by Italy in this connection. In addition, she brought to the attention of the participants the instruments adopted in this respect by the Council of Europe since 1954, the last of which was the European Convention on the Protection of the Archeological Heritage, signed at La Valletta, Malta, on 16 January 1992.
8. During the general debate, the participants repeatedly underlined the alarming increase in the illicit trade with artistic and cultural property. The volume of this trade was almost certain to grow and to become more difficult to detect as national borders become more permeable to commerce and travel. This was already an imminent reality in the European Community, where existing barriers were scheduled to disappear as of 1 January 1993.
9. Illicit trade was also being stimulated by recent development in art markets in developed countries. In fact, prices had been mounting during the last decade and many people saw art objects as a safe investment. This trend would most likely continue in the foreseeable future. High prices made illicit trade and art theft more profitable and thus more attractive.
10. Public awareness of the real dimensions and characteristics of the phenomenon appeared to lag behind the reality of the problem. Not many people seemed to know, for instance, that it ranked second in volume to illicit drug traffic. Perhaps an even smaller number of people was cognizant of the linkages between these two transnational criminal activities. These linkages justified indeed integrating the prevention of crimes against artistic and cultural property in the overall

schemes and policies aimed at combating serious transnational crimes, such as the illicit trade with drugs and arms.

11. Consequently, it was necessary to promote a higher awareness of the problem in question, both among the general public and among public officials. Such awareness was a precondition for the necessary reordering of priorities in this respect. In this connection, some delegations expressed the wish that the United Nations, in co-operation with UNESCO and with the assistance of ICPO/INTERPOL, prepare a document, to be brought to the attention of national authorities, indicating the real dimensions of the problem. If available, statistical data were to be included. ICPO/INTERPOL could be of great assistance in this task. Other delegations felt that, in view of the transboundary nature of the illicit trade, an international patrol should be created for the purpose of pursuing the involved criminals beyond national borders.
12. Several delegations, particularly from developing countries, thought that the problem had to be seen in a broader context. They pointed out that a large share, if not most, of the transboundary illicit trade with artistic and cultural property flowed from developing to developed countries, since the main markets were to be found in the latter. These had, however, rather tolerated this commerce, rather than truly committing themselves to an effective co-operation with developing countries, which were the main victims of these criminal activities. Such laxity could unfortunately be misconstrued as a remnant of colonialist attitudes, which were to be replaced by a new spirit of solidarity and collective responsibility.
13. Further, the same delegations thought that it was mistaken to look at the problem from a purely economic point of view, since such a perspective had prevented that due recognition be given to the moral dimensions of the phenomenon. The constant plundering of the cultural patrimony of a country was bound to inflict grave damage to a people's identity and self-respect. In their opinion, therefore, crimes against the cultural patrimony should be equated to crimes against humanity, and should be pursued accordingly. Criminalization of these activities was fully justified, and could act as a deterrent. An effective sanction could be loss of license for art dealers. New legislation was, in any case, badly needed.
14. Several delegations were of the opinion that bilateral agreements, although valuable and to be encouraged, were marked by severe shortcomings. They could be, as the experience of some countries demonstrated, rendered *de facto* ineffective by the excessive demands for information made by requested countries. Asking, for instance, for the exact date of theft of objects from an archeological site, not always known to the authorities, was demanding information that was impossible to ascertain with any degree of exactitude. Requested countries should be more realistic and less formalistic.
15. An additional obstacle to the recovery of stolen cultural property was the excessive costs incurred by the requesting country when following the judicial proceeding for restitution of stolen or illicitly exported items. In many cases, requesting countries were effectively deterred from initiating legal action by a

consideration of such costs. This was particularly true when the costs were higher than the commercial value of the object. This situation had led a country to buy the stolen object from the possessors rather than to try to recover it by judicial means.

16. In view of this, some delegations felt that countries should demonstrate their willingness to co-operate by establishing simpler and less costly procedures that could lead to a prompt restitution of the stolen objects to their rightful owner. This possibility was, however, unacceptable to other delegations, which felt that this would violate domestic law and constitutional guarantees.
17. Some participants felt that an effective measure would be to institute the obligation of importers to prove the legality of imports by means of an export certificate, to be issued by the relevant authorities of the country of origin. In the absence of such proof, and after a reasonable time, the items in question should be seized and returned to the country of origin. Such a procedure would, however, in the opinion of other participants, unlawfully restrict the free movement of goods being established in some parts of the world, such as the European Common Market. The proposal to establish an international licensing system for art dealers met with similar objections.
18. The creation of focal points in national administration was highly recommendable, since this would facilitate international co-operation and centralize the handling of requests for assistance. These focal points should function in close co-operation with local INTERPOL offices, and link with the United Nations.
19. With respect to the creation of national inventories and the establishment of databases, participants agreed as to their potential value and usefulness. Such registers were indispensable to an effective prevention of crimes against artistic and cultural property. They, however, disagreed concerning their inclusiveness. While some thought that private collections should be included, other felt that this would represent a potential threat to the private sphere.
20. Some difficulty was also expressed with the very concept of cultural property. Drugs could be easily defined and identified, but this was not the case with cultural items. How would a customs officer know that the imported object was of a cultural nature and thus requiring special attention? Probably the whole question of identifying an item was belonging to the cultural patrimony was an idle one. An object as part of the cultural patrimony from the moment the authorities of the country of origin classified it as belonging there, and, therefore, non-exportable. Customs officers could not be expected to possess university degrees in art history or archaeology, but the minimum basic knowledge could be imparted in their training courses.
21. Inventories, in the opinion of some participants, should not be considered as closed. They should remain open so as to allow the inclusion of objects not known at the time they were drawn. Any objects found in archaeological digs should be presumed to belong to the cultural patrimony of the country where the digs were located, regardless of the legal ownership of the surface. This position, however, was difficult to accept for some countries, in so far as it appeared to violate very strongly held conceptions of private property.

22. Inventories and databases were very useful but also costly propositions. As such, they could often be beyond the financial means of many developing countries which, as a matter of fact, usually have more vital tasks to perform with their limited resources. In this situation, the investment needed for the creation of inventories and databases was perceived as possessing a low priority in comparison with other demands. Accordingly, several delegations felt that projects of this kind could not be implemented in the absence of substantive technical assistance. This assistance should include, *inter alia*, such items as evaluations of the objective situation, expert advice on how to perform the tasks at hand in drawing the inventory and establishing the database, training of the required personnel, and provision of equipment, as needed.
23. Participants were convinced of the role to be played by modern technology, particularly communications and electronic information processing, in the establishment and functioning of accurate and rapidly accessible inventories and databases. But it was obvious to all that it would be unrealistic, and perhaps counterproductive, to expect that every country established in the short, or even medium, run, an electronic database. At the beginning at least, it would probably suffice if the inventory took a much more traditional and modest form, such as index cards and other simple systems.
24. As an illustration of the point under discussion, the Arma dei Carabinieri of Italy gave an excellent demonstration of their extremely advanced electronic database. Such database could serve as a model to be followed by interested countries. In fact, the Italian Government felt that the system could be the nucleus for an international network, together with the Canadian Heritage Information Network (CHIN).
25. The representative of IPCO/INTERPOL briefed the Seminar on the establishment, towards the end of 1993, of the INTERPOL Telecommunications Network, linking the central bureau in Lyon, France, with all INTERPOL national offices in member countries. The network, by means of micro-computers, will include text and image retrieval facilities, facilitating thereby the rapid dissemination of relevant information, a fact of great importance for effective police work. The system, however, would be only accessible to law enforcement agencies, a requirement that limited its usefulness to other users, such as museums.
26. The workshop felt that a comprehensive open network, connecting possibly the national databases, and co-ordinated by the United Nations Secretariat in co-operation with UNESCO, would effectively complement existing private and public information networks. This goal was to be pursued in a parallel form to the establishment of national inventories and databases.
27. Membership in existing networks was, however, problematic for developing countries suffering serious financial constraints. This difficulty pointed again at the indispensability of technical assistance, as was repeatedly emphasized by several delegations. In this connection, two delegations signalled the willingness of their respective Governments to explore such assistance.

28. At the conclusion of its works, the meeting was addressed by the Mayor of Courmayeur, who expressed the satisfaction of his city to be able to host such important meeting, adding that he expected other similar international events to take place at Courmayeur in the foreseeable future.
29. The Chairman of the Fondazione Centro internazionale su diritto società e economia which hosted the proceedings, expressing his satisfaction for their results warmly welcomed all participants and in particular the Delegates of the foreign Governments and the Representatives of international Organizations.
30. The Workshop adopted by consensus the Charter of Courmayeur, containing two sets of recommendations, and expressed the wish that they could be brought to the attention of Governments through the Commission on Crime Prevention and Criminal Justice, at its session in 1993, and to the next General Conference of UNESCO. It also expressed the wish that meetings like this should be held at regular intervals among experts from interested countries, for the purpose of keeping the situation under review and of devising appropriate strategies, including the elaboration of technical co-operation projects focused on training, exchange and dissemination of information and linkages through adequate data-banks. Finally, all participants extended their thanks to the organisers of the workshop, for the friendly atmosphere and the generous hospitality.

Index